Dictionary
of Idioms

The Wordsworth
Dictionary
of Idioms

–

Edited by E.M. Kirkpatrick and C.M. Schwarz

Wordsworth Reference

Preface

People tend to be bored by page after page of dull, uninteresting language and so it is important to be able to write and speak in a lively fashion. The use of idioms will greatly enliven one's style of writing and make it more interesting and more entertaining.

This book not only gives the meanings of idiomatic expressions — in language which is simple and easy to understand — but includes example sentences or phrases showing the idioms in actual use. These will be helpful to all users of the book as they capture the "flavour" of the expressions and indicate the context in which they are usually found.

The examples will be particularly helpful to learners of English, as they provide a pattern for them to follow. Mastering idiomatic expressions and reproducing them correctly is one of the most difficult aspects of learning a foreign language.

Trying to find idioms in a dictionary is often not easy. Sometimes they are listed under the first word and sometimes under what is considered to be the most important word in the idiomatic phrase. It is difficult for the user to decide where to look. In this book we have made the task easier by including many cross-references.

The system of cross-referencing not only makes the idioms easier to find but helps to jog the memory of those who can remember only one part of an idiom and not the rest. It will also be helpful to people who are simply browsing through the book looking for inspiration to add colour to their prose.

Many of the idioms have a label to indicate the situation in which they are usually used. For example formal, informal and slang expressions have been labelled (*formal*), (*inf*) and (*sl*) respectively. The labels will not only help people to use the idioms correctly but will prevent them from using them in an inappropriate context which can cause embarrassment.

Several of the idiomatic and figurative expressions in English have interesting origins. Sometimes knowing the origin of a phrase adds to one's understanding of the expression itself. Even when this is not the case, the origins are of interest in themselves. People who are interested in language generally are fascinated by etymologies, and family arguments have been known to start over the origin of an expression. This dictionary will be of help in such disputes.

Abbreviations used in this book

arch	archaic	*ie*	that is
Brit	British	*inf*	informal
c	*circa,* about	*interj*	interjection
C	century	*liter*	literary
derog	derogatory	*neg*	negative
eg	for example	*NY*	New York
esp	especially	*RAF*	Royal Air Force
etc	*et cetera,* and so on	*sl*	slang
euph	euphemistic	*US*	United States
facet	facetious	*usu*	usually
fig	figurative	*vulg*	vulgar

A

A to Z

from A to Z very thoroughly and completely: *He has studied the subject from A to Z.*

A1

A1 (*inf*) of the highest quality; very good: *This material is A1.* [A1 is the highest grading in the scale on which the condition of a ship and its cargo is rated for Lloyd's Register.]

ABC

ABC the simplest and most basic knowledge: *This book gives you the ABC of engineering.*

about

month, week *etc* **about** every alternate month, week: *I go to Manchester and Birmingham week about* (= One week I go to Manchester and one week I go to Birmingham).

above

above (someone's) head *see* **head.**

be, get (a bit) above oneself to have or acquire too high an opinion of oneself; to be or become very conceited: *She's got a bit above herself since she went to live in that district.*

be above suspicion *see* **suspicion.**

absence

leave of absence *see* **leave.**

accident

a chapter of accidents *see* **chapter.**

accord

of one's own accord of one's own free will: *He did it of his own accord, without being forced to.*

with one accord (*formal*) (everybody) in agreement: *With one accord they stood up to cheer him.*

account

bring (someone) to account (*formal*) to make sure that (a criminal *etc*) pays for what he has done: *This murderer must be brought to account.*

by all accounts in the opinion of most people: *By all accounts, he's an excellent golfer.*

call (someone) to account (*formal*) to demand that (someone) explains what he has done and why, *esp* if this was apparently wrong: *He was called to account for his ridiculous behaviour.*

give a good account of oneself (*rather formal*) to do well: *He* *gave a good account of himself (during the match)*.

on my *etc* **account** because of me or for my sake: *You don't have to leave early on my account.*

on no account not for any reason: *On no account must you open that door.*

take (something) into account/take account of (something) to consider (something which is part of the problem *etc*): *We must take his illness into account when assessing his work.*

turn (something) to (good) account to use (a situation *etc*) to one's advantage: *I'm sure I'll be able to turn this information to good account.*

ace

within an ace of very near to: *He was within an ace of success.* [An idiom from the game of dice.]

Achilles

an Achilles' heel *see* **heel.**

acid

the acid test a test which will prove or disprove something beyond doubt: *His leg appears to be completely well again, but the acid test will be the tennis tournament tomorrow.* [From a method of testing for gold by using acid.]

across

across the board *see* **board.**

get (something) across (*inf*) to be or make (something) understood: *The plan seems quite clear to me, but I just can't get it across to anyone else.*

put one across on (someone) (*sl*) to deceive or play a trick on (someone): *He thought he would put one across on his friends by pretending he was going to get married.*

act

an act of God a totally unexpected natural happening which could not have been foreseen or prevented: *His house was not insured against acts of God such as flooding and earthquakes.* [Strictly a legal term, identifying events for which one can expect no legal compensation.]

act the goat *see* **goat.**

act up (*inf*) to behave or act badly or wrongly: *My car always acts up on a long journey.*

catch (someone) in the act to discover (someone) doing something wrong: *The burglars were caught in the act of climbing in through a window.*

2

get one's act together (*inf*) to get oneself organized: *If you're ever going to find a job you'll have to start getting your act together.*

get in on the act (*inf*) to join or copy someone in doing something successful or fashionable, *esp* in order to share in his or her success: *Now that it is obvious that the computer industry is very profitable, a lot of companies are anxious to get in on the act.*

put on an act to pretend: *I thought she had hurt herself, but she was only putting on an act.*

action

action stations a state of readiness for activity: *Action stations! The concert is about to begin!* [Literally, positions taken up by soldiers in readiness for a battle *etc.*]

Adam

Adam's ale (*facet*) water: *We have no wine — you'll just have to have Adam's ale.*

not to know (someone) from Adam not to recognize (someone); not to have any idea who (someone) is: *Jonathan Wright may have been at the party, but I wouldn't know him from Adam.* [Presumably because Adam, the first man according to the Bible, is both the ultimate person one would not know and the archetype of all men.]

add

add up (*inf*) to seem sensible or logical: *I don't understand his behaviour — it just doesn't add up.*

Adonis

an Adonis a beautiful young man: *a bronzed Adonis on the beach.* [In Greek myth, Adonis was the beautiful youth loved by Aphrodite and killed by a boar while hunting.]

advantage

have the advantage of (someone) (*formal*) to recognize (someone) without being recognized oneself: *She stared blankly at the young man who had addressed her and said 'You have the advantage of me'.*

take advantage of (someone or something) to make use of (someone or something) in such a way as to benefit oneself: *She was so kind and generous that people tended to take advantage of her.*

to advantage (*formal*) so that the good points are easily seen: *The evening suit showed off his tall elegant figure to advantage.*

aegis

under the aegis of (someone) (*formal*) with the (moral or financial) support of (someone): *under the aegis of the British* *government.* [*Aegis* is a Greek word for the shield or armour of Zeus or Athena.]

after

the aftermath the situation *etc* resulting from an important, *esp* unpleasant, event: *The country is still recovering from the aftermath of the war.* [This term means literally 'second mowing' and was applied to the new grass that grows in summer after the hay has been cut.]

be after (*inf*) to be looking for or hoping to be given something: *The police are after him*; *What are you after?*

against

be up against it (*inf*) to be in a position where one has to deal with very severe, often apparently impossible difficulties: *We have only just enough money to live on now, and if my husband loses his job we'll really be up against it.*

age

the age of consent the age which a girl must be before a boy or man may legally have sexual intercourse with her: *If you have sexual intercourse with a girl before she reaches the age of consent you can be prosecuted.*

come of age to become old enough to be considered legally an adult (in Britain aged eighteen or over): *My uncle will look after my inheritance until I come of age.*

a/the golden age *see* **gold.**

of a certain age *see* **certain.**

a ripe old age *see* **ripe.**

under age too young, *esp* legally: *She can't come into the nightclub with us — she's under age.*

agony

the agony column (*inf*) the part of a magazine *etc* where letters setting out readers' problems are printed along with advice from a member of the magazine's staff.

agree

strike an agreement *see* **strike.**

ahead

ahead of one's time *see* **time.**

be streets ahead of *see* **street.**

aid

aid and abet to provide help and encouragement in some bad or illegal activity: *His wife aids and abets him in his dishonest deeds.* [Originally a legal term.]

4

what is (something) in aid of? (*Brit inf*) for what reason or purpose is (something) being done *etc*: *What is all this fuss in aid of?*

air

airs and graces (*derog*) behaviour in which a person acts as if he is better or more important than others: *In spite of all her airs and graces she had very few talents.*

clear the air to make a situation simpler and less tense: *The quarrel had not solved any problems, but at least it had cleared the air.*

hot air *see* **hot.**

in the air (*inf*) in existence; current: *suspicion in the air.*

in the open air *see* **open.**

make the air turn blue *see* **blue.**

on the air broadcasting (regularly) on radio or television: *He is on the air almost every week.*

put on airs/give oneself airs to behave as if one is better or more important than others: *She gives herself such airs.*

take the air (*old or facet*) to go for a walk.

thin air *see* **thin.**

up in the air uncertain; undecided: *Our holiday plans are still rather up in the air.*

walk on air *see* **walk.**

alarm

alar(u)ms and excursions confused activity, *esp* disorganized arguments *etc*: *He came back from holiday straight into the alarums and excursions of a major crisis in the office.* [From a stage direction in Shakespeare's history plays calling for a vague representation of the edge of a battle.]

a false alarm *see* **false.**

ale

Adam's ale *see* **Adam.**

alert

on red alert *see* **red.**

on the alert on the watch (for): *We were all on the alert for any sound that might tell us where he was.*

all

all and sundry *see* **sundry.**

all in 1 (*inf*) exhausted: *He was all in after the game.* **2** with everything included: *Is that the price all in?*

all in all considering everything: *We haven't done badly, all in all.*

all my eye *see* **eye.**

all out using the greatest effort possible: *He went all out in his attempt to break the world record.*

all there (*inf*) completely sane; having an alert, intelligent mind and good ideas: *Sometimes I wonder if he's all there*; *She's all there when it comes to looking after her own interests.*

all told *see* **tell.**

be all ears *see* **ear.**

be all over (someone) (*derog*) to treat with great friendliness and affection: *When she found out he was quite famous, she was all over him.*

be all things to all men *see* **thing.**

it is all up with (someone) (*inf*) there is no hope left for (someone): *I'm afraid it's all up with the men who were inside — no-one could have survived the explosion.*

when all is said and done considering all the facts: *When all is said and done I suppose she's lucky to be offered a job at all.*

allowance

make allowances for (someone) to judge (someone) less severely, or require (them) to do less well, than other people: *We must make allowances for Mary — she is not well.*

also

an also-ran *see* **run.**

Amazon

an Amazon (*sometimes derog*) a woman who is strong, energetic or warlike: *He had always pictured her as small and feminine and was surprised when she turned out to be a tall, blonde Amazon.* [From a legendary race of warrior women believed by the Greeks to live in Southern Russia and said to have had their right breasts removed to enable them to draw their bows better.]

amends

make amends to do something to improve the situation after doing something wrong, stupid *etc*: *He gave her a present to make amends for his rudeness.* [From the Old French word for a monetary fine.]

amiss

take (something) amiss (*formal*) to be upset or offended (by something): *He took it amiss that I had not consulted him before acting*; *I was anxious that you should not take my words amiss.* [The original meaning of this phrase was 'to be in error about' — literally 'to miss-take'.]

amount

any amount of *see* **any.**

analysis

in the final/last analysis (*rather formal*) when the problem or situation has been simplified so that only the essentials are left to be considered: *The political situation in his country is extremely complex, but in the final analysis it appears to be a struggle between progressives and conservatives.*

anchor

an anchor-man a person on whom the success of an activity depends, *esp,* on television, the person responsible for the smooth running of a discussion between other people *etc*: *He was the anchor-man for several television current affairs programmes before being given a show of his own.* [Literally, the man at the back of a team competing in a tug-of-war.]

ancient

the Ancient of Days God. [A Biblical epithet for God — Daniel 7:9 — first used in English in the Geneva Bible of 1560.]

the ancients people who lived in ancient times: *the wisdom of the ancients.*

angel

an angel of mercy a person who appears when they are particularly needed, bringing help, comfort *etc*: *Just when we were beginning to feel really thirsty, Mrs Jackson appeared, an angel of mercy, with a pot of tea.*

on the side of the angels basically agreeing with accepted ideas of what is good and bad: *For most of the book Wilkinson appears to be a criminal, but in the last few chapters he proves to be on the side of the angels after all.*

angry

an angry young man a young man who disapproves of the way his parents' generation have run the country *etc* and makes his feelings known. [A term which became popular after being applied to John Osborne, whose play *Look Back in Anger* was first performed in 1956.]

answer

answer back to give a (*usu* impertinent) answer to someone who expects one to do what one is told without argument: *The teacher was angry when the child she was scolding answered her back.*

know all the answers (*usu slightly derog*) to be in complete command of a situation and perfectly able to deal with any developments, *esp* if too proud of this ability: *He is the perfect person to organize the group — he knows all the answers; You can't tell her anything — she knows all the answers.*

any

any amount of (*inf*) a great deal of: *You'll have no difficulty in buying green velvet — there's any amount of it on sale in the shops.*

anybody's guess *see* **guess.**

any day in any circumstances: *I would rather employ you than Muriel any day!*

any old how (*inf*) without any special care: *Her desk is always terribly untidy — she just throws papers and letters into it any old how.*

like anything (*inf*) very strongly or energetically; very much: *As soon as we were out of sight we took to our heels and ran like anything.*

not to get anywhere (*inf*) to make no progress: *We don't seem to be getting anywhere in this discussion.*

apart

be poles apart *see* **pole.**

take (someone or something) apart (*sl*) to deal with or criticize (someone, a plan *etc*) severely: *If you hand in work like that, the teacher will take you apart!*

tell apart (*usu with* **can**, **cannot** *etc*) to recognize the difference between; to distinguish: *I cannot tell the twins apart.*

apology

an apology for (something) (*inf*) an example of poor quality of (something): *That's rather an apology for an essay — do it again!*

appearance

keep up appearances to behave in such a way as to hide the truth (*esp* something bad or unpleasant) from other people: *They haven't much money but they buy expensive clothes in order to keep up appearances.*

put in/make an appearance to attend (a meeting, party *etc*) *usu* only for a short time: *I don't want to stay for the whole meeting, but I'll put in an appearance at the beginning.*

to/by all appearances (*rather formal*) judging by, or basing one's opinion on, what can be seen *etc*: *He is to all appearances a happy man.*

appetite

whet (someone's) appetite *see* **whet.**

apple

an apple of discord (*formal or liter*) something which causes jealousy and fighting: *Aunt Mary's emerald ring proved to be an apple* *of discord* — *within a week of her death the whole family was fighting over who should have it.* [From the golden apple inscribed 'for the fairest' which according to Greek mythology was thrown among the gods by Eris, goddess of discord, and was claimed by Aphrodite, Athene and Hera.]

the apple of (someone's) eye a person or thing which is greatly loved (by someone): *She is the apple of her father's eye.* [Originally a term for the pupil of the eye.]

an apple-pie bed a bed made up (as a joke) in such a way as to be impossible to get into because the top sheet is doubled: *The children made their aunt an apple-pie bed.*

in apple-pie order (*inf*) neat and tidy, with everything in its correct place: *Her desk is always in apple-pie order.* [Origin unknown.]

upset the applecart (*inf*) to spoil plans, obstruct progress *etc*: *The football team were doing very well when their best player upset the applecart by breaking his leg.* [From selling fruit from carts in street markets.]

apron

tied to (someone's) apron-strings (*derog*) ruled by and dependent on (a woman, *esp* one's wife or mother): *He is still tied to his mother's apron-strings and unable to think for himself.*

argue

argue the toss *see* **toss.**

arm

armed to the teeth *see* **teeth.**

the (long) arm of the law (*inf*) the power or authority of the police force: *Although the criminal moved to another town, the long arm of the law soon caught up with him.*

be up in arms to be very angry and make a great protest (about something): *He is up in arms about the decision to close the road.*

chance one's arm *see* **chance.**

keep at arm's length to avoid becoming too friendly with (someone): *She keeps her new neighbours at arm's length.*

lay down one's arms to surrender; to stop fighting or opposing other people: *It will be difficult to persuade the opponents of our plans for the new oil refinery to lay down their arms.*

(someone's) right arm (someone's) main help and support: *In this school the prefects are the headmaster's right arm.*

a shot in the arm *see* **shot.**

take up arms to become actively involved in a dispute, argument *etc*: *The people of the village took up arms to force the local council to build a by-pass, and held rallies and demonstrations which attracted a lot of attention to their campaign.*

twist (someone's) arm (*inf*) to make (someone) do something: *'Do you want a drink?' 'Well, if you're twisting my arm, I'll have a whisky.'*

with open arms *see* **open.**

armour
a chink in (someone's) armour *see* **chink.**

around
have been around (*inf*) to have a great deal of experience of life: *I've been around — I know what people are like.*

ash
the Ashes the trophy, originally imaginary, for which Test matches between Australia and England at cricket are played: *Having won the first two Tests, Australia is now almost certain to retain the Ashes.* [In 1882 the Australian cricket team had a very successful visit to England, and the *Sporting Times* published a mock 'In Memoriam' notice announcing the cremation of the body of English cricket and the taking of the ashes to Australia. Thereafter, English teams were anxious to 'bring back the ashes' by defeating the Australians.]

ask
ask after to make inquiries about the state, *esp* the health, of: *She asked after his father.*

be asking for it/trouble (*inf*) to be behaving as if inviting (something unpleasant): *Going out in cold weather without a coat is just asking for trouble.*

someone's for the asking someone may have something simply by asking: *This table is yours for the asking.*

asleep
be asleep (*inf*) (of arms and legs *etc*) to be numb, *usu* because of pressure on a nerve: *My foot's asleep.*

assure
rest assured *see* **rest.**

attendance
dance attendance on (someone) *see* **dance.**

Attic
Attic salt dry, delicate and refined wit. [A term coined by the Roman writer Pliny.]

attitude

  strike an attitude *see* **strike.**

auction

  a Dutch auction *see* **Dutch.**

avail

  of no avail/to no avail (*formal*) of no use or effect: *He tried to revive her but to no avail; His efforts were of no avail.*

awake

  be awake to to be aware of: *Do you think they're fully awake to the problems involved?*

away

  do away with *see* **do.**

axe

  have an axe to grind to have a personal, often selfish, reason for being involved in something: *I have no axe to grind — I just want to help you.* [Originally US, stemming from a story told by Benjamin Franklin of how a man had once asked him to demonstrate how his father's grindstone worked — and had then produced an axe which he wanted to sharpen.]

B

baby

  be left holding the baby to be the person who has to deal with a problem, organize something *etc* because everyone else has abandoned it: *No sooner had he said that we would do the job than he went abroad, leaving me holding the baby.*

  throw out the baby with the bathwater to be so enthusiastic about changing or reorganizing things and getting rid of old ideas *etc* that one destroys or disposes of things that are essential: *In abolishing the police force because it was corrupt, the revolutionaries had thrown out the baby with the bathwater.*

back

  answer back *see* **answer.**

  backbiting criticizing and speaking evil of a person when he or she is not present: *Constant backbiting by her colleagues led to her resignation.*

  a backhanded compliment *see* **compliment.**

11

a backhander (*inf*) a bribe: *He won the contract for his firm by giving a backhander to the official.*

the back of beyond (*inf derog*) a very remote place: *They live at the back of beyond, somewhere in the Australian bush.* [Originally Scottish and Northern English.]

backpedal to reverse one's opinion or course of action *etc*: *He was forced to backpedal and say the opposite of what he had said originally.* [Literally, to turn the pedals of a bicycle backwards, which on many early models operated the brake.]

backscratching (*derog*) doing favours for other people in return for favours which they do for you: *There is a great deal of back-scratching involved in international politics.*

a back-seat driver a passenger in a car who gives unwanted advice on how to drive it: *Very often back-seat drivers cannot drive.*

a backwater (*usu derog*) a place not affected by what is happening in the world outside, *usu* because of its isolation: *The village where he lives now is rather a backwater.* [Literally, a stretch of water connected to a river but not now in the line of the main flow.]

behind (someone's) back (*inf*) without (someone's) knowledge or permission: *He sometimes bullies his sister behind his mother's back.*

bend over backwards *see* **bend.**

break the back of (something) to complete the heaviest or most difficult part of (a task *etc*): *Now that you've broken the back of the job, have a rest.*

fed to the back teeth *see* **fed.**

get off (someone's) back (*inf*) to stop annoying (someone): *Get off my back! I can't work if you keep on criticizing me.*

get one's own back *see* **own.**

go back on *see* **go.**

have one's back to the wall to be in a very difficult or desperate situation: *He certainly has his back to the wall as he has lost his job and cannot find another one.* [From someone involved in a fight who can retreat no further and is forced to turn and fight from a good defensive position.]

know backwards *see* **know.**

lean over backwards *see* **bend.**

make a rod for one's (own) back *see* **rod.**

put one's back into (something) (*inf*) to do (something) with all one's strength: *He really put his back into making the business profitable.*

put (someone's) back up (*inf*) to anger (someone): *He put my*

12

back up with his boasting. [The image is of a cat, which arches its back when angry.]

stab (someone) in the back *see* **stab.**

take a back seat to take an unimportant position: *At these discussions he always takes a back seat and listens to others talking.*

talk through the back of one's head/neck (*inf*) to talk complete nonsense: *If he told you we were thinking of moving house, he was talking through the back of his neck!*

bacon

bring home the bacon (*inf*) to complete a job, task *etc* successfully: *You can trust William to bring home the bacon!*

save one's (someone's) bacon (*inf*) to (cause someone to) escape unharmed from a difficulty, danger *etc*: *That grant from the government has saved our bacon.*

bad

a bad egg *see* **egg.**

a bad hat *see* **hat.**

bad language *see* **language.**

badly off (for something) not having much (of something), *esp* money: *We can't go on holiday — we are too badly off; We are not badly off for cups but we don't have enough plates.*

be in (someone's) bad books *see* **book.**

give (something) up as a bad job *see* **job.**

go from bad to worse to get into an even worse condition *etc* than before: *Things are going from bad to worse for the firm — not only are we losing money but there's going to be a strike as well.*

go to the bad to become immoral; to behave in a way of which people in general disapprove: *I'm afraid her son has really gone to the bad since he left home — he was prosecuted recently for fraud.*

hit a bad patch *see* **patch.**

in bad odour *see* **odour.**

in a bad way *see* **way.**

make the best of a bad job *see* **best.**

not bad (*inf*) quite good: *'Is she a good swimmer?' 'She's not bad.'*

too bad (*inf*) unfortunate: *It's too bad that your holiday was cancelled; I'm sorry I can't come, but it's just too bad* (= nothing can be done about it).

with a bad grace *see* **grace.**

bag

bag and baggage with all one's belongings, equipment *etc*: *She threw him out of the house bag and baggage.* [A military phrase originally describing an orderly retreat in which neither personal belongings — *bag* — nor army equipment — *baggage* — had to be abandoned.]

a bag of bones (*inf*) a very thin person: *After her illness, she was just a bag of bones.*

a bag of nerves *see* **nerve.**

a bag of tricks (*inf*) all the equipment *etc* required for doing something or connected with something: *The repair man brought out his bag of tricks and mended the washing machine.*

in the bag (*inf*) as certain as if done or complete (in the desired way): *Your appointment as director is in the bag.* [From the bag used in hunting to carry what one has shot *etc*.]

let the cat out of the bag *see* **cat.**

bait

rise to the bait to do what someone has been trying to make one do by means of suggestions, hints, attractions *etc*: *I could see he was trying to make me angry, but I didn't rise to the bait.* [A fishing term.]

baker

a baker's dozen (*old*) thirteen. [It was once customary for bakers to add an extra bun, loaf *etc* to a dozen to be sure that they were not giving short weight.]

balance

in the balance (*formal*) in an undecided or uncertain state: *Her fate is (hanging) in the balance.* [From balance = a pair of hanging scales.]

strike a balance *see* **strike.**

ball¹

have a ball (*sl*) to have a good time; to enjoy oneself: *She was the only woman there, and she was having a ball!*

ball²

have the ball at one's feet to be in a position to become successful: *He has the ball at his feet now — he'll soon be a millionaire!* [From football.]

have the ball in one's court to be responsible for the next development in a situation: *I have answered his letter, so the ball's in his court.* [From racket sports such as tennis.]

on the ball (*inf*) quick, alert and up-to-date: *The manager is increasing profits because he's really on the ball.* [From football.]

play ball (with) (*inf*) to work or act together (with others): *I tried to get him to help but he wouldn't play ball.*

start/set/keep the ball rolling to start or keep something going, *esp* a conversation: *He can be relied on to start the ball rolling at parties.*

balloon

when the balloon goes up (*inf*) when the trouble starts; when something expected (often feared) takes place: *He's always getting us into trouble, but he's never here when the balloon goes up.* [From military observation balloons.]

bananas

be, go bananas (*sl*) to be, go crazy (*esp* with anger): *If your mother sees that mess, she'll go bananas!*

band

beat the band (*sl*) to be especially loud, strong, good or remarkable: *The baby was howling to beat the band; If that doesn't beat the band!* (= I am astonished!). [Originally US.]

jump on the bandwagon (*derog*) to take part in something, or show an interest in something, because it is fashionable or because it is going to be of some (financial) advantage to oneself: *When electronic games became popular, so many toy-manufacturers jumped on the bandwagon that the shops were full of them.* [A *bandwagon* was a large, elaborate, horse-drawn vehicle capable of carrying the band in a circus procession *etc* and thus figuratively any group of people which was showy, popular and successful.]

bang

bang goes (something) (*inf*) that puts a sudden end to (*usu* hopes, plans *etc*): *It cost £50, so bang goes my new dress* (= I will not be able to afford it); *If they take over our firm bang goes my job* (= I will no longer be employed). [From a bursting bubble, balloon *etc*.]

go with a bang (*inf*) to go well; to be very successful: *The party really went with a bang after he arrived.*

bank

bank on (*inf*) to rely on: *I'm banking on his help to run the disco.* [Originally US, meaning 'to use (a sum of money *etc*) to start a bank in a card game'.]

break the bank to leave oneself or someone else without any money: *The price of a cup of coffee won't break the bank, even if we can't afford a meal.* [Literally, to win all the money which the management of a casino is prepared to pay out in one night.]

baptism

baptism of fire a first experience of something, *usu* something difficult, frightening *etc*: *The new typist had her baptism of fire typing a letter for the managing director.* [Originally a theological term.]

bargain

into the bargain in addition; besides: *First I broke my leg and then I got flu into the bargain!*

strike a bargain *see* **strike.**

bargepole

I wouldn't touch (something) with a bargepole (*inf*) I do not wish to have any contact with (something) or to be involved with it in any way: *I think you're very brave to take on that job — I wouldn't touch it with a bargepole!*

bark

his *etc* bark is worse than his bite (*inf*) he sounds angry but he does not actually do anything harmful: *He is always threatening to punish his children, but his bark is worse than his bite.* [The reference is to a dog.]

bark up the wrong tree (*inf*) to attempt to do the wrong thing, or to do something in the wrong way or from the wrong direction: *You're barking up the wrong tree if you think you will be able to influence. the judge.* [Originally US — from raccoon-hunting, in which dogs are used to locate raccoons up in trees.]

barrel

have (someone) over a barrel to be in a position to get whatever one wants from (someone): *I wouldn't help them if I had any choice, but they've got me over a barrel.* [A 19C US expression.]

scraping the (bottom of the) barrel (*derog*) making use of something or someone of very poor quality because it is all that is left or available: *He has run out of material for his newspaper articles and the last few have really been scraping the barrel!*

base

get to/make first base to complete the first stage of a process: *He's so impractical none of his projects ever make first base.* [Literally, in baseball, to complete the first of the four sections of a run.]

basket

put all one's eggs in one basket *see* **egg.**

bat[1]

off one's own bat (*inf*) completely by oneself, without being told (to do something) or given any help: *He did it off his own bat, without consulting anyone else first.* [A phrase from cricket.]

16

bat²
    as blind as a bat completely blind: *Without his spectacles, he's as blind as a bat.*
    have bats in the belfry (*inf facet*) to be slightly (but harmlessly) insane: *The eccentric old woman was generally considered to have bats in the belfry.*
    like a bat out of hell (*inf*) very quickly: *She rushed out of the house like a bat out of hell, thinking she had seen a ghost.*

bat³
    not to bat an eyelid *see* **eye**.

bated
    with bated breath in a very excited and anxious manner: *The crowd watched with bated breath as the fireman brought the child down the ladder.*

bay
    hold/keep (something or someone) at bay to fight off or keep (*eg* hunger or an enemy) from overcoming (*usu* oneself): *I'm just managing to hold disaster at bay*; *The boxer succeeded in keeping his opponent at bay.* [From an old French phrase, originally a hunting term.]

be
    the be-all and end-all the final aim apart from which nothing is of any real importance: *This job isn't the be-all and end-all of existence.* [A Shakespearian phrase, from *Macbeth*, I. vii.]

beam
    broad in the beam (*inf*) wide in the hips: *She's getting very broad in the beam — she's put on a lot of weight.* [Literally used of a ship and meaning 'wide in proportion to its length'.]
    off (the) beam (*inf*) off course or target; inaccurate: *Our original estimate was a long way off the beam.* [An aeronautical idiom from the radio beam used to bring aircraft in to land in poor visibility.]
    on one's beam ends (*inf*) very short of money, and in difficulties because of it: *I can't lend you any money — I'm on my beam ends.* [A nautical term describing a ship lying over on its side and thus in danger of capsizing completely.]

beans
    full of beans (*inf*) full of energy; very cheerful: *She has been ill but she is full of beans now.* [Probably a reference to a horse fed on beans, which are an effective energy-producing food.]
    know how many beans make five (*inf*) to know quite a lot about life and therefore to be able to take care of oneself: *Her*

father didn't worry when she was out late, because he knew she knew how. many beans made five.

spill the beans (*inf*) to give away a secret: *By Monday it was evident that someone had spilled the beans to the newspapers.* [Originally US.]

bear[1]

bear down on (someone) to approach (someone) quickly and often threateningly: *The angry teacher bore down on the child.* [A nautical term, meaning to sail towards another ship *etc* with the wind behind one, and thus with some force.]

bear fruit (*formal*) to produce results: *I hope your hard work will bear fruit.*

bear in mind *see* **mind.**

bear (something) out (*formal*) to support or confirm: *This report bears out what you said.*

bear up to remain brave, strong *etc*, *esp* under a strain: *She's bearing up well after her shock.*

bear with (someone) (*formal*) to be patient with (someone): *Bear with me for a moment and I will explain my scheme in detail.*

bear[2]

like a bear with a sore head (*inf*) in a very bad mood and easily made angry: *When my father has to get up early, he's like a bear with a sore head.*

beard

beard (someone) in his den (*formal*) to face (someone) openly or boldly; to confront (someone): *I bearded the boss in his den because I was determined to get a decision.* [Probably a quotation from Sir Walter Scott — *Marmion*, VI. xiv.]

bearing

find/get one's bearings to find out the details of one's position or situation: *He'll soon get his bearings in his new job.* [Literally, to discover one's position by means of a compass and a known landmark *etc*.]

lose one's bearings to become uncertain of where one is, what one is doing *etc*: *He's confused me so much that I've lost my bearings completely.* [As above.]

beat

beat a path to (someone's) door *see* **path.**

beat a retreat *see* **retreat.**

beat the band *see* **band.**

beat the drum *see* **drum.**

beat (someone) to it to manage to do something before (someone else) can: *She wanted to be the first to welcome him, but she found her sister had beaten her to it.*

if you can't beat them, join them a saying, meaning that if you can't persuade your opponents to change their ideas the most sensible thing to do is to change yours.

off the beaten track away from main roads, centres of population *etc*: *There's no bus service to their house — it's off the beaten track.*

take some/a lot of beating to be of very high quality and therefore difficult to improve upon: *The first competitor's performance will take some beating!*

beauty

beauty is in the eye of the beholder a saying, meaning that everyone decides individually whether something is beautiful or not, and implying that things or people which are considered beautiful by one person are not necessarily beautiful to others.

beaver

eager beaver someone who is very enthusiastic or industrious: *The new assistant always works late — he's a real eager beaver.*

work like a beaver to work very hard and busily: *She works like a beaver getting the house ready for a party.*

beck

at (someone's) beck and call always ready and waiting to carry out (someone's) order or wishes: *She always has plenty of men at her beck and call.* [*Beck* is another form of *beckon*.]

bed

a bed of roses (*inf*) an easy or comfortable place, job *etc*: *Life is not a bed of roses.*

get out of bed on the wrong side to start the day in a bad mood: *You must have got out of bed on the wrong side this morning — you're so grumpy!*

have made one's bed and have to lie in it to be obliged to suffer the disadvantages of a situation one has caused oneself: *I'm sorry their daughter causes them problems, but they always spoilt her — they've made their bed and they must lie in it.*

reds under the bed *see* **red**.

bee

have a bee in one's bonnet to have an idea which has become too fixed in one's mind: *She has a bee in her bonnet about going to America.*

19

make a bee-line for to take the most direct way to; to go immediately to: *Fred always makes a bee-line for the prettiest girl at a party.* [Bees are reputed to fly back to their hive in a straight line.]

think (one or someone) is the bee's knees (*inf, often derog*) to think (one or someone else) is the most admirable and wonderful of all people: *We all know you think you're the bee's knees!*; *All the girls at school think he is the bee's knees.* [1920s US slang.]

beer

not all beer and skittles not consisting only of pleasure, but frequently involving something quite difficult and unpleasant: *You'll soon find out that this job is not all beer and skittles!*

small beer (*formal*) something unimportant: *This is small beer compared with the work he usually does.* [The figurative use of this phrase — literally, 'weak beer' — probably derives from Shakespeare's *Othello*, II. i.]

beg

be going (a-)begging (*inf*) to be unclaimed, unsold or unwanted: *I'll have the last cake if it's going begging.*

beg the question (*formal*) to take for granted the very point that needs to be proved: *Discussing what we should invest our money in begs the question of whether we will have any money to invest.* [From Latin *petitio principiis*, the technical name for this device in medieval logic.]

beg to differ (*formal*) to disagree: *You may think that he should get the job but I beg to differ.*

beggar

beggar description (*formal*) to be so great in some way that the speaker's words cannot describe (it): *Her beauty beggared description.* [A quotation from Shakespeare — *Antony and Cleopatra*, II. i.]

beggars can't be choosers a saying, meaning that if one is in need one must accept whatever one is given whether or not it is what one would have chosen.

behind

behind the times *see* **time**.

fall behind with (something) *see* **fall**.

put (something) behind one to think of (something, *usu* an unpleasant experience) as being in the past or finished: *He has been in a lot of trouble with the police, but he seems to have managed to put all that behind him.*

believe

make believe to pretend (that): *The children made believe they were cowboys and Indians.*

not to be able to believe one's ears/eyes to find it difficult to believe that one has actually heard/seen correctly something which is surprising, shocking, startling *etc*: *When I saw her actually doing some work, I couldn't believe my eyes!*

to the best of my belief (*formal*) as far as I know; to the extent of my knowledge: *To the best of my belief he hasn't been found yet, but his wife will have the latest information.*

bell

as clear as a bell very easy to hear: *His voice was as clear as a bell, although he was phoning from South America.*

as sound as a bell undamaged and in very good condition: *Although the boat was old, it was as sound as a bell.*

bell the cat *see* **cat.**

ring a bell to cause a vague memory of having been seen, heard *etc* before, but not remembered in detail: *His name rings a bell, but I can't remember where I've heard it before.*

saved by the bell (*often interj*) rescued from an unpleasant or difficult situation by something which brings the situation suddenly to an end: *Just as she was about to ask what he was doing, he was saved by the bell when she was summoned by the manager.* [From the bell which signals the end of a round in a boxing match.]

belt

below the belt (of a method of fighting, attacking, competing *etc*) unfair; not following the accepted rules of behaviour: *I know Peter is jealous of John, but I think it was a bit below the belt to embarrass him in front of his girlfriend.* [A phrase from boxing, where a blow below the level of the belt is against the rules.]

tighten one's belt (*inf*) to make sacrifices and reduce one's standard of living: *If the economy gets worse, we shall just have to tighten our belts.*

under one's belt firmly secured and in one's possession (for future use): *She has a university degree under her belt, which should help her to get a job.*

bend

bend/lean over backwards to take great trouble (to do something), *esp* mistakenly or without results: *I bent over backwards to be nice to him because he was a stranger, but he wasn't at all grateful!*

on one's bended knees in a very humble and submissive

manner: *I will only forgive him if he comes to me on his bended knees and says he is sorry!* [*Bended* is an old form of *bent*.]

round the bend (*inf: not usu serious*) mad: *You must be round the bend to swim in the sea in April!*; *Michael's mother is driving me round the bend!* [Originally naval slang.]

benefit

give (someone) the benefit of the doubt to assume that (someone) is innocent or is telling the truth because there is not enough evidence to be sure that he is not: *I am not sure whether his story is true or not, but I'll give him the benefit of the doubt.* [A legal term.]

berth

give (someone or something) a wide berth to keep well away from or avoid (someone or something): *I always give the park a wide berth when I'm out at night.* [A nautical idiom — a *berth* is the amount of space necessary for a sailing ship to manoeuvre safely.]

beside

be beside oneself (with) to be in a state of very great, uncontrolled emotion (as anger, excitement): *She was beside herself with jealousy when her sister got married.*

be beside the point *see* **point.**

best

all the best! (used as a toast, as a farewell *etc*) I hope that you may be happy, successful *etc*: *I wanted to wish her all the best before she left.*

at the best of times when the situation is as favourable as possible — and better than at the time referred to: *He's not a patient person at the best of times, and when he's unwell he's unbearable.*

the best part of most of; nearly (all of): *I've read the best part of two hundred books on the subject.*

do one's (level) best to try as hard as possible: *He'll do his best to get here on time, but he may be late.*

for the best likely or intended to have the best results possible in a particular situation: *I didn't intend to tell him, but now he's found out perhaps it's all for the best.*

have the best of both worlds to benefit from the best features of two different sets of circumstances: *Women with children who have a job they can do at home are often thought to have the best of both worlds.*

make the best of it/a bad job to do all one can to turn a failure, disaster *etc* into something successful: *It is too late to refuse the invitation — you'll just have to make the best of it and try to enjoy yourself.*

past one's best *see* **past.**

put one's best foot forward *see* **foot.**

six of the best *see* **six.**

to the best of my belief *see* **believe.**

with the best (of them) good or well enough to compete with people who are older, stronger, healthier, more experienced *etc*: *He has only one arm but he plays tennis with the best of them; By the time she was ten she could drive a tractor with the best.*

with the best will in the world *see* **will.**

bet

bet one's bottom dollar *see* **bottom.**

hedge one's bets to do something in order to protect oneself from possible loss, criticism *etc*: *We don't know which of them is going to be made manager so we'd better hedge our bets and be nice to both of them.* [Literally, to make sufficient bets on both sides to make sure of not losing anything either way.]

you bet! (*sl*) certainly: *'Do you want to come?' 'You bet I do!'*

better

(someone's) better half *see* **half.**

better late than never *see* **late.**

better off richer; happier in some way: *He'd be better off working as a miner; She'd be better off if she divorced him.*

the better part of most of: *He talked for the better part of an hour.*

for better (or) for worse (*formal*) whatever the result may be: *For better or for worse we were now committed to our course of action.* [From a wedding vow.]

get the better of (someone) to overcome (someone); to win against (someone): *In the third round he began to get the better of his opponent; She should not allow her temper to get the better of her.*

go one better (than someone) to beat (someone) by improving on what they have done, achieved *etc*: *His father was British champion, but he has gone one better and won the European championships.* [Originally US, literally 'to bid one more unit (than someone)' in an auction or a card-game.]

have seen better days (*often facet*) to be in a worse condition or situation than in the past: *My coat has seen better days, but it is very warm; The old man had obviously seen better days* (= was poor and shabbily dressed).

know better *see* **know.**

think better of *see* **think.**

between

between you and me (*facet* **and the cat, bedpost, gatepost** *etc*)/**between ourselves** in confidence: *Between you and me, I think he's rather nice*; *Just between ourselves, I think he has gone away.*

in between times at intervals between other events: *She does not eat much at meals but eats a lot in between times.*

beyond

beyond compare *see* **compare.**

beyond one's ken *see* **ken**.

beyond price *see* **price.**

beyond the pale *see* **pale.**

bid

bid fair to (do something) (*formal*) to seem likely to (do something): *She is bidding fair to be as beautiful as her mother was.*

bide

bide one's time *see* **time.**

big

be big of (someone) (*sl, usu facet*) to be a generous action or speech on the part of (someone) (*usu* implying that he or she is not in fact being generous at all): *It was very big of him to offer us the use of his car, especially as it's actually his father's!*

Big Apple New York.

Big Brother a powerful leader or organization thought to be constantly watching and controlling people's actions: *I would not like to live in that country — you would always have the feeling that Big Brother was watching you.* [From a dictator in George Orwell's book, *Nineteen Eighty-four* (1949).]

big deal! *see* **deal.**

a big fish *see* **fish.**

the big guns *see* **gun.**

a big noise *see* **noise.**

a big shot *see* **shot.**

the big time *see* **time.**

go over big (with) (*sl*) to have a great effect (on); to impress greatly: *His plans to cut taxes went over big with the younger voters.*

have a big mouth *see* **mouth.**

in a big way *see* **way.**

Mr Big (*inf*) the leader or organizer of a group, *esp* one who controls its affairs from a distance: *The police hope that one of the drug-smugglers they have arrested will lead them to Mr Big.*

too big for one's boots (*inf*) conceited; thinking too highly of one's own importance: *His assistant is getting too big for her boots and thinks she runs the office.*

bill

fill the bill (*inf*) to be suitable; to be exactly what is required: *We are looking for a holiday cottage and this will fill the bill.* [Originally US, referring to a handbill or public notice.]

foot the bill to pay (*usu* for something expensive): *Everyone enjoyed the wedding except my father, who was footing the bill.* [Probably from the custom of signing a bill as a promise to pay — originally US.]

top the bill/be top of the bill to be the most important and highly-paid performer in a show at a theatre: *He is top of the bill at the London Palladium this winter.* [From the wording of theatrical notices, with the star performer's name at the top].

bird

a bird in the hand is worth two in the bush a saying, meaning that it is not worth giving up something one already has for only the possibility of getting something better.

the birds and the bees (*facet*) basic information about sexual behaviour in humans: *He is so naive you would think he had never heard about the birds and the bees.* [A popular 19C euphemism.]

a bird's-eye view a view, photograph *etc* from high up: *From the top of the building he had a bird's-eye view of the whole city.*

birds of a feather people of similar interests or personalities, from the saying **birds of a feather flock together**, which means that such people are usually very friendly: *I'm sure you and Debbie will get on — you're birds of a feather.*

an early bird *see* **early.**

(strictly) for the birds (*inf*) something only acceptable to people who are more stupid, weaker, *etc* than oneself; hence, unacceptable: *He says that patriotism is strictly for the birds as far as he is concerned.* [Originally US.]

give, get the bird (*sl*) to send or be sent away in a very definite manner and *usu* rudely: *She went to see him to try to end the quarrel but he gave her the bird so she didn't try again.* [A theatrical idiom, from the custom of audiences hissing — like geese — at performers who do not please them.]

go like a bird (*usu* used of machines, *esp* motor cars) to run very fast and smoothly: *My car is ten years old but she goes like a bird*.

kill two birds with one stone to achieve two of one's aims at once by means of the same action: *If you have to go to London on business next week, you could kill two birds with one stone and do your Christmas shopping at the same time*.

a little bird told me I found out in a way that I do not intend to reveal: *A little bird told me that John is about to lose his job*.

birthday

in one's birthday suit (*facet*) naked: *I couldn't answer the door in my birthday suit, so I hastily put on a dressing-gown*.

biscuit

take the biscuit (*ironic*) to be much worse than everything else: *His latest piece of impertinence really takes the biscuit*. [A British variant of US **take the cake**, which is probably from the giving of cakes as prizes at rural competitions.]

bit[1]

do one's bit (*inf*) to take one's share in a task: *Each of us will have to do his bit if we are to finish the job in time*.

not a bit of it not at all: *You would have expected her to leave early but not a bit of it — she was the last to go*.

thrilled to bits *see* **thrill.**

bit[2]

champing at the bit very impatient: *By the time the bus arrived, the man was champing at the bit*. [Literally, of horses, 'to chew the bit', *ie* with impatience.]

take the bit between one's teeth to go ahead and act on one's own, ceasing to follow instructions, advice *etc* from others: *The interviewer had taken the bit between his teeth and was beginning to ask very awkward questions*. [From a horse's method of escaping from the rider's control.]

bite

bite (someone's) head off *see* **head.**

bite off more than one can chew to try to do more than, or something more difficult than, one can manage: *He's bitten off more than he can chew, trying to renovate his house*.

bite (on) the bullet *see* **bullet.**

bite the dust *see* **dust.**

bite the hand that feeds one *see* **hand.**

have two bites at the cherry *see* **cherry.**

once bitten, twice shy a saying, meaning that if something one has done has turned out badly, one is likely to be very reluctant to do the same thing again: *Once bitten, twice shy — since my marriage ended in divorce, I'm not likely to marry again.*

what's biting you? (*inf*) what is the matter with you?: *What's biting you? You've been irritable all day.*

bitter

a bitter pill (to swallow) (*formal*) something difficult to accept: *She found his betrayal a bitter pill to swallow.*

until/till/to the bitter end up to the very end, however unpleasant *etc*: *The play was very boring, but we stayed until the bitter end; Although the party was very noisy we stayed to the bitter end.* [Probably a nautical expression — 'the bitter end' was the inboard end of an anchor rope or chain, attached in such a way that it could be taken in or paid out as the tide rose or fell. When the chain was paid out to the bitter end, however, no further adjustment was possible.]

black

as black as pitch *see* **pitch**.

be as black as one is painted to be as bad *etc* as others say: *Although he was a criminal, he was not as black as he was painted, and never used violence.*

be in (someone's) black books *see* **book**.

black and blue bruised: *She fell and hurt her arm and it is now all black and blue.*

black out to lose consciousness: *He blacked out for almost a minute.*

a black sheep a member of a family or group who is unsatisfactory in some way: *My brother has always been the black sheep of the family because he has been in prison several times.* [An old proverb held that 'a black sheep is a biting beast'.]

in black and white in writing or print, and therefore by implication in a manner that is accurate or legally binding: *Would you put that down in black and white?*

in the black (*inf*) making a profit; not in debt: *We paid off our overdraft today and we're in the black at last.* [From the use of black ink to make entries on the credit side of a ledger.]

the pot calling the kettle black *see* **pot**.

two blacks don't make a white a saying, meaning that even if someone else has behaved badly in doing you an injury *etc*, you will only make things worse if you also behave badly.

blank

a blank cheque permission to do what one feels necessary with complete freedom: *He's given me a blank cheque to carry out my plan.* [Literally, a signed cheque on which the sum to be paid has not been entered.]

draw a blank (*inf*) to be unsuccessful in a search, enquiry *etc*: *He looked for a cheap fur coat all over town, but drew a blank.* [Literally, to be given an unsuccessful ticket in a lottery.]

blanket

on the wrong side of the blanket (used in the context of family relationships) illegitimately: *He is descended from Charles II — on the wrong side of the blanket, of course.*

a wet blanket (*inf derog*) a person who spoils other people's enjoyment by being depressing: *Don't ask him to the party — he's such a wet blanket!*

blast

(at) full blast at full power, speed *etc*: *He had the radio going (at) full blast* (= as loud as possible).

blaze

blaze a trail *see* **trail.**

blessing

a blessing in disguise something that has proved to be fortunate after seeming unfortunate: *His death in the road accident was a blessing in disguise as he was slowly dying of cancer.* [A quotation from a poem by the 18C poet James Hervey.]

count one's blessings to be grateful for what one has, rather than unhappy about what one does not have: *Every time I hear of someone who is paralysed, I feel we should all count our blessings.*

a mixed blessing *see* **mix.**

blind

blind as a bat *see* **bat**[2].

the blind leading the blind one inexperienced or incompetent person helping another to do something or telling another about something: *If I attempted to explain how this machine works, I'm afraid it would be a case of the blind leading the blind.* [A Biblical reference, to Matthew 15:14 — 'And if the blind lead the blind, both shall fall into the ditch'.]

a blind spot any matter about which someone always shows a lack of understanding: *She's a very reasonable person, but she has a blind spot about her children — she thinks they're perfect.* [Literally, the one point on the retina of the eye where there are no visual cells.]

turn a blind eye *see* **eye.**

blink

    on the blink (*inf*: *usu* of an electrical appliance) not working properly: *My television is on the blink, and I never know whether it's going to work or not when I switch it on.* [From the characteristic flickering lights of a piece of faulty apparatus.]

block

    put one's head on the block *see* **head.**

blood

    bad blood ill-feeling: *There has been bad blood between the two families for years.* [From an old misconception about the cause of angry feeling, resentment *etc*.]

    blood is thicker than water one should have more loyalty to people who are related to one than to other people: *I would prefer to give the money to my friend rather than to my brother but blood is thicker than water.*

    blue blood *see* **blue.**

    fresh/new blood new members of any group of people, who are expected to add liveliness to it: *He has brought vital new blood to the football team.*

    in cold blood deliberately and unemotionally: *He killed them in cold blood.* [From the medieval belief that emotion raised the temperature of the blood.]

    like getting blood out of a stone (*usu* of obtaining something) very difficult: *Getting my father to pay for anything is like getting blood out of a stone!*

    make (someone's) blood boil to make (someone) very angry: *His behaviour really made my blood boil!* [From the medieval belief that certain emotions raised or lowered the temperature of the blood.]

    make (someone's) blood run cold to frighten or horrify (someone) very much: *The terrible scream made her blood run cold.* [As above.]

    new blood *see* **fresh blood** *above.*

    sweat blood *see* **sweat.**

blow

    blow hot and cold (on something or someone) to support and oppose (an idea, person *etc*) in turns: *He blows hot and cold on the plan so that I don't know whether he will eventually help us or not.* [From Aesop's fable of the centaur who believed that, because a man could both warm his hands and cool his food by blowing on them, he must be blowing hot and cold from the same mouth.]

blow it (*sl*) to lose one's chance of success through one's own fault: *I had an opportunity to win the match, but I blew it by being too impulsive.*

blow over to pass and become forgotten: *The trouble will soon blow over.* [Literally, of storm-clouds, to pass over without causing a storm.]

blow one's own trumpet *see* **trumpet.**

blow the gaff *see* **gaff.**

blow the lid off *see* **lid.**

blow the whistle (on) *see* **whistle.**

blow one's top *see* **top.**

see which way/how the wind blows *see* **wind**[1].

strike a blow for (something) to do something definite and noticeable to help (a cause, aim *etc*): *The demonstrators said they were there to strike a blow for freedom.*

blue

blue blood aristocratic ancestry: *They may be poor, but they have blue blood in their family.* [In Spanish *sangre azul*; this term describes Spanish aristocrats of pure, unmixed Germanic ancestry, under whose fair skins the blue veins showed very clearly.]

a blue-eyed boy (*derog*) someone who is a favourite: *He will get promotion — he's the boss's blue-eyed boy.*

the blues (*inf*) low spirits; depression: *He's got the blues today but he's usually cheerful.*

a bluestocking (*derog*) a highly-educated woman; a woman who is interested in serious, intellectual subjects: *She never comes to parties — she's too much of a bluestocking.* [From a group of 18C London ladies who held philosophical evening-parties which at least one guest attended informally dressed in blue worsted stockings.]

a bolt from the blue *see* **bolt.**

in a blue funk *see* **funk.**

make the air turn blue (*inf*) to swear strongly and at some length: *He fairly made the air turn blue when he hit his finger with the hammer!*

once in a blue moon very seldom: *He visits his mother once in a blue moon.* [The moon very occasionally appears to be tinged with blue.]

out of the blue without warning: *He arrived out of the blue, without* *letting us know he was in the area.* [From lightning which strikes out of a clear sky.]

scream/yell blue murder (*inf*) to make a great deal of noise and protest: *Every time the child was put to bed he screamed blue murder.* [Possibly connected with the French oath *morbleu* — 'blue death'.]

true blue unchangingly faithful and loyal: *You can rely on Michael — he's true blue.*

bluff

call (someone's) bluff to demand that (someone) proves the genuineness of a claim, threat or promise which they have made: *We did not really believe he would sue us as he threatened, so we called his bluff and published the story about him.* [From the game of poker.]

board

above board open and honourable; not secret: *We must keep the whole affair above board.* [From card-games, where anything that takes place under the table is likely to be against the rules.]

across the board (*inf*) applying in all cases: *They were awarded wage increases across the board.* [Originally US, from horse-racing — a technical term for betting on the same horse to win, to be placed or to be fourth.]

go by the board to be abandoned or thrown aside: *All my plans went by the board when I lost my job.* [A nautical term meaning 'to vanish overboard' — *board* = 'the ship's side'.]

sweep the board to win everything: *The swimmer swept the board at the Olympics, winning seven gold medals.* [From card-games, where all the money to be won is placed on the 'board'.]

boat

burn one's boats to do something which makes it impossible for one to return to one's former position, way of life *etc*: *I've burnt my boats by resigning, and I haven't got another job.* [A practice by which generals leading an invasion stiffened the resolve of their troops.]

in the same boat (*inf*) in the same, *usu* difficult, position or circumstances: *We're all in the same boat as far as low wages are concerned.*

miss the boat *see* **miss.**

rock the boat (*inf*) to do something which endangers a pleasant or satisfactory situation *etc* in which one shares: *We were all doing very well until he began rocking the boat by asking if our actions were legal and morally justifiable.*

body

    keep body and soul together (*often facet*) to remain alive — *esp* not to die of hunger: *He has to have a snack in the middle of the morning to keep body and soul together until lunchtime.*

    over my dead body *see* **dead.**

bog

    bogged down prevented from making progress: *I'm getting bogged down in all this paperwork.* [Literally — a military term — hindered in movement by mud *etc.*]

boil

    boil down to (*inf*) to mean in effect: *His speech was a long one, but it boiled down to a warning that we would all have to work harder for less money.*

    come to the boil to arrive at a critical state: *Things are coming to the boil in the car industry, and a strike is imminent.* [Literally, to arrive at boiling-point.]

bolt

    a bolt from the blue a sudden, unexpected happening: *His resignation was a bolt from the blue.* [Literally, a flash of lightning out of a cloudless sky.]

    a bolthole a place into which a person can escape: *There's a secret bolthole behind this wall so that we can escape.* [Literally, an exit-hole from a rabbit-warren through which rabbits can escape from a predator.]

    bolt upright absolutely upright: *She sat bolt upright in the chair with her back very straight.* [Literally, 'as upright as a bolt'; where *bolt* = arrow.]

    have shot one's bolt to be unable to do more than one has done: *By the last lap of the race it was obvious that the world champion had shot his bolt and was falling behind.* [The image is of an archer with only one arrow or 'bolt' who is defenceless once he has fired it.]

    make a bolt for it to (attempt to) run away suddenly: *The prisoners made a bolt for it when the guard wasn't looking.*

    the nuts and bolts *see* **nut.**

bomb

    a bombshell a piece of startling and often very bad news: *His resignation was a real bombshell.*

    go like a bomb (*inf*) **1** to move very fast: *My car goes like a bomb.* **2** to sell extremely well; to be very successful: *These pop-records go like a bomb*; *The party is going like a bomb.*

make a bomb (*sl*) to make or earn a great deal of money: *He made a bomb when he sold his house to a film-star.*

bone

as dry as a bone completely dry: *'Is the ground wet?' 'No, it's as dry as a bone.'*

a bag of bones *see* **bag.**

the bare bones the essential facts (of a subject): *He only had time to tell me the bare bones of his scheme.*

bone idle (*inf*) very lazy: *He could find a job but he's bone idle.*

a bone of contention (*formal*) a cause of argument or quarrelling: *Who should inherit their uncle's estate was a bone of contention between the two men for many years.* [From the fact that dogs will fight over a bone.]

feel in one's bones to know by instinct, without having any proof: *Everything seemed to be going well, but I could feel in my bones that something was wrong.*

have a bone to pick with (someone) to have something to disagree, or argue, about with (someone): *I've (got) a bone to pick with you.* [Probably from the fact that two dogs are unlikely to pick at the same bone without fighting.]

make no bones about to have no hesitation about (stating or doing something openly): *They made no bones about (telling us) how they felt.* [An older version, *to find no bones in*, suggests that the reference was originally to bones in soup *etc*.]

near the bone (*inf*) **1** (of a speech *etc*) referring too closely to something which should not be mentioned: *I don't think he realized how near the bone some of his remarks were.* **2** rather indecent: *Some of his jokes were a bit near the bone.*

to the bone 1 thoroughly and completely: *I was chilled to the bone.* **2** to the minimum: *I've cut my expenses to the bone.*

bonnet

have a bee in one's bonnet *see* **bee.**

boo

he *etc* **can't say boo to a goose** *see* **goose.**

book

be in (someone's) good, bad/black books to be in or out of favour with (someone): *The salesman has been in the manager's good books since he increased last year's sales; Ever since he forgot about her birthday, he has been in her black books.*

a bookworm (*inf: sometimes derog*) a person who reads a lot: *He is a real bookworm — he reads ten books a week!*

bring (someone) to book (*formal*) to make (someone) explain, or suffer for, his behaviour: *It was several weeks before the thieves were finally tracked down and brought to book.*

by the book strictly according to the rules: *She will never be sacked — she always does things by the book.*

a closed book (*rather formal*) a subject which one knows nothing about or does not understand: *I'm afraid economics is a closed book to me.*

cook the books *see* **cook.**

get one's books (*sl*) to be dismissed from one's job: *When it was discovered that he never did any work, he got his books at once.*

in my *etc* **book** in my opinion: *In my book your behaviour was perfectly justified.*

an open book something which can be understood easily or whose meaning *etc* is easily seen: *His intentions and plans are always an open book to people who know him.*

read (someone) like a book to understand completely someone's character, reasons for acting as he/she does, *etc*: *He thinks he deceives his wife with his lies, but she can read him like a book.*

suit (someone's) book to be pleasing or favourable to (someone): *If you arrive at six o'clock that suits my book, because I can collect you after work.*

take a leaf out of (someone's) book *see* **leaf.**

throw the book at (someone) to reprimand or punish (someone) severely, *esp* for breaking rules: *He'll throw the book at you if he finds out how you got this information.*

boot[1]

as tough as old boots very tough or (*fig*) strong, *esp* in health.

the boot is on the other foot the very opposite of what used to be the case, or of what is thought to be the case, is true: *You're wrong if you think I borrowed money from Jane — in fact, the boot is on the other foot: she borrowed from me.*

get the boot (*sl*) to be dismissed (*usu* from one's job): *He got the boot for always being late.*

give (someone) the boot (*sl*) to dismiss (someone) (*usu* from their job): *He was late so often that the boss eventually gave him the boot.*

have one's heart in one's boots *see* **heart.**

lick (someone's) boots to flatter (someone) and do everything he or she wants: *She will not join in our campaign for higher wages — she is always too anxious to lick the boss's boots.*

put the boot in (*sl*) to attack someone viciously and unfairly: *When the firm was unable to pay higher wages the employees put the boot in and went on strike although they knew it would bankrupt the firm.* [Literally, 'to kick someone viciously'.]

boot[2]

to boot (*formal*) in addition; also: *She is beautiful, and wealthy to boot.*

born

be born with a silver spoon in one's mouth *see* **silver.**

in all my born days (*inf*) in my life: *I never saw such a thing in all my born days!*

not born yesterday *see* **yesterday.**

not to know one is born *see* **know.**

to the manner born *see* **manner.**

bosom

bosom friend (*inf*) a close friend: *The two teenage girls were bosom friends and went everywhere together.*

bottle

a bottleneck a place where slowing down or stopping of progress occurs, *esp* a narrow part of a road which becomes very crowded with traffic: *There's a bottleneck where the motorway ends and the ordinary road begins*; *The strike has created a bottleneck in the assembly department.*

bottle up to prevent (*eg* one's feelings) from becoming known or obvious: *Don't bottle up your anger — tell him what's annoying you.*

crack a bottle *see* **crack.**

hit the bottle (*derog sl*) to begin to drink too much alcohol: *When his wife died he really hit the bottle and was never really sober for a fortnight.*

on the bottle (*sl*) in the habit of drinking too much alcohol: *She was late for work so often that her boss began to wonder if she was on the bottle.*

bottom

at bottom (*rather formal*) in reality: *At bottom, he's really a very shy person.*

be at the bottom of to be the cause of (*usu* something bad): *What's at the bottom of these nasty rumours?*

bet one's bottom dollar (*inf*) to bet everything one has (*usu* used in an expression of certainty about something): *I would bet my bottom dollar that he gets paid more than you do* (= I am certain that he does). [Originally US.]

bottom drawer *see* **drawer.**

from the bottom of one's heart *see* **heart.**

get to the bottom of to discover the explanation of the real facts of (a mystery *etc*): *I'll get to the bottom of this affair if it takes me a year!*

bound

out of bounds outside the permitted area or limits: *The cinema was out of bounds for the boys from the local boarding-school.*

bow[1]

bowed down with (something) (*formal*) worried or troubled by having to deal with (something difficult *etc*): *He was bowed down with the responsibility of governing the country.*

bow (oneself) out to leave or cease to take part in a situation, project *etc*: *He realized that the situation was getting very difficult and decided that it was time to bow (himself) out.*

take a bow to accept and show that one appreciates applause or recognition: *In this article the man behind the new development plans takes a bow and explains how the idea came to him.* [Literally, to appear on stage at the end of a theatrical performance to acknowledge applause.]

bow[2]

draw the long bow (*formal*) to make statements which go beyond the truth: *When he told us he had captured three bank-robbers single-handed, I felt he was drawing the long bow.* [Origin obscure.]

have more than one string to one's bow to have at least one alternative (to an opportunity, course of action *etc*) already planned or available: *It isn't really vital that he gets this particular job, because he has more than one string to his bow.* [An archer carries a spare bowstring in case one breaks.]

bow[3]

a shot across the bows *see* **shot.**

bowl

bowl over to cause to be overcome by emotion, *esp* gratitude, admiration or grief: *His generosity bowled me over; She was bowled over by his charm.*

Box

Box and Cox two people who never meet and are never in the same place at the same time: *The nightwatchman and the caretaker here are Box and Cox — when one arrives the other goes home.* [From a 19C farce in which two men thus named rent the same room by night and by day respectively.]

boy

a blue-eyed boy *see* **blue.**

a whipping-boy *see* **whip.**

brain

(someone's) brainchild a favourite theory, invention *etc* thought up by (a particular person): *This entire process is Dr Smith's brainchild.*

the brain drain the loss of experts to another country (*usu* in search of better salaries *etc*): *As a result of the brain drain Britain does not have enough doctors.*

a brainstorm a sudden mental disturbance: *He had a brainstorm and murdered his wife.* [Originally a technical medical description for an attack of certain types of mental illness.]

brainwash (someone) to force (a person) to obey, conform, confess *etc* by putting great (psychological) pressure on him or her: *The terrorists brainwashed him into believing in their ideals.*

a brainwave a sudden good idea: *It was a brainwave to come here for our holidays.*

have (something) on the brain to be unable to forget about (something) or to think about anything else: *I've had that piece of music on the brain all day; He has football on the brain and talks about it all the time.*

pick (someone's) brains to ask (someone) questions in order to get ideas, information *etc* from him which one can use oneself: *You might be able to help me with this problem — can I come and pick your brains for a minute?*

rack one's brains to exert one's mind greatly (in trying to think of something): *He racked his brains for the answers.* [From the old instrument of torture called *the rack*.]

branch

root and branch *see* **root.**

brass

as bold as brass (*derog*) very bold and *usu* impertinent: *She walked in late as bold as brass.*

get down to brass tacks (*inf*) to deal with basic principles or matters: *Let's stop arguing about theories and get down to brass tacks.* [Originally US.]

have the brass neck to (do something) (*inf derog*) to be sufficiently shameless and impudent to (do something unacceptable): *He had the brass neck to suggest that I should resign.* [Both *brass* and *neck* are dialect words for 'impudence'.]

the top brass (*often derog*) people of the highest rank (in the army, a business *etc*): *He spends a lot of money on entertaining the top brass.*

brave

put on a brave front/face to pretend that things are going well and that one is perfectly happy: *She puts on a brave front, but I know she is dreadfully worried.*

bread

one's bread and butter (a way of earning) one's living, as opposed to what one does for enjoyment: *Writing novels is my bread and butter, but I prefer to write poetry.*

a breadwinner a person who earns money to keep a family: *When her husband died she had to become the breadwinner.*

know which side one's bread is buttered (on) to know how one should act for one's own advantage: *She won't quarrel with her boss — she knows which side her bread is buttered.*

like one's bread buttered on both sides to want to live *etc* in great comfort or luxury: *Anyone else would have thought it was a good job, but he likes his bread buttered on both sides and he considered he was given too much work to do.*

on the breadline (*inf*) with barely enough money to live on: *The widow and her children were living on the breadline.* [Originally US — breadlines were queues of destitute people waiting for free food from soup-kitchens, especially those run by the government.]

break

break cover *see* **cover.**

break one's duck *see* **duck.**

break even *see* **even.**

break (someone's) heart *see* **heart.**

break in to make (shoes *etc*) less stiff by using them: *You will get blisters if you go climbing in those boots without breaking them in first.* [A technical term for the process of training a young horse to carry a rider *etc*.]

break new/fresh ground *see* **ground.**

break of day (*liter*) dawn: *He left at break of day.*

break ranks *see* **rank.**

break the bank *see* **bank.**

break the ice *see* **ice.**

break the news *see* **news.**

break the record *see* **record.**

break one's word *see* **word.**

breast

make a clean breast of (something) *see* **clean.**

breath

catch one's breath to stop breathing for an instant (often from fear, amazement *etc* or due to physical discomfort): *He caught his breath on seeing the view*; *The sharp pain made him catch his breath.*

get one's breath (back) to regain the ability to breathe properly (*eg* after exercise): *If you want me to climb the rest of the hill you'll have to give me time to get my breath back.*

hold one's breath to stop breathing (often because of anxiety): *He held his breath as he watched the daring acrobat*; *She held her breath and hoped that the burglar wouldn't realize she was behind the curtain.*

out of breath breathless (through running *etc*): *I'm out of breath after climbing all these stairs.*

take (someone's) breath away to make (someone) breathless (with astonishment, delight *etc*): *She took my breath away with her rudeness*; *The view was so beautiful it took his breath away.*

under one's breath in a whisper: *He swore under his breath.*

waste one's breath to say something which is not heeded: *I don't know why I bother talking to you — I'm just wasting my breath!*

breathe

breathe again to be relieved of a great worry *etc*: *Breathe again — the police have gone!*

breathe one's last *see* **last.**

breathing down (someone's) neck 1 close behind (someone): *I ran a fast race, but he was breathing down my neck all the way.* **2** extremely impatient: *He's breathing down my neck for this letter I'm typing.*

a breathing-space a short time in which one can have a rest: *I've only a breathing-space of ten minutes before my next appointment.*

brick

bang one's head against a brick wall *see* **head.**

drop a brick *see* **drop.**

in with the bricks (*inf*) having been in a place, organization *etc*, since the beginning: *The tennis club can't get rid of their treasurer, even although she's not very good, because she's in with the bricks.* [As if built into a building as bricks are.]

like a ton of bricks immediately and heavily: *Margaret wanted to come with us, but her husband came down on the idea like a ton of bricks.*

try to make bricks without straw to try to do a piece of work without the materials, tools *etc* necessary for it: *Trying to prepare a statistical report with the scanty information available was like trying to make bricks without straw.* [A Biblical reference, to Exodus 5.]

bridge

cross a bridge when one comes to it not to bother about a problem that is going to arise in the future until it actually affects one: *Once we get the money we'll have to work out how it is to be allocated, but we'll cross that bridge when we come to it.*

water under the bridge *see* **water.**

brief

hold no brief for (*formal*) not to have any reason to support or speak in favour of: *Contrary to what you obviously think, I hold no brief for any extremist organization.* [A legal term — 'to be employed to conduct a particular case in court'.]

in brief (*formal*) in a few words: *In brief, we have been successful.*

bright

as bright as a button *see* **button.**

bright and early early; in good time: *On the day of the wedding she was up bright and early.*

a bright spark a very lively, cheerful person: *I've met his daughter — she's a bright spark, isn't she?*

look on the bright side to be hopeful and consider the best features of something: *You must look on the bright side — after all, you still have a job.*

bring

bring back/down to earth *see* **earth.**

bring home to *see* **home.**

bring (something) into line *see* **line.**

bring into play *see* **play.**

bring (someone) round 1 to bring (someone) back from unconsciousness: *The smelling-salts brought him round.* **2** to persuade (someone): *We'll bring him round to the idea.*

bring the house down *see* **house.**

bring (someone) to to bring (someone) back to consciousness: *These smelling-salts will bring him to.*

bring (something) to a head *see* **head.**

bring to light *see* **light.**

bring (someone) up short *see* **short.**

bring up the rear *see* **rear.**

bristle

bristle with (*formal*) to be full of: *The warship was bristling with guns*; *They walked through streets bristling with tourists*.

Bristol

shipshape and Bristol-fashion *see* **ship**.

broad

be broad-minded to be ready to allow others to think or act as they choose without criticizing them: *Her parents are broad-minded and allow her to come home very late*.

broad in the beam *see* **beam**.

have broad shoulders *see* **shoulder**.

in broad daylight during the day: *He did not expect to be robbed in broad daylight*.

brother

am I my brother's keeper? I am not responsible for the actions of others.

Big Brother *see* **big**.

broken

broken-hearted overcome by grief: *When the dog died she was broken-hearted*.

a broken home the home of children whose parents are divorced or live apart: *She comes from a broken home*.

a broken reed (*inf derog*) a person who is too weak or unreliable to be depended on (to help, join in an activity *etc*): *John had promised to help her get a job, but he proved to be a broken reed and was of no help at all*.

broom

a new broom *see* **new**.

broth

too many cooks spoil the broth *see* **cook**.

brow

knit one's brows *see* **knit**.

the sweat of one's brow *see* **sweat**.

brown

browned off (*inf*) **1** bored: *I feel really browned off in this wet weather*. **2** annoyed: *I'm browned off with his behaviour*.

in a brown study (*formal*) deep in thought: *She's in a brown study today* (= pays no attention to what you say). [A very old phrase apparently derived from an obsolete meaning of *brown* — 'gloomy'.]

brush

be tarred with the same brush *see* **tar.**

brush (something) aside to pay no attention to (something): *She brushed aside my objections.*

brush up on (something) (*inf*) to refresh one's knowledge of (a subject): *I must brush up on British history.*

give, get the brush-off (*inf*) to reject or be rejected abruptly: *She gave me the brush-off when I asked her to go to the cinema.*

buck

the buck stops here the final responsibility rests here. [For origin see next entry.]

pass the buck (*inf*) to pass on responsibility (to someone else): *Whenever he is blamed for anything, he tries to pass the buck.* [In the game of poker the *buck* is a token object which is passed to the person who wins a jackpot, to remind him that when it is his turn to deal the next hand he must start another jackpot.]

bucket

come down in buckets (*inf*) to be raining heavily: *I can't drive in this rain — it's coming down in buckets.*

a drop in the bucket *see* **drop.**

kick the bucket (*sl*) to die: *They were all just waiting for the old man to kick the bucket so they could get their hands on his money.* [This phrase is recorded in the 18C and may be connected with the wooden frame — called a *bucket* in East Anglia — from which a newly-killed pig was hung.]

weep buckets (*inf*) to weep a great deal: *She wept buckets when she watched the sad film.*

bud

nip (something) in the bud *see* **nip.**

buff

in the buff (*inf: usu facet*) naked: *The beach was crowded with people sunbathing in the buff.* [*Buff* is whitish-yellow leather with the grain removed, once used for military equipment and a similar colour to human skin.]

bug

get the bug (*inf*) to be taken with great enthusiasm (for): *He's got the travel/acting bug.*

Buggins

Buggins' turn one's turn to be promoted *etc* according to some mechanical system, not on merit: *He only became chairman of the committee on the principle of Buggins' turn.*

42

build

build castles in the air *see* **castle**.

build on sand *see* **sand**.

bull

(like) a bull in a china shop (*inf*) (a person who acts) in a very clumsy or tactless way: *He was a bad diplomat, because he tended to approach vital and delicate negotiations like a bull in a china shop.*

hit the bull's-eye/score a bull's-eye to make a remark, do something *etc* which is very apt, appropriate, true or relevant: *As far as Christmas presents were concerned, the family agreed that Aunt Helen had hit the bull's-eye by giving them a sledge.* [Literally, to hit the exact centre section of the dartboard in a game of darts.]

(like) a red rag to a bull *see* **red**.

take the bull by the horns to tackle a difficulty boldly: *If you want to improve the situation you must take the bull by the horns.*

bullet

bite (on) the bullet to accept something unpleasant but unavoidable as bravely as possible: *He disliked being indebted to someone he despised, but he was obliged to bite on the bullet.* [From the practice among army doctors *etc* of giving a patient a soft lead bullet to bite on while setting bones, cleaning wounds *etc*.]

get the bullet (*inf*) to be dismissed: *If you are late for work again you will get the bullet.*

give (someone) the bullet (*inf*) to dismiss (someone).

bully

bully for you *etc* (*sl*; *often facet*) good for you *etc*; that's nice for you *etc*: *'The boss is allowing Anne time off to have her hair done.' 'Bully for her! What about the rest of us?'*

bum

a bum steer (*sl*) a false, misleading or worthless piece of information, set of instructions *etc*: *That exclusive story he promised the newspapers turned out to be a bum steer.* [Literally, in America, a *bum steer* was originally a poor or worthless young bullock.]

give (someone) the bum's rush (*sl*) to get rid of (someone), or force them to leave (a place, a job *etc*), very quickly: *When they found out that she was a member of a terrorist organization, her employers gave her the bum's rush.* [Originally US, presumably from throwing tramps — bums — out of bars *etc*.]

bump

bump into (someone) (*inf*) to meet (someone) by accident: *I bumped into him the other day in the street.*

bump (someone) off (*sl*) to kill (someone): *The hero got bumped off halfway through the play.* [Originally US.]

bump up (*inf*) to raise (prices); to increase the size of: *They have bumped up their charges to make an extra profit.*

bun

have a bun in the oven (*facet*) to be pregnant: *He had to get married because his girlfriend had a bun in the oven.*

bunch

a bunch of fives *see* **five.**

bundle

a bundle of nerves *see* **nerve.**

go a bundle on (*sl*) to like or be enthusiastic about: *I didn't go a bundle on her taste in interior decoration — it was very avant-garde.* [An American expression literally meaning 'to bet a lot of money on'.]

bunk

do a bunk (*sl*) to go away in a hurry, *esp* in order to escape from something: *When he realized the police were after him, he did a bunk with quite a lot of the company's money.*

burden

the burden of proof the responsibility for proving (something, *esp* a point in a court of law): *The burden of proof rests with you.* [A translation of the Latin legal term *onus probandi*.]

burn

burn one's boats *see* **boat.**

burn one's fingers *see* **finger.**

a burning question a question of interest to, and eagerly discussed by, many people: *The burning question in the office was who was to be the next manager.*

burn the candle at both ends *see* **candle.**

burn the midnight oil *see* **midnight.**

a burnt offering (*facet*) a meal, or part of a meal, which has been burnt: *Her husband ate his way through many burnt offerings before she finally learned to cook.* [Literally, a Jewish animal sacrifice, mentioned frequently in the Bible.]

get one's fingers burnt *see* **finger**.

have money to burn *see* **money.**

Burton

    gone for a Burton (*sl*) dead, ruined *etc.* [2nd World War RAF slang — a euphemistic phrase apparently meaning literally 'gone for a drink', *Burton* = 'Burton ale'.]

bus

    a busman's holiday a holiday spent doing something similar to what one does in one's job: *The joiner spent a busman's holiday building a fitted wardrobe in his bedroom.* [Reputedly derived from the story of a certain horse-bus driver who spent his days off travelling back and forward in a bus driven by one of his friends.]

    like the back end of a bus (*inf derog*) very unattractive: *He is quite good-looking, but his wife has a face like the back end of a bus.*

    miss the bus *see* **miss.**

bush

    beat about the bush to approach a subject in an indirect way, without coming to the point: *Stop beating about the bush and tell me what you came for!* [*Beating the bush* is an operation carried out while hunting birds.]

    (the) bush telegraph (*often facet*) the fast spreading of information, *usu* by word of mouth: *The bush telegraph in our office is the most effective way of spreading news.* [An Australian phrase.]

bushel

    hide one's light under a bushel *see* **light.**

business

    the business end (of something) (*inf*) the end or part (of something) that actually does the work: *He prised open the tin with the business end of a screwdriver.*

    funny business *see* **funny.**

    have no business to (do something) (*inf*) to have no right to (do or be doing something): *You've no business to be up at this hour of night — go to bed at once!*

    like nobody's business *see* **nobody.**

    make it one's business to (do something) to be interested or concerned enough to make sure that one (does something): *I make it my business to check that every advertisement our magazine prints is genuine.*

    mean business (*inf*) to intend to do something serious and businesslike; not to be joking: *I could see from the expression on her face as she came in that she meant business.*

    mind one's own business (*not polite*) to attend to one's own affairs, not interfering in other people's: *Why don't you go away and mind your own business?*

monkey business *see* **monkey**.

butter

butterfingers (*inf*) (a name given to) a person who often drops, or is likely to drop, things that he or she is carrying: *Come on, butterfingers, see if you can catch this!*; *I daren't let him do the washing-up — he's such a butterfingers!*

butter (someone) up (*inf*) to flatter (someone) *usu* because one wants him or her to do something for one: *He's always buttering up the boss because he wants promotion.*

know which side one's bread is buttered (on), like one's bread buttered on both sides *see* **bread**.

look as if butter wouldn't melt in one's mouth to appear very innocent, honest, respectable *etc*, *usu* implying that the speaker believes one is not these things: *She sat there looking as if butter wouldn't melt in her mouth, and I think I was the only person who knew that she was responsible for the whole mix-up.*

butterfly

have butterflies (in one's stomach) to feel a fluttering sensation in one's insides as a result of nervousness: *She always gets butterflies before she goes on stage.*

button

as bright as a button (*usu* only of children or animals) (appearing to be) very intelligent and alert: *They have just bought a fox terrier puppy which is very active and as bright as a button.*

buttoned up (*sl*) successfully arranged; safely in one's possession: *The negotiations were all completed and we seemed to have the whole project buttoned up.*

buttonhole (someone) (*inf*) to catch (someone's) attention and hold him in conversation: *He buttonholed me and began telling me the story of his life.* [The word was originally *buttonhold* — 'to catch and hold by the button'.]

buy

buy (someone) off (*inf*) to bribe (someone): *The gangster's friends bought off the police witness.*

I'll buy that (*sl*) I'll accept that explanation (although it seems rather surprising).

buzz

a buzz-word (*inf*) an impressive-sounding but often nearly meaningless word used as part of the jargon of a particular subject *etc*: *'Interface' is a popular buzz-word among pseudo-intellectuals at the moment.*

by

> **by and by** after a short time: *By and by, everyone went home.* [Like *presently*, this phrase originally meant 'at once'.]
>
> **by and large** mostly; considering everything together: *Things are going quite well, by and large.* [A nautical expression, meaning 'both sailing into the wind' — *by* — 'and with the wind' — *large*.]
>
> **by the by(e)/by the way** incidentally: *By the way, have you a moment to spare?*; *I haven't seen her lately, by the bye.* [*By the bye* means literally 'by the way of a secondary route/subject'.]
>
> **let bygones be bygones** to forgive and forget past injuries, quarrels *etc*: *They agreed to let bygones be bygones and not to refer to the incident again.*

C

cahoots

> **in cahoots** (*derog sl*) joined together in a secret partnership, *esp* to do something wrong or dishonest: *His firm was given many government contracts because he was in cahoots with someone in the government.* [Originally US — *cahoot* = partnership, from the French *cahute* = cabin.]

Cain

> **raise Cain** *see* **raise.**

cake

> **eat one's cake and have it** to enjoy the advantages of two alternative courses of action *etc* when it is, or ought to be, impossible to do both at once: *If he wants to be paid more, he will have to accept more responsibility — he can't eat his cake and have it.*
>
> **like hot cakes** *see* **hot.**
>
> **a piece of cake** (*inf*) something very easy: *Winning the race was a piece of cake.*
>
> **a slice of the cake** *see* **slice.**

calf

> **kill the fatted calf** *see* **fat.**

call

    call a halt *see* **halt.**

    call a spade a spade *see* **spade.**

    call (someone's) bluff *see* **bluff.**

    call (something) into question *see* **question.**

    call it a day *see* **day.**

    call it quits *see* **quit.**

    call (something) off to cancel (something): *The party's been called off.*

    call (someone) names *see* **name.**

    the call of nature *see* **nature.**

    call the shots *see* **shot.**

    call the tune *see* **tune.**

    call (someone) to account *see* **account.**

    a close call *see* **close**[1].

calm

    as calm as a millpond *see* **mill.**

camel

    the straw that breaks the camel's back *see* **the last straw** *at* **last.**

can

    carry the can (*sl*) to take the blame: *I'm not going to carry the can for his mistakes.* [Originally naval slang.]

candle

    burn the candle at both ends to waste or use up something in two ways at once, *esp* to work hard during the day from early morning and also stay up late at night studying or enjoying oneself: *The student became ill from going to parties every night and getting up at 5 am to study — he was trying to burn the candle at both ends.*

    the game is not worth the candle the project is too difficult, troublesome *etc* for the advantages it would bring: *I don't work overtime because, with the amount of tax I have to pay, the game isn't worth the candle.* [A literal translation of the French phrase *le jeu n'en vaut la chandelle*, referring to a gambling session in which the amount of money at stake is not sufficient to pay for the candle used up during play.]

    not fit to hold a candle to not good enough to be compared with: *Our new manager is not fit to hold a candle to the previous one.* [Literally, not good enough even to hold a light so that someone else may see to do a job.]

48

canoe

paddle one's own canoe to control one's own affairs without help or control from anyone else: *He would not accept a job in his father's business because he was determined to paddle his own canoe.* [An American idiom of the early 19C.]

cap

cap in hand humbly: *Her son has left home but he'll come back cap in hand when he has run out of money!*

a feather in one's cap *see* **feather.**

if the cap fits from the saying **if the cap fits, wear it**, which means that if you think what has been said applies to you, then you should certainly take notice of it.

put on one's thinking cap *see* **think.**

set one's cap at deliberately to try to attract (a member of the opposite sex): *She set her cap at her boss as soon as she arrived here — she liked the idea of being the manager's wife.* [Possibly a mistranslation from a French nautical expression — *mettre le cap à* — meaning to head towards.]

capital

make capital out of (something) to use (a situation, event *etc*) for one's own advantage: *The politician delivered a clever, witty speech, making capital out of his opponent's failure to appear.*

card

get one's cards (*inf*) to be dismissed (*esp* from one's job): *The workmen knew that as soon as the building was finished most of them would get their cards.*

have/keep a card up one's sleeve to have prepared (but not revealed) an argument, plan of action *etc* to be used as a separate tactic if necessary: *It seemed as if Jim had lost the argument, but as usual he still had a card up his sleeve.* [From cheating at cards.]

on the cards (*inf*) likely: *A February general election is very much on the cards.* [From trying to forecast future events using a pack of playing cards.]

play one's cards close to one's chest to plan or carry out a course of action *etc* without letting anyone know what one intends to do: *I'm sure he has some scheme in mind, but he's playing his cards very close to his chest and I don't know what his scheme is.*

play one's cards right to take the fullest possible advantage of one's chances of success: *She feels that if she plays her cards right she may get the widower to marry her.*

put one's cards on the table to reveal honestly what one's aims are and how one intends to achieve them: *We haven't been entirely frank with one another up to now, but I think the time has come to put our cards on the table.*

stack the cards against (someone) to make it very difficult for (someone) to succeed: *I will do my best to help you, but I'm afraid the cards are stacked against us.*

carpet

on the carpet/mat (*inf*) summoned before someone in authority for (verbal) punishment: *You'll be on the carpet for that.* [From the piece of carpet in front of a desk where someone stands while being reprimanded.]

the red-carpet treatment *see* **red.**

sweep (something) under the carpet to try to put (something unpleasant) out of one's mind, or to hide it from the attention of others: *There was trouble a few years ago about someone stealing our office equipment, but it was all swept under the carpet and we never knew much about it.* [From a simple but unsatisfactory method of making a floor look clean.]

carrot

hold out a carrot to encourage someone to do something by promising a reward: *The parents held out the carrot of a new bicycle to make their son study harder.* [A reference to holding a carrot in front of a donkey to make it reach out for the carrot and so walk faster.]

carry

carry all before one to be very successful: *In his last year as a runner he carried all before him and won all the championships.*

carry (something) off to deal with (a difficult situation, something awkward one is obliged to do *etc*) successfully: *It was a difficult moment, but he carried it off well.*

carry on 1 (*inf*) to behave badly: *The children always carry on when the teacher's out of the classroom.* **2** (*inf derog*) to have a love-affair (with): *She's been carrying on with the milkman for years.*

carry the can *see* **can.**

carry the day (*formal*) to gain victory: *John's arguments carried the day for us.* [Originally a military phrase.]

carry a/the torch for *see* **torch.**

carry weight to have influence: *His opinion carries a lot of weight around here.*

get carried away to be so affected by an emotion as to be unable to be sensible or to control one's actions: *I was so pleased to see them I got carried away and invited all twelve of them for lunch.*

cart

put the cart before the horse to do, plan or say things in the wrong order: *Isn't it rather putting the cart before the horse to redecorate the bathroom when you are planning to put in a new bath soon?*

carte

be given carte blanche (*formal*) to be allowed complete freedom to act as one thinks best: *He has been given carte blanche to select the whole team.* [Literally 'to be given a blank card'.]

case

a case in point (*rather formal*) a relevant example: *Talking of wasting money, my buying this car is a case in point.* [The phrase *in point* meaning 'relevant' was once in general use.]

cash

cash in on (something) (*inf*) to make money or other types of profit by taking advantage of (a situation *etc*): *He is the sort of person who cashes in on other people's misfortunes.*

hard cash *see* **hard.**

cast

cast in the same mould *see* **mould.**

cast pearls before swine *see* **pearl.**

the die is cast *see* **die**[2].

castle

build castles in the air to have dreams and plans which are very unlikely to come true: *I used to build castles in the air about becoming an actress, but when I left school I decided to get a job with more security.*

cat

bell the cat (*formal*) to take the leading part in a dangerous plan of action, *esp* if this is intended to benefit the group to which one belongs: *It was agreed that they must complain to the headmaster, but the question remained of who was to bell the cat.* [From the folk-tale of the mice who decided that it would be of great benefit to them if the cat had a bell put round its neck so that they could hear it coming — however none of them would volunteer to do this.]

the cat's pyjamas/whiskers (*sl*) anything very good: *He thinks he's the cat's pyjamas since he got that job.*

curiosity killed the cat *see* **curiosity.**

grin like a Cheshire cat *see* **Cheshire.**

let the cat out of the bag to let a secret become known unintentionally: *We tried to keep the party a surprise for my mother, but my sister let the cat out of the bag.* [*See* **a pig in a poke,** *at* **pig.**]

like a cat on hot bricks very nervous and unable to keep still: *She was like a cat on hot bricks before her exam.*

like something the cat has brought in (*inf derog*) untidy, soaking wet, or otherwise unpleasant to look at: *He arrived looking like something the cat had brought in.*

not to have a cat in hell's chance *see* **hell.**

play cat-and-mouse with (someone) to amuse oneself by treating (someone who is in one's power) in such a way that they do not know what one is planning to do with them: *Having established a three-goal lead in the first half, our team then played cat-and-mouse with their opponents for the rest of the game.*

put the cat among the pigeons to cause a disturbance, *esp* suddenly: *If the workmen don't get a pay rise it will really put the cat among the pigeons.*

rain cats and dogs to rain very hard: *It's raining cats and dogs — the streets are flooded.*

room to swing a cat the smallest amount of space necessary (to live in, do something in *etc*): *Her kitchen is tiny — there's hardly room to swing a cat.*

see which way the cat jumps to wait and see what is going to happen before making any definite decision or statement about one's own position: *He always waits to see which way the cat is going to jump before committing himself to anything.*

when the cat's away (the mice will play) a saying, meaning that people can be expected to take advantage of the extra freedom of action they enjoy when their boss *etc* is not there.

catch

catch one's breath *see* **breath.**

catch one's death (of cold) *see* **death.**

catch (someone's) eye *see* **eye.**

catch (someone) in the act *see* **act.**

catch it to be punished or scolded: *You'll catch it for breaking that cup if your mother finds out.*

catch (someone) napping *see* **nap.**

catch (someone) on the hop *see* **hop.**

catch (someone) red-handed *see* **red.**

catch sight of *see* **sight.**

catch the sun *see* **sun.**

Catch 22 an absurd situation in which one can never win, being constantly balked by a clause, rule, *etc* which itself can change to block any change in one's course of action. [The title of a novel by J. Heller (1961).]

catch (someone) with his pants down *see* **pants.**

you will not catch me *etc* **doing that** I certainly will not do that: *You won't catch me working late — I don't get paid for it.*

caught

(be caught) with one's pants/trousers down *see* **pants.**

cause

a lost cause *see* **lose, lost.**

caviare

caviare to the general (*formal*) something too sophisticated to be liked or understood by most people: *His poetry is appreciated by experts, but it is caviare to the general.* [A quotation from Shakespeare — *Hamlet*, II. ii.]

ceremony

stand on ceremony to behave in a very formal manner: *Please do not stand on ceremony with me — call me Maggie.*

certain

in a certain condition (*old*) pregnant: *Mrs Walker was in a certain condition which made it unwise for her to take part.*

of a certain age no longer young: *He had discovered from experience that women of a certain age were flattered by the attentions of handsome young men.*

chalk

as different as chalk from cheese very different: *The two brothers are as different as chalk from cheese.*

chalk (something) up to experience to try not to regret that (something unfortunate *etc*) has happened but to try to make sure such a thing does not happen again: *There's no point in worrying about losing so much money — you'll just have to chalk it up to experience.*

not by a long chalk (*inf*) by no means: *You haven't finished yet by a long chalk.* [From the use of chalk lines to mark scores in a game.]

champ

champing at the bit *see* **bit**[2].

chance

chance one's arm (*inf*) to do something risky; to take a risk:

You're really chancing your arm by asking for an increase in salary just now — you'll probably get the sack.

fat chance *see* **fat.**

a fighting chance *see* **fight.**

not to have a cat in hell's chance, not to have a snowball's chance in hell *see* **hell.**

not to have the ghost of a chance *see* **ghost.**

on the off-chance *see* **off.**

a sporting chance *see* **sport.**

with an eye to the main chance thinking about one's own chances of getting profit (out of something): *He became a millionaire by making every decision with an eye to the main chance.* [The main chance was the highest scoring throw in the dice game of hazard.]

change

change colour *see* **colour.**

change hands *see* **hand.**

change horses *see* **horse.**

change one's mind *see* **mind.**

the change of life the menopause: *The change of life makes some women very moody.*

change the subject *see* **subject.**

change one's tune *see* **tune.**

chop and change *see* **chop.**

have a change of heart *see* **heart.**

ring the changes to use, do *etc* a small number of things in a variety of ways: *I only have three shirts and two ties, but I ring the changes with them.* [Literally to ring a small number of church bells one after the other in every order possible.]

chapter

chapter and verse 1 a detailed source for an opinion *etc*: *He wanted us to give him chapter and verse for our belief that his department spent too much.* **2** (*inf*) quoting word for word: *He repeated what you said in your lecture, chapter and verse.* [From the method of referring to texts from the Bible.]

a chapter of accidents a whole series of misfortunes: *The entire episode of the official visit was just a chapter of accidents — everything that could possibly have gone wrong did go wrong.* [The present meaning apparently stems from a play on words — *the chapter of accidents* was originally a term for 'everything that is to happen in the future'.]

charity

as cold as charity very cold: *It was as cold as charity in that cinema.*
[*Charity* = money given to the poor *etc* without feeling for the
particular individuals involved.]

charity begins at home one should look after oneself and one's
relatives first before considering others: *I would like to give some
money towards building a new swimming pool but my family are not well
off and charity begins at home.*

chase

a wild-goose chase *see* **wild.**

cheek

cheek by jowl side by side or close together, *esp* uncomfortably
so: *The duke's family now live in a cottage in the village, cheek by jowl
with the estate workers.*

cheese

cheesed off (*sl*) bored or depressed: *He left his job because he was
cheesed off with it.*

cheese-paring (*derog*) meanness: *I think it would simply be
cheese-paring to stop buying a weekly newspaper.*

cherry

have two bites at the cherry to have a second chance to do
something which one has failed to do or to complete before: *We'd
better take this opportunity now, because we're unlikely to have two bites
at the cherry.* [From the fact that one is not normally expected
to take more than one bite to eat a cherry.]

Cheshire

grin like a Cheshire cat (*slightly derog*) to smile very broadly:
*She just stood there watching me make a fool of myself and grinning like
a Cheshire cat.* [Origin unknown.]

chest

get (something) off one's chest (*inf*) to tell someone else about
(something) that is worrying or upsetting one: *If you've got a
problem you might as well get it off your chest.*

chestnut

an old chestnut an old joke, often no longer funny; a cliché:
I did not find that comedian funny. I'd heard all those old chestnuts before.

pull the chestnuts out of the fire to take control and rescue
someone from a difficult situation: *I am tired of pulling my sister's
chestnuts out of the fire.*

chew

bite off more than one can chew *see* **bite.**

chew the cud *see* **cud**.

chew the fat *see* **fat**.

chicken

the chicken and the egg/which came first, the chicken or the egg? it is difficult or impossible to tell which of two closely related situations, problems *etc* occurred first and caused the other.

chickenfeed (*derog*) something, *usu* a sum of money, very small and unimportant: *That may sound like a large salary to you, but it's chickenfeed to him.*

chickens come home to roost *see* **roost**.

count one's chickens before they are hatched to make plans which depend on something which is still uncertain: *If my father is well enough, I should be able to bring him to see you, but I'm not going to count my chickens before they are hatched.*

no spring chicken (*inf derog*) no longer young: *He's very young to get married, but she is no spring chicken.*

chill

chilled to the marrow *see* **marrow**.

child

child's play (*inf*) something very easy: *Climbing that hill is child's play to the experienced mountaineer.*

with child (*arch or liter*) pregnant: *She is with child.*

chin

keep one's chin up (*inf*) not to be overcome by fear, worry *etc* in a difficult situation: *Keep your chin up — things are bound to get better soon.*

chink

a chink in (someone's) armour a subject *etc* which provides a successful way of attacking or making an impression on (someone who is otherwise not easy to attack *etc*): *As soon as she mentioned his wife she saw from his face that she had found a chink in his armour.*

chip

a chip off the old block (*inf*) someone who is very like one of his parents in personality: *He's just as efficient as his father — a real chip off the old block.*

have a chip on one's shoulder to have rather an aggressive manner, as if always expecting to be insulted, ill-treated *etc*: *He is very difficult to deal with — he's always had a chip on his shoulder about his lack of education.* [19C US — a reference to a man who carries a piece of wood balanced on his shoulder in the hope

56

that someone will give him an excuse for a fight by knocking it off.]

have had one's chips (*sl*) to have had all the chances of success that one is likely to be given and to have failed: *He didn't turn up for the interview, so I'm afraid he's had his chips*. [A reference to gambling tokens.]

when the chips are down (*inf*) at a critical moment; at a point when an important decision must be made: *When the chips are down only your most loyal friends will help you*. [A gambling idiom — literally 'when the bet has been placed'.]

choice
Hobson's choice *see* **Hobson**.

choose
there is nothing to choose between *see* **nothing**.

chop
chop and change to keep altering (something): *I never know which doctor will be on duty when I phone because they're always chopping and changing*.

get the chop (*sl*) to be discontinued or got rid of, *usu* suddenly: *That research project will get the chop because it's too expensive*.

chord
strike a chord (with someone) (*rather formal*) to cause (someone) to remember something: *Her name strikes a chord*.

touch a chord to cause emotion or sympathy in someone: *The orphan's smile touched a chord in the stern old lady's heart*.

circle
come full circle to return to the original position, situation *etc*: *Fifty years ago the horses on this farm were replaced by tractors — now we have come full circle and because of the cost of fuel the farmer is using horses again*. [From the medieval image of the wheel of fortune, constantly turning, on which men rose and fell.]

run round in circles (*inf*) to be very active or busy without achieving anything: *I've been running round in circles trying to organize this party and there seems to be such a lot still to do*.

a vicious circle *see* **vicious**.

claim
stake a claim *see* **stake**.

clanger
drop a clanger *see* **drop**.

clap
clap eyes on *see* **eye**.

clapper

like the clappers (*inf*) very fast indeed: *A couple of fire engines roared past with their sirens wailing, going like the clappers.*

clay

have feet of clay *see* **feet.**

clean

as clean as a whistle *see* **whistle.**

a clean slate a fresh start: *After being in prison, he went back to work with a clean slate.* [From the former use of slates to write on in schools.]

come clean (*inf*) to tell the truth about something, often something about which one has previously lied: *At first he refused to say anything to the police, but finally he came clean.*

give (someone) a clean bill of health to declare that (someone) is fit and healthy: *She had a chest disease but she has been given a clean bill of health.* [Ships were given a clean bill of health before sailing after the absence of infectious disease was certified.]

keep one's nose clean *see* **nose.**

make a clean breast of (something) to confess or admit to (something), often something one has previously denied: *At first he denied the offence, but later he decided to make a clean breast of it.*

make a clean sweep to get rid of everything unnecessary or unwanted: *The new manager made a clean sweep of all the lazy people in the department.*

show a clean pair of heels to escape by running: *The police caught one of the thieves, but the other showed them a clean pair of heels and got away.*

take (someone) to the cleaners (*sl*) to cause (someone) to lose or spend all or a great deal of their money: *His last girlfriend was only interested in his money, and she really took him to the cleaners!*

clear

as clear as crystal *see* **crystal.**

as clear as mud *see* **mud.**

clear (someone's) name *see* **name.**

clear off (*inf*) to go away or leave: *He just cleared off without saying a word.*

clear the air *see* **air.**

in the clear (*inf*) having been freed from suspicion, difficulty or debt: *His wife was suspected of his murder, but now she's in the clear.*

cleft

in a cleft stick not able to decide which to take of two possible courses of action, neither of which is ideal: *We can't decide whether to sell our house before we've bought another or whether we should buy one and then try to sell this one — we're really in a cleft stick.*

climb

climb down (*inf*) to accept defeat; to take back what one has said: *He finally climbed down and accepted our decision.*

clip

clip (someone's) wings *see* **wings.**

cloak

cloak-and-dagger involving or concerning a great deal of plotting and scheming: *Getting the committee to approve his plan entailed a lot of cloak-and-dagger activity.* [The name of a type of 17C Spanish comedy — from the normal dress of the class of character depicted — the current meaning arising from the kind of plot characteristic of the French version of the genre.]

clock

against the clock trying to overcome a shortage of time: *They worked against the clock to get the newspaper out on time.*

put back the clock to return to the conditions *etc* of an earlier time in history: *The union spokesman claimed that the management's decision had put back the clock thirty years in terms of working conditions.*

round the clock the whole day and the whole night: *If we are to get this book published we'll have to work round the clock.*

clockwork

as regular as clockwork perfectly regular(ly): *He comes round for tea at half past three every afternoon, as regular as clockwork.*

like clockwork very smoothly and without faults or problems: *Everything went like clockwork.*

close[1]

at close quarters *see* **quarter.**

a close call/shave a narrow (often lucky) escape: *That was a close shave — that car nearly ran you over.*

sail close to the wind *see* **wind**[1].

close[2]

behind closed doors in private: *The trial will take place behind closed doors.*

a closed book *see* **book.**

close one's eyes to *see* **eye.**

close ranks *see* **rank.**

cloth

cut one's coat to suit/according to one's cloth *see* **coat**.

cloud

cloud cuckoo land (*derog*) an imaginary country where everything is perfect, *usu* implying a lack of understanding of reality: *If he thinks he's going to get the job with those qualifications, he's living in cloud cuckoo land.*

every cloud has a silver lining a saying, meaning that there are always compensations for every apparent difficulty or unpleasantness.

have one's head in the clouds *see* **head**.

on cloud nine very happy: *She has been on cloud nine ever since she was offered the job in Rotterdam.* [Originally US.]

under a cloud under suspicion; in trouble or disgrace: *He wasn't expelled from school, but he certainly left under a cloud.*

clover

in clover (*inf*) in great comfort and contentment: *When he married a wealthy woman he thought that he would live in clover for the rest of his life.*

club

in the club (*facet inf*) pregnant: *Her baby was barely four months old when she discovered she was in the club again.*

join the club! (*inf*) you are in the same (unfortunate) situation that we are in: *If he doesn't like you, join the club! He doesn't like us either.*

clue

be clued up on (something) (*sl*) to be well-informed or knowledgeable about (something): *She's really clued up on the technical side of her job.*

not to have a clue (*inf*) to be ignorant (about something); not to have any knowledge (about something): *'How does that work?' 'I haven't a clue.'; I haven't a clue how to do this.*

clutch

clutch at straws *see* **straw**.

coach

drive a coach and horses through to show the weak points of an argument *etc* and so make it ineffective. [A reference to the fact that the defects (or holes) in the argument are so large that a coach and horses could be driven through them.]

coal

haul (someone) over the coals (*inf*) to reprimand or scold (someone) very severely: *The headmaster really hauled the child over the coals for being absent without permission.*

heap coals of fire on (someone's) head to make (someone) sorry for what they have done by being very kind and forgiving to them: *I knew he had forgotten our anniversary, so I thought I would heap coals of fire on his head by cooking a special dinner.* [A Biblical reference, to Proverbs 25:21–22, repeated in Romans 12:20.]

take/carry coals to Newcastle to take something to a place where there is already a great deal of it: *Taking her flowers is taking coals to Newcastle — her garden is full of flowers.* [For over 150 years Newcastle was the centre which supplied most of the coal in England.]

coast

the coast is clear there is no difficulty or danger (*esp* one already specified) in the way: *She didn't want to meet Father, so I went out to check that the coast was clear before she left.* [Apparently a military term — 'there are no enemy forces near the coast', an important factor in a successful invasion.]

coat

cut one's coat to suit/according to one's cloth to make sure that one's aims *etc* are suitable to the circumstances: *It would be nice to plan to go on a world cruise, but we must cut our coat according to our cloth.*

turn one's coat (*formal*) to change from one side (*esp* in politics) to the other: *Talleyrand was a very astute policitican who survived by turning his coat several times.* [The image is of having a coat which is a different colour inside out.]

cock

a cock-and-bull story an absurd, unbelievable and mostly untrue story: *The tramp told a cock-and-bull story about finding the money hidden in a bottle behind a tree in the park.* [Origin unknown.]

cock a snook at (someone) to express defiance or contempt towards (someone) (originally by means of a rude gesture): *He deliberately doesn't license his car in order to cock a snook at the authorities.*

cock of the walk the most important person in a group: *He is finding it difficult to adjust to his new school after being cock of the walk at his old one.* [*Walk* was the name for the pen in which fighting-cocks were bred and kept.]

go off at half-cock not to be successful because of lack of preparation: *The government's new schemes went off at half-cock.* [At *half-cock*, the firing mechanism of a matchlock gun was raised, but not far enough to engage the trigger. If the gun then fired of its own accord, the shot would obviously be wasted.]

cockle

warm the cockles of the heart to make one feel very warm, happy and comfortable: *The story of her kindness warmed the cockles of their hearts.*

coffin

a nail in (someone's) coffin *see* **nail.**

coin

pay (someone) (back) in his *etc* **own coin** to punish someone for treating one badly by treating them in the same way: *He had kept her waiting so often that she decided to pay him back in his own coin by turning up half an hour late.*

cold

as cold as charity *see* **charity.**

cold comfort (*rather formal*) no consolation at all: *I could tell you that he is as miserable as you are, but that would be cold comfort.*

a cold sweat *see* **sweat.**

get cold feet (*inf*) to lose courage and abandon a plan *etc*: *I was going to apply for the job but I got cold feet.*

give (someone) the cold shoulder (*inf*) to show that one is unwilling to be friendly with (someone) *esp* by deliberately ignoring them: *All the neighbours gave her the cold shoulder because she ill-treated her children.* [Apparently a Scottish expression introduced to standard English by Sir Walter Scott.]

in cold blood *see* **blood.**

in cold storage *see* **store.**

in the cold light of day *see* **light.**

knock (someone) cold *see* **knock.**

leave (someone) cold (*inf*) to fail to impress (someone): *Everyone told me it was a wonderful film, but I must say it left me cold.*

leave (someone) out in the cold to neglect or ignore (someone): *You can't invite half your relatives to your wedding and leave the others out in the cold!*

throw cold water on/over to discourage; to lessen enthusiasm for: *She often has good ideas but her boss throws cold water on all of them.*

colour

change colour to become very pale or very red in the face because of emotion such as fear, anger *etc*: *He changed colour when he saw the woman whom he thought he had killed.*

a horse of a different colour *see* **horse.**

lend colour to (something) to make (something) appear more likely, believable or reasonable: *Some pieces of evidence were found which lent colour to Mrs Adams's account of what had happened.*

local colour *see* **local.**

nail one's colours to the mast (*formal*) to commit oneself to an opinion or course of action in a way that makes it impossible to change one's mind: *He nailed his colours to the mast by writing a newspaper article attacking government policy.* [A naval idiom — lowering a ship's flag was the traditional signal of surrender, and nailed colours obviously cannot be lowered.]

off-colour (*inf*) not feeling very well: *He was a bit off-colour the morning after the party.*

show oneself in one's true colours to show or express one's real (and *usu* unattractive) character, opinion *etc*: *He pretends to be very generous, but he showed himself in his true colours when he refused to give money to charity.* [From the former use of coloured ribbons and badges to show allegiance to a person or party.]

with flying colours with ease and great success: *He passed his exams with flying colours.* [A naval phrase — *colours* = flags.]

column

the agony column *see* **agony.**

come

come a cropper *see* **crop.**

come back/down to earth *see* **earth.**

come clean *see* **clean.**

come hell or high water *see* **hell.**

come in for (something) to receive or be the target for (abuse, criticism *etc*): *She came in for a lot of criticism over her controversial speech.*

come in handy *see* **handy.**

come into one's own *see* **own.**

come into play *see* **play.**

come of age *see* **age.**

come off it! (*inf*) don't be ridiculous (*esp* in trying to persuade someone of something they do not believe): *Come off it — stop pretending and tell me the truth!*

come out in the wash *see* **wash.**

come out into the open *see* **open.**

come to grief *see* **grief.**

come to grips with *see* **grip.**

come to light *see* **light.**

come to nothing *see* **nothing.**

come to rest *see* **rest.**

come to one's senses *see* **sense.**

come to that/if it comes to that if you want to take absolutely all the facts into consideration: *I'm not one of her admirers — come to that, I don't even like her much.*

come to the point *see* **point.**

have it coming to one (*inf*) to deserve the bad luck, punishment *etc* that one is going to get: *Don't feel sorry for him — he had it coming/he's got it coming to him.*

comfort

cold comfort *see* **cold.**

(one's) creature comforts *see* **creature.**

commission

out of commission (*inf*) not in a usable, working condition: *The car's out of commission just now.* [A naval phrase — a warship *in commission* is under the command of an officer and ready to put to sea. It would be *out of commission* if laid up or under repair.]

common

common-or-garden (*derog*) ordinary; not unusual in any way: *She was anxious to point out that what we were eating was not common-or-garden stew, but carbonade de boeuf.* [From the *common or garden variety*, a frequent description of the least exotic form of a plant.]

company

keep company (with) (*old*) to be friendly (with), *esp* as a boy- or girlfriend: *They have kept company for more than two years; She has kept company with him for a long time.*

keep (someone) company to go, stay *etc* with (someone): *I'll come too and keep you company.*

compare

beyond compare (*very formal*) so great, good *etc* as to have no rival: *Her beauty is beyond compare.*

compliment

a back-handed/left-handed compliment a remark *etc* that is intended to be or seems like a compliment, but in fact is not: *He said he liked me a lot better then the last time he met me, which I thought was rather a back-handed compliment.*

the compliments of the season (*formal*) a greeting especially appropriate to a certain time of year, *esp* Christmas: *He came round on Boxing Day to bring us a bottle of wine and offer us the compliments of the season.*

con

    the pros and cons *see* **pro.**

concrete

    a/the concrete jungle (*inf derog*) modern cities when considered to be unattractive, dangerous or primitive places to live: *You have to be tough to survive in the concrete jungle.*

confidence

    a confidence trick the trick of a swindler who first gains someone's trust and then persuades him to hand over money: *The rich old lady realized she had been the victim of a confidence trick.*

    take (someone) into one's confidence to tell one's private thoughts, plans, secrets *etc* (to someone): *He decided to take her into his confidence.*

    a vote of confidence *see* **vote.**

conscience

    in all conscience (*formal*) being fair and reasonable: *In all conscience, I can't bring myself to do it.*

contention

    a bone of contention *see* **bone.**

contradiction

    a contradiction in terms a statement, idea *etc* which contains a contradiction: *Is a poor landowner a contradiction in terms?*

conversation

    a conversation piece something which is so unusual in some way as always to cause a discussion (and often kept deliberately for that purpose): *He had a hideous bronze statuette on the sideboard which made a useful conversation piece at dinner-parties.* [In art, a *conversation piece* is an informal painting of a group of people. The modern meaning may have arisen from a misunderstanding or from a joke.]

convert

    preach to the converted to speak enthusiastically about something, recommend a course of action *etc*, to a person or persons who already agree with one: *The trouble with holding a protest rally is that all the speakers are preaching to the converted.*

cook

    cook (someone's) goose *see* **goose.**

    cook the books to make false records, *esp* accounts, in order to hide the evidence of illegal or immoral behaviour: *He had been cooking the firm's books for years and had embezzled £250 000.*

too many cooks spoil the broth a saying, meaning that a project is likely to be hindered rather than helped if too many people are involved in organizing it.

what's cooking? (*inf*) what is planned or about to happen: *Two of the committee members were whispering in a corner, and we wondered what was cooking.*

cookie

that's the way the cookie crumbles (*inf*) that's what the situation is; that's just what one would expect to happen: *I'm sorry you'll be on duty over Christmas, but that's the way the cookie crumbles.* [Originally US.]

cool

as cool as a cucumber *see* **cucumber**.

cool one's heels *see* **heel**.

keep, lose one's cool (*sl*) not to, to become angry, over-excited or confused: *If you keep your cool you won't fail; Whatever he says to you, you must not lose your cool.*

play it cool (*inf*) to deal with a situation, problem *etc* in a calm way: *If you play it cool you'll probably get the job.*

cop

cop it (*sl*) to be punished: *You'll really cop it when your dad sees the mess you've made.*

not much cop (*derog sl*) not very good, desirable or useful: *This cheap saw is not much cop; He turned out to be not much cop as an actor.*

corn

tread on (someone's) corns to hurt (someone's) feelings: *He is very tactless and is always treading on other people's corns.*

corner

cut corners to use less money, effort, time *etc* when doing something than was thought necessary, often giving a poorer result: *You can't cut corners if you want the building to be of good quality.*

a tight corner *see* **tight**.

turn the corner to get past the worst part of a difficulty or danger: *We've turned the financial corner and business is improving steadily; He was very ill, but he's turned the corner now.*

correct

stand corrected *see* **stand**.

corridor

the corridors of power (*formal*) the higher levels of government administration: *Few people have a clear idea of how things are decided in the corridors of power.* [A phrase invented by C. P. Snow, in *Homecomings*, 1956.]

cost

at all costs no matter what the cost or outcome may be: *We must at all costs avoid being seen.*

cost, pay the earth *see* **earth.**

not cost a penny *see* **penny.**

to (someone's) cost in a way that causes (someone) disadvantage, discomfort *etc*: *The new boss seems very kind and friendly, but I have discovered to my cost that he is not* (= he has been very unkind to me).

counsel

keep one's (own) counsel (*formal*) to keep something secret: *She considered sharing her problem, but decided to keep her own counsel.*

count

count one's chickens before they are hatched *see* **chicken.**

out for the count exhausted, deeply asleep or unconscious: *As soon as he laid his head on the pillow he was out for the count.* [Literally, in boxing, to be knocked unconscious and counted out.]

stand up and be counted *see* **stand.**

counter

under the counter (used of giving or receiving, *esp* buying and selling) secretly or illegally; not in the official manner: *The shop was not licensed to sell alcohol, but supplied many people with whisky under the counter.*

country

go to the country to find out the opinion of the electorate on a political question by holding a general election: *Having been defeated in Parliament on this crucial issue, the Prime Minister decided to go to the country.*

courage

Dutch courage *see* **Dutch.**

have the courage of one's convictions (*rather formal*) to be brave enough to act according to one's opinions: *If she thinks her employers are immoral, she should have the courage of her convictions and resign from her job.*

pluck up (the) courage/screw up one's courage (to do something) finally to become brave enough (to do something): *She plucked up (the) courage to ask a question.*

course

  (there are) horses for courses *see* horse.

  stay the course *see* stay.

court

  be laughed out of court *see* laugh.

  have a friend at court *see* friend.

  pay court to (someone) (*old*) to try to win the affection or love of (someone): *He paid court to the duke's daughter.*

Coventry

  send (someone) to Coventry not to allow (someone) to associate with others; to refuse to speak to (someone) (*usu* because of something they have done): *His workmates sent him to Coventry because he worked during the strike.* [The most likely explanation for this phrase is that it is from an incident during the English Civil War when groups of Royalists captured in Birmingham were sent for safe-keeping to the Parliamentary stronghold of Coventry.]

cover

  break cover to appear suddenly from a hiding-place: *The bank-robber disappeared for some months before breaking cover in South America.* [A hunting term.]

  cover up for (someone) to try to prevent the dishonest, illegal *etc* deeds of (someone) from being discovered, by concealing the truth, lying *etc*: *He's been covering up for his friend's absence by telling lies.*

cow

  a sacred cow *see* sacred.

  till the cows come home for a very long time: *We could cheerfully sit here talking till the cows come home.*

crack

  at crack of dawn very early in the morning: *We shall have to set out for the airport at crack of dawn.*

  crack a bottle open a bottle (of an alcoholic drink *etc*): *After dinner we cracked a bottle of port and smoked cigars.*

  crack a joke to tell a funny story; to make a funny remark: *The comedian in the concert kept cracking jokes.*

  crack down on (*inf*) to take strong action against: *The police are cracking down on vandals in this area.*

  a fair crack of the whip a fair and sufficient period of importance, dominance *etc*: *Each of the three speakers was given a fair crack of the whip.*

get cracking (*inf*) to get moving quickly; to get busy: *We'll have to get cracking if we want to catch that train!*

a hard nut to crack *see* **nut.**

have a crack (at) (*inf*) to have a try at; to make an attempt to: *I've never driven a lorry that size before, but I'll have a crack at it.*

not all it's *etc* **cracked up to be** (*sl*) not as good as it is said to be.

cramp

cramp (someone's) style *see* **style.**

creature

(one's) creature comforts (*often facet*) things (food, alcohol, warmth *etc*) contributing to (one's) physical pleasure: *His house is most luxurious — he likes his creature comforts.* [A 17C phrase.]

credit

be a credit to (someone or something)/do (someone or something) credit (*formal*) to bring honour or respect to (someone or something): *Your son is a credit to you; Your honesty does you credit.*

creek

up the creek (*sl*) in serious difficulties: *If he doesn't arrive in time, we shall really be up the creek.* [2nd World War slang.]

creep

give (someone) the creeps (*inf*) to make (someone) feel fear and disgust: *Spiders in the bath give me the creeps.*

cricket

as lively as a cricket very lively: *My great-aunt is ninety-two, but she's still as lively as a cricket.*

not cricket (*fig*) unfair or not sportsmanlike: *It's definitely not cricket to cheat in exams.*

crocodile

crocodile tears pretended tears of grief: *They're only crocodile tears — she hated her cousin and she's not really sorry he's dead.* [The crocodile was once reputed to weep bitterly, either to attract the attention of potential victims (Hakluyt's *Voyages*, 1600) or while eating them (Mandeville's *Travels*, 1400).]

crop

come a cropper (*inf*) to meet misfortune: *That child's so cheeky he's bound to come a cropper soon.* [A hunting phrase for 'take a serious fall', probably from *neck and crop* = completely.]

crop up (*inf*) to happen or appear unexpectedly: *I'm sorry I'm late, but something important cropped up just as I was leaving.*

cross

at cross purposes (of two or more people) misunderstanding one another because of talking or thinking about different things: *I think we've been talking at cross purposes.*
cross one's fingers *see* **finger**.
cross (someone's) mind *see* **mind**.
cross my heart *see* **heart**.
cross swords *see* **sword**.
cross the Rubicon *see* **Rubicon**.
dot one's i's and cross one's t's *see* **dot**.
have one's wires crossed *see* **wire**.

crow

as the crow flies measured in a straight line, not following the route one would have to take on the ground: *We're fifty miles from London as the crow flies.*

crunch

when the crunch comes/when it comes to the crunch when the actual moment of testing or trial arrives: *When it came to the crunch, she decided to stay with her father rather than her mother.*

crush

have a crush on (*inf*) (*usu* of a young girl or boy) to have a great (sexual) liking for (someone); to be in love with (someone): *She has a crush on John Smith/the new gym mistress.*

cry

be crying out for (something) to be in urgent and obvious need of (something): *My garden is crying out for some rain.*
cry one's eyes out *see* **eye**.
cry for the moon *see* **moon**.
a crying need something urgently requiring notice or attention: *There is a crying need for more hospitals.*
a crying shame a very great shame: *It's a crying shame that no-one will give the poor child a home!*
cry off (*inf*) to cancel (an engagement or agreement): *After promising to come to the party, she cried off at the last moment.*
cry over spilt milk *see* **spill**.
cry wolf *see* **wolf**.
a far cry from a long way from; something quite different from: *This job is a far cry from the last one I had.* [Apparently from a Gaelic saying introduced to standard English by being quoted in Sir Walter Scott's *Rob Roy*.]

for crying out loud (*sl*) an expression of frustration, anger, impatience *etc*: *Oh, for crying out loud! That's the third time I've phoned the office and no-one has answered.*

in full cry enthusiastically pursuing something: *The women rushed into the sale in full cry after the bargains.* [Literally used of hunting dogs.]

a shoulder to cry on *see* **shoulder.**

crystal

as clear as crystal very clear; very easy to understand: *The water was as clear as crystal; His instructions were as clear as crystal.*

a crystal ball something which helps one to see into the future: *How should I know what is going to happen? Do you think I have a crystal ball?*

cuckoo

cloud cuckoo land *see* **cloud.**

cucumber

as cool as a cucumber very calm and not at all upset or worried: *Everyone was rushing about madly except the bride, who was as cool as a cucumber.*

cud

chew the cud (*fig*) to think deeply to oneself: *He sat chewing the cud for hours, but never wrote anything down.* [Literally of cows *etc*, to bring food from the first stomach back into the mouth and chew it again.]

cudgel

take up the cudgels on behalf of (someone or something) to defend (a person, cause *etc*) vigorously: *She's taken up the cudgels on behalf of women's rights.*

cue

take one's cue from (someone) to copy the way (someone) is reacting to a situation *etc*: *Taking our cue from Bill, we all tried to look surprised at what Susan was saying.* [Literally, in the theatre, to use the words of another actor as a signal to speak, move *etc*.]

cuff

off the cuff without planning; unprepared: *He spoke entirely off the cuff, with no notes.* [Probably from the reputed habit of speech-makers of scribbling brief headings on the celluloid cuffs of their evening-shirts.]

culture

culture vulture (*derog*) someone who is more than normally interested in painting, music, drama *etc*: *The Experimental Theatre*

Workshop was very popular with culture vultures, but incomprehensible to the general public.

cup

(someone's) cup of tea (*inf: usu in neg*) the sort of thing (someone) likes or prefers: *Classical music is not really my cup of tea.*

in one's cups (*old or facet*) under the influence of alcohol: *He becomes very indiscreet in his cups.*

there's many a slip 'twixt cup and lip *see* **slip**.

cupboard

cupboard love attachment to a person because of the material things (food *etc*) which they can provide: *My cat is particularly friendly when I'm cooking, but I know it's just cupboard love.*

a skeleton in the cupboard *see* **skeleton**.

curiosity

curiosity killed the cat showing too much interest in other people's affairs can be dangerous or harmful to one.

curl

make (someone's) hair curl *see* **hair**.

curry

curry favour with (someone) to seek (a) favour from (someone) by flattery: *She wants a rise in her pay, so she's trying to curry favour with the boss.* [Originally *curry favel*, from the Old French *estriller fauvel*. *Fauvel* — 'chestnut horse' — was the name of a centaur in a romance, and as centaurs traditionally symbolized the subhuman, it is possible that 'grooming Fauvel' was a metaphor for 'making oneself the servant of an unworthy creature'.]

curtain

be curtains for (someone) (*inf*) to be the end or death of (someone): *It was nearly curtains for him when the runaway car mounted the pavement.* [A theatrical idiom.]

a curtain raiser a first subject for discussion, first action *etc*, which is not the most important one planned, but which is useful to get things started or to show how things are likely to continue: *As a curtain raiser to his school career, he set off the fire-alarm on his first day.*

the Iron Curtain *see* **iron**.

ring down the curtain on (something) (*formal*) to end (a project *etc*): *We have decided to ring down the curtain on that deal — it's not economic.* [A theatrical image, from the bell used as a signal to lower the curtain at the end of a performance.]

cut

a cut above (someone or something) (obviously) better than (someone or something): *He's a cut above the average engineer.*

cut a long story short *see* **story.**

cut and dried (*often derog*) fixed and definite: *Her views on this are very cut and dried.* [Originally describing one form — as opposed to fresh — in which herbs were sold.]

cut and thrust (*formal*) (fierce) competition: *The cut and thrust of big business frightened him.* [From sword-fighting.]

cut back on (something) to reduce (something) considerably: *The government is planning to cut back on public spending.*

cut both ways (*inf*) to affect both parts of a question, have advantages to both people involved, have both good and bad points *etc*: *That argument cuts both ways!*

cut one's coat according to one's cloth *see* **coat.**

cut corners *see* **corner.**

cut (someone) dead *see* **dead.**

cut (someone) down to size *see* **size.**

cut it fine *see* **fine.**

cut it out (*impolite*; *inf*) to stop (doing something wrong): *He kept interrupting me until I told him to cut it out.*

cut no ice *see* **ice.**

cut off one's nose to spite one's face *see* **nose.**

cut one's own throat *see* **throat.**

cut one's teeth on *see* **teeth.**

cut (someone) to the quick *see* **quick.**

cut up (*sl*) very upset: *She was very fond of her godfather and was terribly cut up when he died.*

cut up rough *see* **rough.**

not cut out for (something) not naturally suited to or able for (something): *I am not cut out to be a housewife — I have no interest in home-making.*

cylinder

firing on all cylinders (*inf*) working at full strength or perfectly: *Our department can process a hundred orders a day when we're firing on all cylinders.* [Literally used of an internal-combustion engine, for instance of a car.]

73

D

dab

    a dab hand (at something) (*inf*) an expert (at something): *He's a dab hand at carpentry.*

daddy

    the daddy of them all (*inf facet*) the most extreme example (*esp* bad or astonishing) of anything: *I've had hangovers before, but the one I had on that occasion was the daddy of them all.*

    a sugar daddy *see* **sugar.**

dagger

    at daggers drawn (*formal*) ready to start fighting or quarrelling at any minute: *They've been at daggers drawn for years.*

    cloak-and-dagger *see* **cloak.**

    look daggers at (someone) to look at (someone) in a hostile manner: *I realized I had said something wrong when I saw my wife looking daggers at me from the other side of the room.*

daily

    daily dozen *see* **dozen.**

daisy

    as fresh as a daisy very bright, active and untired: *After a night without sleep we were all exhausted except Ann, who was as fresh as a daisy.*

damage

    what's the damage? (*inf facet*) what is the total cost?: *'What's the damage?' he asked the waiter.*

damn

    damn all (*inf*) nothing at all: *He said he would help us, but up to now he's done damn all.*

    damn (someone or something) with faint praise to condemn (someone or something) indirectly by not praising enthusiastically enough: *She said my dress was very suitable, which I thought was damning it with faint praise.* [A quotation from Alexander Pope's *Epistle to Dr Arbuthnot.*]

    do one's damnedest (*inf*) to do one's very best: *I may not be able to get there on time, but I'll do my damnedest!*

    not to give a damn (*inf*) not to care in the least: *I'm sorry, but I don't give a damn for his opinion!*; *He was unemployed, but he didn't give a damn.*

    not worth a damn (*inf*) completely worthless: *Since he knows nothing about it, his opinion isn't worth a damn!*

Damocles

the sword of Damocles *see* **sword.**

damp

a damp squib something which is expected to be exciting, effective *etc* but which completely fails to be so: *The debate turned out to be a damp squib as none of the important speakers turned up.*

dance

dance attendance on (someone) to have to wait near (someone) ready to carry out their wishes: *She expects everyone to dance attendance on her.*

lead (someone) a (merry) dance to keep (someone) constantly involved in a series of problems and irritations: *I believe their teenage daughter leads them a merry dance.*

dander

get one's dander up (*inf*) to (cause one to) become angry or hostile: *By this time he had got his dander up and was becoming angry; Rudeness always gets his dander up.* [Originally northern dialect and US.]

Darby

a Darby and Joan a devoted elderly married couple: *They were a real Darby and Joan — always so concerned for one another's comfort.* [From a poem by Henry Woodfall in the *Gentleman's Magazine*, 1735.]

dark

a dark horse a person about whose abilities *etc* little is known: *We knew how three of the four competitors would perform, but the fourth was a dark horse.* [19C racing slang.]

in the dark in a state of ignorance or unawareness (*esp* of particular facts): *You two may know what you're talking about, but the rest of us are completely in the dark.*

keep it dark (*inf*) to keep (something) a secret: *They're engaged to be married but they want to keep it dark.*

not to darken (someone's) door not to dare to visit (someone's) house: *He gave her the money, but told her never to darken his door again or he would call the police.*

a shot in the dark *see* **shot.**

dash

cut a dash to cause oneself to have an impressive (*usu* smart or fashionable) appearance: *He cuts quite a dash in his purple suit.*

date

out of date 1 old-fashioned: *His ideas are very out of date.* **2** no longer able to be (legally) used; no longer valid: *Your ticket is out of date.*

to date (*formal*) up to the present time: *This is the best entry we've received to date.*

up to date 1 completed *etc* up to the present time: *I try to keep my correspondence up to date.* **2** modern and in touch with the latest ideas and fashion: *This method is very up to date.*

daunt

nothing daunted (*formal: often facet*) not at all discouraged; not frightened or made less enthusiastic *etc*: *She was an old lady but, nothing daunted, she hit her attacker over the head with her umbrella.*

Davy Jones

Davy Jones's locker (*usu facet*) the bottom of the sea: *The ship sank and all the gold she was carrying is now in Davy Jones's locker.* [For obscure reasons, 18C seamen gave the name Davy Jones to the ruler of the evil spirits of the sea.]

dawn

at crack of dawn *see* **crack.**

dawn on (someone) to become suddenly clear to (someone): *It suddenly dawned on me what he had meant.*

day

all in a/the day's work *see* **work.**

as happy as the day is long very happy, *esp* in how one is spending one's time: *In the summer my children spend their whole time in the orchard, as happy as the day is long.*

at the end of the day when everything has been considered and final decisions are being made: *I don't suppose what we do now will make much difference at the end of the day.*

call it a day (*inf*) to bring something to an end; to stop (*eg* working): *I haven't finished this piece of work but I'm so tired that I'll have to call it a day; They were engaged to be married but they quarrelled so much that they decided to call it a day.* [This phrase originally meant 'to reckon what one has already done to be a full day's work', and thus by inference 'to stop work early'.]

carry the day *see* **carry.**

day in, day out every day without exception: *Day in, day out she has to look after the baby.*

daylight robbery *see* **rob.**

his *etc* **days are numbered** he is about to die, to be dismissed from his job *etc*: *If she continues to behave like that, her days in this firm are numbered.*

have a field day *see* **field**.

have had one's day (*inf*) to be past the most successful *etc* period of one's life: *Steam trains have had their day*. [Probably from the saying **every dog has his day**, which means that everyone can expect to enjoy a period of success at some time.]

have seen better days *see* **better**.

in this day and age at the present (advanced) period of time: *You don't expect people to live in such primitive conditions in this day and age*.

live from day to day to think only about the present without making any plans for the future: *We did not know how long it would take for him to recover, so we just lived from day to day*.

make (someone's) day to make (someone) very happy: *It made the old lady's day when she received a bunch of flowers*.

name the day (*rather facet*) to announce a date for something, *esp* the date on which one is to be married: *Have Norman and Margaret named the day yet?*

not to be (someone's) day to be a day on which (someone) is not able to be successful, or on which things go wrong for them: *It just isn't my day — the car broke down, my lunch engagement was called off, and I burned a cake I was baking*. [As **have had one's day** *above*.]

one of these days (*inf*) at some time in the near future: *I shall look in and see you one of these days*.

one of those days (*inf*) a day on which everything goes wrong: *I was exhausted when I got home from work — it had been one of those days*.

the order of the day *see* **order**.

the other day not long ago: *Mr Smith can't have moved house — I saw him just the other day*.

save the day to prevent something from going wrong, from failing *etc*: *We thought we were stranded but his offer of a lift saved the day*.

see daylight 1 to approach the end of a long task: *Clearing out the attic took me weeks, but at last I began to see daylight*. **2** to understand suddenly: *He puzzled over her joke for some minutes before he saw daylight*.

some day at some time in the future: *She hopes to get married some day*.

that will be the day (*inf*) that is very unlikely: *'Perhaps your husband will buy you flowers for your birthday.' 'That'll be the day!'*

[Originally Australian, possibly from German *der Tag* — 'the day (of victory)' — a favourite catch-phrase of the German forces during the 1st World War, much parodied by Allied troops.]

those were the days the time we are talking about was a good one: *When I was a child, an ice-cream cost a halfpenny — those were the days!*

to this day even now; up to the present time: *To this day we have no idea who was the real thief.*

win the day to be successful: *Common sense will win the day.* [A military phrase — literally, 'to win the battle'.]

dead

as dead as a/the dodo *see* **dodo.**

cut (someone) dead to ignore (someone) completely, *esp* by acting as if one had not seen them: *I must have offended her, because last time we met she cut me dead.*

dead beat (*inf*) exhausted or very tired: *She was dead beat after doing her spring cleaning.*

a dead duck (*inf*) a project, person *etc* unlikely to continue or to survive: *I'm afraid the African project is a dead duck — we can't afford it; If he walks into that ambush, he's a dead duck!*

a dead end a situation *etc* from which it is impossible to progress: *I enjoyed my job in Italy, but it was a dead end and I had to come home eventually.* [Literally, a road closed off at one end.]

a dead loss (*inf*) something completely useless or unprofitable: *That shop is a dead loss — they never have anything I want.*

(the) dead of night the middle of the night: *No-one will see us leaving if we go at (the) dead of night.*

a dead ringer for (someone) *see* **ring.**

dead set on (something) determined or very anxious (to obtain) (something): *My wife is dead set on that house; I'm dead set on going to America.*

the dead spit of *see* **spit.**

dead to the world fast asleep: *When he arrived home at midnight his wife was already dead to the world.* [Probably from the use of this phrase in a religious context to describe the situation of a person who had entered a convent or monastery.]

flog a dead horse *see* **horse.**

over my dead body an expression showing that one is strongly opposed to a certain proposal, plan *etc*: *That woman will be invited* to our party *over my dead body!*; 'Could he perhaps use your car?' 'Over my dead body!'

step into dead men's shoes to take over the job, position *etc* of someone who has died, or of someone who has left in unfortunate circumstances: *The only way you get promotion in that firm is by stepping into dead men's shoes.*

I *etc* **would not be seen dead with, in** *etc*: I have a very strong dislike of (a person, an article of clothing *etc*): *I would not be seen dead in the hat my mother-in-law was wearing.*

stop dead *see* **stop**.

deaf
fall on deaf ears *see* **ear**.
turn a deaf ear to (something) *see* **ear**.

deal
big deal! an ironic expression indicating that one is not very impressed by something one has just been told: *'The shop offered to mend the faulty radio free of charge.' 'Oh, big deal! Surely they might have offered you your money back!'*

a raw deal *see* **raw**.
a square deal *see* **square**.

dear
dear knows I do not know at all: *She ran out of the house screaming, and dear knows where she is now!*

for dear life extremely fast, hard, busily *etc*: *As the exam drew to an end, many of the students were still scribbling for dear life.*

death
at death's door on the point of dying: *I'm surprised she recovered, because the last time I saw her I thought she was at death's door.* [From the version of Psalm 107:18 in the Church of England Prayer Book — 'Their soul abhorred all manner of meat; and they were even hard at death's door'.]

be in at the death to be present during the final stages of a course of events, especially a hunt of some kind: *Since she had been one of those most involved in collecting evidence against him, it was fitting that she should be in at the death when he was arrested.* [A hunting term.]

catch one's death (of cold) (*inf*) to get a very bad cold: *If you go out in that rain without a coat you'll catch your death (of cold).*

a death-trap a place, building *etc* in which one is in danger of being killed or harmed: *Old buildings without fire-escapes are real death-traps!*

dice with death *see* **dice.**

hang/hold on like grim death *see* **grim.**

the kiss of death *see* **kiss.**

like death warmed up (*often facet*) in a very poor state, *esp* appearing ill, exhausted *etc*: *He always looks like death warmed up first thing in the morning.*

put the fear of death into *see* **fear.**

sick to death of (something) *see* **sick.**

deck

clear the decks to tidy up, *esp* to remove everything unnecessary in preparation for starting an important task: *The kitchen was rather untidy, so I thought I'd better clear the decks before I started preparing dinner.* [Originally an operation to prepare a warship for battle.]

deep

be thrown in at the deep end to have to start an activity, job *etc* with little experience or by doing something quite difficult: *The first day I arrived at school I was thrown in at the deep end by being given one of the problem classes to teach.* [From the 'deep end' of a swimming pool.]

go off the deep end to express strong feelings in a very strong, often angry, manner: *He really went off the deep end when he heard that she had forgotten to book the tickets.*

in deep water in difficulties or trouble: *He found himself in deep water when he took over the management of the firm.*

degree

give (someone) the third degree (*inf*: *often facet*) to question (someone) very intensely, using very severe methods: *Every time I get home late, my parents give me the third degree about where I've been and what I've been doing.* [From an interrogation method involving bullying and ill-treatment once used by the American police.]

to the nth degree *see* **n.**

delicate

in a delicate condition (*old euph*) pregnant: *Mrs Osborne was not present as she was in a delicate condition once again.*

deliver

deliver the goods *see* **goods.**

depart

the departed (*euph*) a person who is or people who are dead: *You mustn't speak ill of the departed.*

a new departure a change of purpose or method in doing

something: *The release of a jazz record represents a new departure for a folk singer.*

depth

in depth deeply and thoroughly: *I have studied the subject in depth.*

out of one's depth in a situation with which one cannot deal: *I felt rather out of my depth during the discussions as I didn't understand a word.* [Literally, in water deeper than one can stand up in.]

deserts

get one's just deserts *see* **just.**

design

have designs on (something) to be trying to get (*usu* something belonging to someone else): *He has designs on my job.*

desire

leave a lot to be desired (*rather facet*) not to be very good or satisfactory: *Her cooking leaves a lot to be desired.*

devil

between the devil and the deep blue sea faced with a choice between two risky or undesirable courses of action *etc*: *Faced with a choice between starving to death and emigrating, they were between the devil and the deep blue sea.*

devil take the hindmost a short form of the phrase **every man for himself and devil take the hindmost,** meaning that everyone acts (or should act) only to benefit himself without thinking about what is happening to other people: *You have to be ruthless to succeed in the world — it's a case of devil take the hindmost.*

the devil to pay serious trouble: *There will be the devil to pay when your mother sees this mess!* [From legendary bargains made with the devil, in which the bargainer usually agreed to give the devil his soul at a later date in payment for immediate worldly success *etc*.]

give the devil his due to be fair to someone one dislikes or disapproves of: *Her husband is terribly bad-tempered although, to give the devil his due, he is always very pleasant to me.*

needs must when the devil rides *see* **need.**

play the devil's advocate to put forward objections to a plan, arguments against something *etc* in order to test the arguments for it: *Although he appeared to be very hostile to the proposal, as soon as it was accepted it became obvious that he had only being playing devil's advocate and was as enthusiastic as the rest.* [The devil's advocate — *advocatus diaboli* — was the man given the rôle of opposing the canonization of a saint in the medieval Church, 'putting the devil's point of view' and thus ensuring that the evidence for canonization was sound.]

talk of the devil here comes the very person we have just been speaking about: *I was just wondering the other day if you ever see John now — well, talk of the devil! Here he is coming along the road!* [From the saying *talk of the devil and see his horns*, which originally expressed the superstition that talking about evil gave it power to appear, happen *etc*.]

diamond

a rough diamond a person who is (probably) basically good and valuable, but who looks unattractive and/or behaves in a rude, uncivilized manner: *The hero of a Western film is often a rough diamond.*

dice

dice with death (*often facet*) to do something very risky (and dangerous): *He diced with death every time he took a short cut across the main railway line.*

load the dice against (someone) to take away any chance (someone) has of succeeding at something: *The dice were loaded against him and he had to give in.* [From a method of cheating in gambling games by using dice with a weight inside, tending to make them show the same score every time.]

no dice (*sl*) an expression used to indicate lack of success: *I tried to get him to help us, but no dice.*

die[1]

die hard to struggle hard against death or to take a long time to disappear *etc*: *Old customs die hard.*

like a dying duck *see* **duck.**

never say die a saying, meaning that one should never give up and admit that one has been defeated.

die[2]

the die is cast a step has been taken which makes the future inevitable: *I'm not sure that I want to leave this job after all but the die is cast — I've handed in my resignation.* [In Latin *jacta alea est*, traditionally Julius Caesar's comment on crossing the River Rubicon into Italy with his army in 49 BC, thus effectively declaring war on the Roman administration.]

difference

sink our, your *etc* **differences** *see* **sink.**

split the difference to settle an argument by agreeing that each side should give up half of the thing, *esp* an amount of money, that is being argued about: *You want £20, I'm offering £10, so let's split the difference and I'll give you £15.*

dig

dig in (*inf*) to make an energetic start on something, *esp* eating a meal: *She put a pot of stew on the table and we all dug in.*

dig in one's heels *see* **heel.**

dignity

beneath (someone's) dignity not fitting to what (someone) thinks their position in the world is; too lowly or ordinary (an action) for (someone) to do: *Now she is the manager, she thinks it is beneath her dignity to answer the telephone.*

stand on one's dignity (*rather formal*) to be ready to take offence very easily: *She tended to stand on her dignity and did not like being made fun of.*

dilemma

on the horns of a dilemma in a position where it is necessary to choose between two undesirable courses of action *etc: His decision left her on the horns of a dilemma as she could not decide whether to risk offending him or agree to something she disapproved of.* [In medieval rhetoric a *dilemma* was a way of arguing which consisted of proving that one of two statements must be true, both being damaging to one's opponent's case. It was likened to a two-horned animal. In choosing which of the two statements he preferred to admit as the truth, the opponent was pictured as having to throw himself on to one or other of the 'horns'.]

dim

take a dim view of (*inf*) to disapprove of: *I take a dim view of his attitude to his parents.*

dine

dine out on (*inf*) to be socially successful because one possesses *eg* interesting information: *It was such a good story, even if untrue, that he dined out on it for years.*

dip

dip into to look briefly at (a book) or to study (a subject) in a casual manner: *I've dipped into his book on Shakespeare, but I haven't read it right through.*

a lucky dip *see* **luck.**

dirt

dirt cheap (*inf*) very cheap: *She got that car dirt cheap.*

do (someone's) dirty work to do an unpleasant task or morally wrong action on behalf of (someone else): *He wanted me to do his dirty work for him.*

do the dirty on (*sl*) to play an unpleasant, mean trick on: *He began to realize that they had done the dirty on him and left him to pay the bill.*

wash one's dirty linen in public *see* **linen.**

discord

an apple of discord *see* **apple.**

discretion

discretion is the better part of valour it is wise not to take unnecessary risks: *I thought of joining in the fight to help him but decided that discretion was the better part of valour and went away.*

distance

come, be within striking distance *see* **strike.**

keep one's distance not to be too friendly; not to come too close: *After he had been so rude to me I was careful to keep my distance; He was very pleasant to everyone in the office, but he kept his distance.*

ditchwater

as dull as ditchwater very boring or uninteresting: *The lecture was as dull as ditchwater.*

do

I *etc* **could do with/could be doing with (something)** it would be better if I had or did (something): *I could do with a cup of coffee; This house could be doing with a coat of paint; You could do with a wash.*

do (someone) a good turn *see* **turn.**

do away with (someone or something) 1 to get rid of (something), *esp* to abolish it officially: *They did away with uniforms at that school years ago.* **2** (*inf*) to kill (someone), *esp* secretly: *He's afraid someone might try to do away with him.*

do (someone) down (*Brit inf*) to cheat or overcome (someone) in some way: *He enjoys doing other people down.*

do (someone) in (*very inf*) to kill (someone): *The general opinion about the missing woman was that someone had done her in.*

do justice (to) *see* **justice.**

do one's nut *see* **nut.**

do or die to succeed or to die, ruin oneself *etc* in trying to succeed: *The football team arrived at the match determined to do or die.*

do (someone) out of (something) (*inf*) to prevent (someone) from getting (something), *esp* by using dishonest methods: *He feels he has been done out of a day's holiday.*

84

do (someone) over (*sl*) to give a severe beating to (someone): *A group of thugs came round to his house one night and did him over.*

do (someone) proud *see* **proud.**

do the honours *see* **honour.**

do the trick *see* **trick.**

do one's (own) thing *see* **thing.**

do time *see* **time.**

do (something) up to repair, redecorate *etc* (something) in order to put it into a better condition than before: *I will have to do my car up a bit before I sell it — it's very rusty.*

fair do's *see* **fair.**

nothing doing! *see* **nothing.**

take some doing to be very difficult: *He is more untidy than you are, and that takes some doing!*

doctor

what the doctor ordered the very thing that is needed: *At this moment a cup of tea is just what the doctor ordered.*

dodo

as dead as a/the dodo completely dead or no longer fashionable, useful, popular *etc*: *That kind of hairstyle is as dead as a dodo.* [From a flightless bird discovered on the island of Mauritius in the early 17C and extinct by 1700.]

dog

be top dog *see* **top.**

dog eat dog (of) a situation in which one has to compete ruthlessly in order to survive or be successful: *He is not ambitious and hates the dog-eat-dog business world.*

a dog in the manger someone who tries to prevent another person from having or doing something which he himself does not want, cannot do *etc*: *He's a real dog in the manger — even though he doesn't have a car he won't let anyone else use his garage.* [The image is of a dog which lies in the hay-rack of a cow-shed, thus preventing the cattle from eating the hay.]

dog Latin *see* **Latin.**

a dogsbody someone who is given odd jobs, *esp* unpleasant ones, to do: *She acts as secretary and general dogsbody to the firm.*

a dog's breakfast/dinner (*inf*) an untidy mess: *What a dog's breakfast you've made of your homework!*

every dog has his day *see* **have had one's day** *at* **day.**

go to the dogs (*inf*) to be ruined, *esp* to ruin oneself: *He seems to have gone completely to the dogs and spends all his time in the pub.*

in the doghouse (*inf*) in disgrace: *He forgot his wife's birthday, so he's in the doghouse.* [The image is of someone banished from the house and forced to take shelter in an outdoor kennel.]

lead a dog's life to lead an unhappy life, *esp* because one is ruled by a person who makes one unhappy: *He leads a dog's life, living with his mother — she won't let him do anything she disapproves of.*

let sleeping dogs lie a saying, meaning that one should not try to reform or improve a situation, people *etc* who might cause trouble but are not doing so at present: *I don't think you should mention the fence to the neighbours — I think you should let sleeping dogs lie.*

doggo

lie doggo (*inf*) to remain in hiding without giving any sign of one's presence; not to do anything that would draw attention to oneself: *They hoped if they lay doggo for a bit the teacher would forget to ask them for their homework.*

dollar

bet one's bottom dollar *see* **bottom**.

done

done for (*inf*) ruined or about to be killed *etc* without there being any hope of rescue or recovery: *We're done for if we stay here and the bomb goes off.*

done to a turn *see* **turn**.

have done with *see* **have**.

(not) the done thing (not) acceptable behaviour: *It used to be the done thing to send your hostess flowers after a dinner party.*

donkey

donkey's ages/years (*inf*) a very long time: *I haven't seen him in donkey's ages.* [From a pun on 'donkey's ears' — which are very long.]

donkey work hard, unrewarding part of any task: *We now have a computer to do the donkey work.*

talk the hind leg off a donkey (*derog*) to talk a great deal and for a long time: *I like his little girl, but she would talk the hind leg off a donkey!*

door

at death's door *see* **death**.

behind closed doors *see* **close**[2].

have a foot in the door *see* **foot**.

keep the wolf from the door *see* **wolf**.

not to darken (someone's) door see **dark**.

on (someone's) doorstep very close to where (someone) lives: *The Welsh mountains are on our doorstep.*

out of doors outside; not in a house *etc*: *We like to eat out of doors in summer.*

show (someone) the door to make (someone) leave the house: *The landlord came round to try to make us pay extra rent, but my husband soon showed him the door.*

dose

a dose of (someone's) own medicine see **medicine**.

go through (something) like a dose of salts (*inf*) to finish (something) very quickly: *She's very efficient — she goes through all the paperwork like a dose of salts.* [From the use of Epsom salts as a purgative.]

dot

dot one's i's and cross one's t's to take great care over details: *She makes a good organizer because she is always careful to dot her i's and cross her t's.*

from/since the year dot for a very long time: *Our family has lived in this village since the year dot.* [The year dot implies 'a year too long ago to be specified'.]

on the dot (of) exactly (at) (a given time): *The train left at nine o'clock on the dot; The train left on the dot of nine (o'clock).* [From the dots marking the minutes on a clock face.]

double

at the double very quickly: *He came up the road at the double and rushed into the house.* [A military term — literally, at twice the normal marching pace.]

double back to turn and go back the way one came: *The fox doubled back and went down a hole near to where it had started.*

double Dutch see **Dutch**.

see double see **see**.

doubt

a doubting Thomas a person who will not believe something without strong proof. [In the Bible, Thomas was the apostle who refused to believe that Jesus had risen from the dead until he had touched him.]

down

be, go down with to be or become ill with: *The children all went down with measles one after the other.*

down-and-out (*derog*) (a person) having no money, no means of earning a living, and no hope of ever doing so: *They are volunteer workers in a hostel for down-and-outs.*

down-at-heel shabby, untidy and not well looked after or well-dressed: *The hotel looked rather down-at-heel and had obviously seen better days* (= once been much more prosperous). [Literally, of shoes, having worn-down heels.]

down in the dumps *see* **dumps.**

down in the mouth *see* **mouth.**

down on one's luck *see* **luck.**

down the drain *see* **drain.**

down-to-earth practical and not concerned with theories, ideals or possibilities: *He has a very down-to-earth approach to the subject.*

down tools (*inf*) to stop working: *When the man was sacked his fellow-workers downed tools and walked out.*

down under (*often facet*) in or to Australia or New Zealand: *How are you enjoying life down under?*

fall down on *see* **fall.**

get down to to begin working seriously at or on: *I must get down to writing some letters.*

go downhill to become worse and worse: *We expected him to die, I suppose, because he's been going steadily downhill for months.*

have a down on (*inf*) to be very hostile or opposed to: *He has a down on university students and won't rent his flat to them.*

play down *see* **play.**

sell (someone) down the river *see* **river.**

suit (someone) down to the ground *see* **ground.**

talk down to (someone) *see* **talk.**

dozen

a baker's dozen *see* **baker.**

daily dozen physical exercises done every day, *usu* every morning: *I do my daily dozen every morning when I get up.*

(talk) nineteen to the dozen *see* **nineteen.**

drain

down the drain (*derog inf*) completely wasted: *We had to scrap everything and start again — six months' work down the drain.*

draught

feel the draught to be unpleasantly aware of difficult conditions, *esp* lack of money: *People haven't so much money these days, and firms making luxury goods are really feeling the draught.*

draw

back to the drawing-board I will have to start again from the very beginning and make new plans (said when a project has failed, been rejected *etc*): *That's not very successful, is it? — Ah well, back to the drawing-board.* [From the fact that many projects begin with a design sketch.]

the days/nights are drawing in the days are getting quickly shorter and the nights longer, as happens in early autumn: *Now that the days are drawing in I like to leave work early and get home before dark.*

draw a blank *see* **blank.**

draw a veil over *see* **veil.**

draw in one's horns *see* **horn.**

draw the line *see* **line.**

draw the teeth of *see* **teeth.**

long drawn out going on for a long time: *The meeting was so long drawn out that we missed our train.*

drawer

(someone's) bottom drawer bed-linen, table-linen *etc* which a girl is given or collects for use in her own house when she gets married: *My mother gave me several spare pairs of sheets for my bottom drawer.*

out of the top drawer (*often facet*) from the upper social classes: *It was a very smart wedding although the bridegroom was not exactly out of the top drawer.*

dream

go like a dream to progress *etc* very well: *My new car goes like a dream; It was a complicated operation, moving office, but it went like a dream.*

dress

dressed to kill (*inf*) dressed in one's best clothes, *esp* in clothes designed to attract attention: *He was dressed to kill for the interview.*

a dressing-down (*inf*) a scolding: *His boss gave him a dressing-down for being late so often.*

drib

dribs and drabs (*inf*) very small quantities: *I'm doing the spring cleaning in dribs and drabs as I feel like it.*

drift

catch/get the drift (of something) (*inf*) to understand the general meaning or subject (of what is being said *etc*): *I couldn't hear you clearly, but I got the drift of what you said.*

drink

be meat and drink to *see* **meat.**

drink (something) in to take (something) in rapidly or eagerly: *The audience were fascinated, drinking in his every word.*

drink like a fish *see* **fish.**

drink to (someone's) health *see* **health.**

drink (someone) under the table *see* **table.**

drip

a dripping roast something which continues to provide profit for a long time and without a great deal of effort: *His share in the oil-well proved to be a dripping roast, and he lived very well on the proceeds.*

drive

as pure as the driven snow (*facet*) completely pure: *I don't care whether she's evil or as pure as the driven snow!*

be driving at (*inf*) to be trying to say or suggest: *I don't know what he was driving at, but it sounded rude.*

drive (something) home to (try to) make (something) completely understood or accepted: *The manager drove home the need for everyone to try to save the firm's money.*

drive (someone) up the wall *see* **wall.**

drop

at the drop of a hat immediately and needing only the slightest reason or excuse: *He expects me to dash off to Paris at the drop of a hat, whether or not it's convenient.*

drop a brick/clanger to mention a subject or communicate a piece of information to a person or persons to whom one should not have mentioned it, *esp* to do so in such a way that the mistake cannot be covered up: *You certainly dropped a brick when you mentioned Jack to her — they were divorced two years ago.*

drop by (*inf*) to visit someone casually and without being invited: *I'll drop by on my way home if I've time.*

drop in (*inf*) to arrive informally to visit someone: *Do drop in if you happen to be passing!*

a drop in the bucket/ocean a tiny part of the quantity which is needed: *The work we can do in this area is, of course, just a drop in the ocean.* [A Biblical reference, to Isaiah 40:15.]

drop off (*inf*) to fall asleep: *I was so tired I dropped off in front of the television.*

a drop of the hard stuff *see* **hard.**

drop out to withdraw, *esp* from a course at university *etc* or from the normal life of society: *There are only two of us going to the theatre now Mary has dropped out; She's dropped out of college.*

let (something) drop to allow (something) to become known (as if) by accident: *I didn't ask her if he had written — she let it drop in the course of conversation.*

name dropping *see* **name.**

the penny drops *see* **penny.**

you could hear a pin drop *see* **pin.**

drown

drown one's sorrows to take an alcoholic drink in order to forget a disappointment *etc*: *Ah well, since neither of us won the competition, let's go and drown our sorrows together.*

drum

beat the drum (for something or someone) to try to attract public notice (to something or someone): *We try to persuade well-known personalities to beat the drum for our latest product.* [From the former use of a drum to attract attention to a person making an announcement in a public place *etc*.]

drum (someone) out to send (someone) away in disgrace, *esp* publicly: *He was drummed out of his bridge club for cheating.* [From the military use of drums to emphasize the dismissal of an officer from his regiment for misconduct *etc*.]

drunk

as drunk as a lord *see* **lord.**

punch-drunk *see* **punch.**

roaring drunk *see* **roar.**

dry

as dry as a bone *see* **bone.**

dry (someone) out (*inf*) to cure or make better (an alcoholic): *He went to a nursing-home to be dried out.*

a dry run an attempt at carrying out a procedure, *esp* if complicated or requiring very careful timing *etc*, made beforehand in order to practise: *The organizers of the procession made a dry run the week before to ensure that all would go smoothly on the day.*

dry up (*inf*) (of a speaker) to forget what to say, *eg* in a play: *He dried up in the middle of a scene.*

go dry (*inf*) (of a place) to cease to have any shops, public houses *etc* that sell alcohol: *Our village went dry some years ago when our only pub closed down.*

high and dry *see* **high.**

home and dry *see* **home.**

duck

be like water off a duck's back *see* **water.**

break one's duck to have one's first success, *esp* in playing a game: *She had entered for the competition for five years before she eventually broke her duck and won a medal*. [A cricketing term — no score in cricket is called a *duck*, from *duck egg*, a reference to the shape of the figure 0.]

a dead duck *see* **dead.**

a lame duck (*sometimes derog*) a helpless or inefficient person: *Her house is always full of lame ducks who need help*.

like a dying duck (*derog*) (behaving) in a weak, pathetic and sad manner: *I would feel more sympathy with her if she wouldn't mope about the house like a dying duck!*

a sitting duck *see* **sit.**

duckling

an ugly duckling *see* **ugly.**

dump

(down) in the dumps in a state of depression or low spirits: *He's down in the dumps today*.

dust

bite the dust (*inf: often facet*) to cease to exist; to be unsuccessful: *That's another scheme that's bitten the dust*. [A phrase, meaning simply 'to die', much used in 19C adventure stories and 20C Westerns.]

throw dust in (someone's) eyes to (attempt to) deceive (someone): *She only mentioned the possibility in order to throw dust in my eyes*. [From a method of temporarily blinding an enemy.]

Dutch

double Dutch (*inf*) nonsense: *I couldn't understand what he was saying — it was double Dutch to me*.

a Dutch auction a kind of auction at which the auctioneer begins by asking for a high price and then reduces it until someone offers to pay the price he is asking.

Dutch courage an artifical courage gained by drinking alcohol: *He needed some Dutch courage before asking her to marry him*. [Either from a belief that the Dutch were heavy drinkers or from the fact that gin was introduced into England by the Dutch followers of William III.]

go Dutch (*inf*) to pay each for oneself (at a restaurant, cinema *etc*): *Since neither had much money, they always went Dutch when they went out together*. [An American phrase, from a kind of party — a *Dutch lunch* — to which all the guests are expected to contribute food.]

like a Dutch uncle in a scolding manner: *Just because he's older than me doesn't give him the right to talk to me like a Dutch uncle!* [Supposedly from the Dutch reputation for severe family discipline.]

dye

dyed-in-the-wool (*derog*) of firmly fixed opinions: *He's a dyed-in-the-wool Tory.* [Once a technical term for yarn dyed before being spun, implying that a person's attitudes *etc* were acquired very young — in figurative use by the 16C.]

E

eager

eager beaver *see* **beaver.**

ear

about (someone's) ears all around (someone) (used of something falling on top of someone or attacking someone): *The house is so dilapidated it is likely to fall about our ears at any moment.*

be all ears (*inf*) to listen with keen attention: *The children were all ears when their father was describing the car crash.*

be wet behind the ears *see* **wet.**

my *etc* **ears are burning** someone elsewhere is talking about me: *Your ears should have been burning this morning — the manager was singing your praises to the rest of us.* [The belief that one's ears grow hot when someone is talking about one is mentioned by the Roman writer Pliny.]

fall on deaf ears not to be listened to: *His advice fell on deaf ears.*

a flea in one's ear *see* **flea.**

give (someone) a thick ear *see* **thick.**

go in one ear and out the other (of advice, instructions *etc*) not to make any lasting impression: *I keep telling that child to work harder but my words go in one ear and out the other.*

have (someone's) ear (*formal*) to be sure that someone will pay attention to what you say and will do what you ask *etc*: *He is a very influential man and is known to have the king's ear.*

have/keep one's ear to the ground to pay attention to, and keep oneself well informed about, all that is happening around one: *If you keep your ear to the ground you'll soon find a new job.* [From a reputed Red Indian tracking technique.]

lend an ear (*usu facet*) to listen: *If you will all lend an ear, I shall explain the arrangements for our staff outing.*

pin back one's ears (*inf*) to listen carefully: *I could hear that they were discussing our proposal, so I pinned back my ears to find out what they thought of it.*

play (something) by ear to play (a piece of music) without using printed music: *They asked him to play the piano at the party, but he could not play by ear and he had no music with him.*

play it by ear (*inf*) to do what a situation requires as and when it is required, without making a fixed plan beforehand: *I don't know how he is going to react at the meeting, so we had better just play it by ear.* [From previous idiom.]

prick up one's ears *see* **prick.**

set (someone) by the ears to cause trouble between or among (two or more people): *They got on well enough together until the question of promotion set them all by the ears.*

turn a deaf ear to (something) deliberately to ignore or refuse to take any notice of (something): *They tried to persuade her not to go, but she turned a deaf ear to their advice.*

up to one's ears (in) deeply involved (in): *I'm up to my ears in work*; *He's up to his ears in trouble/debt.*

walls have ears *see* **wall.**

you can't make a silk purse out of a sow's ear *see* **silk.**

early

an early bird (*inf*) a person who gains advantage by acting more promptly than others: *You have to be an early bird if you want to get a bargain at an auction sale.* [From the saying **the early bird catches the worm**, meaning that those who act most promptly are the ones most likely to be successful in obtaining what they want.]

it's early days it is too soon to know, have results *etc*: *Our new secretary seems to be very efficient, but it's early days yet.*

earth

bring, come back/down to earth to (cause to) start being aware of the practical details of life after a period of dreaming, great happiness *etc*: *He was planning what he would do after school when the teacher's voice suddenly brought him back to earth*; *They were thrilled when the baby arrived, but came back to earth suddenly when he cried all night.*

cost, pay the earth (*inf*) to cost, pay a great deal of money: *Eating in hotels costs the earth*; *She paid the earth for that fur coat!*

go to earth (*rather formal*) to disappear into a hiding-place: *The police could not find the thief — he had gone to earth.* [A hunting term used of a fox which escapes into its hole.]

like nothing on earth (*inf*) extremely ill, ugly, untidy *etc* (*usu* an exaggeration): *You look like nothing on earth in that dress; If I drink too much wine, I feel like nothing on earth the next morning.*

move heaven and earth *see* **heaven.**

not to have an earthly (*inf*) **1** to have not the slightest chance of success: *He has entered the tennis competition but he hasn't an earthly.* **2** to have no knowledge or information about: *'Do you know where he is now?' 'No, I haven't an earthly.'* [A contraction of *not to have an earthly hope* — originally a religious reference — and thus by analogy *not to have an earthly idea.*]

on earth a phrase added to a question for emphasis: *What on earth are you doing?; Why on earth did you do that?*

pay the earth *see* **cost the earth** above.

run (someone or something) to earth to find (someone or something) after a long search: *He had been looking for a copy of that book for a long time and finally ran one to earth in Edinburgh.* [A hunting term — 'to chase or hunt a fox into its hole'.]

the salt of the earth *see* **salt.**

easy

as easy as falling off a log *see* **log.**

easier said than done more difficult to do than it sounds: *Getting seats for the theatre is easier said than done.*

easy come, easy go a saying, referring to something (money *etc*) which someone gets without much effort and which they are therefore quite happy to lose, spend *etc* in a casual manner: *He has a different girlfriend every time I see him — it's a case of easy come, easy go, I think.*

easy on the eye (*inf*) pleasant to look at: *He likes his secretary to be easy on the eye as well as efficient.* [Originally US.]

go easy on (someone or something) (*inf*) **1** not to make things difficult for (someone): *Go easy on her — she's very young.* **2** not to use too much of (something): *Go easy on the wine — there isn't much left.*

take it easy 1 not to work *etc* hard or energetically; to avoid using much effort: *Take it easy — you don't have to finish the job until tomorrow; The doctor told him to take it easy.* **2** (*usu in imperative*) not to get upset, angry *etc*: *Take it easy! There's no need to lose your temper.*

eat

    eat one's cake and have it *see* **cake.**

    eat one's heart out *see* **heart.**

    eat humble pie *see* **humble.**

    eat like a horse *see* **horse.**

    eat (someone) out of house and home *see* **house.**

    eat one's words *see* **word.**

    I'll eat my hat *see* **hat.**

    what's eating you? (*inf*) what is bothering you?: *What's eating you? You've been grumpy all day.*

ebb

    at a low ebb in a poor or depressed state: *She was at a low ebb after the operation.* [Literally, of the tide, 'very far out'.]

edge

    edge (someone) out to remove or get rid of (someone) gradually: *I feel that our new chairman is trying to edge out those committee members who disagree with him.*

    get a word in edgeways *see* **word.**

    have the edge on/over (someone) to have an advantage over (someone): *In the tennis match he had the edge on his opponent at the start but was beaten in the end.* [Originally US.]

    on edge uneasy, nervous or irritable: *She was on edge when waiting for her exam results.*

    set (someone's) teeth on edge *see* **teeth.**

egg

    a bad egg (*inf*) a completely worthless person: *I never really liked her husband — I always felt he was a bad egg.*

    egg (someone) on (*inf*) to urge (someone) on (to do something): *He egged on his friend to steal the radio; She egged him on to·apply for a better job.* [From the Old Norse verb *eggja* = to urge on — no connection with the noun *egg*.]

    have egg on one's face (*inf*) to be left looking foolish: *If I hold a party and no-one turns up, I'll have egg on my face, won't I?*

    a nest-egg *see* **nest.**

    put all one's eggs in one basket to depend entirely on the success of one scheme, plan *etc*: *You should apply for more than one job — don't put all your eggs in one basket.*

    teach one's grandmother to suck eggs to try to show someone more experienced than oneself how to do something they can already do: *I've been organizing fêtes for years, and I know how to do it — don't teach your grandmother to suck eggs!*

eight

 a figure of eight a pattern, movement *etc* in the shape of the figure 8: *The skater did a series of figures of eight.*

 one over the eight (*sl*) one drink too many: *By the way he was talking, I suspected that he had had one over the eight.*

elbow

 elbow-grease (*inf facet*) hard work; energy: *If you use a bit of elbow-grease you'll get that floor clean.*

 elbow-room space enough for moving or doing something: *Get out of my way and give me some elbow-room!*

 more power to his elbow *see* **power.**

 out at elbow (*formal*) ragged; shabby; worn out: *He always wears that old jacket although it is out at elbow.*

El Dorado

 El Dorado a place where it is easy to make money (often only in theory, or in the imagination): *America was believed by many emigrants to be El Dorado, the land of opportunity.* [This name — in Spanish 'the gilded one' — was given to a legendary 16C South American chieftain and later to his fabulously wealthy kingdom, which was believed to exist somewhere in the jungles of South and Central America.]

element

 in one's element in the surroundings that are most natural or pleasing to one: *He is in his element when he is organizing something*: [Literally referring to the four 'elements' of medieval science — fire, earth, air and water — to one of which every creature was believed to belong by nature.]

elephant

 a white elephant something which is useless and a nuisance or which causes much trouble while doing little good: *That enormous wardrobe your mother gave us has been nothing but a white elephant.* [In Thailand, where white elephants were traditionally treated like royalty, the king was reputed to bestow one on courtiers with whom he was displeased, because the cost of its upkeep was likely to ruin them.]

eleven

 at the eleventh hour at the last possible moment; only just in time: *The child was saved from the kidnappers at the eleventh hour.* [A Biblical reference, to the parable of the labourers in the vineyard — Matthew 20.]

empty

empty vessels make most noise it is usually the most foolish people, and those whose views are least valuable, who are the most concerned to make their opinions known. [Quoted by Shakespeare, *Henry V*, IV. iv, but certainly older.]

end

a dead end *see* **dead.**

at a loose end *see* **loose.**

at the end of one's tether emotionally exhausted because of worry, anger *etc*; having no more patience: *I'm at the end of my tether, and if the phone rings once more, I'll scream!* [From a grazing animal which can only go a certain distance from the peg to which it is tethered.]

at the end of the day *see* **day.**

at one's wits' end *see* **wit.**

be the end of (*not usu used seriously*) to cause the death of: *That child will be the end of me!*

come to a sticky end *see* **sticky.**

the end justifies the means a saying, meaning that if the result of an action is good, it doesn't matter whether the action itself was morally right or not.

the end of the road/line the point beyond which one can no longer continue or survive: *A management spokesman said that another strike might well mean the end of the road for the company.*

end up (*inf*) to end or finish (in a certain way); to do something in the end: *He said he would not go, but he ended up by going*; *He refused to believe her, but he ended up apologizing.*

get (hold of) the wrong end of the stick *see* **stick.**

keep one's end up (*inf*) to perform one's part in something equally as well as all the others who are involved: *Everyone else is so good at what they are doing that he has a hard job keeping his end up.* [A cricketing term — 'not to lose one's wicket'.]

make (both) ends meet to live within one's income; not to get into debt: *The widow and her four children found it difficult to make ends meet.* [The French version of this phrase, *faire joindre les deux bouts de l'année*, suggests that the 'ends' are the start and finish of one's yearly income.]

no end (of) (*very inf*) very much: *I feel no end of a fool*; *I liked it no end.*

enemy

how goes the enemy? what time is it? [Popularized by appearing in Dickens's *Nicholas Nickleby*, but in fact coined by Frederic Reynolds in his play *The Dramatist* (1789).]

enfant

an enfant terrible a child or young person, or a person, organization *etc* with new, unconventional ideas, who embarrasses older or more conventional people, organizations *etc* by the things he says and the attitudes he expresses: *I think our MP is something of an enfant terrible, and I'm not sure that his colleagues approve of everything he says.* [*Les enfants terribles* was the title of a series of prints by the 19C French caricaturist Paul Gavarni.]

enter

enter the lists *see* **lists.**

envy

be the envy of (someone) to be envied by (someone): *Her piano-playing was the envy of her sisters.*

equal

all things being equal *see* **thing.**

err

err on the side of (a quality *etc*) to be guilty of a fault, or what might be seen as a fault, in order to avoid an opposite and greater fault: *It is better to err on the side of leniency when punishing a child.*

errand

a fool's errand a useless journey: *I came to help him, but I can see that it was a fool's errand — he has no need of my assistance.*

run errands to do jobs (for someone): *He runs errands for his mother.*

error

trial and error *see* **trial.**

essence

of the essence (*formal*) of the greatest importance: *Patience is of the essence in training animals.*

establishment

the Establishment (*Brit*) the people, as a group, who hold important positions in a country, society or community: *Young people often distrust the Establishment.*

eternal

the Eternal City Rome.

the eternal triangle an emotional situation involving two women and a man or two men and a women: *In this novel Katy*

loves Ben, but Ben loves Caroline — the classic eternal triangle, in fact.
[Coined by a book reviewer in the *Daily Chronicle* in 1907.]

even

be, keep on an even keel *see* **keel.**

break even to make neither profit nor loss: *I spent £100 and made £100, so overall I broke even.*

even money a situation in which either of two possibilities is equally likely: *It is even money whether he will be made Home Secretary or Chancellor of the Exchequer.*

get even with (someone) (*inf*) to be revenged on (someone): *He tricked me, but I'll get even with him.*

have an even chance to be equally likely to be successful or unsuccessful: *We have an even chance of success.* [A gambling term.]

event

be wise after the event *see* **wise.**

in the event in the end; as it happens/happened/may happen: *In the event I did not need to go to hospital.* [From an otherwise obsolete meaning of *event* = result.]

in the event of (something) (*formal*) if (something) occurs: *In the event of his death you will inherit his money.*

every

every man jack *see* **jack.**

every now and then *see* **now.**

every other *see* **other.**

evidence

turn King's/Queen's evidence (of an accomplice in a crime) to give evidence against his partner(s) with the result that his own sentence is less severe: *He was sentenced to two years' imprisonment for his part in the crime because he turned Queen's evidence. His accomplices were sentenced to five years.* [*Evidence* here means 'witness(es)'.]

evil

the evil eye *see* **eye.**

put off the evil hour to postpone something unpleasant: *She knew she would have to break the bad news to her mother, but she decided to put off the evil hour by writing to her aunt first.*

ewe

a ewe lamb (*usu facet*) a person, project *etc* which is one's dearest possession: *Her youngest son is her ewe lamb.* [A Biblical reference, to the man in II Samuel 12:3 who 'had nothing save one little ewe lamb. . .'.]

example

make an example of (someone) to punish (someone) as a warning to others: *The judge decided to make an example of the young thief and sent him to prison for five years.*

set (someone) an example to act in such a (good) way that others will copy one's behaviour: *Teachers must set (their pupils) a good example.*

exception

the exception proves the rule the fact that an exception has to be made for a particular example of something proves that there is a general rule: *I know that what I have said does not apply to Brian, but I think in his case the exception proves the rule.* [A legal maxim — in full *the exception proves the rule in cases not excepted*.]

take exception to (something) to object to or take offence at (something): *The old lady took exception to the rudeness of the children.*

exhibition

make an exhibition of oneself (*derog*) to behave foolishly in public: *The little girl made an exhibition of herself by screaming loudly at her mother.*

expect

be expecting (*inf euph*) to be pregnant: *His wife is expecting again.*

expense

at the expense of (someone or something) causing harm, embarrassment *etc* to (someone or something): *She pursued her ambitions at the expense of her marriage.*

eye

all my eye (*sl*) simply not true: *He told me how sorry they were that they were unable to help, but that was all my eye.*

the apple of (someone's) eye *see* **apple.**

catch (someone's) eye to make (someone) notice one: *We wanted the bill for our meal, but I could not catch the waiter's eye.*

clap/lay/set eyes on (someone or something) (*inf*) to see (someone or something), *esp* for the first time: *I wish I'd never laid eyes on her!*

close one's eyes to (something) to ignore (something, *esp* something blameworthy): *She closed her eyes to her children's misbehaviour.*

cry one's eyes out (*inf*) to weep bitterly: *She cried her eyes out when he married someone else.*

easy on the eye *see* **easy.**

the evil eye the supposed power of causing harm by a look: *Nothing is going right for me — I think he put the evil eye on me.*

eyeball to eyeball (*inf*) in direct confrontation, for the purpose of frank and firm discussion: *The Prime Minister has never discussed the matter with the President eyeball to eyeball.*

an eye for an eye a punishment exactly the same as the offence committed: *She wants him to lose his job as he made her lose hers — she believes in the principle of an eye for an eye.* [A Biblical reference, to Exodus 21:23, often considered to sum up the stern moral code of the Old Testament.]

an eye-opener (*inf*) something which reveals an unexpected fact *etc*: *Our visit to their office was a real eye-opener — they're so inefficient!*

an eyesore (*inf*) something (*esp* a building) that is ugly to look at: *That new skyscraper is a real eyesore!*

in a twinkling of an eye *see* **twinkle.**

in one's mind's eye in one's imagination: *If you try hard you can see the room in your mind's eye.* [Probably from Shakespeare — *Hamlet* I. ii, 'I see my father . . . in my mind's eye, Horatio' — although the image had been used before.]

keep an eye on (someone or something) 1 to watch (someone or something) closely: *You must keep an eye on the price of bread.* **2** to look after (someone or something): *Keep an eye on the baby while I am out!*

keep a weather eye (open) *see* **weather.**

keep one's eyes peeled/skinned to watch carefully (for something): *This is the right street — keep your eyes skinned for a house with a red front door.*

make eyes at (someone) to look at (someone) with sexual interest or admiration: *Stop making eyes at that blonde!*

the naked eye the eye unassisted by spectacles, a telescope, a microscope *etc*: *He went on watching them through his binoculars until they were close enough to be seen with the naked eye.*

not to bat an eyelid to appear to feel no surprise, distress *etc*: *He didn't bat an eyelid when I told him he was sacked.*

not to be able to take one's eyes off (someone or something) not to be able to stop watching (something): *He couldn't take his eyes off the girl.*

one in the eye (for) (*inf*) a direct rejection or refusal (for): *The men's decision to accept the pay offer was one in the eye for the militants who had wanted them to strike.*

open (someone's) eyes to (something) to make (someone) see or understand (something of which they were not previously aware): *His trip to Africa opened his eyes to the poverty of underdeveloped countries.*

a private eye *see* **private.**

pull the wool over (someone's) eyes *see* **wool.**

see eye to eye (*usu in neg*) to be in agreement: *We've never seen eye to eye about this matter.* [From an interpretation of an obscure phrase in the Bible — Isaiah 52:8 — which the New English Bible retranslates as 'see with their own eyes'.]

see with half an eye to see without difficulty: *Anyone could have seen with half an eye that she was upset.*

a sight for sore eyes *see* **sight.**

a smack in the eye *see* **smack.**

there's more to (something) than meets the eye (something) is more complicated, or better, than it appears: *There is more to my job than meets the eye.*

turn a blind eye (to something) to pretend not to see or notice (something): *Because he works so hard, his boss turns a blind eye when he comes in late.*

up to one's eyes in (something) deeply involved in (something): *She is up to her eyes in school work just at the moment — the exams are next week.*

with an eye to (something) with (something) as an aim: *He always worked with an eye to promotion.*

with an eye to the main chance *see* **chance.**

with one's eyes open with full awareness of what one is doing: *I knew what the job would involve — I went into it with my eyes open.*

F

face

at face value as being as valuable *etc* as it appears: *You must take this offer at face value.* [Literally, as being worth the value printed on the face of a coin, bank-note, stamp *etc*.]

be staring (someone) in the face (*inf*) to be very obvious or easy (for someone) to see: *The reason for his behaviour was staring us in the face; I couldn't see the book I wanted, although it was staring me in the face.*

cut off one's nose to spite one's face *see* **nose.**

face (someone) down to assert one's superiority over (someone) merely by looking stern: *He was always able to face down people who interrupted him when he was making a speech.*

his *etc* face fell he looked suddenly disappointed: *When she heard she had been disqualified her face fell.*

face to face both or all people concerned actually being present: *They finally met face to face to discuss the problem.*

face up to (something) to meet or accept (something) boldly: *He faced up to his difficult situation.*

fly in the face of (something) to oppose or defy (something); to treat (something) with contempt: *She always flew in the face of public opinion.* [Originally used of a dog attacking a person.]

give (something) a facelift to carry out improvements intended to make (something, *eg* a building) look better: *Several million pounds will be spent giving this mining village a facelift.* [From *face-lifting*, an operation to raise the skin of the lower face, and thus eliminate wrinkles.]

grind the face(s) of (someone) to govern (someone) cruelly, by imposing harsh taxation *etc*: *He was accused of grinding the faces of the working class.* [A Biblical reference, to Isaiah 3:15.]

have a face like a fiddle *see* **fiddle.**

have a long face to look unhappy or disapproving: *There were many long faces among the children when they heard there would be no school treat that year.*

in the face of (something) in spite of having to deal with (something): *He succeeded in the face of great difficulties.* [Literally, this phrase originally meant 'in the presence of'.]

laugh on the other side of one's face *see* **laugh.**

let's face it if one is to be honest: *Let's face it, none of us like him very much.*

lose face to suffer a loss of respect or reputation: *You will really lose face if you are defeated in the tennis match against a younger player.* [This phrase, and **save face** *below*, were first used by English-speaking residents in China. *Lose face* is a translation of the Chinese *tiu lien.*]

make/pull a face to twist one's face into strange expressions: *That rude child is making faces at me; He pulled faces at the baby to make it laugh.*

on the face of it as it appears at first glance (*usu* deceptively): *On the face of it, the problem was quite easy, but it actually turned out* *to be very difficult.*

put a good face on it to give the appearance of being satisfied *etc* with something when actually one is not: *Now it's done we'll have to put a good face on it, but I am not pleased with it.*

save (one's/someone's) face to prevent (oneself/someone else) from appearing stupid or wrong: *I refuse to accept the responsibility for that error just to save your face — it's your fault.* [See **lose face** above.]

set one's face against (something) to oppose (something) very determinedly: *There is no point trying to persuade him — he has set his face against the project and he won't change his mind.* [A Hebrew idiom from the Bible — Leviticus 20:3.]

show one's face (*usu in neg*) to be sufficiently confident or unashamed to be able to go to a particular place: *After making such a fool of myself I'll never be able to show my face in there again.*

a slap in the face *see* **slap.**

to (someone's) face while (someone) is present: *You wouldn't be brave enough to say that to his face!*

fact

the hard facts *see* **hard.**

fag

a/the fag-end (*inf*) the very end of something: *The new teacher arrived at the fag-end of the autumn term; He only heard the fag-end of the conversation.* [Originally a term for the last section of a piece of cloth, often woven with odd remnants of yarn.]

fail

words fail me *see* **word.**

faint

faint heart never won fair lady a saying, meaning that it is necessary to be bold to achieve what one desires.

not to have the faintest (*inf*) not to know at all: *'Do you know where he went?' 'No, I haven't the faintest.'* [A contraction of **not to have the faintest idea.**]

fair

all the fun of the fair *see* **fun.**

bid fair to *see* **bid.**

by fair means or foul in any possible way, just or unjust: *I intend to win by fair means or foul.*

fair and square straight or directly: *He hit him fair and square on the chin.*

fair do's/fair's fair (*inf*) an expression appealing for, or agreeing to, fair play, complete honesty *etc*: *Come on, fair do's — I babysat for you; now it's your turn to babysit for me; Fair's fair — it's your turn to do the washing-up.*

fair game something which it is quite reasonable and permissible to attack, laugh at *etc*: *It is generally accepted that politicians are fair game for journalists.* [A hunting term.]

fair play honest treatment; an absence of cheating, biased actions *etc*: *He's not involved in the contest — he's only here to see fair play.*

the fair sex (*usu facet*) women: *He has very little success with the fair sex.*

fairweather friends people who are only friendly to one so long as everything is going well for one: *As soon as he found himself in trouble over money, all his fairweather friends deserted him.*

in a fair way to likely to succeed in: *He is in a fair way to becoming a millionaire — he already owns three companies.*

play fair *see* **play.**

faith

in (all) good faith sincerely: *She made the offer in all good faith.*

fall

fall about (*inf*) to collapse (with laughter): *When I told the joke to my children they fell about laughing.*

fall back on (something or someone) (*inf*) to use (something), or to go to (something or someone) for help, finally when everything else has been tried: *Whatever happens you'll have your father's money/your father to fall back on.*

fall behind with (something) to become late in (regular payment, letter-writing *etc*): *Don't fall behind with the rent!*

fall by the wayside *see* **wayside.**

fall down on (something) (*inf*) to fail in (something): *He's falling down on his job.*

fall flat (*inf*) (*esp* of jokes *etc*) to fail completely or to have no effect: *His booby-trap fell flat; His attempt at humour fell flat.*

fall for (something or someone) (*inf*) **1** to be deceived by (something): *I made up a story to explain why I had not been at work and he fell for it.* **2** to fall in love with (someone): *He has fallen for your sister.*

fall foul of *see* **foul.**

fall from grace *see* **grace.**

fall in to join a group of people doing something: *As the queue of people passed us, we fell in at the rear.* [Literally, of soldiers, to take places in ranks.]

fall into place *see* **place.**

fall in with (someone or something) 1 to join with (someone) for company: *On the way home we fell in with some friends.* **2** to agree with (a plan, idea *etc*): *They fell in with our suggestion.*

fall off to become smaller in number or amount: *Theatre audiences often fall off during the summer.*

fall on (something) to begin to do something with (something) (*esp* to eat it) very eagerly or vigorously: *They fell hungrily on the food; She fell on the photographs he had brought and began passing them round.* [Literally, to attack.]

fall on deaf ears *see* **ears.**

fall on one's feet *see* **feet.**

fall out to quarrel: *I have fallen out with my brother; She and her friends are always falling out.*

fall over oneself (*inf*) to very busy and put oneself to a great deal of trouble (to do something): *As soon as the film star appeared in the restaurant, all the waiters fell over themselves to see that she had everything she wanted.*

fall short (*often with* **of**) to be not enough or not good enough *etc*: *The money we have falls short of what we need.*

fall through (of plans *etc*) to fail or come to nothing: *We had planned to go to Paris, but the plans fell through.*

fall to (*old*) to begin enthusiastically, *esp* eating: *The food was put on the table and they fell to eagerly.*

pride goes before a fall *see* **pride.**

riding for a fall *see* **ride.**

false

a false alarm a warning of something which does not in fact happen: *We were told there was a bomb in that parcel but it was a false alarm.*

false pretences acts or behaviour intended to deceive people: *He got the money by/on/under false pretences.* [A legal term.]

a false start a beginning in some activity which is unsuccessful and so has to be repeated: *After several false starts he eventually made a success of his business.* [Literally, a start to a race that has to be repeated, *eg* because one of the runners has left the starting-point before the correct signal has been given.]

a false step a mistake: *He made a false step in not informing the police.*

familiarity

    familiarity breeds contempt a saying, meaning that one ceases to be fully aware of and to appreciate the qualities (beauty, goodness, danger *etc*) of something one knows very well.

family

    a family tree (a plan showing) a person's ancestors (and sometimes his descendants): *If you want to know the relationship of the present Queen of Britain to the Stuart kings you must consult her family tree.*

    in the family way (*euph*) pregnant: *It was obvious that Mr Martin's wife was in the family way.*

    run in the family to be a feature found in many members of a particular family: *Athletic skill runs in our family; I'm not surprised he is going bald — it runs in the family.*

fancy

    fancy oneself (*inf*) to think of oneself as being, or as likely to be, good (*esp* at a particular thing): *She always fancied herself as an actress.*

    fancy free not in love with anyone: *She went out with many men in the days when she was fancy free, but after she met her future husband she gave them all up.* [Probably from Shakespeare — *A Midsummer Night's Dream* II. i.]

    (someone's) fancy man (*derog sl*) (someone's) male lover: *I thought she was quite amusing, but I didn't think much of her fancy man.*

    take a fancy to (someone or something) to become fond of (someone or something), often suddenly or unexpectedly: *He bought that house because his wife took a fancy to it.*

    take (someone's) fancy to be liked or wanted by (someone): *When my wife goes shopping she just buys anything that takes her fancy.*

    tickle (someone's) fancy *see* **tickle**.

far

    far and away by a very great amount: *He is far and away the cleverest boy in the class.*

    far be it from me (*usu ironic*) I have no right or desire (to do something): *Far be it from me to tell you how to do your job, but isn't that a silly thing to do?*

    a far cry from *see* **cry**.

    so far, so good the operation has been successful up to now: *We've built the walls of the shed — so far, so good. Now we have to build the roof.*

fashion

   after a fashion in a way, but not very well: *He can speak French after a fashion.*

fast

   play fast and loose (*inf*) to do what one likes (with); to act irresponsibly (with): *He played fast and loose with his father's money.* [From the name of an old trick in which one player made loops in a piece of string which the other player tried to secure by thrusting a stick through them — however this was never possible because of the way the loops were constructed.]

   pull a fast one (on someone) (*inf*) to deceive (someone): *He certainly pulled a fast one on me.* [Literally, to bowl a fast ball in cricket.]

   stand fast *see* **stand.**

fat

   chew the fat (*sl*) to have a chat or discussion: *I want to come to a decision quickly rather than waste time chewing the fat.*

   fat chance (*inf*) not at all likely: *Will he get the job? Fat chance — he has no qualifications.*

   the fat is in the fire trouble has been started off (by something happening) and something remarkable can be expected to happen: *The fat's in the fire now that he has discovered about his wife's lover.*

   a fat lot of (*sl*) not much: *It's a fat lot of use coming round to see me when I'm out at work!*

   kill the fatted calf to have a great celebration to welcome someone, *esp* someone whom one has not seen for a long time. [A Biblical reference, to the parable of the Prodigal Son — Luke 15.]

   live off the fat of the land (*often derog*) to live in a very luxurious manner: *His opponents accused him of living off the fat of the land and not doing any work.* [A Biblical reference, to Genesis 45:18.]

fate

   a fate worse than death (*inf: often facet*) a dreadful happening: *Having to eat her cooking for a whole week would be a fate worse than death!* [Originally coined as a euphemism for seduction or rape.]

father

   the father and mother of a very extreme (*esp* bad) example of: *There'll be the father and mother of a row if your wife sees you like that!*

be gathered to one's fathers (*arch or facet*) to die. [A Hebrew idiom, from the Bible — Judges 2:10.]

like father, like son a saying, meaning that someone is like his father in some way.

fault

find fault with (someone) to criticize or scold (someone), *esp* unreasonably, for something they have done: *He hates his teacher because she is always finding fault with him.*

to a fault (*formal*) excessively; to too great an extent: *He was generous to a fault and embarrassed his friends by his lavish gifts.*

favour

curry favour with *see* **curry.**

fear

no fear (*inf*) not likely: '*Are you thinking of getting married?*' '*No fear, I like being a bachelor.*'

put the fear of death/God into (someone) (*inf*) to terrify (someone): *He is an appalling driver, and driving with him puts the fear of God into me.*

strike fear into (someone) *see* **strike.**

there is not much fear of (something) it is not likely that (something will happen): *There's not much fear of him leaving the firm, I'm sorry to say.*

feather

featherbed (someone) to make things easy for (someone): *He was featherbedded in his early life by his father's immense wealth.*

a feather in one's cap something one can be proud of: *That prize he won was quite a feather in his cap.*

feather one's (own) nest (*derog*) to gain money for oneself or to make oneself rich while serving others in a position of trust: *All the time he has been a member of the committee he has been feathering his own nest.*

fine feathers make fine birds a saying, meaning that people often appear attractive *etc* because they are expensively dressed.

make the feathers fly to attack suddenly with great effect: *He stormed into the office to complain and made the feathers fly.* [A reference to an animal attacking poultry.]

ruffle (someone's) feathers to upset, distress or annoy (someone) slightly: *She was a placid person, but his rudeness had ruffled her feathers quite a bit.*

show the white feather to show signs of cowardice: *He refused to join the protest, and the others accused him of showing the white feather.*

[A white feather in the tail was a sign of inferior breeding in a fighting-cock.]

you could have knocked me down with a feather (*inf*) I was astonished: *You could have knocked me down with a feather when he introduced this girl as his wife!*

fed

fed up (*inf*)/**fed to the back teeth** (*sl*) tired; bored and annoyed: *I'm fed up with all this work!; Oh, do shut up! I'm fed to the back teeth with the sound of your voice!*

feel

feel at home *see* **home**.

feel free (to) you may do (what you wish): *Feel free to ask if you need any help.*

feel in one's bones *see* **bone**.

feel small *see* **small**.

feel the draught *see* **draught**.

feel the pinch *see* **pinch**.

get the feel of (something) (*inf*) to become accustomed to (something): *Once I got the feel of my new car, I enjoyed driving it.*

feet

be/sit at (someone's) feet to admire (someone) greatly and be greatly influenced by them: *She was so beautiful and charming that half of London was at her feet within a month.*

be rushed off one's feet to be extremely busy: *Just before Christmas the staff in the shop are always rushed off their feet.*

fall/land on one's feet to have some unexpected good luck, *esp* after or because of something bad or unpleasant: *He lost his job last year, but he really fell on his feet — he is now doing the same job for someone else at a higher salary.*

find one's feet to become able to cope with a new situation: *The new job was difficult at first, but she soon found her feet.*

get cold feet *see* **cold**.

have feet of clay to have a weakness which was previously unsuspected: *She discovered that the film star had feet of clay when she read in a magazine that he admitted neglecting his children.*

have both feet/have (both) one's feet on the ground to act always with good sense: *I don't worry about her — she's got both feet on the ground and I know she won't do anything silly.*

have two left feet *see* **left**.

put one's feet up to take a rest by lying down or sitting with one's feet supported on something: *I look forward to getting home* *and putting my feet up.*

sit at (someone's) feet *see* **be at (someone's) feet** *above*.

stand on one's own (two) feet to manage one's own affairs without help: *I won't always be here to help you — it's time you learned to stand on your own two feet.*

sweep (someone) off his *etc* **feet** to affect (someone) with strong emotion or enthusiasm: *She was swept off her feet by* (= fell violently in love with) *a dark, handsome stranger.*

fell

at one fell swoop *see* **swoop**.

fence

rush one's fences to act in too much of a hurry, without enough care: *Don't rush your fences — I think you should plan more carefully what you are going to do.* [A horse-riding idiom.]

sit on the fence to (appear to) remain neutral and not take sides (in a dispute *etc*): *You can't sit on the fence for ever — sooner or later you'll have to commit yourself.* [An early 19C US idiom, implying that one is undecided on which side of the fence to come down.]

fetch

fetch and carry to go back and forward getting things which are needed: *The old lady wanted someone to fetch and carry for her as she could no longer walk very well.*

fetch up (*inf*) to come finally to a halt (in a particular place): *She got on an express train by mistake and fetched up in Manchester.* [A nautical term.]

fettle

in fine/good fettle in good health or good spirits: *He was ill when I saw him last, but he seems in fine fettle now.*

fiddle

as fit as a fiddle extremely healthy: *He is eighty-eight, but he is as fit as a fiddle.*

have a face like a fiddle not to look cheerful or happy: *Having lunch with her wasn't much fun — she just sat there with a face like a fiddle, saying nothing.*

on the fiddle (*sl derog*) dishonest: *He's always on the fiddle.*

play second fiddle (to someone) *see* **second**.

field

have a field day (*usu facet*) to spend time in great activity or with great success: *She had a field day in the shops when she went out to spend her year's clothes allowance all at once; The reporters had a field* *day when the princess got married.* [A *field day* was literally a military review, or a series of (large scale) field exercises for the army.]

play the field *see* **play.**

fifth

a fifth-columnist one of a group of people in a town, country *etc* who try to help the people with whom that town or country is at war: *The fortress was captured with the aid of the fifth-columnists who opened the gates to the enemy in the middle of the night.* [In 1936, during the Spanish Civil War, General Mola encircled Madrid with four columns of troops. He claimed, however, that he could count on the help of *la quinta columna* — 'the fifth column' — within the city.]

fig

not to give a fig for (something) (*old*) not to care about (something) at all: *I don't give a fig for what he thinks.*

fight

a fighting chance a chance of success if a great effort is made: *Yesterday the doctors thought he would die, but today they say he has a fighting chance.*

fighting fit in very good physical condition: *I've been ill, but I'm fighting fit again now.*

fight it out to argue until a decisive end is reached: *Fight it out among yourselves which of you is to go.*

fight shy of (something) to avoid: *He fought shy of introducing her to his wife.* [Apparently a term from prize-fighting.]

live like fighting-cocks to have the best of food and drink: *I don't see why your whole worthless family should live like fighting-cocks at my expense!* [Fighting-cocks were very carefully looked after and well fed.]

put up a good fight to fight or compete well or bravely: *She put up a good fight in the finals of the tennis competition, but was defeated.*

figment

a figment of one's imagination (*formal*) something one has imagined and which has no reality: *That rich uncle in America he talks about is just a figment of his imagination.*

figure

a figure of eight *see* **eight.**

that figures (*sl*) this is what I would expect: *He has gone away? That figures — he always disappears without warning.* [Originally US.]

file

in Indian/single file (moving along) singly, one behind the other: *They went downstairs in single file*; *The children trotted along the path in Indian file*. [From the usual method of travel of American Indians.]

the rank and file *see* **rank.**

fill

fill in (for someone) (*inf*) to do (someone's) job temporarily: *I'm filling in for his secretary while she's in hospital.*

fill (someone) in (*inf*) to give (someone) all the necessary information: *I've been away — can you fill me in on what has happened?*

fill out to become rounder or fatter: *She used to be very thin, but she has filled out a bit now.*

find

finders keepers (*inf*) a saying, *esp* used by children, meaning that a person who finds something is entitled to keep it.

find fault with (someone) *see* **fault.**

find one's feet *see* **feet.**

find it in one's heart *see* **heart.**

find one's/its (own) level *see* **level.**

fine

cut it fine (*inf*) to allow barely enough (time, money *etc*) for something that must be done: *If you want to catch the noon train, you're cutting it a bit fine.*

fine feathers make fine birds *see* **feather.**

go through (something) with a fine-tooth(ed) comb to search, or look at (something) very carefully: *There must be a mistake somewhere, so I suggest you go through all the records with a fine-tooth comb.* [From the standard method of finding and removing lice and fleas.]

finger

be all fingers and thumbs, my *etc* **fingers are all thumbs** (*inf*) to be, I am, very awkward and clumsy (for the moment) in handling or holding things: *She could not undo the string of the parcel — she was all fingers and thumbs.*

cross one's fingers to hope for good luck: *I am crossing my fingers and hoping that I get the job.* [From an old superstition.]

get one's fingers burnt/burn one's fingers to suffer because one has interfered, taken part in buying and selling of shares *etc*: *Several people have got involved in her problems and burned their fingers doing so*; *He got his fingers badly burned speculating in oil shares.*

get/pull one's/the finger out (*rather vulg*) to begin working, doing one's job thoroughly or efficiently *etc*: *The boss told him if he didn't get his finger out he would shortly find himself without a job; If it annoys you so much, why don't you get the finger out and do something about it!* [RAF slang.]

have a finger in the pie/in every pie (*inf: often derog*) **1** to have an interest or share in a plan, business *etc* or in several plans, businesses *etc*: *He was so anxious for the scheme to do well that I knew he had a finger in the pie.* **2** to be involved in everything that happens: *Mrs Jones likes to have a finger in every pie in the village.*

have (something) at one's fingertips to know all the details (of a subject) thoroughly: *He has the history of the firm at his fingertips.*

have green fingers *see* **green.**

keep one's finger on the pulse *see* **pulse.**

let (something) slip through one's fingers to lose (an advantage *etc*) which one had the chance of getting for oneself: *I will never forgive myself for letting such an opportunity slip through my fingers.*

not to lift a finger (*inf*) to do nothing: *She did not lift a finger to prevent his arrest.*

point the finger at (someone) to call attention to (someone) by blaming them for something: *Although I do not wish to point the finger at anyone in particular, certain people in this office have not been working as well as they might.*

put one's finger on (something) to point out or describe (something) exactly; to identify (something): *He put his finger on the cause of our financial trouble; You put your finger on it when you told him he was a lazy good-for-nothing.*

to one's fingertips completely or perfectly: *She is an artist to her fingertips.*

twist (someone) round one's little finger to make (someone) act exactly as one wants: *She can twist her father round her little finger and she always gets her way.*

work one's fingers to the bone to work extremely hard: *His mother worked her fingers to the bone to send him to university.* [Literally, to wear the flesh off one's fingers by working.]

finish
    the finishing touches the final details which complete a work of art *etc*: *They had a meeting to put the finishing touches to their plan.*

fire
    add fuel to the fire *see* **fuel.**

the fat is in the fire *see* **fat.**

fire away (*inf*) to begin doing something; to go ahead: *I'm ready to start writing down what you're going to say — fire away!*

a firebrand a person who causes political or social trouble or excitement: *He was a real firebrand in his youth, but he has lost his political enthusiasm now.* [Literally, 'a piece of burning wood'.]

firing on all cylinders *see* **cylinder.**

hang fire to delay or to be delayed: *Our plans for the new factory are hanging fire at the moment.* [A term applied to flintlock guns in which, because of the firing mechanism, there was sometimes a delay between the pulling of the trigger and the gun firing.]

have several irons in the fire *see* **iron.**

like a house on fire *see* **house.**

open fire (on someone or something) to begin shooting (at someone or something): *The enemy opened fire (on us) before we reached safety.*

play with fire to do something dangerous or risky: *She knew she was playing with fire by having an affair with a married man.*

there's no smoke without fire *see* **smoke.**

under fire being criticized or blamed: *The government is under fire for its economic policy.* [Literally, being shot at.]

first

at first hand obtained *etc* directly: *I was able to obtain information about the accident at first hand.*

first and foremost (*formal*) first of all; before anything else: *First and foremost we must thank you for your help.*

(in) the first flush of *see* **flush.**

first refusal *see* **refusal.**

first thing before doing anything else: *I haven't time to discuss your proposal tonight, but I'll see you first thing tomorrow; She does exercises every morning first thing.*

get to/make first base *see* **base.**

in the first place *see* **place.**

not to know the first thing about (something) (*inf*) to know nothing about (something): *I'm afraid I don't know the first thing about cars.*

of the first water (*formal*) of the highest quality: *She was a beauty of the first water; He is a television journalist of the first water.* [A technical term for a completely colourless diamond — in the 18C diamonds were graded into three 'waters'. The idiom may derive originally from Arabic.]

fish

    a big fish (*sl*) an important or leading person: *He works in the Ministry of Defence, and I think he's quite a big fish.* [From the saying **a big fish in a small pond.**]

    drink like a fish (*derog*) to drink too much alcohol: *He's a kindly man, but he drinks like a fish and is quite unreliable.*

    fish in troubled waters (*derog*) to take advantage of a disturbance, difficulties, problems *etc* to obtain benefits for oneself: *During the war, his company had been quietly fishing in troubled waters by selling electronic communication systems to both sides.*

    have other fish to fry to have something else to do or to attend to (and therefore unable to devote all one's attention to the subject being discussed): *He did not seem to be interested in the project, and they suspected that he had other fish to fry.*

    like a fish out of water in an uncomfortable or unaccustomed situation; ill at ease: *The middle-aged woman felt like a fish out of water at her daughter's party.*

    make fish of one and flesh of another (*formal*) to treat one thing (unfairly) as being different from another: *I'm afraid the two situations are directly parallel, and it would not be right to make fish of one and flesh of another.*

    neither fish nor flesh nor good red herring neither one thing nor another: *The author seems undecided as to whether his book should be a light novel or a serious biography, with the result that it is neither fish nor flesh nor good red herring.*

    a pretty kettle of fish *see* **kettle.**

    a queer fish (*inf derog*) a person with odd habits, or a person whose personality one does not understand: *I like William, but he's a queer fish and you never know how he will react to what you say.*

    there's plenty more fish in the sea a saying, used when an opportunity of some sort has been lost, meaning that more opportunities of the same kind can be expected to arise.

fist

    hand over fist *see* **hand.**

fit

    by fits and starts irregularly; often stopping and starting again: *He did his work by fits and starts.*

    fit as a fiddle *see* **fiddle.**

    fit like a glove *see* **glove.**

    have/throw a fit (*inf*) to behave wildly because of extreme feelings, *esp* of anger, fear or reluctance (*usu* an exaggeration): *If your mother sees you in that state, she'll have a fit!*

see/think fit (*usu with* **to**) to consider that some action is right, suitable *etc*: *I won't tell you what to do — you may do as you see fit (to do).*

five

a bunch of fives (*old sl*) a clenched fist (when used to strike someone *etc*): *I turned round — and got a bunch of fives in the face.*

fix

fix on (something) (*inf*) to decide or choose (something): *Have you fixed on a date for your party yet?*

fix (someone) up with (something) (*inf*) to provide (something) for (someone): *Can you fix me up with a car for tomorrow?*

flag

a flag of convenience a foreign flag under which ships are registered in order to avoid taxes *etc* at home: *All their ships are registered under flags of convenience.*

show the flag to appear at a gathering *etc* in order to make sure that the firm, country *etc* to which one belongs is not forgotten by others: *We feel that since all the other insurance companies will be represented at the conference, someone from this firm should go to show the flag.*

flake

flake out (*inf*) to collapse from tiredness or illness: *I rush about so much during the day that I just flake out in the evenings.*

flash

a flash in the pan a sudden brief success which is not likely to happen again: *She did pass one exam, but it was just a flash in the pan.* [In a flintlock gun the spark from the flint ignited a pinch of gunpowder in the priming pan, from which the flash travelled to the main charge in the barrel. If this then failed to go off, only 'a flash in the pan' resulted.]

flat

fall flat *see* **fall.**

flat out (*inf*) as fast, energetically *etc* as possible: *He ran flat out down the road; She worked flat out to get it finished.*

in a flat spin (*sl*) in a state of confused excitement: *My daughter is getting married on Saturday, and my wife has been in a flat spin all week.* [An aviation term, probably from the 1st World War. A plane descending in circles while remaining nearly horizontal — 'flat' — quickly went out of control.]

that's flat I am telling you definitely: *I'm not doing it, and that's flat!*

flea

    a flea in one's ear (*often facet*) a sharp scolding: *The old lady thought he was impertinent and sent him away with a flea in his ear; He got a flea in his ear from his boss for forgetting to put the date on his letters.*

    a flea market (*inf*) a shop *etc* selling second-hand goods, *orig esp* clothes: *She buys a lot of her more bizarre clothes in a flea market.* [From the famous *Marché aux Puces* in Paris.]

    a flea-pit (*derog*) a public building, *esp* a cinema or theatre, of an inferior kind, which is or appears to be infested with fleas *etc*: *One of the cinemas in this town is very nice, but the other one is a real flea-pit!*

flesh

    flesh and blood 1 (someone's) relations; family: *She is my own flesh and blood.* **2** human nature: *It is more than flesh and blood can tolerate.*

    the flesh-pots luxurious living: *She is enjoying herself among the flesh-pots of Hollywood.* [A Biblical reference, to Exodus 16:3.]

    get/have one's pound of flesh *see* **pound.**

    make fish of one and flesh of another *see* **fish.**

    make (someone's) flesh creep to cause (someone) to feel as if horrible creatures are crawling all over them; to horrify (someone): *That science fiction story really made my flesh creep.*

    neither fish nor flesh nor good red herring *see* **fish.**

    the spirit is willing but the flesh is weak *see* **spirit.**

    a thorn in (someone's) flesh *see* **thorn.**

flight

    a flight of fancy (*usu facet*) an example of rather too free a use of the imagination: *They thought secretly that when she likened the falling snow to dancing fairies she was merely indulging in a flight of fancy.*

    top-flight (*formal*) of the highest class: *She is a top-flight secretary.*

fling

    have a final fling to enjoy the last period of gaiety (before a change in one's circumstances *etc*): *On the last night of the holiday they decided to have a final fling and visit the town's most expensive nightclub.*

flog

    flog a dead horse *see* **horse.**

flood

before the Flood (*facet*) a very long time ago: *Some of her ideas date from before the Flood*. [A reference to the Great Flood in the Bible — Genesis 7:9].

floor

hold the floor to be the dominant person at a meeting, party *etc* because one talks a great deal: *When she arrived at the party, she found that a man with a loud voice was holding the floor*. [*The floor* here is the main area of a Parliamentary chamber, where the delegates sit.]

take the floor (*rather formal*) **1** to rise to speak to a group of people: *The chairman asked Mr Smith to take the floor*. **2** to begin to dance: *The young couple took the floor and waltzed round the room*.

wipe the floor with (someone) to defeat (someone) completely: *He tried to argue with his wife about the matter, but she wiped the floor with him*.

flower

the flower of (*formal*) the best of: *The flower of the nation died on the battlefield*.

flush

a busted flush (*sl*) something that has to be abandoned as a failure: *He had to admit that his plans for expansion had been a busted flush*. [Literally, in poker, a sequence of cards which the player is unable to complete in time to win the hand.]

(in) the first flush of (something) (in) the early stages of (something) when a person is feeling fresh, strong, enthusiastic *etc*: *He is no longer in the first flush of youth*; *In the first flush of victory they thought they had won the war, but there were more battles to come*.

fly

fly a kite *see* **kite.**

fly-by-night (*derog*) not able to be trusted, *esp* used of someone who is likely to disappear without notice: *You should not do business with fly-by-night companies*.

a flying visit a very short, often unexpected, visit: *She paid her mother a flying visit before she went back to university*.

fly in the face of *see* **face.**

a fly in the ointment something that spoils something or makes something less perfect, less valuable *etc*: *I enjoy my job — the fly in the ointment is that I start early in the morning*. [Possibly a Biblical reference, to Ecclesiastes 10:1 — 'Dead flies cause ... ointment ... to send forth a stinking savour'.]

fly off the handle *see* **handle.**

get off to a flying start to have a very successful beginning: *Our new shop has got off to a flying start.* [Literally, a flying start is a beginning to a race where all the competitors are already moving.]

a high flier *see* **high.**

let (something) fly (at someone or something) to throw, shoot or send out (something) violently; to strike at or speak sharply to (someone): *He aimed carefully and let fly (an arrow) at the target; She let fly at him for being late.*

pigs might fly *see* **pig.**

send (someone/something) flying (*inf*) to hit or knock (someone or something) so that he or it falls down or falls backward: *The children rushed through the shop and sent all the goods flying.*

there are no flies on (someone) (*inf*) there is no lack of intelligence and cunning in (someone): *I'm sure he realized what you were doing — there are no flies on John!*

time flies *see* **time.**

with flying colours *see* **colour.**

I *etc* **would like to be a fly on the wall** I would like to be present (at a meeting, conversation *etc*) without being seen so that I could see and hear what happens without taking part: *When she finds out where he was, she's going to ask a lot of questions — and I'd like to be a fly on the wall at that interview!*

he *etc* **wouldn't hurt a fly** he is very gentle: *Our dog looks fierce, but really he wouldn't hurt a fly.*

foam

foam at the mouth (*inf*) to be extremely angry: *The children's work was particularly bad that day, and by the afternoon the teacher was foaming at the mouth.*

fog

not to have the foggiest (idea) (*inf*) to have no knowledge or ideas about something: *I haven't the foggiest (idea) why he left so suddenly.*

follow

follow in (someone's) footsteps *see* **foot.**

follow one's nose *see* **nose.**

follow suit (*formal*) to do just as someone else has done: *He went to bed and I followed suit after a few minutes.* [Literally, in card games, 'to play a card of the same suit as the one played by the last player'.]

food

food for thought something which can or has to be considered carefully: *My conversation with the priest gave me a great deal of food for thought.*

fool

a fool's errand *see* **errand.**

a fool's paradise a happy state caused by something which is deceptive or not to be trusted: *People who think the economic situation will improve shortly are living in a fool's paradise.*

make a fool of (someone) to make (someone) appear ridiculous or stupid: *He made a real fool of her by promising to marry her and then leaving her when he had spent all her money.*

make a fool of oneself to act in such a way that people consider one ridiculous or stupid: *He didn't want to make a fool of himself by asking her to the party when he knew that she would refuse to go.*

more fool you *see* **more.**

nobody's fool a sensible person: *He tells her lies, but she's nobody's fool and she doesn't believe them.*

play the fool (*not inf*) to act in a foolish manner, *esp* with the intention of amusing other people: *He always played the fool when the teacher left the classroom.*

suffer fools gladly *see* **suffer.**

foot

the boot is on the other foot *see* **boot**[1].

follow in (someone's) footsteps to do the same as (someone) has done before one: *When he joined the police force he was following in his father's footsteps.*

get off on the wrong foot to make a bad beginning: *She got off on the wrong foot by being half an hour late for her interview.* [A reference to marching out of step.]

have a foot in the door to have completed the first stage towards achieving a *usu* difficult aim: *If you can get any sort of job at all in a newspaper office you may not become a journalist at once, but you will have a foot in the door.*

have one foot in the grave (*facet inf*) to be not far from death, *esp* because of being old (*usu* an exaggeration): *The trouble with teenagers is that they think anyone over twenty-five has one foot in the grave!*

not to put a foot wrong not to make a mistake of any kind: *In all the delicate negotiations, the diplomat never put a foot wrong.*

put one's best foot forward to make the best attempt possible:

If you put your best foot forward you will complete the work in time.

put one's foot down (*not formal*) to be firm about something: *He wanted to go to Spain, but I put my foot down and refused to let him go.*

put one's foot in it (*inf*) to do or say something stupid: *I really put my foot in it when I asked about his wife — she has just run away with his friend!*

set foot in (somewhere) to arrive at or on (somewhere): *As soon as he set foot in the hotel he knew it would be unsuitable for his mother's holiday.*

force
force (someone's) hand *see* **hand**.
from force of habit *see* **habit**.

fore
to the fore (*formal*) in the front; easily seen; prominent: *He has recently come to the fore in local politics.* [Originally a Scots/Irish expression.]

fork
fork (something) out (*inf*) to pay, *usu* unwillingly; to hand over (*usu* money): *I'll have to fork out the cost of the meal.*

speak with a forked tongue (*facet*) to tell lies; to attempt to deceive others. [An idiom reputedly used by North American Indians.]

form
be good, bad form (*formal*) according to or not according to custom: *It's bad form to laugh at a funeral.*

be in good form (*not formal*) to be in a good mood: *She's in good form after her holiday.*

fort
hold the fort to take temporary charge (of a job, task *etc*): *I can't leave my children alone, but in the mornings my daily woman will hold the fort if I have to go out.* [A military image from a once-popular Moody & Sankey hymn.]

forty
forty winks (*inf*) a short sleep: *He always has forty winks after dinner.*

forward
look forward to (something) to wait with pleasure for (something which is going to happen): *I am looking forward to seeing you; She is looking forward to the Christmas holidays.*

123

foul

    fall foul of (someone or something) (*formal*) to get into a position where (someone or something) is hostile to or angry with one: *At an early age he fell foul of the law.* [A nautical term used of a ship which becomes entangled with another ship.]

    foul play (*formal*) a criminal act, *esp* involving murder: *A man has been found dead and the police suspect foul play.* [A long-established legal term.]

four

    on all fours (*inf*) on hands and knees: *He went up the steep path on all fours.*

free

    a free-for-all (*usu derog*) an argument, discussion *etc* in which everybody is allowed to express their opinions without control: *The discussion opened quietly, but soon became a free-for-all.*

    a free hand freedom to do whatever one likes: *He gave her a free hand with the servants.*

    make free with (someone or something) (*derog*) **1** to behave in too friendly and informal a way towards (someone): *His wife suspected him of making free with the typists in the office.* **2** (*often facet*) to eat or drink large quantities of (*usu* something which belongs to someone else): *He came into the sitting-room to find his guests making free with his best brandy.*

    make so free as to (*rather formal*) to be bold enough to: *If I might make so free as to offer some advice, I think you should have nothing to do with the plan.*

    scot-free *see* **scot.**

    with a free hand generously or liberally: *She spread cream on top of the cake with a free hand.*

French

    take French leave to be absent or on holiday, *esp* from work or military duty, without permission: *The soldier took French leave because he wanted to see his girlfriend.* [From the 18C French custom of leaving a party without saying goodbye to the host or hostess.]

fresh

    fresh as a daisy *see* **daisy.**

    fresh blood *see* **blood.**

Freud

    a Freudian slip a mistake, *esp* the use of the wrong word *etc* while speaking, that is supposed to indicate an unconscious thought: *The police spokesman made an obvious Freudian slip when he* said the whole matter of racial prejudice in the case was being considered by the Public Persecutor. [From the theories of the psychologist Sigmund Freud.]

Friday

    a Man Friday *see* **man.**

friend

    have a friend at court (*formal*) to have a friend in a position where his influence is likely to be useful to one: *Of course she has a friend at court — her husband is the sales manager of the firm.*

frighten

    frighten (someone) out of his wits *see* **wit.**

fro

    to and fro *see* **to.**

frog

    have a frog in one's throat to be hoarse: *Your voice sounds funny — have you got a frog in your throat?*

front

    the front of the house in a theatre, all the activities such as selling tickets and programmes which involve dealing directly with the audience: *He supervised the shifting of the scenery, the lighting and various other backstage activities, while his wife was in charge of the front of the house.*

fruit

    bear fruit *see* **bear**[1].

fry

    have other fish to fry *see* **fish.**

    out of the frying-pan into the fire a saying, meaning that someone has got out of a difficult or dangerous situation only to find themselves in a worse one.

    small fry (*derog*) unimportant people or things: *The local politicians are just small fry — we must convince the people in power.*

fuel

    add fuel to the fire to make an angry person angrier, an argument more heated *etc*: *Just as the discussion seemed to be becoming more rational Mary added fuel to the fire by saying that people should only talk about things they understood.*

full

    at full blast *see* **blast.**

    at full pelt *see* **pelt.**

    at full stretch *see* **stretch.**

    at full tilt *see* **tilt.**

be full of oneself (*inf derog*) to have a good opinion of oneself; to be conceited: *She is so full of herself that people dislike her.*

come full circle *see* **circle.**

come to a full stop *see* **stop.**

full steam ahead *see* **steam.**

full up completely filled: *The bus was full up when it arrived at our stop and none of us could get on.*

in full (*formal*) completely: *Write your name in full*; *He paid his bill in full.*

in full cry *see* **cry.**

in full swing *see* **swing.**

in the fullness of time (*formal or liter*) when the proper time (has) arrived; eventually: *In the fullness of time her son was born*; *In the fullness of time he will be promoted to manager.* [An idiom from the Bible — Galatians 4:4].

to the full (*formal*) as much as possible: *They all enjoyed life to the full.*

fun

all the fun of the fair (*often facet*) all the amusements *etc* suitable to the occasion: *We spent Christmas going to parties, carol-singing and generally enjoying all the fun of the fair.*

like fun (*sl*) **1** very quickly, hard or strongly: *We were all working like fun to get it finished.* **2** (*facet*) not at all: *'I think you should go.' 'Like fun I will.'*

make fun of (someone) to laugh at (someone), *usu* unkindly: *They made fun of her because she wore such old-fashioned clothes.*

poke fun at (someone) *see* **poke.**

funeral

that's my *etc* **funeral** (*often in neg*) that is something for me in particular to worry about: *If he wants to do something illegal, that's his funeral, but there's no reason why you should get involved.*

funk

in a blue funk (*sl*) in a state of terror or extreme fear: *She was in a blue funk about going to the dentist.* [Apparently originally Oxford University slang.]

funny

funny business (*inf*) tricks or deceptions *etc*: *The hijackers told the pilot that if he tried any funny business they would shoot him.* [Originally theatrical slang for comic action performed by a clown *etc*.]

funny ha-ha 'funny' meaning 'amusing' (as opposed to **funny peculiar**).

funny peculiar 'funny' meaning 'queer' or 'odd' (as opposed to **funny ha-ha**): *'The office I work in is a very funny place.' 'Funny peculiar or funny ha-ha?'*

fur

the fur was flying a fight or serious argument was taking place: *His ex-wife met his girlfriend at the party, and within minutes the fur was flying.* [From fights between animals.]

fury

like fury (*inf*) with great effort, enthusiasm *etc*: *She got into the car and drove like fury in order to be there on time.*

fuss

make a fuss (*inf*) to complain: *You will have to make a fuss if you want your money back in place of those damaged goods.*

make a fuss of (someone) (*inf*) to pay a lot of attention to (someone): *He always makes a fuss of his grandchildren.*

G

gab

the gift of the gab (*inf derog*) the ability to persuade (a person *etc*) to do, believe *etc* whatever one wishes: *Politicians need to have the gift of the gab.*

gaff

blow the gaff (*sl*) to tell (something secret) to someone: *When the police arrived, the thieves realized that someone had blown the gaff.*

gain

gain ground *see* **ground**.

gain time *see* **time**.

nothing ventured, nothing gained *see* **nothing**.

gallery

play to the gallery to try to become popular by doing, saying *etc* what would appeal to the less educated, less sophisticated section of the population, a group *etc*. [A theatrical expression. The cheapest seats in a theatre are in the gallery.]

game

fair game *see* **fair**.

the game is not worth the candle *see* **candle**.

the game is up the plan or trick has failed or has been found out: *The thief knew the game was up when he saw the policeman.*

give the game away *see* **give.**

a mug's game *see* **mug.**

the name of the game *see* **name.**

play a losing game *see* **lose.**

play the game to act fairly and honestly: *Reading other people's letters is not playing the game.*

garden

lead (someone) up the garden path to mislead (someone) or cause them to take a wrong decision, direction *etc* in a very gradual and not an obvious manner: *He realized that she had been leading him up the garden path and had no intention of marrying him.*

gasp

at one's last gasp just about to collapse, die, give up *etc*: *I'm surprised he's still alive — I thought he was at his last gasp when I saw him six months ago.* [A Biblical reference — to II Maccabees 2:32 in the Apocrypha.]

gauntlet

run the gauntlet (of) to suffer or be exposed to criticism, blame, danger *etc* (of): *The government always has to run the gauntlet of the trade unions; She had to run the gauntlet of her neighbours' disapproval.* [*Running the 'gatlopp'* was a Swedish military punishment in which the culprit had to run between two lines of men with whips who struck him as he passed. The phrase came into English during the Thirty Years' War — about 1640 — and *gatlopp* was soon replaced by a word more familiar to English speakers.]

throw down the gauntlet to make a challenge: *He threw down the gauntlet by calling his opponent a liar.* [From the traditional method of challenging an opponent to fight.]

gentle

the gentle sex (*often facet*) women: *Karate might seem to some to be an unsuitable sport for the gentle sex.*

get

be getting on for (*inf*) to be close to (a particular age, time *etc*): *It's getting on for three o'clock; He must be getting on for sixty at least.*

get away from it all (*inf*) to go away somewhere, or have a holiday somewhere, where one does not need to think about one's job, one's family, one's problems *etc*.

get off with (someone) (*sl*) to form a close, often sexual, relationship with (someone), *eg* at a dance, party: *He is always trying to get off with someone.*

get set *see* **set.**

tell (someone) where to get off/where he *etc* gets off (*Brit inf*) to tell (someone) that his bad, arrogant *etc* behaviour will not be tolerated: *He was trying to tell me how to do my job, but I soon told him where to get off.*

ghost

give up the ghost (*formal or facet*) to die, cease to work *etc*: *My car has given up the ghost, I'm afraid.* [An idiom from the Bible — Acts 7:23.]

not to have the ghost of a chance (*inf*) to have no chance of success at all: *He's entered for the big competition, but the standard is so high that he doesn't have the ghost of a chance.*

gift

the gift of the gab *see* **gab.**

a Greek gift *see* **Greek.**

look a gift horse in the mouth to criticize something which has been given to one: *The washing-machine Bob's mother gave us doesn't always work very well, but we shouldn't look a gift horse in the mouth.* [Looking at a horse's teeth is the standard way of telling its age, and thus its value.]

gild.

gild the lily *see* **lily.**

gilt

take the gilt off the gingerbread to spoil the attractiveness of a plan, situation *etc*: *It seemed like a very glamorous job, but discovering that we had to start at 6 am rather took the gilt off the gingerbread.* [Up to the middle of the 19C, gingerbread was often sold baked in fancy shapes and decorated with gold leaf.]

give

give (something) a miss *see* **miss.**

give and take a willingness to grant or allow a person *etc* something in return for being granted something oneself: *There must be some give and take in discussions between trade unions and management.*

give (someone) a piece of one's mind *see* **mind.**

give as good as one gets *see* **good.**

give (something) away to cause or allow (information, one's plans *etc*) to become known, *usu* accidentally: *Don't give me away;*

He gave away our hiding-place.

give (someone) hell *see* **hell.**

give (someone) his head *see* **head.**

give in to stop fighting *etc* and admit that one has been defeated: *The only way to win a war is to keep fighting and never think about giving in.*

give or take (something) (*inf*) adding or taking away (something) within certain limits: *I weigh sixty-five kilos, give or take a kilo* (= I weigh between sixty-four and sixty-six kilos).

give out (*inf*) to come to an end or be used up: *At this point my patience/money gave out.*

give (someone) pause *see* **pause.**

give rise to *see* **rise.**

give the game/show away (*inf*) to let a secret, trick *etc* become known (*usu* accidentally): *Don't laugh or you'll give the game away.*

give (someone) the works *see* **work.**

give up (something) to stop doing (something), seeing, eating or using (something), or trying to do (something): *I can't understand this problem — I'll have to give up; I must give up smoking; I have given up meat and become a vegetarian.*

give up the ghost *see* **ghost.**

give vent to *see* **vent.**

what gives? (*sl*) what is happening?; what is the matter?: *Everyone seems to be in a bad mood — what gives?*

glad

  glad rags (*facet inf*) one's best clothes, worn for special occasions: *I'll have my glad rags on for the party.* [Originally US, c 1900.]

glass

  people who live in glass houses shouldn't throw stones a saying used to warn people that it is unwise to criticize others *etc* if one is in a position where one could be criticized (*esp* for the same thing) oneself. [A proverb which dates back to the 14C.]

glory

  Old Glory the Stars and Stripes, the national flag of the United States of America. [The name is said to have been coined in 1831 by William Driver of Salem, Mass.]

glove

  be hand in glove *see* **hand.**

  fit like a glove to fit perfectly: *This suit fits like a glove.*

  the gloves are off (*inf*) the serious fighting or argument is about to begin: *Up to today both sides have been cautious, but after the President's speech this afternoon the gloves are off and we can expect some hard words.* [The reference is probably to boxing gloves.]

handle (someone or something) with kid gloves *see* **kid.**

glutton

a glutton for punishment (*not derog*) someone who seems eager to continue to do something difficult, unpleasant or unrewarding: *Our treasurer, being a glutton for punishment, has agreed to continue to do the job for another year.*

gnash

gnash one's teeth *see* **teeth.**

gnome

the gnomes of Zurich the big international bankers: *Much of the world's money is controlled by the gnomes of Zurich.* [Traditionally, gnomes were considered to be guardians of the earth's treasures.]

go

at one go all at the same time: *The boys had a competition to see who could eat the most ice-cream at one go.*

be going on (*inf*) to be near or close to (a time, age *etc*): *He must be going on (for) eighty.*

from the word go from the very beginning: *I want accuracy from the word go.*

give (someone or something) the go-by (*sl*) to ignore (someone) in an unfriendly way; to ignore (something) or not to deal with it: *It was very rude of her to give us the go-by like that; I think we'll give all her stupid suggestions the go-by.*

go against the grain *see* **grain.**

go back on (something) to fail to carry out (a promise *etc* to do something): *I never go back on my word.*

go for (someone or something) 1 (*inf*) to attack (a person, animal *etc*) physically or in words: *The two dogs went for each other as soon as they met; The newspapers went for the Prime Minister over the government's tax proposals.* **2** (*sl*) to be attracted by (a person, thing *etc*): *I go for redheads in short skirts.*

go for nothing *see* **nothing.**

go great guns *see* **gun.**

go in for (something) to take part in (something) or to do (something) as a hobby, job, subject for study, habit *etc*: *My son is going in for medicine.*

go native *see* **native.**

go off *see* **off.**

go places *see* **place.**

go short *see* **short.**

go slow *see* **slow.**

go steady *see* **steady.**

go the whole hog *see* **hog.**

go through with (something) to do or finish doing (something which is difficult, unpleasant or disapproved of): *I'm going to go through with this in spite of what you say.*

go to (someone's) head *see* **head.**

go to pot *see* **pot.**

go to the wall *see* **wall.**

go to town *see* **town.**

go to work on *see* **work.**

go wrong *see* **wrong.**

have a go (*inf*) to make an attempt: *I don't know if I can do it, but I'll have a go.*

it goes without saying (that) it is obvious and doesn't need to be stated (that): *It goes without saying that I didn't win — I never win.*

make a go of (something) (*inf*) to make a success of (something): *He has never owned a shop before, but I think he'll make a go of it.*

no go (*inf*) unsuccessful; useless; not getting approval or agreement: *I asked if he would agree to our plans, but it's no go, I'm afraid.*

on the go very busy or active: *He's always on the go from morning till night.*

goat

act the goat (*inf*) to behave intentionally in a silly way; to play the fool: *Do stop acting the goat and try to be serious.*

get (someone's) goat (*inf*) to annoy or irritate (someone): *What got my goat was the way she kept laughing at my mistakes.* [Early 20C US, of obscure derivation.]

separate the sheep from the goats *see* **sheep.**

god, God

an act of God *see* **act.**

God rest his soul *see* **rest.**

the gods (*inf*) the top balcony in a theatre: *We had to sit in the gods — we couldn't get any better seats.* [From the position of the top balcony directly under the ceiling, which was often painted with clouds.]

God's (own) country (*esp US*) the country, or part of the country, to which one belongs.

in the lap of the gods *see* **lap.**

put the fear of God into *see* **fear.**

think one is God's gift to (something or someone) (*derog inf*) to have a very high opinion of one's ability to do something or of one's attractiveness to someone: *He thinks he is God's gift to competitive tennis/women.*

a tin god *see* **tin.**

gold

as good as gold (used *esp* of children) very well-behaved: *Their little girl is as good as gold when they take her out visiting.*

a gold-digger (*derog sl*) a woman who is friendly towards men merely for the sake of the presents they give her: *She married him because he is wealthy — she's a real gold-digger.*

a/the golden age (*liter*) **1** an imaginary time in the past of great happiness: *The Golden Age was generally believed to have existed at the beginning of the world.* **2** any time of great achievement, *esp* in art, literature *etc*: *The sixteenth century was the golden age of Italian art.*

a golden boy a young man of great talent who is expected to become famous in his career: *He was hailed as the golden boy of athletics and was said to be certain to win a medal at the Olympic games.*

golden egg/goose *see* **goose.**

a golden handshake a large amount of money given to a person who is leaving a job, *esp* to one who is forced to leave it: *Although the firm gave him a golden handshake, he was very depressed at losing his job.*

a golden opportunity a very good or favourable chance: *When you were speaking to the boss you should have asked for a higher salary — you missed a golden opportunity.*

the golden rule the rule which is the most important (for a particular person, in carrying out a particular purpose *etc*): *When you are making pastry, the golden rule is to work quickly.* [Originally the golden rule was specifically that one should do to others as one would wish them to do to oneself.]

a gold-mine (*inf*) a source of wealth or profit: *That clothes shop is an absolute gold-mine.*

silence is golden *see* **silence.**

worth its/one's weight in gold *see* **weight.**

good

all in good time *see* **time.**

all to the good *see* **to the good** *below*.

as good as almost; virtually: *He as good as called me a thief; The job's as good as done.*

be as good as one's word to keep one's promises; to do what one has promised to do: *He said he would lend me the money if I needed it, and he was as good as his word.*

be in (someone's) good books *see* **book**.

be on to a good thing (*inf*) to be in a situation, job *etc* which is particularly good, pleasant, desirable *etc*: *He does nothing all day and gets paid for it — he's really on to a good thing there!*

be up to no good (*inf*) to be doing, or to be about to do, something wrong or illegal: *There's something odd about the way that fellow is behaving — I'm sure he's up to no good.*

do a power of good *see* **power**.

for good and all (*inf*) for ever; permanently: *He's not going to France for a holiday — he's emigrating for good and all.*

for good measure *see* **measure**.

give as good as one gets (in an argument, fight *etc*) to be as successful as one's opponent; to do as much harm as one's opponent does; to give as good arguments or replies as one's opponent does: *I didn't think he would have the courage to argue with the boss, but he certainly gave as good as he got.*

(a) good-for-nothing (*derog*) (someone who is) useless and lazy: *That boy's a lazy good-for-nothing (rascal).*

a good job *see* **job**.

goodness knows I do not know at all: *Goodness knows how much money she earns; Where they are now, goodness knows.* [A euphemism for *God knows*.]

good riddance to *see* **rid**.

good show! *see* **show**.

have a good mind to *see* **mind**.

have a good thing going (*sl*) to have arranged a particularly pleasant or profitable position, relationship *etc*: *He gets paid a lot of money and he has very little to do — he's got a good thing going there!*

have seen good service *see* **service**.

in good hands *see* **hand**.

in good heart *see* **heart**.

in good nick *see* **nick**.

in good time *see* **time**.

in good voice *see* **voice**.

in good working/running order *see* **order**.

in (someone's) own good time *see* **time.**

make good (*inf*) to be successful: *He had very little money when he arrived, but through hard work and ability he soon made good.*

make good time *see* **time.**

make good use of *see* **use.**

no news is good news *see* **news.**

put in/say a good word *see* **word.**

take (something) in good part *see* **part.**

throw good money after bad *see* **money.**

to goodness a phrase used for emphasis: *I wish to goodness you'd make up your mind!*; *Surely to goodness you know how old your father is!*

to good purpose *see* **purpose.**

to the good 1 (*also* **all to the good**) to someone's benefit: *'John said he was bringing a friend.' 'That's all to the good — we need all the help we can get!'* **2** (*inf*) richer; with gain or profit of (a certain amount): *After buying and selling some of these paintings, we finished up £100 to the good.*

goods

(deliver) the goods (*sl*) (to do) what one has promised to do, what one is expected to do, or what is required *etc*: *He said he could easily arrange the loan for us, but I don't think he can deliver the goods.* [Originally US.]

goods and chattels (*facet inf*) all movable property: *They had to hire a van to bring their son's goods and chattels home from college.* [An old legal term.]

goose

cook (someone's) goose (*inf*) to ruin completely (someone's) chances of success *etc*: *I'm afraid he's cooked his goose by being an hour late for his interview.*

kill the goose that lays the golden eggs to destroy something (sometimes referred to as **a golden goose**) which is a source of profit to oneself, *usu* in the false hope of making more profit by doing so. [From a fable by Aesop, in which the owner of the goose killed it to get immediate access to the many golden eggs he believed were inside it, only to discover that there were none.]

he *etc* **can't/couldn't/wouldn't say boo to a goose** he is very timid: *She ought to have complained about it, but she's so quiet she wouldn't say boo to a goose.*

what's sauce for the goose is sauce for the gander *see* **sauce.**

a wild-goose chase *see* **wild.**

gooseberry

play gooseberry (*inf*) to be with two other people (*usu* people who are in love) who wish that one was not there: *I'm certainly not coming with you and your fiancée — I hate playing gooseberry.* [Apparently originally Devonshire dialect for 'act as a chaperone', but the derivation is obscure.]

grab

how does that grab you? (*sl*) what do you think of that?: *If I borrow my father's car, you can have mine for the day — how does that grab you?*

up for grabs (*sl*) ready to be taken, bought *etc*: *Land in the new colonies was up for grabs and could be claimed by whoever got there first.*

grace

fall from grace to lose one's privileged and favoured position: *He was chief adviser to the king for several years before he fell from grace and had to retire to his estates.* [A religious term.]

a saving grace a good quality that makes (someone or something) less bad then he, it *etc* would have been: *His speeches are boring but they have the saving grace of being short.*

with a bad, good grace in a bad-tempered and rude or pleasant and good-tempered manner: *There was nothing he could do but concede the argument with a good grace; She wasn't at all pleased to see us, and invited us in with a very bad grace.*

grade

make the grade (*inf*) to do as well as necessary (in an examination, job *etc*): *We'll have to wait until we get the results of the exam before we know whether you have made the grade or not.* [Originally a US railroading phrase, used of a locomotive which succeeded in climbing a steep section of track.]

grain

go against the grain to be against a person's wishes, feelings *etc*: *It goes against the grain for me to tell lies.* [A woodworking expression — it is easier to cut or plane wood with the grain than against (*ie* across) it.]

take (something) with a grain of salt *see* **salt.**

grandmother

teach one's grandmother to suck eggs *see* **egg.**

grant

take (something or someone) for granted 1 to assume that (something) is true, will happen *etc* without checking: *I just took* *it for granted that you had been told about this.* **2** to treat (someone, something) casually, without giving him or it much thought, attention or kindness: *I wish people would stop taking me for granted*; *People take electricity for granted until their supply is cut off.*

grape

the grapevine (*inf*) an informal means of passing news, rumours *etc* from person to person *eg* in an office: *This isn't official but I did hear through the grapevine that he is leaving.*

sour grapes saying or pretending that something is not worth having because one cannot obtain it: *He said he had never wanted to be made the manager anyway but I'm sure it was just sour grapes.* [From Aesop's fable of the fox who, having failed to reach a bunch of grapes growing above his head, went away saying, 'I see they are sour'.]

grasp

grasp the nettle *see* **nettle**.

grass

the grass is always greener on the other side of the fence a saying, meaning that one always tends to feel that others are in a better or more favourable position than oneself, or that one would be in a better position if circumstances were different. [From the habit of cows *etc* of grazing through the fence separating them from the next field.]

the grass roots the ordinary people in an association, trade union, country *etc* as opposed to those who take decisions: *There is some dissatisfaction at the grass roots about our union's policies.*

a grass widow a woman whose husband is temporarily not living with her: *I'm a grass widow at the moment — my husband is playing cricket in Australia.* [Originally 'an unmarried woman who has borne a child', possibly from the fact that many illicit sexual encounters took place out of doors.]

let the grass grow under one's feet to delay or waste time: *The Managing Director is not a man who lets the grass grow under his feet when there are decisions to be made.*

put (someone) out to grass to cause (someone) to retire as no longer useful: *It is time that the government put some of its longer-serving ministers out to grass.* [Literally, to turn (a horse) permanently out into a field at the end of its working life.]

a snake in the grass *see* **snake**.

grasshopper

knee-high to a grasshopper *see* **knee**.

grave

have one foot in the grave *see* **foot.**

turn in one's grave (*inf*) (of someone who is dead) to be disturbed in one's rest by displeasing events in the world of living people (not intended literally): *Your grandfather would turn in his grave if he could see you acting like that.*

gravy

the gravy train (*sl*) a position in which one has much more chance than other people of obtaining advantages for oneself: *Many people think that a job with the Civil Service gives one automatic access to the gravy train.* [From the slang meaning of *gravy*, easy gain or profit.]

grease

grease (someone's) palm *see* **palm.**

great

go great guns *see* **gun.**

great minds think alike *see* **mind.**

Greek

the Greek calends never. [The *calends* was the first day of the Roman month, but was not a part of the Greek calendar — the phrase was coined by the Emperor Augustus.]

a Greek gift a dangerous gift: *The arms with which the country has been supplied may turn out to be a Greek gift in the event of a civil war.* [From the story of the Trojan horse, told in Virgil's *Aeneid* ii, which was apparently a gift from the Greeks but which was actually a trick leading to the fall of Troy.]

it's (all) Greek to me (*inf*) I don't understand: *The doctors were discussing my illness, but what they were saying was Greek to me.* [A quotation from Shakespeare's *Julius Caesar*, I. ii.]

green

be green to be without training or experience; to be easily fooled: *He's green but he'll soon learn what to do; Only someone as green as you would believe a story like that.*

a green belt open land surrounding a town or city: *You will not get permission to build houses in that area — it is a green belt.*

the green-eyed monster jealousy: *I'm afraid Susan is in the grip of the green-eyed monster, and that's why she's so unpleasant to her sister.* [A quotation from Shakespeare — *Othello*, III. iii.]

the green light (*inf*) permission to begin (doing) something: *We can't start until we get the green light; We can't start until he gives us the green light.*

have green fingers, (*US*) **a green thumb** (*inf*) to be skilled at gardening: *My mother's garden is beautiful — she certainly has green fingers.*

not to be as green as one is cabbage-looking (*inf*) not to be as stupid or as easily fooled as people might think: *He thought he would trick me but I'm not as green as I'm cabbage-looking and I wasn't fooled.*

grey

a grey area a part of a subject *etc* where it is difficult to distinguish between one category *etc* and another: *I'm afraid the question of who is responsible for publicity is a grey area — several people are involved.*

a grey eminence a person who is very influential but remains in the background: *The Foreign Office acted as a grey eminence influencing Cabinet decisions during the last government.* [From the French *Eminence Grise* — 'the cardinal in grey' — the nickname given to Cardinal Richelieu's secretary and adviser, Père Joseph, who was a Capuchin friar and wore a grey habit.]

grief

come to grief to be unsuccessful, suffer some bad luck *etc*: *The project came to grief; You'll come to grief if you go on like that.*

grim

hang/hold on like grim death (*inf*) to take a very firm hold (of something) in difficult circumstances: *The runaway horse galloped wildly along the street with the rider hanging on like grim death.*

grin

grin and bear it (*inf*) to put up with something unpleasant without complaining: *He doesn't like his present job but he'll just have to grin and bear it till he finds another.*

grin like a Cheshire cat *see* **Cheshire.**

grind

back to the grindstone (*inf facet*) back to work: *Lunchtime is over — now it's back to the grindstone.*

grind the face(s) of (someone) *see* **face.**

have an axe to grind *see* **axe.**

keep (some)one's nose to the grindstone to (force someone to) work hard, without stopping: *The new boss does hardly any work although he keeps his workers' noses to the grindstone.*

grip

get a grip (on oneself) to stop being foolish, afraid *etc*: *She started to panic but managed to get a grip on herself.*

get/come to grips with (something) to deal with (a problem, difficulty *etc*): *You must get to grips with your financial problems or you will go bankrupt.*

lose one's grip to lose control or understanding (of something): *It's time the manager retired — he's losing his grip.*

grist

grist to the mill something which brings profit or advantage: *Selling these matches only brings in a little money but it's all grist to the mill.* [*Grist* = 'corn for grinding' *ie* something to keep the mill profitably operating.]

grit

grit one's teeth *see* **teeth.**

ground

break new/fresh ground to deal with a new subject for the first time: *Our firm is breaking new ground with this project.* [Literally, to plough up land which has not previously been cultivated.]

gain ground to become more generally accepted or influential: *His views were once scoffed at but are now gaining ground rapidly.*

get (something) off the ground to get (a project *etc*) started: *We must try to get the campaign off the ground by the middle of next week.* [A phrase from aviation.]

give ground to be forced to move away from a strong position: *She was attacked by many opponents in the debate, but refused to give ground on the main issues.* [A military idiom.]

have both feet on the ground *see* **feet.**

have/keep one's ear to the ground *see* **ear.**

hold/stand one's ground to refuse to give in or make concessions: *He stood his ground and answered all her accusations.* [A military idiom.]

let (someone) in on the ground floor to take (someone) in to a business *etc* on the same terms as the people who started it: *After some discussion the committee decided to let the chairman's son in on the ground floor.*

lose ground to lose one's advantage; to lose one's good, strong or leading position: *The leader of the political party said that he was worried because his party was losing ground.* [A military idiom.]

on one's own ground dealing with a situation *etc* which one knows and understands: *He knew little about the theoretical side of management, but he was on his own ground when it came to solving problems.*

run (someone or something) to ground to hunt out or track down (someone or something): *She finally ran to ground the book she wanted in a second-hand bookshop.* [A hunting term.]

shift one's ground to change one's opinions, arguments *etc*: *It's impossible to prove him wrong because he keeps shifting his ground.* [A military idiom — 'to alter the position in which one has drawn up one's army'.]

stand one's ground *see* **hold one's ground** *above.*

suit (someone) down to the ground to suit (someone) completely or perfectly: *That arrangement will suit me down to the ground.*

thin on the ground *see* **thin.**

grow

grow on (someone) (*inf*) to become gradually liked (by someone): *I didn't like the painting at first, but it has grown on me.*

grow out of (something) to stop doing, liking *etc* (something) as one grows older: *He'll eventually grow out of sucking his thumb.*

Grub

Grub Street (of writings) of very poor quality: *He calls himself an author, but his work is pure Grub Street.* [From a street in London — now renamed — once the home of many inferior writers.]

guard

catch (someone) off guard to do something to (someone) or cause (someone) to do something when he is surprised or not prepared to prevent it: *I didn't mean to tell him our secret but he caught me off guard.* [A fencing/boxing term.]

the old guard *see* **old.**

on one's guard (*often with* **against**) prepared for something to happen and ready to prevent it: *He was trying to trick me but I was on my guard all the time:* [A fencing/boxing term.]

guess

anybody's guess (*inf*) something that no-one can be certain about: *What the result of our negotiations will be is anybody's guess at present.*

guess what? an interjection used to introduce a piece of *usu* surprising news: *Guess what? She's not coming after all!*

your guess is as good as mine (*inf*) I have no idea: *There's no point in asking me how much he earns — your guess is as good as mine.*

guest

be my guest (*inf: only in the imperative*) please do (the thing you are wanting to do): *'May I have a look at these books?' 'Be my guest.'*

guinea-pig

a guinea-pig (*sometimes derog*) a person used as the subject of an experiment: *We'd like to use you as a guinea-pig to test some of our theories.*

gum

gum up the works (*inf*) to cause a machine, a system of working *etc* to break down: *He produced so many rules and regulations for the office that he gummed up the works completely.*

up a gum tree (*inf*) in a very difficult or hopeless position: *If I don't get the information I need by tomorrow, I'll be up a gum tree.* [From the usual place of refuge of a hunted opossum.]

gun

be gunning for (someone) (*inf*) to try to attack or criticize (someone): *He has been gunning for me ever since I was rude about his new book.*

the big guns (*inf*) the important people in any group, organization *etc*: *The manager appears to run his branch himself, but all the important decisions are made by the big guns at the head office in London.*

go great guns (*inf*) to be doing well; to be moving steadily towards one's goal: *The blue team was going great guns on the far side of the arena.* [A term — in the form *blow great guns* — originally used of a high wind making a sound like cannon fire.]

jump the gun (*inf*) to start before the proper time: *He jumped the gun by applying for the job before it was advertised.* [Literally, to make a false start in a race.]

spike (someone's) guns to spoil (an opponent's) plans by making it impossible to carry them out: *He planned to cause trouble at the meeting but we spiked his guns by holding it on a different night without telling him of the change.* [A military term — captured enemy guns which could not be moved were made useless by driving a metal spike into the touch-hole.]

stick to one's guns to hold to one's position in an argument *etc*: *No-one believed her story but she stuck to her guns.*

gut

hate (someone's) guts (*sl*) to dislike (someone) very strongly: *She used to love him but she hates his guts now.*

gutter

the gutter press (*derog*) such newspapers as give a great deal of space to scandal and gossip: *The gutter press was full of stories of the actress's divorce today.*

H

habit

    from force of habit because one is used to doing (something): *I didn't mean to smoke that cigarette — I just took it from force of habit.*

hackle

    make (someone's) hackles rise to make (someone) angry: *Her unnecessary rudeness made my hackles rise.* [From the long feathers — *hackles* — on the necks of certain birds, including fighting-cocks, which are raised when the bird is angry.]

hair

    get in (someone's) hair (*inf*) to annoy (someone): *During the school holidays the children keep getting in my hair.*

    hair of the dog (*inf facet*) an alcoholic drink taken in the morning by someone who has drunk too much the night before: *He believed firmly that a hair of the dog was the best cure for a hangover.* [From the phrase **a hair of the dog that bit you**, formerly a recipe recommended as a cure for rabies.]

    hair-raising terrifying: *The explorer told some hair-raising stories about his adventures.*

    have (someone) by the short hairs to have complete power over (someone): *His boss has him by the short hairs because he knows he could not get a job elsewhere.*

    keep one's hair on (*inf*) to remain calm and not become angry: *Keep your hair on — I'm working as fast as I can.*

    let one's hair down (*inf*) to behave in a free and relaxed manner: *I've had enough of formal meetings — tonight I'm going to a party to let my hair down.*

    make (someone's) hair curl/stand on end to horrify or terrify (a person): *That horror film really made my hair stand on end; Some of the stories she tells about her boss would make your hair curl!*

    not to turn a hair to remain calm: *He didn't turn a hair when the madman ran towards him waving a knife; He did it without turning a hair.*

    split hairs to make small, unnecessary distinctions; to worry about unimportant details: *There's no need to split hairs about who actually did what — we both had a hand in it.*

    tear one's hair (*inf*) to show great irritation or despair: *He was tearing his hair by the time he'd finished marking the exam papers.*

half

    at half mast *see* **mast.**

(someone's) better half (*inf*) (someone's) wife or husband: *I don't know where we're going on holiday — ask my better half.*

by half (*inf*) to too great an extent: *He's too clever by half.*

do things by halves (*inf; usu in neg*) to do things in an incomplete, careless *etc* way: *He never does things by halves — his parties are always very lavish affairs.*

go halves (with someone) (*inf*) to share the cost of something (with someone): *I'll go halves with you in a bottle of lemonade* (= in buying a bottle of lemonade).

go off at half-cock *see* **cock.**

half a loaf is better than no bread *see* **loaf.**

half-baked (*sl*) stupid: *She is full of half-baked ideas.*

have half a mind to *see* **mind.**

meet (someone) halfway to reach an agreement (with someone) by meeting some of his demands in return for his meeting some of one's own: *You can't expect them to make all the concessions — you'll have to be prepared to meet them halfway.*

not half (*sl*) very much so: *'Are you enjoying yourself?' 'Not half!'*

see with half an eye *see* **eye.**

halt

call a halt (to something) to stop; to put an end to: *I've had enough — let's call a halt; Let's call a halt to these stupid arguments.*

ham

ham-fisted (*inf derog*) clumsy: *He can't tie a knot in that rope — he's too ham-fisted.* [Literally, having hands which are the size of hams and are therefore clumsy.]

hammer

come under the hammer to be sold at an auction: *It is many years since one of his paintings last came under the hammer, and it is difficult to predict what price they would fetch now.* [A reference to the hammer with which an auctioneer indicates that a sale has been made.]

give (someone) a hammering (*sl*) to beat (someone) severely: *His father gave him a hammering for stealing.*

go/be at it hammer and tongs to fight or argue violently: *No-one knew how the argument began, but within a few moments they were (going) at it hammer and tongs.* [The reference is to a blacksmith holding a piece of heated iron in his tongs and striking it repeatedly with his hammer.]

hammer away at (something) (*inf*) to keep working on (a problem *etc*): *We'll hammer away at this until we get it solved.*

hammer (something) home to make great efforts to make a person realize or understand (something): *We'll have to hammer home to them the problems we face with this project.*

hand

at first hand *see* **first.**

at hand (*formal*) available; able to be used; ready for use when needed: *Help is at hand.*

at second hand *see* **second.**

be hand in glove (with someone) to be very closely associated (with someone), *usu* in a bad sense, for a bad purpose: *Some well-known politicians have been found to be hand in glove with leading gangsters.* [The idiom was originally *hand and glove* — *ie* as close as can be imagined.]

bite the hand that feeds one to be ungrateful to someone who has helped one: *She felt that her protégé had bitten the hand that fed him by making unkind remarks about her in public.* [A quotation from an essay by Edmund Burke.]

change hands to pass into different ownership: *This car has changed hands three times.*

close/near at hand near: *The bus-station is near at hand.*

a dab hand at *see* **dab.**

force (someone's) hand to force (someone) to do something either which he does not want to do or sooner than he wants to do it: *I did not want to sack him — but he forced my hand by always being late.* [A French idiom, from card-playing.]

a free hand *see* **free.**

get one's hands on (someone or something) (*inf*) **1** to catch (someone who has *usu* done something bad): *If I ever get my hands on him, I'll make him sorry for what he did!* **2** to get or obtain the use of (something): *I'd love to get my hands on a car like that.*

give/lend a (helping) hand to help or assist someone: *I'm always ready to give a helping hand to anyone who needs it; When we moved house my brother came to lend a hand.*

go hand in hand (with) to be found always in close connection (with): *Poverty and crime go hand in hand.* [Literally, of two or more people, to walk with one person holding the hand of another.]

a golden handshake *see* **gold.**

hand (something) down to pass on (a precious object, a belief, a tradition *etc*) from one generation to the next: *These customs have been handed down from father to son since the Middle Ages.*

hand over fist (*inf*) in large amounts; very quickly: *He's making* *money hand over fist in that shop.* [Originally a nautical term expressing steady and rapid progress, such as can be achieved by hauling on a line with one hand after another.]

his *etc* **hands are tied** he is unable to act as he would wish because of something which prevents him: *My hands are tied as far as going on holiday is concerned as I cannot get away from work until the new manager is appointed.*

hands down (*inf*) very easily: *He's not very good at chess — you'll win hands down.* [A racing term, referring to a jockey who relaxes his hold on the reins because he sees he is winning easily.]

hands off! (*inf*) do not touch or take (something): *Hands off (those cakes)!*

have a hand in (something) (*formal*) to be one of the people who have caused, done *etc* (something): *Did you have a hand in the building of this boat/in the success of the project?*

have (something) handed to one on a plate *see* **plate**.

have one's hands full (*inf*) to be very busy: *She must have her hands full with those four children to look after.*

have, get the upper hand *see* **upper**.

have the whip hand *see* **whip**.

high-handed *see* **high**.

in good hands receiving care and attention: *Your husband will soon be well again — he's in good hands here.*

in hand 1 not used *etc*; remaining: *Of the £60 we collected, we've spent £50, so we still have £10 in hand; These two football teams have won the same number of points but one of them has a game in hand (= has played one game less than the other).* **2** (*formal*) being dealt with; being done *etc*: *We have received your complaint about the smell and the matter is now in hand.* [Originally used of a horse which responds easily to the rider or to the driver's hand on the reins.]

keep one's hand in (*inf*) to remain good or skilful at doing something by doing it occasionally: *I still sometimes play a game of billiards, just to keep my hand in.* [*Have one's hand in* was an idiom, dating from the Middle Ages, for 'to be in practice'.]

know a hawk from a handsaw *see* **hawk**.

lay (one's) hands on (someone or something) (*inf*) **1** to reach or find (something one is looking for): *Your report is on my desk, but I can't just lay (my) hands on it at the moment.* **2** to catch (someone who has *usu* done something bad): *If I ever lay (my) hands on the person who stole my car, he'll wish he hadn't.*

lend a hand *see* **give a hand** *above*.

live (from) hand to mouth to be able to get only what one needs at present, without having anything extra to save up: *They are so poor they just live from hand to mouth and never have any money in the bank.* [The implication is that whatever money comes into one's hand is immediately used to feed oneself.]

many hands make light work a saying, meaning that a job becomes much easier if there are a number of people to help to do it.

near at hand *see* **close at hand** *above.*

an old hand *see* **old.**

on hand near; present; ready for use *etc*: *We always keep some candles on hand in case there's a power failure*; *You'd better be on hand in case you are needed.*

(left) on one's hands (*inf*) left over; remaining; not sold *etc*: *We were left with a lot of rubbish on our hands at the end of the sale.*

out of hand 1 unable to be controlled: *The angry crowd was getting out of hand.* **2** (*formal*) quickly; without thinking, waiting *etc*: *The soldiers shot the bandits out of hand* (= without a trial).

play into (someone's) hands to do exactly what (an opponent or enemy) wants one to do: *By accepting the money he has played right into my hands.* [Literally, in card games, to play so as to benefit another player.]

show one's hand to allow one's plans or intentions to become known: *It is unlike him to show his hand so clearly — I suspect he has a purpose in doing so.* [From card games.]

a show of hands *see* **show.**

take (someone) in hand to look after, discipline or train (someone): *These young hooligans need to be taken in hand.* [As **in hand** *above*.]

take one's life in one's hands *see* **life.**

throw in one's hand to abandon a plan, course of action *etc*: *He threw in his hand after only one week at the job.* [From the method of resigning in card-games.]

try one's hand at (something) (*inf*) to see if one can do (something): *He tried his hand at farming*; *I think I'll try my hand at swimming.*

turn one's hand to (something) to (have the ability to) do (a job *etc*): *He can turn his hand to anything, from painting to engineering.*

wash one's hands of (someone or something) to say that one is no longer willing to be involved in a (project *etc*) or to be responsible for (a project, a person *etc*): *He told them that if they*

147

wouldn't listen to his advice, he would wash his hands of them/their schemes. [A Biblical allusion, to the action of Pontius Pilate (Matthew 27:24) symbolizing his dissociation from the wish of the people to crucify Jesus.]

you have (got) to hand it to (someone) you must give (someone) the praise or admiration which they deserve: *You've got to hand it to him — he said he'd be a millionaire one day and he's done it.* [Originally US.]

handle

a handle to one's name (*inf*) a title: *I think he had a handle to his name — Sir Somebody or Lord Something.*

fly off the handle (*inf*) to lose one's temper: *He flew off the handle when he heard that the boys had raided his garden again.* [Originally US — the allusion is to an axehead which flies off the handle while one is using it.]

handle (someone or something) with kid gloves *see* **kid**.

handy

come in handy (*inf*) to be useful: *I'll put these bottles in the cupboard — they might come in handy some day.* [This phrase, and others with *come in*, originally applied to fruit and vegetables *etc* coming in to season just when they are most needed.]

hang

I'll *etc* **be hanged if I'll (do something)** (*old inf*) I am determined not to (do something): *She said she'd be hanged if she would agree to such a stupid idea.* [A euphemism for *I'll be damned if . . . .*]

get the hang of (something) (*inf*) to learn, or begin to understand, how to do (something): *It may seem difficult at first, but you'll get the hang of it after a few weeks.* [An American expression, originally meaning 'to become accustomed to and learn the use of (tools *etc*)'.]

hang about/around 1 to stand around doing nothing: *I don't like to see all these youths hanging about (street corners).* **2** to be close to (a person) frequently: *I don't want you hanging about my daughter.* **3** (*sl*) to wait: *Hang about! I think we're being offered a cup of coffee.*

hang by a thread *see* **thread**.

hang fire *see* **fire**.

hang one's head *see* **head**.

a hanging matter (*inf*) a serious question, offence *etc*: *It might be interesting to know who it was who took that telephone call, but it's hardly a hanging matter.* [Literally, a crime punishable by death.]

hang on (*inf*) to wait: *Will you hang on a minute — I'm not quite ready.*

hang on like grim death *see* **grim.**

hang out (*sl*) to live or spend one's time: *Where does he hang out nowadays?*

hang together to agree or be consistent: *His statements just do not hang together — he must be lying.*

hang up to put the receiver back after a telephone conversation: *I tried to talk to her, but she hung up.*

hang up one's hat *see* **hat.**

hung up (on) (*sl*) obsessed (with): *She is really hung up on the campaign for women's rights — she never talks about anything else.*

thereby hangs a tale *see* **tale.**

happy

as happy as a lark *see* **lark.**

as happy as a sand-boy *see* **sand.**

a happy event (*euph usu facet*) a birth: *I hear Mary has a baby son — when did the happy event take place?*

happy-go-lucky not worrying about what might happen: *She is such a happy-go-lucky person — she is never upset by anything.*

a happy hunting-ground (*inf*) a place where one often goes, *esp* to obtain something or to make money: *She collects old bottles, and the local dump is her happy hunting-ground; The wreck of the famous liner was a happy hunting-ground for souvenir-seekers.* [From the name of the Red Indians' Paradise.]

a happy medium a sensible middle course between two extreme positions: *You can surely find some happy medium between starving yourself and over-eating.*

trigger-happy *see* **trigger.**

hard

as hard as nails *see* **nail.**

be hard on (someone) 1 to punish or criticize (someone) severely: *Don't be too hard on the boy — he's too young to know that he was doing wrong.* **2** to be unfair to (someone): *I know we can't make exceptions to our rules, but it's a bit hard on those who did nothing wrong.*

be hard put to it (to do something) to have difficulty (in doing something): *I'd be hard put to it to finish making this dress by this evening.*

hard-and-fast (of rules) that can never be changed or ignored: *There are no hard-and-fast rules about the use of hyphens in English.*

[A nautical phrase, describing a ship which has run aground.]

hard-bitten (*inf*) (of people) tough; toughened by experience; stubborn: *She's become really hard-bitten since her divorce.* [Originally a term applied to dogs, meaning 'biting hard'.]

hard-boiled (*inf*) unfeeling and not influenced by emotion: *It would be a very hard-boiled politician who did not take pity on the plight of these unfortunate people.* [Originally US.]

a hard case (*inf*) a person who is difficult to deal with or reform: *Some of the criminals in this prison are real hard cases.*

hard cash (*inf*) coins and bank-notes, as opposed to cheques *etc*: *I prefer to be paid in hard cash for a job like this.*

a hard core a part of something which is very difficult to change, *esp* the most loyal or stubborn members of a group *etc*: *He was supported by a hard core of MPs who were opposed to any kind of concession to the reformers.*

hard done by (*inf*) unfairly treated: *We gave him a fair share of the money but he still says he has been hard done by.*

the hard facts facts that cannot be denied: *I don't care what he says — the hard facts are that the mistakes were mainly caused by him.*

hard-headed clever; practical; not influenced by emotion: *Successful businessmen must be shrewd and hard-headed.*

hard lines (*inf*) bad luck: *Hard lines! I'm afraid you haven't won this time.* [Apparently a nautical idiom, probably referring to ropes stiffened by ice.]

a hard-luck story (*often derog*) the story of a person's bad luck and suffering, *usu* intended to gain sympathy for the person concerned: *I'm tired of listening to his hard-luck stories — he brought all his misfortunes on himself.*

a hard nut to crack *see* nut.

hard of hearing (*euph*) rather deaf: *He is a bit hard of hearing now.*

hard on (someone's) heels close behind (someone): *The thief ran off, with two policemen hard on his heels.*

hard-pressed in difficulties: *We will be hard-pressed to find the money to pay the staff this week.*

(a drop of) the hard stuff (*facet inf*) (some) alcoholic drink, *usu* spirits and *esp* whisky: *What we need now is a drop of the hard stuff!*

a hard time (of it) trouble, unpleasantness, difficulty, worry *etc*: *The audience gave the speaker a hard time of it at the meeting; The* *speaker had a hard time (of it) trying to make himself heard.*

hard up (*inf*) not having much *esp* money: *I'm a bit hard up at the moment; You must be hard up for boyfriends* (= You must have difficulty in finding boyfriends) *if you are going out with him.* [Probably originally nautical slang — meaning literally 'aground'.]

take a hard line to take strong action on something, or hold firmly to decisions, policies *etc* that have been made: *The government is taking a hard line over its new pay policy.*

hare

run with the hare and hunt with the hounds to try to be on both sides of an argument *etc* at once.

start a hare to introduce a subject of conversation, problem *etc* which is not important to the main issues being considered: *I don't want to start a hare, but I have been wondering if the council will give you permission to make these alterations at all.* [Literally, to cause a hare to leave its hiding-place, something likely to distract hounds engaged in, for example, a fox-hunt.]

hark

hark back (to) (*formal*) to refer to (something that has been said or done earlier): *Harking back to what you said last night, I think a decision will need to be made soon.* [A hunting term — *hark back* is a command to hounds and their handlers to double back and try to pick up a lost scent.]

harm

out of harm's way in a safe place: *I put the vase on a high shelf out of harm's way during the children's party.*

harp

harp on (something) (*inf*) to keep on talking or to talk too much (about something): *She keeps harping on his faults.* [A reference to the old idiom *harp on one string* — *ie* to become boring on a subject.]

hash

make a hash of (something) (*inf*) to spoil (something) completely; to do (something) badly: *I made a complete hash of that translation.*

settle (someone's) hash (*sl*) to deal with (someone) in such a way that they cease to be a nuisance, or are unable to do what they intended to do: *He thinks he's going to marry my daughter but I'll soon settle his hash!* [Apparently a cooking term of obscure implication.]

151

haste

the more haste/hurry the less speed a saying, meaning that by hurrying too much one makes more mistakes *etc*.

hat

at the drop of a hat *see* **drop.**

a bad hat a bad and worthless person: *I knew her husband was a bad hat long before he was sent to prison.*

hang up one's hat to move into a house, office *etc* for a long stay: *The official sent from London to supervise the reorganization has hung up his hat in the County Buildings.*

hats off to (a particular person) (*inf*) everyone should admire and praise (a person): *Hats off to Mrs Smith for the best meal I've had in years!*

a hat trick 1 (in cricket) the putting out of three batsmen by three balls in a row. **2** (in football) three goals scored by one player in a match: *He scored a hat trick.* **3** any action done successfully three times in a row: *I've got a hat trick — that's the third car I've sold today.* [The cricketing meaning is the original one: it is claimed that the feat described entitled a bowler to a new hat from his club.]

I'll eat my hat (*inf*) I shall be amazed (used to express a strong belief that what one thinks, is saying *etc* is true): *If it wasn't your little brother that broke my window, I'll eat my hat!*

keep (something) under one's hat (*inf*) to keep (something) secret: *Keep it under your hat, but I'm getting married next week.*

knock (someone or something) into a cocked hat (*inf*) to damage or ruin (someone or something); to surpass completely: *My husband's illness has knocked our holiday plans into a cocked hat; Their luxury flat knocks our house into a cocked hat.*

old hat (*inf*) something very old-fashioned: *His theories are old hat nowadays.*

pass/send round the hat (for someone) to ask for or collect money (on someone's behalf): *When Tom had an accident and was out of work, his colleagues passed round the hat for him.* [From a traditional method of making impromptu collections of money.]

take one's hat off to (someone) (*inf*) to admire (someone) for doing something: *I take my hat off to that woman for bringing up five children on her own.*

talk through one's hat (*inf*) to talk nonsense: *Don't believe what he says — he always talks through his hat.*

throw one's hat into the ring to make a challenge: *Last night*

Mr Edwards threw his hat into the ring and announced that he would stand for election to the party leadership. [From a method of making a challenge to prize-fighters at a showground *etc.*]

wear another hat/several hats to speak or act as the holder of a different official position, several official positions: *Since there are only three people on our committee, we all have to wear several hats.*

hatch

batten down the hatches to prepare for trouble, a quarrel *etc*: *I've just seen the boss coming up the stairs looking furious, so we'd all better batten down the hatches.* [From preparations for a storm on a ship at sea.]

hatches, matches and dispatches (*facet inf*) the announcement of births, marriages and deaths in the newspapers.

hatter

as mad as a hatter utterly crazy; completely insane: *He's very clever but as mad as a hatter.* [Hatmaking used to involve treating fur with nitrate of mercury, prolonged exposure to which could result in a nervous illness interpreted in those days as a symptom of insanity.]

haul

haul (someone) over the coals *see* **coal.**

a long haul (*inf*) a long or tiring job *etc*: *Writing dictionaries can be a long haul; The journey from Edinburgh to London is rather a long haul.*

have

have a go *see* **go.**

have done with (something) to stop or put an end to (something): *Let's have done with all this quarrelling.*

have had it (*inf*) to be dead, ruined *etc*: *The bullet went into his brain — he's had it, I'm afraid.*

have it coming to one *see* **come.**

have it in for (someone) (*inf*) to dislike (someone) and therefore be unpleasant to or try to cause trouble for them: *I don't know why he has it in for me — I've always been nice to him.*

have it in one *etc* to have the courage or ability (to do something): *I hear she told her boss to stop shouting at her — I didn't think she had it in her.*

have it off (with someone) (*sl*) to have sexual intercourse (with someone); to have an affair (with someone): *There's a rumour that he's having it off with his secretary.*

have it out (with someone) to argue (with someone) in order to put an end to some disagreement: *This argument has been going on for weeks, so I'm going to have it out with her once and for all.*

have (someone) on (*Brit inf*) to try to make (someone) believe something which is not true: *You're having me on — that's not really true, is it?*

have something on (*inf*) to be busy: *She has (got) something on every afternoon this week.*

have (someone) up (*Brit inf*) to make (a person) appear in court to answer some charge: *He was had up for drunken driving.*

have what it takes (*inf*) to have the qualities or ability that one needs to do something: *He has what it takes to make a good officer; He would like to be a doctor but he hasn't got what it takes.*

let (someone) have it (*inf*) to attack (someone) suddenly and vigorously with words or blows: *We'll wait till he comes out, then we'll let him have it.*

havoc

play havoc with (something) to cause a lot of damage to (something); to ruin (something): *The rain played havoc with our garden party arrangements.*

hawk

know a hawk from a handsaw to be able to judge between things fairly well: *It's no use telling me he is a nice person — I know a hawk from a handsaw and I think he is thoroughly untrustworthy.* [A Shakespearian quotation — *Hamlet*, II. ii.]

watch (someone) like a hawk to watch (someone) very carefully and alertly: *If you don't watch that little boy like a hawk, he gets into mischief.*

hay

go haywire (*inf*) to stop working properly; to go crazy: *Our computer has gone haywire — we can't get any sensible answer from it.* [Originally US, probably from the use of *haywire* to describe an inefficient and makeshift organization — *ie* one in which the equipment was held together with pieces of wire *etc*.]

hit the hay (*facet inf*) to go to bed: *You lot might be intending to stay up all night, but I think I'll hit the hay.* [Originally US.]

like looking for a needle in a haystack *see* **needle**.

make hay (while the sun shines) to make use of an opportunity while it is available to one: *We have been given an unexpected holiday tomorrow, so I think I'll make hay while the sun shines and get started on the spring-cleaning.* [From the fact that haymaking is only possible in fine weather.]

head

above (someone's) head (*inf*) too difficult for (someone) to understand: *What he said was well above their heads — he should have made his talk much simpler.*

bang one's head against a brick wall to try in vain to make someone understand something, agree with one's point of view *etc*: *I keep telling her that she should change her job, but I'm just banging my head against a brick wall.*

bite/snap (someone's) head off to answer (someone) sharply and angrily: *I only asked if I could help and she bit my head off — I think she's upset.*

bring (something) to a head, come to a head to (cause something to) come to a state of climax or crisis when urgent action is needed: *The government's difficulties were brought to a head by the miners' strike; The government's difficulties came to a head when the miners went on strike.*

bury one's head in the sand to avoid trying to deal with a problem, danger *etc* by ignoring it or deliberately knowing nothing about it: *He had suspected for some months that his son was taking drugs, but he had buried his head in the sand and refused to admit it, even to himself.* [From the old belief that the ostrich reacted to danger by burying its head in the sand, thinking that being unable to see it could not be seen.]

by a short head *see* **short.**

get (something) into (someone's) head (*inf*) to make (someone) recognize that (something) is true, necessary *etc*: *I can't get it into his head that he will never be an artist.*

give (someone) his head to allow (someone) to do what they want with regard to something: *His ideas may sound a bit odd but I think we should still give him his head.* [Literally, *to give a horse its head* means to slacken one's hold on the reins.]

go to (someone's) head (of praise, success *etc*) to make (someone) arrogant, foolish, careless *etc*: *All the publicity he has had because of his book has gone to his head.* [Literally (of alcoholic drinks) to make someone slightly drunk, from the way in which alcohol in the body appears to behave.]

hang one's head to look ashamed or embarrassed: *We all hung our heads when our team was last in the competition.*

have a head for (something) to be good at (dealing with something): *He has a head for figures and finds arithmetic easy; I hate climbing — I have no head for heights.*

have a (good) head on one's shoulders to be calm, clever and sensible: *Most of the children just screamed, but Emma has a head on her shoulders and she put the fire out with a bucket of water.*

have a roof over one's head *see* **roof.**

have one's head in the clouds to be dreaming and not attending to what is going on: *I could see that she had her head in the clouds and was not listening to a word I was saying.*

have one's head screwed on the right way (*inf*) to behave sensibly: *Robert has his head screwed on the right way — if he gets lost he'll ask someone for directions.*

head over heels completely: *He fell head over heels in love.* [Literally, 'turning a complete somersault'.]

heads will roll (*slightly facet*) someone will get into very serious trouble: *If this project is not an overwhelming success, heads will roll!* [From the use of the guillotine to execute criminals.]

hit the headlines (*inf*) to attract a great deal of attention and interest from the newspapers, television *etc*: *He has been hitting the headlines recently with a series of important scientific discoveries.*

hold a pistol to (someone's) head *see* **pistol.**

hold one's head up not to feel ashamed, guilty *etc*: *If you had been sent to prison, your family would never have been able to hold up their heads in this town again.*

keep one's head to remain calm and sensible, *eg* in a crisis or sudden difficulty: *She kept her head when she found the flats were on fire — if she had panicked, many people might have died.*

keep one's head above water (*inf*) to get or earn enough money, profits *etc* to remain out of debt: *We're not making a lot of money in the shop, but we are keeping our heads above water.*

knock (something) on the head (*inf*) to destroy or put an end to (a plan *etc*): *She wanted to go to Crete for a month with her boyfriend, but her father soon knocked that plan on the head.* [From a method of slaughtering animals.]

lose one's head to become angry or excited, or to act foolishly, *eg* in a crisis or sudden difficulty, or when someone does something wrong *etc*: *I must apologize — I rather lost my head when I thought you had burned the only copy of my manuscript.*

make headway to go forward; to make progress: *We're not making much headway with this new scheme.* [A nautical idiom — *headway* is a contraction of *ahead-way*, ie 'progress forwards'.]

need one's head examined (*inf*) to be foolish, stupid or slightly insane: *If you think I'm going to work on a Saturday, you must need* *your head examined!*

not (quite) right in the head *see* **right**.

not to be able to make head or tail of (something) (*inf*) to be unable to understand (something): *I can't make head or tail of these instructions.*

off/out of one's head (*inf*) mad: *You must be off your head to go for a picnic on such a cold day.*

off the top of one's head (*inf*) without much thought; without making sure that what is said *etc* is correct: *When asked what the company's profits were, he said he could only give them some figures off the top of his head.*

on your *etc* **own head be it** you will bear the responsibility for any harm caused by your actions or wishes: *He insists on going to the football match even though he has a bad cold, so on his own head be it if he catches pneumonia.*

(be/go) over (someone's) head 1 (in a way which is) too difficult (for someone) to understand: *What he said was/went over the heads of the children in the audience.* **2** when others (seem to) have a better right (to something): *He was promoted over the heads of three people who were senior to him.*

a price on (someone's) head *see* **price**.

put one's head on the block/in a noose to put oneself into a position where one could easily be harmed: *By admitting to the boss that she was the one who made the mistake, I think she's put her head on the block.*

put our *etc* **heads together** (*inf*) to discuss a plan, problem *etc* among ourselves: *I'm sure Anne and I can come up with an idea for a wedding present if we put our heads together.*

rear its ugly head (*inf*: used of something unpleasant or unwelcome) to appear or happen: *I'm afraid the question of money reared its ugly head again at our committee meeting.*

soft in the head (*inf*) stupid or unintelligent: *If you think I'm going to play football in this weather you must be soft in the head!*

take it into one's head 1 to come to believe, *usu* wrongly, that something is true *etc*: *He's taken it into his head that everybody hates him.* **2** to decide to do something, *usu* implying that it is foolish: *He's taken it into his head to have a cold shower every morning.*

talk one's head off *see* **talk**.

talk through the back of one's head *see* **back**.

turn (someone's) head to make (someone) conceited *etc*: *Success has turned his head.*

two heads are better than one a saying, meaning that two people working together are more likely to be able to find a solution to a problem *etc* than one person alone.

health

    drink to (someone's) health to drink a toast (to someone), wishing him good health, often using the words 'Your health!'.

heap

    knock/strike (someone) all of a heap (*inf*) to astonish (someone) *usu* so completely that they are not able to do or say anything: *When she said they were married she knocked me all of a heap — I never dreamed of it!* [This phrase first appears in a play by Sheridan.]

hear

    hear tell of (someone or something) (*old*) to hear of or about (someone or something): *I have heard tell of his courageous actions.*

    I *etc* will, would not hear of (something) I will or would not allow (someone to do something): *He would not hear of her going home alone, and insisted on going with her.*

heart

    after (someone's) own heart (of people) of exactly the type someone likes: *You're a man after my own heart.* [A Biblical reference — I Samuel 13:14.]

    at heart (*formal*) really; basically: *He seems rather stern but he is at heart a very kind man.*

    break (someone's) heart to cause (someone) great sorrow: *If you leave her, it'll break her heart.*

    by heart so that one has (a poem, a set of facts *etc*) accurately and completely in one's memory: *He has to learn all the kings and queens of England by heart by next week.*

    cross my *etc* heart (*inf*) said *esp* by children to emphasize the truth of what is being said, (sometimes accompanied by a movement of the hand making an X over the heart): *I promise I'll do it, cross my heart.*

    do (someone's) heart good (*old*) to give (someone) a feeling of pleasure: *It would do your heart good to see the enthusiasm of these young people.* [Probably deriving from Shakespeare — *A Midsummer Night's Dream*, I. ii.]

    eat one's heart out to make oneself ill by being unhappy, by longing for something one cannot have *etc*: *The little girl was eating her heart out because she was not allowed to have a dog.*

    faint heart never won fair lady *see* **faint.**

find it in one's heart (to do something) (*formal*) to manage or persuade oneself (to do something): *Can you find it in your heart to forgive me?*

from the bottom of one's heart very much; very sincerely: *She thanked him from the bottom of her heart for all his help.*

give (someone) heart failure (*inf*) to give (someone) a very bad shock: *When I looked up and saw my little boy at the top of the tree, it gave me heart failure!*

have a change of heart to change a decision *etc, usu* to a better, kinder one: *He's had a change of heart — he's going to help us after all.*

have a heart! (*inf*) show some pity or kindness: *Have a heart! He'll never be able to do all that unless we help him.*

have a heart of gold to be a very kind, generous, worthy person: *My landlady is rather fierce-looking, but she has a heart of gold.*

have (something) at heart (*formal*) to have or feel a kind concern for or interest in (something): *He never shows it, but he has the interest of his workers at heart.*

have one's heart in one's boots to be very depressed or lacking in hope: *The boy's heart was in his boots as he arrived home because he knew his mother would be angry with him for tearing his jersey.*

have one's heart in one's mouth to be extremely worried and anxious: *His heart was in his mouth as he watched the firemen trying to reach the child on the roof of the burning building.*

have one's heart in the right place to be basically kind, generous *etc* even though not always appearing to be so: *He seems rather bad-tempered when you first meet him, but his heart is in the right place.*

have one's heart set on (something) *see* **set one's heart on (something)** *below.*

heartache (a feeling of) great sadness, *eg* as caused by the loss of, or the failure to get, a person's love: *The end of their affair was accompanied by a great deal of heartache and many tears.*

heart and soul completely; with all one's attention and energy: *She devoted herself heart and soul to working for the church.*

heartfelt (*formal*) sincere: *I offer you my heartfelt thanks for your help.*

my *etc* heart goes out to (someone) I feel pity, sympathy *etc* for (someone): *My heart goes out to men who have to work outside in this cold weather.*

my *etc* heart is not in (something) I am not really eager or enthusiastic (to do something): *He continued to entertain after his wife's death, but it was obvious that his heart was not in it any longer.*

my *etc* **heart sinks** I feel depressed and lose hope, cheerfulness *etc*: *My heart sank when I saw the amount of washing-up there was to do after the party.*

a heart-throb (*facet sl*) someone (*esp* a singer, actor *etc*) who is very attractive to (young) persons of the opposite sex: *Rudolf Valentino was the great heart-throb of the silent movies.*

a heart-to-heart (*inf*) an open and sincere talk, *usu* in private: *After our heart-to-heart I felt more cheerful.*

heart-warming causing a person to feel pleasure: *It was heart-warming to see the happiness of the children.*

in good heart (*rather formal*) **1** in a good, healthy condition: *The land had been carefully tended for years and was in good heart.* **2** in good spirits and full of courage: *He was pleased to find that after four hours of fighting his men were still in good heart.*

in one's heart of hearts in one's deepest and most hidden thoughts and feelings: *Although she tried to be hopeful, in her heart of hearts she knew her mother was dying.*

lose heart to become discouraged: *After more than fifty unsuccessful attempts to get a job, he began to lose heart.* [Moral courage was once thought to be created in the heart.]

my heart bleeds for you *etc* (*ironic*) I am very sympathetic towards you (implying that one is not at all sympathetic because one does not feel that the other person is in a particularly bad position): *My heart really bled for him when I heard he was now so poor he had to sell one of his four holiday homes.*

not to have the heart (to do something) not to want or be unkind enough (to do something unpleasant): *I don't have the heart to tell him that everyone laughed at his suggestions.*

put new heart into (someone) to make someone once again more cheerful and hopeful: *The news of the naval victory put new heart into the tired soldiers.* [As **lose heart** above.]

set one's heart on (something)/have one's heart set on (something) to want (something) very much: *He had set his heart on winning the prize*; *He had his heart set on winning.*

sick at heart (*rather liter*) very sorrowful and unhappy: *By evening they knew that there was no more hope of finding the men alive and, sick at heart, they gave up the search.*

take heart (*formal*) to become encouraged or more confident: *The soldiers took heart when they heard that reinforcements were coming.*

[As **lose heart** *above*.]

take (something) to heart **1** to be made very sad or upset (by something): *You mustn't take his unkind remarks to heart.* **2** to pay great attention to (something): *He seems to have taken my criticisms to heart — his work has improved a lot since I spoke to him.*

to one's heart's content as much as one wants: *During the summer, she can play in the garden to her heart's content.*

tug at the heartstrings (*not inf*) to appeal to one's feelings, *esp* of pity: *The forlorn expression on the child's face tugged at the teacher's heart-strings.* [In medieval anatomy, the heartstrings were thought of as nerves or sinews which braced and supported the heart.]

warm the cockles of the heart *see* **cockle.**

wear one's heart on one's sleeve to show one's feelings openly: *I think he was really disappointed when he didn't get the job, but he is not a person who wears his heart on his sleeve.* [Probably a Shakespearian quotation — *Othello*, I. i.]

with a heavy heart *see* **heavy.**

with all one's heart very willingly or sincerely: *I hope with all my heart that you will be happy.*

heat

a heatwave a period of very hot weather: *We had a sudden heatwave in the middle of May.*

in/on heat (of female animals) sexually aroused in the breeding season: *They are planning to mate their spaniel bitch when she is in heat.*

in the heat of the moment while influenced by the excitement or emotion caused by something: *In the heat of the moment, he vowed revenge on his attackers, but later realized this would be unwise.*

take the heat out of (something) to make (a quarrel, a difficult situation *etc*) less emotional and disturbing: *They hoped that a period of calm would take the heat out of the political situation.*

turn on the heat (*sl*) to put pressure on someone by treating them cruelly or very severely: *He was afraid that they would turn on the heat if he did not tell them what they wanted to know.*

heather

set the heather on fire to cause a great deal of general interest and excitement: *His book is rather dull — I don't think its publication will set the heather on fire.*

heave

heave in sight to come into sight; to appear: *After we had been* *walking for about an hour, the farmhouse hove into sight.* [A nautical idiom.]

give (someone) the (old) heave-ho (*sl*) to tell (someone) to leave; to get rid of (someone): *She has just given her boyfriend the old heave-ho.* [Originally US.]

heaven

for heaven's sake an expression used to show anger, surprise *etc*: *For heaven's sake, will you stop making that noise!*; *Why did you do that, for heaven's sake?*

heaven knows 1 I don't know at all: *Heaven knows what he's trying to do.* **2** certainly: *Heaven knows, I ought to have seen that I couldn't trust him.*

(good) heavens (*interj*) an expression of surprise, dismay *etc*: *Heavens! I forgot to buy your birthday present.*

the heavens opened (*facet*) there was a sudden downpour of rain: *We had just started to play tennis when the heavens opened and we all got soaked.*

in (the) seventh heaven extremely happy: *When she won the prize she was in the seventh heaven.* [From the mystical Jewish cabbala, a system of belief which held that there were seven heavens in ascending order of excellence. The Muslims have a similar belief.]

manna from heaven *see* **manna.**

move heaven and earth to do everything that one possibly can: *He moved heaven and earth to get them to agree to this plan.*

stink to high heaven (*inf*) to have a very strong and unpleasant smell: *That rotten meat stinks to high heaven.*

thank heavens an expression used to show that a person is glad something or someone is all right, satisfactory *etc*: *Thank heavens he isn't coming!*

heavy

heavy going (*inf*) (something) causing difficulty in doing, understanding or making progress: *I found his book very heavy going*; *It's heavy going but we'll finish the job eventually.* [Literally 'damp, sticky ground', especially when there is to be hunting or racing on it.]

heavy-handed not showing good judgement or good taste; made in too dramatic, shocking, lengthy, emphatic *etc* a way: *He paid me some rather heavy-handed compliments*; *The film shows a very heavy-handed treatment of its theme.*

lie heavy on *see* **lie.**

162

make heavy weather of (something) (*inf*) to find great difficulty in doing (something which should usually be easy to do): *He said he'd finish the job in half an hour, but he seems to be making rather heavy weather of it.* [A nautical idiom used of a ship — 'to handle badly in difficult conditions.']

with a heavy heart (*liter*) with a feeling of sadness: *I say this with a heavy heart.*

hedge

hedge one's bets *see* **bet.**

look as if one had been dragged through a hedge backwards (*derog inf*) to be extremely untidy: *You can't go out without brushing your hair — you look as if you had been dragged through a hedge backwards.*

heel

an Achilles' heel a person's one weakness, way in which they can be injured *etc*: *He was a ruthless businessman but his uncritical love for his daughter was his Achilles' heel.* [From the legendary Greek hero, whose mother, a sea-nymph, dipped him in the River Styx as a baby to make him invulnerable. Only his heel, by which she was holding him, remained unprotected, and he was finally killed by an arrow in the heel.]

bring (someone) to heel to make (someone) obey and behave as one wishes: *The Prime Minister is finding it difficult to bring his rebellious ministers to heel.*

dig in one's heels (*inf*) to refuse to do, allow *etc* something: *I'm going to dig in my heels over this — it must be done the way I say.*

down-at-heel *see* **down.**

hard on (someone's) heels *see* **hard.**

head over heels *see* **head.**

kick/cool one's heels (*inf*) to be kept waiting for some time: *Although I arrived on time for the meeting, I was left kicking my heels for half an hour.*

set (someone) by the heels (*old*) to put (someone) in prison: *The thieves were finally set by the heels.*

show a clean pair of heels *see* **clean.**

take to one's heels (*inf*) to run away: *The thief took to his heels when the policeman arrived.*

turn on one's heel to turn round or away suddenly, *usu* with the intention of moving in the opposite direction: *When he finished talking, he turned on his heel and walked away.*

hell

all hell breaks loose there is sudden and complete (unpleasant) confusion, uproar *etc*: *It was a quiet party until one guest punched someone, then all hell broke loose and within moments a full-scale fight was in progress.* [A quotation from Milton's *Paradise Lost*.]

come hell or high water whatever difficulties have to be overcome: *I am going to get my autobiography published come hell or high water!*

for the hell of it (*inf*) for no particular reason; just for fun: *The boys said they had set fire to the house just for the hell of it.*

give (someone) hell (*inf*) to treat (someone) very severely, *esp* to scold (someone) severely: *If he has a drink with his friends after work his wife gives him hell.*

hellbent (on something) (*inf*) determined (to do something): *I've told him it will be dangerous, but he's hellbent on going.*

hell for leather very fast: *They saw two young motorcyclists going hell for leather down the road.* [Possibly from *all of a lather* and certainly applied originally only to riding on horseback.]

not to have a cat in hell's chance/a snowball's chance in hell (*inf*) not to have any chance at all: *He doesn't have a cat in hell's chance of keeping his job under the new management.*

play (merry) hell with (*inf*) to harm or damage: *Curry plays hell with my weak stomach.*

raise hell *see* **raise.**

what the hell! (*inf*) what does it matter; I don't care: *If I buy that dress I shall have no money for the rest of the month, but what the hell!*

helm

at the helm in charge or in control: *There's a new man at the helm of the company.* [Literally, 'steering the ship'.]

help

give/lend a helping hand *see* **hand.**

a helpmeet a partner who helps one, *esp* a wife or husband: *The marketing side of his business is handled by his wife and helpmeet, Angela.* [A Biblical reference, from a misinterpretation of Genesis 2:18 'an help meet for him', *ie* 'a suitable help for him'.]

help oneself (to something) 1 to give oneself or take (food *etc*): *Help yourself to another cake*; *'Can I have a pencil?' 'Certainly — help yourself.'* **2** (*inf facet*) to steal (something): *He just helped himself to my jewellery.*

hen

henpecked (*inf*) (of a man) ruled by his wife: *He never does*

anything without asking his wife first — he's completely henpecked.
[From the fact that hens do in fact peck feathers out of the plumage of cocks.]

like a hen on a hot griddle very nervous and excited: *She's expecting a phonecall from her boyfriend — she's been like a hen on a hot griddle all evening.*

here

the hereafter (*formal*) life after death: *He believed that he would be rewarded in the hereafter for living a good life on earth.*

here's to (someone or something) used as a toast to the health, success *etc* of (someone or something): *Here's to the success of the new company.*

neither here nor there not important: *His opinion of us is neither here nor there.*

herring

(packed) like herring in a barrel very closely packed: *Far more people turned up than was expected, and they were packed into the hall like herring in a barrel.*

neither fish nor flesh nor good red herring *see* **fish.**

a red herring *see* **red.**

hide

hide one's light under a bushel *see* **light.**

neither hide nor hair of (someone or something) no trace at all of (someone or something): *She said her solicitors lived in Banks Street, but I could find neither hide nor hair of them.*

on a hiding to nothing (*sl*) in a situation where one cannot win, no matter what one does: *After two years of trying to become a singer, he realized he was on a hiding to nothing and gave up.* [Reputed to be a boxing idiom.]

tan (someone's) hide to beat (someone): *When that boy comes back, I'll tan his hide for not telling us where he was going!* [The reference is to leather-making.]

high

for the high jump (*sl*) about to be punished *etc* because one has done something wrong: *If the boss finds out that you broke that machine, you'll be for the high jump.* [Originally army slang.]

high and dry in a difficult position, unable to continue normally: *Her husband has left her high and dry without any money.* [A nautical idiom, for a boat stranded on a beach *etc*.]

(hunt) high and low (*inf*) (to search) everywhere: *I've hunted high and low for that book.*

high and mighty (*derog inf*) thinking, or behaving as if one thinks, that one is very important: *There's no reason for you to be so high and mighty — you're no-one special.*

high as a kite (*sl*) very happy, excited or drunk, or very much under the influence of drugs: *It must have been a good party — Tom was as high as a kite when he got home.*

a highbrow 1 a person who is interested in things such as classical music, great literature *etc*: *I am not a highbrow — I enjoy popular music.* **2** of things such as classical music, great literature *etc*: *The books he reads are too highbrow for me — I prefer a good cowboy story.*

high-falutin, high-faluting (*inf*) very, *usu* too, showy or grand: *She's too high-falutin to speak to her workers when she meets them in the street.* [19C US, probably an elaboration of *high-flown*.]

a high flier a person who is ambitious or who has natural characteristics which will cause him or her to be successful: *Their new managing director is a very high flier.*

high-handed (*derog*) **1** (of people) acting without thought or consideration for others: *He is so high-handed — he never consults anyone else before acting.* **2** (of actions *etc*) done without thought or consideration for others: *People dislike his high-handed attitude.*

a high spot an especially good part or section of something: *The speech made by Mr Brown was one of the high spots of the meeting.* See also **hit the high spots** below.

hightail it (*inf*) to hurry away: *If you don't want to meet him, you'd better hightail it out of here, because I see him coming now.* [Originally US, from the raised tail of a fleeing animal.]

hit the high spots (*inf*) to reach a high level: *Their concert was enjoyable but it never really hit the high spots.*

it is *etc* **high time** (*inf*) something ought to be or have been done *etc* by this time: *It is high time that this job was finished*; *It's high time someone told him to stop being stupid.*

on one's high horse difficult to argue with *etc*, *eg* because one is determined to show that one is very important or that one has not been shown enough respect *etc*: *As soon as anyone criticizes him, he gets on his high horse.* [A high horse was the charger of a mounted knight, and riding one was a sign of superior rank.]

riding high *see* **ride.**

run high (of feelings, tempers *etc*) to be excited, angry *etc*: *Feelings ran high at the meeting held to protest against the new motorway.* [Literally used of the sea, when there is a strong current and a high tide, or high waves.]

hill

    as old as the hills very old: *My husband's great-aunt is as old as the hills, but she's very fit.*

    over the hill (*inf*) past one's best; (too) old: *Although thirty-four is old for a footballer, Smith is certainly not over the hill.*

hind

    devil take the hindmost *see* **devil.**

hint

    take a/the hint (*inf*) to understand what (a person) is hinting at, and do what (the person) wants: *I keep making jokes to my secretary about her coming to work late every day, but she never takes the hint.*

hit

    hit a man when he is down *see* **man.**

    hit-and-run 1 (of a driver) causing injury to a person and driving away without stopping or reporting the accident. **2** (of an accident) caused by such a driver. [Originally a term for a tactic in baseball, with no connection in meaning to its present use.]

    hit it off (*inf*) to become friendly: *We hit it off as soon as we met; I hit it off with him.*

    hit (up)on (something) (*inf*) to find (an answer *etc*) by chance: *We've hit on the solution at last.*

    hit-or-miss without any system or planning; careless: *hit-or-miss methods.*

    hit the hay *see* **hay.**

    hit the headlines *see* **head.**

    hit the jackpot *see* **jackpot.**

    hit the nail on the head *see* **nail.**

    hit the roof *see* **roof.**

    make a hit (with someone) (*inf*) to make oneself liked or approved of (by someone): *That young man seems to have made quite a hit with your daughter.*

    a smash hit *see* **smash.**

hive

    hive (something) off (*inf: often derog*) **1** to give (some work, part of a job *etc*) to some other person, firm *etc*: *If we can't meet the schedule, we can hive off some of the work to another firm.* **2** to make (part of an organization) independent: *We can hive off part of the company and make it a separate firm.*

Hobson

Hobson's choice the choice between taking what one is offered and getting nothing at all: *Since this is the only kind of wheelbarrow I can find for sale it's a case of Hobson's choice.* [Reputedly from a 17C Cambridge livery-stable keeper, who only offered customers the hire of the horse nearest the door.]

hog

go the whole hog (*inf*) to do something completely: *I've bought a new dress — I think I'll go the whole hog and buy shoes and a handbag.* [Probably from the fact that *hog* was once a slang word for a shilling.]

hoist

hoist with one's own petard *see* **petard.**

hold

get hold of (someone or something) (*inf*) **1** to manage to speak to (someone): *I've been trying to get hold of you by phone all morning.* **2** to get, buy or obtain (something): *I've been looking for a copy of that book for years, but I've never managed to get hold of one.*

have a hold over (someone) to have power or influence over (someone): *He has a strange hold over that girl.*

hold (the line) (of a person who is making a telephone call) to wait while the person one is calling comes to the telephone, finishes what he is doing *etc*: *Mr Brown is busy at the moment — will you hold the line or would you like him to call you back?*

hold (something) against (someone) to dislike, have a bad opinion of *etc* (a person *etc*) because one knows that that person has done something bad, wrong *etc*: *I don't hold his foolish remarks against him.*

hold a pistol to (someone's) head *see* **pistol.**

hold (something) down to keep or be allowed to stay in (a job): *He is incapable of holding down a job.*

hold forth (*usu derog*) to talk or give one's opinions, often loudly, at great length and forcefully or dogmatically: *The prime minister held forth for hours on the success of his government.* [Originally meaning 'to preach' — a Biblical reference to Philippians 2:16, 'holding forth the word of life'.]

hold good to be true or valid; to apply: *Does that rule hold good in every case?*

hold one's head up *see* **head.**

hold it! (*inf*) stop or wait: *Hold it! Don't start till I tell you to.*

hold off (*inf*) (of weather conditions) to stay away: *I hope the* *rain holds off.*

hold on like grim death *see* **grim.**

hold out on (someone) (*inf*) to keep back money, information *etc* from (someone): *He says he knows nothing about it, but I think he's holding out on us.*

hold one's own *see* **own.**

hold one's peace *see* **peace.**

hold sway *see* **sway.**

hold the floor *see* **floor.**

hold the fort *see* **fort.**

hold (someone) to (something) to make (someone) keep (a promise), follow a (decision) *etc*: *You had better not promise anything rash, because you know I will hold you to it!*

hold one's tongue *see* **tongue.**

hold (someone) to ransom *see* **ransom.**

hold water *see* **water.**

hold with (something) to approve of (something): *He doesn't hold with smoking.*

hold your horses *see* **horse.**

no holds barred no restrictions on what is fair, allowed *etc*: *From the tone of his speech it was clear that there would be no holds barred in the election campaign.* [From wrestling, where certain holds are sometimes not allowed to be used in a match.]

hole

burn a hole in (someone's) pocket *see* **pocket.**

hole-and-corner carried out in a secretive manner, suggesting dishonesty: *I hate hole-and-corner affairs — let's have this whole problem dealt with in an open and frank manner!*

make a hole in (something) (*inf*) to use a large part of (something): *Buying a car made a large hole in my savings.*

pick holes in (something) (*inf*) to criticize or find faults in (an argument, theory *etc*): *He sounded very convincing, but I'm sure one could pick holes in what he said.*

holy

holier-than-thou (*derog*) behaving towards other people in a way which shows one thinks one is better, *esp* more holy and virtuous, than they are: *She always has such a holier-than-thou attitude to people who get into trouble — as if she never did anything wrong herself!* [A Biblical reference, to Isaiah 65:5 '. . . come not near to me, for I am holier than thou'.]

the holy of holies (*facet*) a very special place right inside a building *etc*: *The shopkeeper disappeared into the holy of holies at the back of the shop where he kept his books.* [A literal translation of the Hebrew name of the inner sanctuary in the Jewish Temple, where the Ark of the Covenant was kept.]

a holy terror (*inf*) **1** a person who is feared: *The boss is a holy terror when he's angry.* **2** a badly-behaved child: *Her little boy is a right holy terror.*

home

bring (something) home to (someone) to prove (something) to (someone) in a way which makes it impossible not to believe it: *The sudden epidemic brought it home to the townspeople that the town's drains were in need of replacement.*

do one's homework (*inf*) to prepare for a meeting *etc* by making sure one knows all the relevant figures, facts *etc*: *The Home Secretary has tried to impress us by quoting a lot of statistics, but those of us who have done our homework know that his facts are wrong.*

drive (something) home *see* **drive.**

feel at home to feel as relaxed as one does in one's own home or in a place or situation one knows well: *I always feel at home in France when I go there on holiday.*

home and dry having succeeded in what one wanted to do *etc*: *I wasn't sure that I could put this clock back together, but if I can fit this last wheel back in, I think I'll be home and dry.* [Probably from cross-country running.]

a home from home (*inf*) a place where one feels as relaxed, happy *etc* as when one is at home: *You have been in this jail so often, you must regard it as a real home from home by now!*

a home truth a plain statement of something which is unpleasant but true (about a person, his behaviour *etc*) said directly to the person: *I'm not putting up with his bad behaviour any longer — it's time someone told him a few home truths about how to behave in public.*

make oneself at home to make oneself as comfortable, or to behave in as relaxed a way, as one would at home: *Make yourself at home while you're waiting — help yourself to coffee if you want some.*

nothing to write home about (*inf*) not very exciting, important *etc*: *The concert was nothing to write home about.*

honest

honest Injun (*facet*) truthfully: *I didn't break the plate, honest Injun!* [Originally an American children's phrase, possibly from an assurance of reliability once demanded from Indians by white settlers.]

make an honest woman of (someone) (*facet*) to marry (a woman, originally one with whom one has already had sexual relations): *He lived with his secretary for five years before she persuaded him to make an honest woman of her.*

honour

do the honours (*formal or facet*) to do what is expected of a person who has guests, *esp* serve food *etc* to them: *The wine is over there — will you do the honours?*

honourable mention *see* **mention.**

hook

by hook or by crook (*inf*) by some means or another; in any way possible: *I'll get her to marry me, by hook or by crook.* [Origin obscure.]

hook, line and sinker (*inf*) completely; in all details: *He fell for the story hook, line and sinker* (= He believed all the lies he was told). [A fishing idiom, from a fish which swallows not only the hook but the entire end section of the line.]

off the hook (*sl*) free from some difficulty or problem: *If he couldn't keep the terms of the contract, he shouldn't have signed it — I don't see how we can get him off the hook now.* [From fishing.]

hoop

put (someone) through the hoop to cause (someone) to suffer something unpleasant: *The interviewer certainly put their spokesman through the hoop!* [Probably from circus performers.]

hoot

not to give/care a hoot/two hoots (in hell) (*inf*) not to care in the least: *He doesn't care two hoots what anyone thinks of him.*

hop

catch (someone) on the hop (*inf*) to do something (to someone) when they are not prepared: *He wasn't expecting to be asked such detailed questions — we rather caught him on the hop.*

hopping mad (*inf*) very angry: *I was hopping mad when he told me he'd crashed the car.*

hop it (*Brit sl*) to go away: *You'd better hop it before someone finds you here.*

keep (someone) on the hop to keep (someone) busy, active, alert *etc*: *The boss never tells us when he is going to inspect our work — he likes to keep us on the hop all the time.*

hope

hope against hope to continue hoping (that something will (not) happen *etc*) when there is no reason or no longer any reason for this hope: *Their cat had been missing for six weeks but they were still hoping against hope that it would come back to them.* [A Biblical allusion, to Romans 4:18.]

not to have a hope (in hell) of (something) (*inf*) to be certainly not going to do, be, have *etc* (something): *He hasn't a hope of getting this done by the end of the week.*

pin one's hopes on *see* **pin.**

raise (someone's) hopes to give (someone) good reason to believe that something will (not) happen, has (not) happened *etc*: *I don't want to raise your hopes too much, but I've heard that you are being considered for the manager's job.*

while there's life there's hope *see* **life.**

horn

draw in one's horns to behave in a quieter manner, *esp* to spend less money: *Our new carpet cost a lot of money, so we'll have to draw in our horns for the rest of the summer.* [The reference is to a snail.]

horn in on (something) (*derog inf*) to join in (an activity *etc*) without being wanted or invited: *She's always horning in on private conversations and insisting on giving us her views.*

on the horns of a dilemma *see* **dilemma.**

hornet

stir up a hornet's nest to do something which causes a great deal of anger and resentment: *He really stirred up a hornet's nest when he tried to change the way the office is run!*

horse

change horses in midstream to alter one's views, plans *etc* in the middle of a project: *Although it might have been wiser to have approached the job with different priorities, we can't now change horses in midstream.* [Apparently an image either coined or popularized by Abraham Lincoln.]

a dark horse *see* **dark.**

eat like a horse to eat a great deal: *It is amazing that Mary is so thin, because she eats like a horse.*

flog a dead horse to try to make people interested in a subject which everyone has already fully discussed, which is no longer interesting *etc*: *Doesn't he know he's flogging a dead horse trying to interest us in his savings scheme?*

hold your horses wait a moment; don't go so fast: *Hold your horses! You can't move the bookcase until I've taken the books out!* [From driving a carriage.]

a horse laugh a loud, harsh laugh: *His horse laugh could be heard throughout the hotel lounge.*

a horse of a different colour something or someone of a completely different kind: *Most of her friends are quiet and conventional, but Brian is a horse of a different colour.*

horseplay rough and noisy play: *It's harmless for children to indulge in horseplay.*

horse sense plain good sense: *It's sometimes safer to rely on horse sense than on the advice of one's colleagues.*

(there are) horses for courses certain people are better suited to do certain jobs, *esp* certain particular tasks: *There were many more senior people in his department who might have been sent on the mission, but it was a case of horses for courses.* [An allusion to the theory that certain racehorses are most likely to win on certain racecourses and that this factor should influence the races they are entered for, the odds offered by bookmakers *etc*.]

the iron horse *see* **iron.**

lock the stable door after the horse has bolted *see* **stable.**

look a gift horse in the mouth *see* **gift.**

on one's high horse *see* **high.**

put the cart before the horse *see* **cart.**

straight from the horse's mouth from a well-informed and reliable source: *I got that story straight from the horse's mouth.* [Possibly originally used for 'infallible' tips in horse-racing.]

wild horses would not (do something *etc*) *see* **wild.**

a willing horse someone who is willing to work, to help people *etc*: *Poor Helen is a willing horse and seems to do three-quarters of the work of the whole committee.* [An allusion to a saying which exists in several forms, *eg* **a willing horse never wants work**, all of which mean that if one member of a group *etc* is prepared to do all the work, the others will give him or her all the work to do.]

you can take a horse to (the) water but you can't make it drink a saying, meaning that one cannot actually force someone else to perform an action, only encourage him or her to do it.

hot

blow hot and cold *see* **blow.**

hot air (*inf*) boastful words, promises that will not be kept *etc*: *Most of what he said was just hot air.*

a hotbed of (something) a place where (something unpleasant) grows or increases rapidly: *That country is a hotbed of disease/revolution.* [Literally, a *hotbed* is a heated bed of soil in a greenhouse *etc* for forcing plants.]

hot-blooded 1 passionate; having strong sexual feelings: *He is too hot-blooded to keep away from women for long.* **2** easily made angry; excitable: *She is too hot-blooded to accept criticism calmly.* [From the medieval belief that emotion raised the temperature of the blood.]

hotfoot (*inf*) in a great hurry: *He arrived hotfoot from the meeting.*

a hothead a person who is easily made angry or who is inclined to act suddenly and without sufficient thought for the consequences: *Don't be such a hothead — if you rush off and say that to the boss he'll sack you at once!*

a hot line (*inf*) a line of quick communication between two (*usu* important) people *etc* for use in emergencies: *The American president has a hot line to Moscow;* (*facet*) *That man claims to have a hot line to God.*

hot on (something) (*inf*) fond of (something); interested in and enthusiastic about (something): *She is very hot on equal opportunities for women.*

hot stuff (*sl*) **1** a person *etc* of a high quality, ability *etc*: *He is hot stuff with a trumpet.* **2** a person who has strong sexual passions: *She's really hot stuff!*

hot under the collar cross and/or embarrassed: *He got quite hot under the collar at the amount of undeserved praise he was receiving.*

in hot water (*inf*) in trouble: *You will be in hot water if you're late again.*

in the hot seat (*inf*) in an uncomfortable or difficult position: *The Prime Minister is really in the hot seat over this problem.* [Originally US slang for 'in the electric chair'.]

like hot cakes (*inf*) (of selling, disappearing *etc*) very quickly: *These old books are going/selling like hot cakes.*

make it hot for (someone) to make things unpleasant or impossible for (someone): *If he fails to do his homework once more, the teacher is going to make it hot for him.*

piping hot *see* **pipe.**

red hot *see* **red.**

hour

after hours after the end of a working day or after the time during which a shop *etc* is normally open: *People are not allowed to buy beer in public houses after hours.*

at all hours (*inf*) at irregular times, *esp* late at night: *He comes home at all hours.*

at the eleventh hour *see* **eleven.**

in (someone's) hour of need (*formal or facet*) at a time when (someone) is in need of help: *I knew you would help me in my hour of need.*

the rush hour *see* **rush.**

the small hours *see* **small.**

house

as safe as houses completely safe: *I know the children are as safe as houses when Gillian is looking after them.*

bring the house down to produce great applause or laughter: *At the school entertainment, his impersonation of the headmaster brought the house down.* [A theatrical phrase.]

eat (someone) out of house and home to be so expensive to feed and keep that the person who is paying cannot afford it: *His wife's huge dog is eating him out of house and home.*

houseproud (*rather derog*) very concerned about the appearance of one's house: *She is very houseproud and makes all her guests put on slippers before they walk on her carpets.*

keep open house to be prepared to entertain anyone who arrives: *They keep open house for all their daughter's friends.*

like a house on fire (*inf*) **1** very well: *The two children got on like a house on fire* (= played *etc* together in a happy, friendly way). **2** very quickly: *I'm getting through this job like a house on fire.*

on the house paid for by the provider: *The car-hire firm offered us a car for a week on the house as compensation for our ruined holiday.* [Originally US and applied only to drinks paid for by the landlord of a public house.]

how

and how (*sl*) yes indeed; very much so: *'That was a terrific party last night.' 'And how!'* [Originally US.]

any old how *see* **any.**

how about (*inf*) **1** I would like to suggest: *'Where shall we go tonight?' 'How about the cinema?'* **2** what is he *etc* going to do?; what does he *etc* think?: *I rather like that picture. How about you?*

how come? (*inf*) for what reason?: *How come I didn't get any cake?* [Originally US.]

hue

a hue and cry a loud protest: *There will be a great hue and cry about this decision.* [An Anglo-Norman legal term, *hu et cri*, for the customary summons to the public to join the hunt for the perpetrator of a crime. [*Hue* may originally have meant 'noise', including the sound of trumpets *etc*, as opposed to *cry*, 'shouting'.]

huff

in a/the huff (*inf derog*) being or becoming silent because one is angry, displeased *etc*: *He is in the huff; He went off in a huff.*

hum

hum and haw to make sounds which express doubt, uncertainty *etc*: *He obviously didn't know the answer to my question — he just stood there humming and hawing.*

make things hum to cause everything to work quickly and smoothly: *He really makes things hum when he comes into the office — it's much quieter when he's not here.*

human

the milk of human kindness *see* **milk.**

humble

eat humble pie to humble oneself, *eg* by admitting a mistake: *You'll have to eat humble pie if he's proved right.* [*Humble pie* was a dish made from the offal (*umble*) of deer and eaten by estate servants as opposed to estate owners.]

hump

be over the hump to have passed a crisis or difficulty: *John won't be really fit and well for some weeks yet, but at least he's over the hump.*

hunt

a happy hunting-ground *see* **happy.**

(hunt) high and low *see* **high.**

run with the hare and hunt with the hounds *see* **hare.**

hurry

the more hurry the less speed *see* **haste.**

hush

hush-hush (*inf*) secret: *The plans are very hush-hush.* [1st World War military slang for an especially important secret military or naval project, specifically for the development of tanks.]

hush money (*sl*) money which is paid to a person to persuade him not to make certain facts known to someone else: *The criminals gave the boy hush money when they realized that he had overheard their plans for the robbery.*

hush (something) up (*inf*) to prevent (something) becoming known to the general public: *Their affair was hushed up to prevent a scandal.*

Hyde

Hyde *see* **Jekyll.**

I

ice

break the ice to overcome the first shyness *etc* in a new situation: *Let's break the ice by inviting our new neighbours for a meal.*

cut no ice to have no effect: *This sort of flattery cuts no ice with me.* [Originally 19C US.]

just/only the tip of the iceberg only a small, visible, part of a very much larger hidden problem, state of affairs *etc*: *It is believed that the few thousand people who are prepared to admit that they cannot read are only the tip of the iceberg.* [From the fact that an estimated 90% of an iceberg is hidden underwater.]

on ice put aside for use, attention *etc* at a later date: *We'll put these plans on ice for the time being.* [From a method of preserving perishable food.]

(skating) on thin ice in a risky or dangerous position: *When you try to give him advice you are (skating) on thin ice — he is likely to resent it very much.*

ill

go ill with (someone or something) to end in danger or misfortune for (someone or something): *Unless he can explain his actions satisfactorily to the manager, things will go ill with him.*

ill-gotten gains (*formal or facet*) money got in a bad or unlawful way: *He's living in South America on the ill-gotten gains from the bank-robbery.*

it's an ill wind (that blows nobody any good) a saying, meaning that almost every unfortunate *etc* happening benefits someone in some way, used to indicate that the speaker recognizes that some good has come of an apparent misfortune: *If we hadn't had to cancel our holiday, we would have been on the plane that crashed, so I suppose it's an ill wind.*

take it ill (*formal*) to be offended (that): *She will take it ill if you refuse her invitation.*

illusion

be under an/the illusion (that) to have a false impression or belief (about something): *She is under the illusion that he is honest although he is obviously cheating her.*

image

the spitting image *see* **spit**.

imagination

a figment of one's imagination *see* **figment**.

immemorial

  from time immemorial from a time beyond anyone's memory or written records; for a very long time: *That family has lived in the village from time immemorial.* [In legal phraseology, *immemorial* means 'before the beginning of legal memory', *ie* before the accession of Richard I in 1157.]

impression

  be under the impression that to have the (often wrong) feeling or idea that (something is the case): *I was under the impression that you were paying for this meal.*

in

  fall in *see* fall.

  in for (something) (*inf*) likely to experience (something, *usu* something bad): *We're in for some bad weather.*

  in for it (*inf*) about to experience trouble; likely to be punished: *You're in for it, now that you've broken the window again!*

  in on (something) (*inf*) to know (something); to have a share in (something): *I'm in on the secret.*

  the ins and outs (*inf*) the complex details (of a plan *etc*): *He alone knows all the ins and outs of this scheme.*

  (well) in with (someone) (*inf*) very friendly with (someone): *He is well in with a lot of important people.*

  there is *etc* **nothing in it 1** there is no truth, no importance or no difficulty in the matter: *I heard a rumour that he was leaving, but there is nothing in it; Any fool can make a skirt — there is nothing in it!* **2** there is no important difference between two or more things, scores *etc*: *As the swimmers reached the last hundred metres of the race, there was nothing in it between first and second.*

inch

  every inch completely; entirely; in every way: *He is every inch a nobleman.*

  give him *etc* **an inch (and he'll take an ell/a yard/a mile)** a saying meaning that it is unwise to make any concession at all to a person because he will take advantage of the concession to obtain even more.

Indian

  an Indian summer a time of fine, still weather in autumn: *The Indian summer we had this year was an unexpected bonus for ice-cream manufacturers.* [From a feature of the N American climate, probably named simply because when it was first observed the country was inhabited by Indians.]

in Indian file *see* **file.**

innings

have a good innings (*Brit*) to live for a reasonable length of time, or to enjoy a reasonably long period of success or power: *Uncle James had a good innings — he lived to be ninety-two.* [A cricketing term.]

inside

know (something) inside out *see* **know.**

instance

in the first instance (*formal*) as the first step in an action: *If you wish to join the club, you should apply to the secretary in the first instance.* [A legal term: *instance* here means 'a legal process in a court of law', and *the second instance* would be an appeal.]

insult

add insult to injury to behave badly towards someone whom one has already harmed in another way: *Having cut off our electricity in error, the Electricity Board added insult to injury by charging us for the cost of reconnection.* [A quotation from Edward Moore's play *The Foundling*, of 1748.]

intent

to all intents (and purposes) (*formal*) almost exactly; in all important ways: *There are slight differences between the two plans, but to all intents (and purposes) they are the same.* [A legal term.]

interest

in an interesting condition (*old euph*) pregnant: *He told us that his wife was once more in an interesting condition.*

in one's *etc* **(own) (best) interest(s)** bringing, or in order to bring, advantage, benefit, help *etc* to oneself: *It would be in our own interest to help him, as he may be able to help us later; It is in my best interests to invest in this firm.*

in the interest(s) of (something) (*formal*) in order to get, achieve, increase *etc* (something): *The political march was banned in the interests of public safety.*

a vested interest *see* **vested.**

iron

have several, too many *etc* **irons in the fire** to be involved in, or doing, several *etc* things at the same time: *Even if this project fails, he has several other irons in the fire.* [The reference is to blacksmith's work. It is only possible to work iron successfully at the correct temperature, and, while it useful to have some

-179-

spare pieces heating in case of failure, it is unproductive to heat too many at once.]

the Iron Curtain the barrier, considered to exist between Communist countries and other countries, that prevents free communication and trading: *I have a nephew living behind the Iron Curtain.* [The idiom dates from *c* 1920, but was made popular by Winston Churchill's use of it in a speech in 1946. It may derive ultimately from the use of an iron curtain as a fire precaution in theatres.]

the iron hand/fist in the velvet glove a strong or ruthless type of government *etc* which is hidden by a surface appearance of softness and courtesy.

the iron horse (*old*) railway engines: *Emigration to the American West was greatly assisted by the coming of the iron horse.*

rule (someone) with a rod of iron to control (a person or persons) very severely and sternly: *He used to lead a riotous life before his marriage, but his wife rules him with a rod of iron.* [An apparent Biblical reference to Psalm 2.]

strike while the iron is hot to act *etc* while the situation is favourable: *On hearing of his inheritance she struck while the iron was hot and asked him to repay the money he owed her.* [An idiom from blacksmith's work.]

issue

make an issue of (something) to make (something) the subject of an argument: *I don't agree with your proposal, but I don't want to make an issue of it.*

the point at issue (*formal*) the question that is being discussed: *The point at issue is not whether we would like a holiday, but whether we can afford one.*

take issue with (someone) (*formal*) to disagree with (someone): *I take issue with you on the question of education.*

itch

have an itching palm to be very greedy for money: *It cost us a lot of money to get papers to leave the country — we had to see a lot of officials and they all had itching palms.* [An old superstition held that an itching palm meant that one was about to receive money.]

ivory

an ivory tower (*derog*) a way of living in which one is protected from all the difficult and unpleasant features of life: *You live in an ivory tower — you have no idea of the problems faced by ordinary* *people!* [A phrase — *la tour d'ivoire* — coined in 1837 by the French poet Charles Augustin Sainte-Beuve.]

J

jack, Jack
    all work and no play makes Jack a dull boy *see* **work.**
    before you can say Jack Robinson very quickly: *If we all help, we'll get the job done before you can say Jack Robinson.* [Origin unknown.]
    every man jack (*inf*) everybody: *Every man jack of us must help.* [Probably from the prevalence of Jack as a Christian name.]
    a jack-of-all-trades (*sometimes derog*) someone who can and does work at a number of different jobs (*usu* doing none of them particularly well): *He is a jack-of-all-trades who will take on almost any piece of work he is offered, from laying concrete to mending cars.*

jackpot
    hit the jackpot (*inf*) to win or obtain a lot of money or success: *He must have hit the jackpot with the sales of his last gramophone record.* [The jackpot is a pool of money in poker which continues to accumulate without being won until someone is able to begin the betting with a pair of jacks or better.]

jam
    (there will be) jam tomorrow a saying, indicating that the speaker believes that benefits, prosperity, happiness *etc* which are promised will never in fact come: *For years politicians have persuaded the people of this country to put up with hardships by promising them jam tomorrow.* [From Lewis Carroll's *Alice Through the Looking-Glass*, in which the Red Queen offers Alice a job with 'Twopence a week, and jam every other day . . . jam tomorrow and jam yesterday — but never jam today'.]
    money for jam *see* **money.**
    want jam on it (*facet derog*) to be dissatisfied with an already favourable state of affairs: *He already earns a huge wage for a twenty-hour week — does he want jam on it?*

Jekyll
    a Jekyll and Hyde a person with two sides to his personality, often one good and one bad: *I found her difficult to deal with because*

*she was such a Jekyll and Hyde that I never knew how she would behave
in any situation.* [From the hero of Robert Louis Stevenson's novel
Doctor Jekyll and Mr Hyde.]

jet

   the jet set (*often derog*) very wealthy people who enjoy a life of
   frequent travel (by jet) and expensive holidays: *I haven't liked
   that part of France since the jet set started going there.*

job

   give (something) up as a bad job (*inf*) to decide that something
   is not worth doing, or impossible to do, and so stop doing it:
   *I could not persuade him to practise the piano, and finally gave it up as
   a bad job.*

   a good job (*inf*) a lucky or satisfactory state of affairs: *It's a
   good job that she can't hear what you're saying; He has lost his trumpet,
   and a good job too!*

   have a job (*inf*) to have difficulty (doing something, to do
   something, with something): *I've had quite a job with this essay; He
   has a hard job to pay all the bills; You'll have a job finishing all this
   work tonight.*

   a job lot a mixed collection (*eg* of goods) *esp* if of poor quality:
   *I bought this clock in a job lot at an auction and I'm surprised that it
   works.*

   just the job (*inf*) entirely suitable; exactly what is needed: *These
   gloves are just the job for gardening.*

   make the best of a bad job *see* **best.**

   on the job working: *The policeman was not allowed to drink while
   he was on the job; Since I'm on the job, do you want me to put up the
   towel-rail as well as the mirror?*

   a put-up job *see* **put.**

Job

   a Job's comforter a person who intends to comfort someone
   in distress but who in fact makes things worse: *My mother is a
   real Job's comforter when I'm ill — she comes to see me and tells me how
   ill I look and how much worse I'm going to feel before I'm better.* [From
   the three friends of Job in the Bible.]

jockey

   jockey for position to try to push one's way into a favourable
   position: *The senior staff in this firm are all jockeying for position.* [A
   jockey was originally a horse-trader, a profession generally
   regarded as characterized by deviousness, if not outright
   dishonesty.]

join
>**join the club** *see* **club.**

joint
>**put (someone's) nose out of joint** *see* **nose.**

joke
>**beyond a joke** past the limit of being humorous: *His attitude towards women is beyond a joke.*
>
>**crack a joke** *see* **crack.**
>
>**it's no joke** (*inf*) it is a serious or worrying matter: *It's no joke when water gets into the petrol tank.*
>
>**joking apart/aside** let us stop joking and talk seriously: *I feel like going to Timbuctoo for the weekend — but, joking apart, I do need a rest!*
>
>**a practical joke** *see* **practical.**
>
>**a standing joke** *see* **stand.**

jolly
>**jolly (someone) along** (*inf*) to keep (someone) in a good temper in order to gain his goodwill or co-operation: *He might help you, if you jolly him along a bit.* [Originally US.]
>
>**the Jolly Roger** the black flag with a white skull and crossbones reputed to be flown by pirate ships. [It appears that Roger was thought of as being the name of the person whose skull appears on the flag — *jolly* is ironic. Another, early 18C, name was *Old Roger*.]

Jones
>**keep up with the Joneses** to make sure that one remains equal socially with one's neighbours by doing the same things, buying the same type of car, television *etc*: *Since they live in a wealthy neighbourhood, they find it difficult to keep up with the Joneses.* [From the title of a comic strip by Arthur R Momand which appeared in the New York *Globe* from 1913 until the early 1940s.]

jowl
>**cheek by jowl** *see* **cheek.**

joy
>**be (someone's) pride and joy** *see* **pride.**
>
>**no joy** (*sl*) no luck, news, information *etc*: *The police have been searching for the child for two days, and no joy.*
>
>**wish (someone) joy of (something)** *see* **wish.**

judgement
>**sit in judgement on (someone)** to take upon oneself the responsibility of criticizing (others): *The old man was always sitting in*

judgement on his neighbour's gardening abilities.

juice

stew in one's own juice (*inf*) to suffer as a result of one's own stupidity *etc*: *If she doesn't like her new job she'll just have to stew in her own juice — she shouldn't have left her previous one.*

jump

for the high jump *see* **high.**

jump down (someone's) throat *see* **throat.**

a jumping-off place/point a place from which to start: *If you want to get to Finland, Newcastle is the best jumping-off place.*

jump on the bandwagon *see* **band.**

jump out of one's skin *see* **skin.**

jump the gun *see* **gun.**

jump the queue *see* **queue.**

jump to it (*inf*) to hurry up: *If you don't jump to it you will miss the train.*

jungle

concrete jungle *see* **concrete.**

the law of the jungle *see* **law.**

just

get one's just deserts to suffer the fate or results *etc* which one deserves (*esp* if bad): *He'll get his just deserts one day!*

just so 1 very neat and ordered: *He likes everything in his house to be just so, and gets upset if even an ornament is out of place.* **2** precisely; exactly: *'We can't expect any results until Friday.' 'Just so.'*

just the job *see* **job.**

justice

do (someone or something) justice/do justice to (someone or something) 1 to treat (someone) fairly or properly: *It would not be doing him justice to call him lazy when he's so ill.* **2** to fulfil the highest possibilities of (someone); to get the best results from (someone or something); to show (someone or something) fully or fairly: *I was so tired that I didn't do myself justice in the exam; The portrait is good, but doesn't do justice to her beauty.* **3** (*facet*) to consume (a meal *etc*) with a good appetite: *You've certainly done justice to the pie!*

poetic justice *see* **poetic.**

K

keel

be, keep on an even keel to be, keep or remain in a calm and untroubled state: *He kept the business on an even keel in spite of the many changes in staff.* [A nautical idiom.]

keel over (*inf*) to fall over (*usu* suddenly or unexpectedly): *She seemed to be perfectly well and then she just keeled over in the middle of the kitchen.*

keen

as keen as mustard *see* **mustard**.

keep

for keeps (*inf*) permanently: *Do you mean I can have it for keeps?*; *She's coming home tomorrow for keeps.*

in keeping with (*formal*) suited to: *He has moved to a house more in keeping with his position as an MP.*

keep an eye on *see* **eye**.

keep an open mind *see* **open**.

keep at arm's length *see* **arm**.

keep at it (*inf*) to go on doing something, *esp* to continue to work at something until one succeeds or finishes: *You'll get through all that work by tomorrow if you keep at it.*

keep company (with) *see* **company**.

keep one's cool *see* **cool**.

keep one's (own) counsel *see* **counsel**.

keep one's distance *see* **distance**.

keep one's end up *see* **end**.

keep one's hair on *see* **hair**.

keep one's hand in *see* **hand**.

keep one's head *see* **head**.

keep one's head above water *see* **head**.

keep in mind *see* **mind**.

keep in with (someone) (*inf*) to remain friendly with (someone), *usu* for a special reason: *It's a good idea to keep in with the police in case you need their help one day.*

keep it up (*inf*) to carry on doing something at the same speed or as well as one is doing it at present: *Your work is good — keep it up!* [Probably from the game of shuttlecock, the main aim of which was to keep the shuttlecock in the air. The idiom was originally applied to prolonged drinking parties *etc.*]

keep one's nose clean *see* **nose**.

keep on at (someone) (*inf*) to urge (someone) constantly (to do something): *She kept on at me to write to him.*

keep pace with *see* **pace.**

keep (someone) posted *see* **post.**

keep (someone) right *see* **right.**

keep one's shirt on *see* **shirt.**

keep sight of *see* **sight.**

keep tabs on *see* **tab.**

keep one's temper *see* **temper.**

keep the peace *see* **peace.**

keep the wolf from the door *see* **wolf.**

keep time *see* **time.**

keep oneself *etc* **to oneself** (*inf*) to tell others very little about oneself, and not to be very friendly or sociable: *Our new neighbours keep themselves to themselves.*

keep (something) to oneself not to tell anyone (something): *He kept his conclusions to himself.*

keep track of (someone or something) *see* **track.**

keep (something) under one's hat *see* **hat.**

keep (something) under wraps *see* **wrap.**

keep up appearances *see* **appearance.**

keep up with the Joneses *see* **Jones.**

keep one's word *see* **word.**

ken

beyond one's ken outside the extent of one's knowledge or understanding: *Such things are beyond my ken, I'm afraid.* [*Ken*, in the 17–18C, meant 'range of sight'.]

kettle

the pot calling the kettle black *see* **pot.**

a pretty kettle of fish (*inf*) a mess or awkward situation: *Oh dear, this is a pretty kettle of fish!* [Origin obscure.]

key

(all) keyed up (*inf*) excited; tense: *The actress always gets keyed up before a performance*; *The child is all keyed up about the party.* [A musical idiom — *key up* means 'to tune to a higher pitch'.]

kick

for a kick-off (*sl*) in the first place or to start (an argument or complaint *etc*): *You can forget about having lunch early for a kick-off — there's too much to be done.* [From the first kick of the match in football.]

for kicks (*sl*) in order to get a thrill; for fun: *These young criminals beat people up for kicks.*

kick oneself (*inf*) to be annoyed with oneself because one has been stupid or has made a mistake *etc*: *You'll kick yourself when I tell you what the answer is — it's very simple.*

kick one's heels *see* **heel.**

kid

handle (someone or something) with kid gloves to deal with (a person or situation) in a delicate and tactful manner: *She has a terrible temper and has to be handled with kid gloves.*

kid's stuff (*sl*) something very easy and undemanding: *He's a trained accountant, so balancing the society's books should be kid's stuff to him.*

kill

be in at the kill to be present at the most exciting or advantageous moment: *All the neighbours were in at the kill when the old lady's furniture was being sold.* [A hunting term.]

curiosity killed the cat *see* **curiosity.**

dressed to kill *see* **dress.**

kill the fatted calf *see* **fat.**

kill the goose that lays the golden eggs *see* **goose.**

kill time *see* **time.**

kill two birds with one stone *see* **bird.**

make a killing (*inf*) to make a great deal of money, a large profit *etc*: *During the tourist season he sold souvenirs at street corners and made a killing.* [Originally a racing term meaning 'to win a great deal of money'.]

kin

one's next of kin (*legal*) one's nearest relative(s): *You must inform his next of kin of the accident.*

kind

in kind (*formal*) in the same way or with the same treatment: *He spoke rudely to her and she replied in kind.*

nothing of the kind not at all what is/was expected, supposed *etc*: *I thought he would be helpful, but he was nothing of the kind — he was positively rude*; *'Aren't you an actress?' 'Nothing of the kind — I'm a teacher.'*

of a kind (*derog*) scarcely deserving the name: *We received hospitality of a kind at their house but we had to have a meal at a restaurant on the way home.*

two of a kind *see* **two.**

king

a king's ransom *see* **ransom.**

take the king's shilling (*hist*) to join the army. [From the method of joining, which was by accepting a shilling from the recruiting officer as an advance on wages.]

turn King's evidence *see* **evidence**.

kingdom

go/be sent *etc* **to kingdom come** (*usu facet*) to die: *If the bomb exploded we would all be blown to kingdom come.* [From the phrase 'thy kingdom come' in the Lord's Prayer.]

till kingdom come for a very long time: *I can't get my wife away from parties — she'd be quite happy to sit there chatting till kingdom come.* [As previous entry.]

kiss

the kiss of death (*usu facet*) something (*esp* if apparently helpful) which causes ruin, death *etc*: *A recommendation from him would be the kiss of death — he is very unpopular.* [A Biblical reference, to the kiss by means of which Judas betrayed Jesus — Matthew 26; Mark 14.]

kite

fly a kite (*inf*) to start a rumour about a new project *etc* in order to find out whether or not people would support it if it was really put into operation: *It was difficult to tell if the changes he was talking about were being seriously considered or if he was just flying a kite.* [From the use of kites to discover the direction and strength of the wind.]

high as a kite *see* **high.**

kitten

as weak as a kitten very weak: *She was as weak as a kitten after her illness.*

have kittens (*inf*) to be very nervous, upset or angry: *She didn't get home last night until 2 am and her mother was having kittens wondering where she was.*

knee

bring (someone) to his *etc* **knees** to make (someone) humble; to make (someone) realize that they have been defeated: *Napoleon brought his enemies to their knees; Poverty brought him to his knees.*

knee-high to a grasshopper (*facet*) very small: *He has been interested in trains every since he was knee-high to a grasshopper.* [Originally US.]

knickers

get one's knickers in a twist (*impolite inf*) to become worried or excited: *Don't get your knickers in a twist — no-one will expect you to make a speech!*

knife

have one's knife in (someone) (*inf*) to be continually hostile or unfair towards (someone): *He would love to get me into trouble — he's had his knife in me for years.*

knit

knit one's brows (*formal*) to draw together or wrinkle the brows; to frown: *He knit his brows as he read the closely-written letter.*

knock

knock (someone) all of a heap *see* **heap.**

knock around/about 1 to move about (in) a casual manner without a definite destination or purpose: *He spent six months knocking around Europe seeing the sights and living as cheaply as possible.* **2** to be present without doing anything in particular: *Three youths were knocking around outside the cinema when the incident occurred.*

knock (something) back (*inf*) to eat or drink (something), *esp* quickly and/or in large quantities: *He knocked back three pints of beer in the space of ten minutes.*

knock (someone) cold (*inf*) to make (someone) unconscious by a blow: *The beam swung round, hit him on the back of the head and knocked him cold.*

knock (someone) for six *see* **six.**

knock (someone or something) into a cocked hat *see* **hat.**

knock (something) into shape *see* **shape.**

knock it off! (*sl*) stop it!: *Oh, knock it off, Bill, you've been criticizing Jim all afternoon!*

knock off 1 (*inf*) to stop (working): *What time do you knock off in this factory?* **2** (*sl*) to steal (something): *He was caught trying to get rid of a lot of cigarettes he had knocked off from a local tobacconist's.*

knock (something) on the head *see* **head.**

knock spots off *see* **spot.**

knock the living daylights out of (someone) *see* **live**[1].

knock the stuffing out of *see* **stuff.**

you could have knocked me down with a feather *see* **feather.**

knot

at a rate of knots very quickly: *As soon as the policeman appeared, the boys went off down the street at a rate of knots.* [A nautical idiom.]

get knotted (*sl*) a scornful expression of annoyance, refusal to do what one is asked, disbelief *etc*: *When my brother suggested I might like to do his washing, I told him to get knotted.*

tie oneself/someone (up) in knots to get oneself, someone else into a confused or difficult situation: *She tied herself up in knots trying to explain tactfully why she didn't want him to come.*

know

before one knows where one is very quickly and *esp* before one has time to understand a problem, situation *etc* fully: *We allowed him to borrow the car once, and before we knew where we were he was out in it every night and we had to take the bus.*

for all I *etc* **know** because I do not know anything about the subject (*usu* implying either that one ought to have been informed or that one has no interest): *For all I know she might be dead — I haven't heard from her for years.*

in the know (*inf*) having information possessed by a small group of people and not by those outside it: *People in the know tell me that she has got the job.*

know a hawk from a handsaw *see* **hawk**.

know all the answers *see* **answer**.

know a thing or two *see* **thing**.

know (something) backwards/inside out to know extremely well or perfectly: *He knows the road to London backwards*; *He knows the publishing business inside out.*

know better to be too wise or well-taught (to do something): *He should have known better than to trust them.*

know (someone) by sight *see* **sight**.

know-how (*inf*) the practical knowledge and skill to deal with something: *I didn't have the know-how to be able to benefit from the situation.*

know one's onions *see* **onion**.

know one's place *see* **place**.

know the ropes *see* **rope**.

know the score *see* **score**.

know what's what *see* **what**.

know where one stands *see* **stand**.

know which side one's bread is buttered (on) *see* **bread**.

not to know one is born (*derog*) to lead a very trouble-free, protected life: *His mother does everything for him — he doesn't know he is born!*

not to know one's own mind *see* **mind**.

there's no knowing it is impossible to know: *It is very exciting* *going to one of his parties — there's no knowing who will be there.*

what do you know (*inf: esp US*) an expression of surprise: *What do you know? I thought that man over there died last year.*

I wouldn't know (*inf*) I am not in a position to know: *'Is that the new hotel?' 'I wouldn't know — I'm a visitor here myself.'*

you never know it is possible (that): *'Will she come?' 'I don't think so, but you never know.'*

knowledge

come to (someone's) knowledge to be discovered by (someone): *It has come to my knowledge — never mind how — that some of my pupils were not in school yesterday.*

to one's knowledge (*rather formal*) according to what one has been told, knows *etc*: *'Has Henry been invited?' 'Not to my knowledge.'*

knuckle

knuckle down (to something) to start working seriously (at something): *I don't really want to start studying for my exams but I'll just have to knuckle down to it.*

knuckle under (*inf*) to give in (to someone else): *When we have disagreements, it's always me who has to knuckle under and do what I'm told.*

near the knuckle (*inf*) rather too indecent: *Some of the stories she was telling the other guests were very near the knuckle — I was most embarrassed.*

L

labour

a labour of love a job *etc* which one does for one's own satisfaction or pleasure (or for that of someone whom one loves) and for which one is usually not paid: *It took her a long time to make her daughter's wedding-dress — but it was a real labour of love.*

lady

a ladies' man a man who likes the company of women: *He was not much of a ladies' man, and preferred to be with his male friends.*

a lady-killer (*inf: usu derog*) a man who is said to be very popular with women: *He thinks he's a lady-killer but most women find him boring.*

lamb

as well be hanged for a sheep as a lamb *see* **sheep.**

a ewe lamb *see* **ewe.**

like a lamb to the slaughter quietly and without arguing or complaining (used of someone going into danger or difficulty, about to be punished *etc*): *She went off to start organizing the meeting like a lamb to the slaughter, not realizing what an unpleasant task she had taken on.* [A Biblical reference, to Isaiah 53:7.]

two shakes of a lamb's tail *see* **shake.**

lame

a lame duck *see* **duck.**

lamp

smell of the lamp (*usu derog*) (of books *etc*) to show signs that the writer has done a lot of research for or revision of his book: *His best novels were written quickly — anything he spent a lot of time over tended to smell of the lamp.*

land

a land of milk and honey an area which is very fertile: *The early settlers found the Oregon was a land of milk and honey.* [A Biblical quotation, from Exodus 3:8, describing the Promised Land of the Israelites.]

the Land of Nod *see* **nod.**

a landslide victory a victory in an election by a very large majority of votes: *The election resulted in a landslide victory for the Opposition.*

land up (*inf*) to finish or come eventually to be (in a certain, *usu* the wrong, place or a certain, *usu* bad, condition): *He wanted to go to London, but got on the wrong train and landed up in Bristol; If you go on like that, you'll land up in jail.* [A nautical idiom.]

land (someone) with (something) (*inf*) to give or pass (a job, an object *etc* which is unpleasant or unwanted) to (someone else): *She was landed with the job of telling him; They landed me with the things no-one else wanted.*

a no-man's-land *see* **man.**

see how the land lies to look at the conditions, state of affairs *etc* which exist before taking an action or making a decision: *I can't say what I'll do until I get there — I shall have to see how the land lies.* [A nautical idiom, literally implying 'to see where exactly one is'.]

spy out the land *see* **spy.**

language

bad language (*inf*) swearing: *He uses too much bad language.*

speak the same language (as someone) to have a good mutual understanding (with someone), having similar tastes and thoughts: *John and I like each other well — we speak the same language.*

strong language *see* **strong.**

lap

in the lap of luxury in very luxurious conditions: *We lived in the lap of luxury and didn't have to pay a penny!*

in the lap of the gods (of a situation) left to chance, so that it is impossible to affect what happens or even to know what will happen: *I've done as much as I can to make sure things go well — from now on it's in the lap of the gods.* [A Greek idiom found frequently in Homer.]

large

as large as life *see* **life.**

loom large *see* **loom.**

lark

as happy as a lark very happy: *The little girl spent the afternoon digging on the beach as happy as a lark.*

get up with the lark to rise early in the morning: *She gets up with the lark and does most of the housework before breakfast.*

lash

lash out (*inf*) to spend money in large quantities: *For our anniversary, we decided to lash out and have a really big party.*

last

as a/in the last resort *see* **resort.**

at (long) last in the end, *esp* after a long delay: *At long last she arrived, about two hours late*; *Oh, there he is at last!*

breathe one's last (*liter euph*) to die: *At four o'clock in the morning, the nation's greatest statesman breathed his last.*

the last person someone who is very unlikely, unwilling *etc* to do something; someone that it is dangerous, unsuitable *etc* to do something to: *She's the last person you would suspect of such a thing*; *John is the last person they should have treated like that — he has a very bad temper.*

last resting-place *see* **rest.**

the last straw a fact, happening *etc* which, when added to all other facts or happenings, makes a situation finally impossible to bear: *Everything was going wrong, and his message was the last straw — she just burst into tears.* [An allusion to the saying **it is the last straw that breaks the camel's back**, which means that when one trivial annoyance, worry *etc* is added to another there comes a point when the addition of yet one more causes a disaster.]

the last word 1 the final remark in an argument *etc*: *She always must have the last word!* **2** the final decision: *The last word on the project rests with the manager.* **3** (*inf*) something very fashionable or up-to-date: *Her hat was the last word in elegance.*

on one's last legs very near to falling down or collapsing with exhaustion, old age *etc*: *My washing-machine is on its last legs — I've had it twenty-five years.*

see, hear the last of (someone or something) to see or hear of (someone or something) for the last time: *I think we've seen the last of him!*; *You haven't heard the last of this!*

latch

a latchkey child a child who frequently comes home to an empty house, and therefore carries a key to the door with him or her: *Many of the pupils in the school are latchkey children whose parents are both out at work until half past five or six o'clock at night.*

latch on to (someone or something) 1 to join oneself to (a person, group *etc*): *They have acquired a stray dog which latched on to them in the park one day.* **2** to get and keep hold of (an object *etc*): *You stay here and keep this table for us to sit at and I'll go and see if I can latch on to a couple of extra chairs.* **3** to come to understand (an idea *etc*): *The children soon latched on to the idea that reading was fun.*

late

better late than never a saying, meaning that it is better that something should happen, occur *etc* rather later than one would have wished than not at all.

late in the day when a project, activity has been going on for some time, *esp* if it is considered to be too late to make proposed changes, decisions *etc*: *I don't think it will be possible to incorporate your suggestions in our report so late in the day — the final version is already being typed.*

lather

in a lather (*inf*) very excited or upset: *She was all in a lather over the preparations for the party.* [Literally applies to horses.]

Latin

dog Latin very incorrect Latin (as compared to Classical Latin): *The book had an inscription in dog Latin on the title page.*

laugh

be laughed out of court to cause so much amusement or scorn (*usu* by what one says, is asking *etc*) that one's complaint, case *etc* is not fully considered: *I don't think you should ask for a 70%*

pay rise — you'll be laughed out of court.

be laughing to be (about to be) in a good position, with no further worries, problems *etc*: *If our new product doesn't sell well, we might be in difficulties, but if it does sell well, we're laughing.*

have the last laugh to succeed or to be proved right, after suffering a great deal of scorn, disbelief *etc*: *We all thought he was a fool to want to publish his memoirs, but he had the last laugh because the book was a bestseller.* [An allusion to the saying **he who laughs last laughs longest**, *ie* 'the final victory is the most complete one'.]

a horse laugh *see* **horse.**

a laughing-stock someone who is laughed at: *If I wear that hat, I'll be the laughing-stock of the village.*

laugh (something) off to treat (injuries, problems *etc*) as unimportant: *We were impressed by the way he laughed off the difficulties of being handicapped.*

laugh on the other side of one's face to be made to feel disappointment or sorrow (by implication, deservedly) after seeming to be lucky or successful: *The thieves were delighted that they had apparently thrown off the police but they laughed on the other side of their faces when they were stopped for speeding on the motorway.*

laugh up one's sleeve *see* **sleeve.**

no laughing matter a very serious matter: *To have mumps at forty-five is no laughing matter.*

laurel

look to one's laurels to be careful not to lose a position or reputation because of better performances *etc* by others: *If you want to win the race you had better look to your laurels and start training.* [From the laurel wreath with which the Greeks crowned poets, winners at the Pythian games *etc.*]

rest on one's laurels to keep a position or reputation because of past successes without actually doing anything more: *I think it used to be a good school, but it has been resting on its laurels for twenty years or so.* [As previous entry.]

law

the (long) arm of the law *see* **arm.**

be a law unto oneself not to obey rules or orders: *I can't say that she will agree to do it — she's a law unto herself.* [A Biblical reference, to Romans 2:3.]

have the law on (someone) (*inf: usu* used as a threat) to make sure that legal action is taken against (someone who is breaking the law): *I'll have the law on you, you thief!*

the law (*inf*) the police: *The thief was still in the building when the law arrived.*

the law of the jungle the rules for succeeding or surviving in a difficult or dangerous situation by the use of force *etc*: *He soon discovered that the criminal underworld he had joined was governed by the law of the jungle and that the most ruthless members were the most successful.* [A phrase coined by Rudyard Kipling.]

lay down the law to state something in a way that indicates that one expects one's opinion and orders to be accepted without argument: *He tried to lay down the law to us when he first arrived, but soon discovered that we just ignored him.*

the letter of the law *see* **letter.**

take the law into one's own hands to obtain justice in a way not involving the law, the police *etc*: *The riotous mob took the law into their own hands and hanged the murderer.*

lay

lay about one to strike blows in all directions: *He seized a long piece of wood and laid about him with it.*

lay down one's arms *see* **arm.**

lay down the law *see* **law.**

lay (one's) hands on *see* **hand.**

lay into (someone) to attack (someone) strongly, *esp* to beat (someone) thoroughly: *He laid into his attacker with his walking-stick*; *He was late again this morning, and the boss really laid into him.*

lay it on the line *see* **line.**

lay it on thick *see* **thick.**

lay it on with a trowel *see* **trowel.**

lay (someone) low *see* **low.**

lay off 1 to dismiss (employees) temporarily: *Because of a shortage of orders, the firm has laid off a quarter of its workforce.* **2** (*inf*) to stop (doing something): *I told him to lay off following me or he'd be sorry!*

lay (something) on the line *see* **line.**

lay oneself open to (something) *see* **open.**

lay (someone) to rest *see* **rest.**

lay waste *see* **waste.**

lead[1]

lead (someone) by the nose *see* **nose.**

a leading light (*sometimes facet*) a very important and influential person (in a certain field): *She is one of the leading lights of the new movement in education.* [Literally a nautical term for a light used with other marks as a guide to the entrance of a harbour, a channel *etc*.]

a leading question a question asked in such a way as to suggest the answer the questioner wants to hear: *It was a leading question to ask the witness if it was not the case that the man he saw was bald.* [A legal term.]

lead (someone) on to deceive (someone) by causing them to have false hopes: *She led us on to believe that we would be paid for our work.*

lead the way to go first (*esp* to show the way): *Our country has led the way in the field of electronics for years.*

lead (someone) up the garden path *see* **garden.**

lead up to (something) to prepare (to do something, for something to happen *etc*) by steps or stages: *He talked for a long time and seemed to be leading up to something.*

lead[2]

swing the lead (*sl*) to neglect one's work, *usu* inventing excuses to hide the fact; to try to make others believe something that is not true, in order to hide one's own mistakes, inefficiency *etc*: *Two or three of the people working on this project are really keen, but most of the others are swinging the lead.* [Originally naval slang.]

leaf

take a leaf out of (someone's) book to use (someone) as an example: *It would be better if you took a leaf out of Mary's book and arrived early.*

turn over a new leaf to begin a new and better way of behaving, working *etc*: *He has been in jail several times, but now he seems to have turned over a new leaf.* [Literally, to start writing on a fresh page of a notebook *etc*.]

league

be top, bottom of the league to be best, worst in a particular area of activity, quality *etc*: *When it came to holding parties, the children in my son's class thought that Stuart's mother was top of the league.* [From the grouping of clubs in soccer *etc*.]

in league with (someone) having joined together with (a person, organization *etc*), *usu* for a bad purpose: *The police did not know that he was in league with a group of bank-robbers, or they would have questioned him more closely.*

not in the same league as (someone) not as able, as important, as good *etc* as (someone): *He is quite a talented musician, but he is not in the same league as his wife — she is a genius.*

leak

    leak out to come to be known by the public: *It was some months before the news of their secret engagement leaked out.*

lean

    lean on (someone) (*sl*) to use slight force to persuade (someone) to do something *etc*: *I'll have to lean on her a bit — I don't think she's working hard enough.*

leap

    by leaps and bounds extremely rapidly and successfully: *The building of the new sports complex is going ahead by leaps and bounds.*

    a leap in the dark an action, decision *etc* whose results cannot be foreseen: *Since he was quite unknown as an artist, employing him to paint such an important picture was rather a leap in the dark.*

lease

    give (someone or something) a new lease of life to cause (someone or something) to have a longer period of active life, usefulness *etc* than they would otherwise have had: *Dyeing my suede coat has given it a new lease of life; He was given a new lease of life by an operation to replace a valve in his heart.*

least

    least said, soonest mended a saying, meaning that the less one says in a difficult situation, the less one is likely to offend or hurt someone.

    to say the least not to exaggerate in any way: *When I admitted I'd forgotten our date, she was rather annoyed, to say the least.*

leave

    leave (someone) alone not to disturb, upset or tease (someone): *Why can't you leave your little brother alone?*

    leave (someone) in the lurch *see* **lurch.**

    leave of absence permission to be away (from one's duty *etc*), or the time that one is permitted to be away: *He was granted (a week's) leave of absence to attend his sister's wedding.*

    leave/let well alone *see* **let.**

    take French leave *see* **French.**

    take it or leave it *see* **take.**

    take leave of one's senses *see* **sense.**

leeway

    make up leeway to recover from a setback, disadvantage *etc* which has caused one to fall behind others, a schedule *etc*: *He had a lot of leeway to make up at school after his illness.* [A nautical idiom — *leeway* is the (unwanted) progress sideways made by

a sailing ship in response to the sideways pressure of the wind
— as opposed to **headway**, 'progress forwards'.]

left

have two left feet (*inf*) to be clumsy or awkward, *eg* in dancing:
*I don't like dancing with Jim because he has two left feet and keeps
treading on my toes.*

left, right and centre (*inf*) in large quantities: *We will not make
any money if we hand out free tickets for the concert left, right and centre.*

leg

get one's sea legs *see* **sea.**

give (someone) a leg up (*inf*) to help (someone) to achieve
something: *He would never have become a director of the company if
his father-in-law had not given him a leg up.* [Literally, to support
someone's leg and foot to help them to climb up on to something.]

not to have a leg to stand on (*inf*) to have no way of excusing
one's behaviour, justifying one's requests *etc*: *She hasn't got a leg
to stand on if she's forgotten to write, because I reminded her every day
for a week.*

on one's last legs *see* **last.**

pull (someone's) leg (*inf*) to try as a joke to make (someone)
believe something which is not true: *You haven't really got a black
mark on your face — he's only pulling your leg.*

stretch one's legs *see* **stretch.**

legion

their name is legion (*rather formal*) there are a very great many
of them: *I don't know how many people have written complaining, but
their name is legion.* [A Biblical reference, to Mark 5:9.]

lemon

the answer is a lemon one is given an unsatisfactory answer
or no answer at all. [US, of obscure origin.]

lend

lend a hand *see* **hand.**

lend an ear *see* **ear.**

lend itself to (something) to be suitable for or adapt easily to:
This room lends itself to formal occasions.

length

at length (*formal*) **1** in detail; taking a long time: *She told us at
length what had been decided.* **2** at last: *At length, we began to understand
what he wanted.*

go to any lengths to do anything, no matter how extreme,
dishonest, wicked *etc* (to get what one wants): *I'm not surprised*

that she's having an affair with the boss — she'll go to any lengths to get promotion.

let

    let alone (someone or something) not to mention (someone *etc*); without taking (someone *etc*) into consideration: *It will cost us a fortune for the food, let alone the wine!*

    let (someone) down to disappoint or fail to help (someone) when necessary *etc*: *She felt he had let her down by not coming.*

    let fly *see* **fly.**

    let oneself go 1 to act without attempting to restrain oneself: *She really let herself go at the party and had a wonderful time.* **2** to lose interest in and cease to take trouble over one's appearance, the way one lives *etc*: *She used to look very smart, but she has let herself go since her husband left her.*

    let go (of something) to stop holding (something): *Will you let go of my coat!*; *When he was nearly at the top of the rope he suddenly let go and fell.*

    let (someone) have it *see* **have.**

    let (someone) in for (something) to cause (someone) to be involved in (something unpleasant or difficult): *When I agreed to do the job, I didn't know what I was letting myself in for, or I would have refused.*

    let (someone) in on (something) (*inf*) to share (a secret *etc*) with (someone): *I think we'll have to let your mother in on our plans.*

    let off steam *see* **steam.**

    let on 1 to pretend, or allow (something untrue) to be believed: *I let on that I had never heard of him.* **2** to reveal or show: *I didn't let on that I knew him.*

    let (something) slide *see* **slide.**

    let (something) slip *see* **slip.**

    let the grass grow under one's feet *see* **grass.**

    let/leave well alone to allow things to remain as they are, in order not to make them worse: *I know her television doesn't work very well, but she is perfectly happy with it and I think you should let well alone in case you break it.*

    to let available to be rented: *Their house is to let, so they must have moved away.*

letter

    the letter of the law an interpretation of the law which follows exactly what it says (as opposed to what the writer actually meant): *What he did was illegal according to the letter of the law, but* *he would never be sent to prison for it.* [A Biblical reference, to II Corinthians 3:6.]

a red-letter day *see* **red.**

to the letter exactly; following every detail: *He followed his father's instructions to the letter.*

level

do one's level best *see* **best.**

find one's/it's (own) level to find the place, rank *etc* to which one/it naturally belongs: *She felt she had found her own level as an assistant and had no ambition to become the manager of the firm; The government let the pound find its own level against foreign currencies.* [Originally used of two connected bodies of liquid, meaning 'to arrive at a common level'.]

level-headed calm and having good sense: *He is very level-headed and can think quickly in an emergency.*

level pegging (*inf*) (of two or more people *etc*) doing equally well, having equal scores *etc*: *The two teams at the top of the football league are level pegging at the moment.* [Probably from scoring by means of pegs and numbered holes.]

on the level (*sl*) fair; honest: *Is his offer on the level?* [Originally US, probably from the idea that *level*, like *straight* and *square*, implies rightness.]

liberty

at liberty to (do something) free, permitted *etc* to (do something): *I am not at liberty to reveal the source of my information.*

take liberties with (someone or something) to treat (someone or something) with too much freedom, without enough respect or in an indecent manner: *The director of this play has taken terrible liberties with Shakespeare's lines.*

take the liberty of (doing something) (*formal*) to do (something) without permission: *I took the liberty of moving the papers from your desk — I hope you don't mind.*

lick

a lick and a promise (*inf*) a short and not very thorough wash or clean: *Since it was late she gave the children only a lick and a promise before bed.*

lick (someone or something) into shape (*inf*) to put (something) into a more perfect form or make (someone) more efficient: *It only took him half an hour to lick the rough draft of the letter into shape and send it.*

lick one's lips *see* **lip.**

201

lid

blow the lid off (something) (*sl*) to expose (a scandal *etc*): *The television report blew the lid off their illegal operation.*

put the (tin) lid on (something) (*sl*) to add the final unpleasant detail to (something very unsatisfactory *etc*): *When I found my train home had been cancelled, it just put the (tin) lid on a really ghastly trip!*

lie[1]

give the lie to (something) (*formal*) to show (a statement *etc*) to be false: *Her pale face gave the lie to her assurance that she felt quite well.* [Literally, this phrase means 'to call (someone) a liar'.]

lie in one's teeth (*inf*) to lie very obviously and shamelessly: *When he said he didn't know we were dissatisfied, he was lying in his teeth but I pretended to believe him.*

a white lie *see* **white.**

lie[2]

lie heavy on (someone) to be a worry or a burden to (someone): *The responsibility lay heavy on him.*

lie in wait (for someone or something) to be waiting to catch or attack (someone or something): *As he left the building, she was lying in wait for him, hoping to be able to speak to him.*

lie low *see* **low.**

the lie of the land the details of any particular situation: *I'll write you a report as soon as I've studied the lie of the land in the department.* [A nautical idiom — literally 'the direction and characteristics of the coastline'.]

see how the land lies *see* **land.**

take (something) lying down (*usu in neg*) to accept or suffer (something) without arguing, complaining or trying to avoid it: *I do not intend to take this insult lying down, and will write to my lawyer!*

life

as large as life in person; actually: *I went to the party and there was John, as large as life.* [Literally 'life-size', used of a painting, sculpture *etc*.]

for dear life *see* **dear.**

for the life of me (*inf*) even if it was necessary in order to save my life: *I couldn't for the life of me remember his name!*

have the time of one's life *see* **time.**

the life and soul of the party a person who is very active, enthusiastic, amusing *etc* at a party: *He sings, tells jokes and dances with all the girls — he's the life and soul of the party.*

the life of Riley (*sl*) an easy, troublefree life: *It's all very well* *for him — he married an heiress and has been living the life of Riley ever since.* [Origin obscure.]

a matter of life and death *see* **matter.**

not on your life! (*inf*) certainly not!: *'Will you get married?' 'Not on your life!'*

see life (*not formal: often facet*) to find out how other people live, *esp* if they live strangely or not respectably: *He thought he would be a better writer if he spent some weeks in the slums of Naples, seeing life.*

take one's life in one's hands to take the risk of being killed or (*loosely*) attacked *etc*: *He took his life in his hands when he entered the burning building to try to rescue the child; I took my life in my hands and asked for a rise in salary.*

to the life exactly (like): *When he put on that uniform, he was Napoleon to the life.*

while there's life there's hope a saying, meaning that one should not despair of a situation while it is still possible for it to improve.

lift

not to lift a finger *see* **finger.**

thumb a lift *see* **thumb.**

light

according to one's lights (*formal*) following one's own standards: *He was a good father according to his lights, but very strict.* [Apparently a translation of a French idiom — *lights* in French means 'mental ability'.]

bring to light to reveal or cause to be noticed: *The scandal was brought to light by a journalist.*

come to light to be revealed or discovered: *New evidence concerning the recent murder has come to light.*

go out like a light (*inf*) to fall quickly and deeply asleep: *I was so tired when I got to bed that I went out like a light.*

hide one's light under a bushel to hide, or try not to attract attention to, one's talent or ability: *Elizabeth is an excellent pianist but she tends to hide her light under a bushel and won't play in public.* [A Biblical allusion, to Matthew 5:15 — 'Neither do men light a candle, and put it under a bushel, but on a candlestick ... let your light so shine before men that they may see your good works'.]

in the cold light of day when a plan *etc* is considered in a practical manner, not in an atmosphere of emotion: *We made all*

203

sorts of plans over drinks at his house, but in the cold light of day back at the office none of them seemed likely to achieve any success.

in the light of (something) (*formal*) taking into consideration (information acquired *etc*): *The theory has been abandoned in the light of modern discoveries.*

a leading light *see* lead[1].

light-fingered likely to steal: *Don't leave your handbag for a moment — this place is full of light-fingered people!*

make light of (something) to treat (something) as unimportant: *He had a bad fall, but made light of his cuts and carried on.*

many hands make light work *see* hand.

see the light 1 (often **see the light of day**) to be discovered, produced *etc*: *That was one of our projects which never saw the light (of day) at all.* **2** (*often facet*) to be converted to someone else's point of view *etc*: *She finally saw the light and agreed to follow our suggestions.*

shed/throw light on (something) to make (a reason, subject *etc*) clearer: *This letter sheds light on the reasons for his actions at the time.*

lightning

as quick as lightning very quickly: *The dog grabbed the meat and was out of the shop as quick as lightning.*

lightning never strikes in the same place twice a saying, meaning that an unusual accident, mishap *etc* is very unlikely to be repeated exactly.

like (greased/a streak of) lightning very quickly: *The child ran down the street like (greased) lightning and disappeared round the corner.*

like

a likely story! (*inf*) I don't believe you, him *etc*: *'She says she spent the whole evening working!' 'A likely story — she was probably watching TV!'*

the likes of (*inf*) people such as: *An important person like Mr Macdonald won't want to have lunch with the likes of us!*

not likely! (*inf*) certainly not!: *'Would you be willing to put your head in a lion's mouth?' 'Me? Not likely.'*

lily

gild the lily to add unnecessary decoration, exaggeration *etc* to something: *I think it would be gilding the lily to wear diamonds with that dress — you look beautiful without any jewellery at all.* [An adaptation of a quotation from Shakespeare's *King John*, IV. ii — 'To gild refined gold, to paint the lily . . . Is wasteful and ridiculous excess.']

lily-livered (*liter*) cowardly: *Stand up and fight, you lily-livered scoundrel!* [Probably a direct quotation from Shakespeare — *Macbeth*, V. iii — from the old scientific belief that the liver of a coward contained no blood.]

limb

    out on a limb having ideas or opinions not shared by others; in a dangerous or disadvantageous position: *In making his views on the subject known, he had put himself out on a limb, as no-one agreed with him.* [The reference is to being isolated on a branch of a tree out of contact with the main trunk.]

limbo

    in limbo (*formal*) forgotten, neglected or cast aside: *Plans were completed last year, but the whole project has been in limbo since then.* [A Latin term — 'on the border' — for the region in the borderland of Hell held by orthodox Catholic theology to be inhabited by the souls of the unbaptized and the righteous who lived before Christ.]

limelight

    in the limelight in a situation or position where one attracts a great deal of attention from the public: *Members of the Royal Family spend their whole lives in the limelight.* [From a type of brilliant light formerly used for spotlights in theatres.]

limit

    the limit (*inf*) only just able to be tolerated: *That firm is the limit! This is the sixth time they have sent us faulty goods!*

    the sky's the limit *see* **sky.**

line

    all along the line (*not formal*) at every point in a process *etc*: *I have been telling him all along the line that we were not approaching the problem in the most sensible manner.* [A military idiom.]

    be in (someone's) line (of country) to be the kind of thing (someone) understands, likes, can deal with *etc*: *I'm afraid making such decisions is not in my line*; *Barney is a fanatical golfer — cricket is not in his line of country.*

    bring (something) into line to make (something) agree with, the same as *etc*, a number of other things: *These changes will bring our procedures into line with those of other European countries.*

    draw the line to fix a limit *esp* for what one is prepared to do: *No, there I draw the line — I will not invite him to my party!*

    hard lines *see* **hard.**

in line for (something) likely to get or to be given (something): *He is in line for promotion.*

hold the line *see* **hold.**

a hot line *see* **hot.**

in, out of line with (something) (*formal*) in or out of agreement or harmony with: *His statement is in line with his previous attitude to the subject; His views are out of line with those of his colleagues.*

lay it on the line (*inf*) to speak frankly in order to make a subject, *esp* one's orders, opinions, conditions *etc*, quite clear: *I thought he might have misunderstood my position, so this time I really laid it on the line.* [Originally US.]

lay (something) on the line (*inf*) to risk losing (money, one's job *etc*): *He really laid his reputation on the line to persuade them to sponsor his play.* [Originally US.]

the line of least resistance a course of action *etc* that will cause the least trouble, argument or difficulty: *Seeing that they were all determined that she should go with them, she chose the line of least resistance and agreed.* [A technical term from engineering.]

line one's pockets *see* **pocket.**

on the lines of (something) in a particular manner or direction, similar to (something else): *The workers wished to make a deal with the management on the lines of the one that had recently come into operation in the steel industry.*

read between the lines to understand something from a situation, statement *etc* which is not actually stated: *She said she was managing all right, but reading between the lines I could see she was tired.* [From a method of sending secret messages by writing in invisible ink between the lines of another message.]

shoot a line (*sl*) to exaggerate, *esp* in order to boast about oneself: *He told us how much the company relied on his skill and expertise, but we knew he was just shooting a line.* [Originally US.]

step out of line to behave in a way different from what is usual or accepted: *He's very pleasant as long as you do what you're told, but if you step out of line you're in trouble.* [A military image, of lines of soldiers.]

take a hard line *see* **hard.**

toe the line *see* **toe.**

linen

wash one's dirty linen in public to have a discussion or argument in public, in a manner which attracts attention *etc*, about private problems, scandals *etc*: *If you contest the divorce case* *your wife is bringing against you, it will simply result in a lot of washing of dirty linen in public.*

lion

a lion-hunter (*derog*) a person who tries to become friendly with famous people, invites them to parties *etc*: *The young actor was overwhelmed to find he was now the target of all the lion-hunters in London.* [The use of the word *lion* to mean 'celebrity' is from the phrase *to see the lions* — 'to see all the noteworthy attractions of a place' (celebrities being ironically included) — which itself derives from the custom of including a visit to see the lions (kept until the 1830s in the Tower of London) as an essential part of sightseeing in the city.]

the lion's share the largest share: *When his money was divided, his wife got the lion's share.* [In the wild, the lion does in fact get the first and largest share of meat killed by the lionesses in his pride.]

put one's head in the lion's mouth to place oneself in a dangerous position: *She put her head in the lion's mouth by asking the boss for a pay rise.* [From a celebrated circus trick.]

throw (someone) to the lions to put (someone else) in a position where they will be attacked (*usu* to protect oneself): *She threw her assistant to the lions by telling the manager that he, not she, had been responsible for the mistake.* [From the Roman entertainment in which prisoners were attacked and killed by wild animals.]

lip

keep a stiff upper lip to appear very determined and unaffected by emotion: *It was difficult to know how James felt about the affair, because he always believed in keeping a stiff upper lip.*

lick one's lips (*inf*) to look forward to something with pleasure, *esp* because one expects to benefit from it: *The popular newspapers were licking their lips at the prospect of a really big political scandal.*

my *etc* lips are sealed (*often facet*) I am unable to reveal (something secret): *She told me what she was giving you for your birthday — but my lips are sealed!*

pay lip-service to (something) (*formal*) to pretend to agree with and approve of (an idea, way of thinking *etc*) without really doing so: *She has stopped even paying lip-service to the rules.*

there's many a slip 'twixt cup and lip *see* **slip.**

list

enter the lists (*rather formal*) to join in a contest or argument: *He did not wish to take sides in the dispute, but was forced to enter the* *lists to defend his reputation.* [Literally, 'to take part in a tournament', the *lists* being the arena used for jousting.]

listen

listen in 1 (*old*) to listen to a radio broadcast: *If you listen in tonight you'll hear my brother talking about his new play.* **2** (*often with* **on**) to listen intentionally to a telephone conversation, to a message intended for someone else *etc*: *It was impossible to discuss anything private over the telephone, as the operator was in the habit of listening in (on our conversations).*

listen to reason *see* **reason.**

little

make little of (something) (*rather formal*) **1** to treat (something) as unimportant, not serious *etc*: *He made little of his injuries.* **2** not to be able to understand (much of) (something): *I could make little of his instructions.*

live¹

beat/knock the living daylights out of (someone) to beat (someone) severely: *If I catch you near my personal belongings again, I'll knock the living daylights out of you!*

live and let live to tolerate other people's actions and expect them to tolerate one's own: *They thought differently about most things, but worked together on a principle of live and let live.* [Apparently from a Dutch proverb.]

live by one's wits *see* **wit.**

live (something) down to continue living in a normal way until (a wrong action, mistake *etc*) is forgotten: *It took her a long time to live down the scandal caused by her arrest.*

live from hand to mouth *see* **hand.**

live in sin *see* **sin.**

live it up (*sl*) to live in a rather too active and expensive manner: *When he went to Paris on business he wasted the firm's money by living it up in the night clubs.*

live like fighting-cocks *see* **fight.**

live like a lord *see* **lord.**

live up to (someone or something) to behave as well *etc* as (someone) or in a manner worthy of (something): *He found it difficult to live up to his brother; She did not live up to her early promise as a pianist.*

live up to one's reputation *see* **reputation.**

live²

a live wire (*inf*) a person who is full of energy and enthusiasm:

He is very quiet but his sister is a real live wire. [Literally, a wire with an electric current running through it.]

as lively as a cricket *see* **cricket.**

load

get a load of (*sl*) listen to, look at or pay attention to: *Get a load of this, folks! According to this newspaper we're about to lose our jobs!*

a loaded question a question intended to lead someone into saying, admitting or agreeing to something which he is unwilling to do: *The police kept asking him loaded questions.* [The reference is to 'loaded' dice, which are weighted so as to have a tendency always to show the same score, and thus to make it possible to cheat.]

a load off one's mind relief from something which has been worrying one: *If you could do the accounts it would be a load off my mind, because I'm no good at figures.*

loaf

half a loaf is better than no bread a saying, meaning that one should not be ungrateful for what one achieves, is given *etc*, even if it is not all that one wanted, because it is better than nothing.

use one's loaf (*inf*) to use one's brain (to act in a sensible way *etc*): *You would be able to understand his point of view if you used your loaf!*

local

local colour details in a story *etc* which are characteristic of the time or place in which it is set: *His description of the harbour added a bit of local colour to an otherwise boring book.*

lock

lock, stock and barrel completely or with all the various parts included: *They moved the business lock, stock and barrel to a new office.* [From the three main components of a gun.]

lock the stable door after the horse has bolted *see* **stable.**

under lock and key in a place which is locked: *I always keep all my medicines under lock and key so the children can't get hold of them.*

log

as easy as falling off a log (*inf*) very easy: *The machine is so well-designed that learning how to use it is as easy as falling off a log!*

sleep like a log (*inf*) to sleep very well: *After my hard day's work I slept like a log.*

loggerheads

at loggerheads (*rather formal*) quarrelling: *We have been at log-gerheads with the neighbours for years.* [A *loggerhead* was a long iron bar with a ball at the end used, when heated, for melting buckets of tar and pitch. It was probably an obvious weapon among shipwrights *etc*.]

loins

gird up one's loins (*arch or facet*) to prepare for energetic action: *Since the job had to be done, we girded up our loins and set to work*. [A Biblical phrase, from the fact that the Hebrews wore loose, flowing robes which were impractical for working or travelling in unless they were fastened up with a girdle.]

lone

a lone wolf a person who prefers to be by himself, without companions: *I am rather a lone wolf — I like to go on holiday by myself*.

long

be, get *etc* **long in the tooth** *see* **tooth**.

draw the long bow *see* **bow**[2].

go a long way to(wards) *see* **way**.

have a long face *see* **face**.

in the long run in the end; considering (something) over a period of time: *We thought we would save money, and for a week or two we did, but in the long run our spending was the same as usual*.

the long and the short of it (*inf*) the story *etc* told in a few words: *I made a mistake, and that's the long and the short of it!*

the long arm of the law *see* **arm**.

a long haul *see* **haul**.

a long shot *see* **shot**.

long-winded (*derog*) (of a speaker or his speech) tiresomely long: *I haven't time to listen to long-winded explanations!*

not long for this world (*euph*) about to die: *Mrs Williams isn't at all well — I'm sure she's not long for this world, poor soul*.

look

by the look(s) of (someone or something) judging from the appearance of (someone or something) it seems likely or probable (that): *By the looks of him, he won't live much longer*; *It's going to rain by the look of it*.

have a look of (*inf*) to look like; to resemble: *She has a look of her mother*.

look after (someone or something) to attend to or take care of (someone or something): *She is paid to look after the children*; *The secretary looks after all the complaints we receive*.

look down one's nose at *see* **nose**.

look down on (someone or something) to think of (someone or something) as being inferior: *She has always looked down on us for not having a car.*

look forward to *see* **forward.**

look in on (someone) (*inf*) to visit briefly and without invitation: *I decided to look in on Paul and Carol on my way home.*

look sharp *see* **sharp.**

look small *see* **small.**

look smart *see* **smart.**

look snappy *see* **snap.**

look the other way *see* **way.**

look to one's laurels *see* **laurels.**

look up 1 to improve or become better: *Things have been looking up lately and most of my worries have disappeared.* **2** to pay a visit to (a person): *I hadn't seen them for months so I thought it was time I looked them up.*

look up to (someone) to respect the conduct, opinions *etc* of (someone): *He has always looked up to his father.*

not much to look at (*inf*) plain or unattractive: *My dog is not much to look at, but he's very intelligent.*

not to get/have a look-in (*inf*) not to have any attention paid to one: *She is so beautiful that no-one else has a look-in when she's here.*

loom

loom large to be a very important influence, possibility *etc, esp* if likely to cause a problem or danger: *The threat of war loomed large during the emergency talks*; *The plans for her wedding loomed large in all her conversation.* [Originally a nautical term for the sudden appearing of a shadowy shape.]

loop

loop the loop (of aeroplanes *etc*) to move in a complete vertical loop or circle: *At the air display the pilots kept looping the loop.*

loose

at a loose end (*inf*) with nothing to do: *He went to the cinema because he was at a loose end.*

have a screw loose *see* **screw.**

on the loose (*inf*) enjoying a time of freedom: *She was worried about how much money her husband would spend during his weekend on the loose in London.*

lord, Lord

as drunk as a lord (*inf*) very drunk: *He went out to a reunion last night and came home as drunk as a lord.*

live like a lord to live in a very rich and luxurious manner: *He will find it difficult to adjust to life in Britain after living like a lord in the East Indies for twenty years.*

one's lord and master (*facet*) one's husband: *I don't know if we can afford to come with you to the dance — I'll have to ask my lord and master!*

lord it over (someone) (*inf*) to act like a lord, or like a master, towards (someone): *He thinks he is important enough to lord it over everyone else here.*

Lord knows who, what *etc* I do not know who, what *etc*, (and I don't believe anyone else does): *Lord knows how much trouble this is going to cause us; She went off to some party with Lord knows who.*

loss

cut one's losses to decide not to spend any more time, money *etc* on something unprofitable on which one has already wasted time, money *etc*: *I have put a lot of effort into trying to get this project started, but I have finally decided to cut my losses and abandon the idea.*

a dead loss *see* **dead.**

lose, lost

get lost (*inf*) a rude way of saying 'go away!': *Oh, get lost — I'm sick of having to listen to you!*

lose one's cool *see* **cool.**

lose face *see* **face.**

lose one's grip *see* **grip.**

lose ground *see* **ground.**

lose one's head *see* **head.**

lose heart *see* **heart.**

lose one's nerve *see* **nerve.**

lose oneself in (something) to have all one's attention taken up by (something): *to lose oneself in a book.*

lose out to suffer loss or be at a disadvantage: *She lost out by being ill and missing the party.*

lose one's rag *see* **rag.**

lose one's reason *see* **reason.**

lose sight of *see* **sight.**

lose sleep *see* **sleep.**

lose one's temper *see* **temper.**

lose the thread *see* **thread.**

lose the toss *see* **toss.**

lose touch *see* **touch.**

lose track of (someone or something) *see* **track.**

lose one's voice *see* **voice.**

lose one's way *see* **way.**

a lost cause an aim, ideal *etc* that cannot be achieved: *Trying to ban violence on television is a lost cause nowadays.*

lost on (someone) (*inf*) wasted, or having no effect, on (someone): *She has no sense of humour and his jokes are lost on her.*

lost to (something) (*formal*) no longer, or not, feeling in a certain way *etc*: *She was lost to all sense of shame.*

play a losing game to attempt to do something, carry on an argument *etc* in which it is obvious that one is not going to succeed: *By the end of the year it was obvious that we were playing a losing game in our campaign to avert closure of the factory.*

love

for the love of Mike (*inf*) an expression of exasperation or surprise: *For the love of Mike, will you sit down and stop pacing up and down the room!* [Originally an Irishism.]

not for love or money (*inf*) not in any way at all: *We couldn't get a taxi for love or money.*

there's no love lost between them they dislike one another. [This phrase originally meant exactly the opposite — the shift in meaning is unexplained.]

low

be low on (something) (*inf*) not to have much or enough of: *I'll have to go to the supermarket — we're low on coffee and sugar.*

(hunt) high and low *see* **high.**

keep a low profile *see* **profile.**

lay (someone) low (of an illness) to make (someone) ill: *I was laid low by pneumonia just before my exams.*

lie low to stay quiet or hidden: *The criminal lay low until the police stopped looking for him.*

the low-down (*sl*; *esp US*) information, *esp* confidential and/or damaging, about (a person, organization or activity): *On his first day in his new job, he managed to get the low-down on how the firm was run from one of the other employees.*

luck

down on one's luck (*formal or liter*) experiencing misfortune: *He used to be wealthy, but he's down on his luck now.*

a hard-luck story *see* **hard.**

a lucky dip a situation in which one has to accept whatever is given to one, happens *etc* without being able to make a choice: *Since none of us had ever seen any of them before, choosing a partner to* dance with was rather a lucky dip. [Literally, a fairground sideshow etc in which one chooses a parcel at random in a tub full of bran.]

push one's luck (*inf*) to risk complete failure by trying to gain too much when one has already been reasonably successful: *I think he's pushing his luck to ask for another day off this week.*

strike (it) lucky to have good luck in a particular matter: *We certainly struck lucky in choosing that school.* [An idiom from the gold- and silver-mining camps of the 1850s and 60s.]

take pot-luck *see* **pot.**

thank one's lucky stars (*inf*) to be grateful for one's good luck: *You can thank your lucky stars he didn't notice your mistake!*

third time lucky *see* **third.**

tough luck *see* **tough.**

try one's luck (at something) to try to do (something at which one may or may not be successful): *He was not sure whether he would be able to find their house, but he decided to try his luck.* [*Try* here means 'test'.]

worse luck! (*inf*) most unfortunately!: *He's allowing me to go, but he's coming too, worse luck!*

lull

lull (someone) into a false sense of security to lead (someone) to believe that everything is going well, in order to attack when they are not expecting it: *Helen thinks he has given up the fight, but Lucy says he is just trying to lull them into a false sense of security.*

lumber

be/get lumbered with (someone or something) (*inf*) to be given an unpleasant, unwanted responsibility or task: *I've been lumbered with her kids for the weekend; I got lumbered with driving her home.*

lump

if you don't like it, you can lump it (*inf*) whether you like the situation or not, you'll have to endure it: *I know working here is not very pleasant, but if you don't like it you can lump it.*

lunatic

the lunatic fringe (*derog*) the more extreme or ridiculous members of a group: *Our movement is essentially non-violent, but I'm afraid we cannot answer for the actions of some of the lunatic fringe.*

lurch

leave (someone) in the lurch (*inf*) to leave (someone) in a difficult situation and without help: *Soon after their child was born* *he went off and left her in the lurch.* [A *lurch* is a position at the end of certain games (such as cribbage) in which the loser has lost by an enormous margin, or in some games scores no points at all.]

lute
    a rift in the lute *see* **rift.**

luxury
    in the lap of luxury *see* **lap.**

M

mackerel
    a sprat to catch a mackerel *see* **sprat.**

mad
    hopping mad *see* **hop.**
    like mad (*inf*) wildly, desperately, very quickly *etc*: *We lit the fuse and ran like mad.*
    mad as a hatter *see* **hatter.**
    midsummer madness *see* **midsummer.**
    there is method in his *etc* **madness** *see* **method.**

made
    be made for (someone or something) (*inf*) to be ideally suitable for (someone or something): *John and Mary were made for each other.*
    made to measure *see* **measure.**

maid
    an old maid *see* **old.**

maiden
    a maiden lady (*formal*) a middle-aged or elderly unmarried woman: *She was a very respectable maiden lady who bred budgerigars.*
    a maiden speech (*esp Brit*) a Member of Parliament's first speech: *He made a memorable maiden speech to the House of Commons.*
    a maiden voyage a ship's first voyage: *The Titanic sank on her maiden voyage in 1912.*

main
    in the main (*formal*) mostly: *In the main, I find this composer's music pleasant to listen to.*
    splice the mainbrace *see* **splice.**
    with an eye to the main chance *see* **chance.**

with might and main *see* **might.**

make

be the making of (someone) to be the thing or person that ensures the success or improvement of (someone): *Two years in the navy will probably be the making of him!*

have the makings of (something) (*formal*) to have the clear ability for becoming (something): *Your son has the makings of an excellent engineer.*

in the making (*formal*) being made or formed at this very moment: *A revolution is already in the making — we must take care.*

make a day, night of it to spend a whole day, night enjoying oneself in some way: *As we wanted to visit the area, we decided to make a day of it and take a picnic.*

make a face *see* **face.**

make a fool of *see* **fool.**

make a go of *see* **go.**

make a meal of *see* **meal.**

make a name for oneself *see* **name.**

make a night of it *see* **make a day of it** *above.*

make a pass at *see* **pass.**

make a play for *see* **play.**

make a point of *see* **point.**

make as if to (do something) (*formal*) to behave as if one were about to (do something): *He made as if to hit me, but he was only pretending.*

make a stand *see* **stand.**

make believe *see* **believe.**

make do (with something) to use (something) as a poor quality or temporary alternative to the real thing: *There's no meat in the house, so we'll just have to make do with potatoes.*

make eyes at *see* **eye.**

make good *see* **good.**

make hay while the sun shines *see* **hay.**

make heavy weather of (something) *see* **heavy.**

make it (*inf*) to be successful: *We've made it at last — our products are selling all over the world.*

make it up (*inf*) to become friends again after a quarrel: *It's time you two made it up (with each other).*

make light of *see* **light.**

make one's mark *see* **mark.**

make merry *see* **merry.**

make much of *see* **much.**

make-or-break involving the important test that brings final success or failure to (a person, a project *etc*): *Next year will be a make-or-break year for the firm.*

make one's peace with *see* **peace.**

make one's point *see* **point.**

make the best of it/a bad job *see* **best.**

make the grade *see* **grade.**

make the most of *see* **most.**

make tracks *see* **track.**

make up for (something) to supply a reward, substitute *etc* for (disappointment, damage, loss of money or time *etc*): *This will make up for all the occasions when you've lost; Next week we'll try to make up for lost time.*

make up one's mind *see* **mind.**

make up to (someone) (*inf*) to try to gain the favour or love of (someone) by flattery *etc*: *She's always making up to the teacher by bringing him presents.*

make one's way *see* **way.**

make way *see* **way.**

on the make (*sl*) trying to make a profit (often unfairly large or illegal): *Don't trust him to give you a bargain — he's always on the make.*

man

be a marked man *see* **mark.**

be one's own man to be independent, not relying on, or controlled by, anyone else: *He's not his own man now that his mother-in-law has come to stay!*

every man jack *see* **jack.**

hit a man when he is down to attack someone who is already suffering under a misfortune, disappointment, setback *etc*: *To dismiss John from his job when his wife has just left him would be hitting a man when he is down.* [From a prohibited action in prizefighting.]

a man-about-town a man who lives and acts fashionably and in a sophisticated way: *He has become quite a man-about-town since he inherited his great-uncle's fortune.*

a Man Friday a general servant or employee who does all kinds of jobs: *He is employed as a Man Friday in a small boat-hire firm to keep the books, answer the telephone and do minor repairs to the boats.* [From the native who acts as Robinson Crusoe's servant — 'my man Friday' — in Daniel Defoe's book of 1719.]

the man in the street the ordinary, typical, average man: *The man in the street often has little interest in politics.*

a man of his word someone who is known to keep promises: *If he said he would come, he will come — he's a man of his word.*

the man of the moment the person who is dealing with, or is best able to deal with, the present situation, *esp* political: *Because of his frequent diplomatic missions to troubled parts of the world, he is often considered to be the man of the moment.*

a man of the world (*sometimes facet*) a sophisticated man who is not likely to be shocked or surprised by most things: *You can speak freely in front of John — he's a man of the world.*

man to man as one man to another; openly or frankly: *They talked man to man about their problems.*

a marked man *see* **marked.**

a no-man's-land an area which lies between two subjects, areas of interest *etc* and is usually not governed by any rules or conventions: *His book deals with the uneasy no-man's-land between sociology and politics.* [Originally the name of a piece of wasteland on the north side of medieval London where executions were carried out; later most notably applied to the wasteland between the German and Allied trenches in the 1st World War.]

odd man out *see* **odd.**

a right-hand man *see* **right.**

to a man (*rather formal*) every one, without exception: *They voted to a man to accept the proposal.*

manger

a dog in the manger *see* **dog.**

manna

manna from heaven something good which comes to one unexpectedly or by chance, *esp* as a help or comfort in difficulty: *She was very bored in hospital, and welcomed a bundle of old magazines brought from a friend as manna from heaven.* [A Biblical reference, to Exodus 16:15.]

manner

in a manner of speaking in a certain way; to a certain extent: *I suppose, in a manner of speaking, you could call me an engineer.*

to the manner born (*facet*) (as if) accustomed since birth to a particular occupation, rôle *etc*: *He speaks in public as if to the manner born.* [A Shakespearian quotation, from *Hamlet*, I. iv.]

many

many hands make light work *see* **hand.**

many happy returns *see* **return.**

map

put (a place) on the map (*inf*) to cause (a place) to be important: *The recent events in that town have certainly put it on the map.*

march

get one's marching orders (*inf*) to be dismissed (from a job *etc*): *She got her marching orders and was told never to come back.* [A military term.]

steal a march on (someone) to gain an advantage, *esp* in time, over (someone), *esp* in a secretive manner: *We stole a march on our rivals by issuing our new formula shampoo two weeks before they launched theirs.* [A military term, meaning to move an army unexpectedly while the enemy is resting.]

mare

a mare's nest a supposed discovery of something which turns out to be imaginary: *He is not a very reputable researcher — he is always discovering mares' nests.*

marine

tell that to the marines (*inf*) I do not believe you. [Originally continuing ' — the sailors won't believe it', this phrase derives from the seaman's contempt for the marine's ignorance of the sea.]

mark

be a marked man to be in danger because enemies are trying to harm one: *You are a marked man — your boss is trying to find a reason to sack you.* [*Marked* here means 'watched'.]

beside/off/wide of the mark (*formal*) off the target or subject: *His guess was rather wide of the mark.* [From archery.]

be up to the mark to reach the required or normal standard: *His work hasn't been up to the mark for some time.* [Probably from the use of a mark to represent a standard height or length for measuring goods *etc* against.]

get off the/one's mark to begin an undertaking *etc*, *esp* quickly, without wasting any time: *If you want to buy that house you had better get off the mark before someone else puts in an offer.* [From track athletics.]

make one's mark to make a permanent or strong impression: *He is beginning to make his mark as an actor.*

mark (something) down, up to bring down or increase the price of (an article for sale in a shop): *This jacket has been marked down from £10 to £8.*

mark time *see* **time.**

quick off the mark acting promptly: *The garage-owner was very quick off the mark — when he heard there was a threat of a petrol shortage he immediately put his prices up by 5p a gallon.* [Literally, starting quickly in a race.]

a soft mark *see* **soft.**

market

be in the market for (something) (*inf*) wishing to buy (something): *Are you in the market for second-hand furniture these days?*

be on the market to be for sale: *Her house has been on the market for months.*

marrow

chilled/frozen to the marrow extremely cold: *I forgot my coat and came home chilled to the marrow.* [The reference is to the marrow in the centre of one's bones.]

mass

in the mass considered as a whole, not separately: *Although there may be many sensitive, thinking people in this town, in the mass the population is bigoted and unsympathetic.*

the masses (*derog*) the ordinary people, *esp* of the working class: *I think we should have a new opera house — I don't care what the masses think.*

mast

at half mast (*facet*) (of socks, trousers *etc*) falling down: *When he was a small boy, he always arrived at school with his shirt-tail hanging out and his socks at half mast.* [Literally used of a flag flown half-way up a mast or flagpole, often signalling a death.]

before the mast (*old*) as an ordinary sailor, not as an officer or in a position of responsibility: *He spent thirty years before the mast on voyages from London to Valparaiso.* [From the position of the crew's quarters in a ship.]

nail one's colours to the mast *see* **colour.**

master

an old master *see* **old.**

a past master *see* **past.**

mat

on the mat *see* **on the carpet** *at* **carpet.**

match

be a match for (someone) to be as good at something or as successful as (someone), *esp* to be able to resist successfully a strong personality *etc*: *She very nearly bullied us into going with her,* *but John was a match for her and in the end she went by herself; When it comes to running, Tom is a match for anyone.*

meet one's match 1 to have to deal with someone who is able successfully to resist one: *John's mother has been ruling her family for years, but she's met her match in her new daughter-in-law.* **2** to meet or have to compete with someone who is as good at something as, or better than, one is oneself: *Joan talks a lot, but I think she's met her match in her new flatmate.*

material

raw material *see* **raw.**

matter

as a matter of course as something that one expects automatically to happen, be done *etc*: *You don't have to ask her — she'll do it as a matter of course.*

be the matter (*often with* **with**) to be the/a trouble, difficulty or thing that is wrong: *Is anything the matter?; What's the matter with you?; He would not tell me what the matter was.*

for that matter (used *eg* when referring to some alternative or additional possibility) as far as that is concerned: *I could go this afternoon, or, for that matter, I could go tomorrow.*

a matter of 1 used in giving quantity, time *etc* approximately: *This job will only take a matter of minutes.* **2** used in saying what is involved or necessary: *It's a matter of asking her to do it.*

a matter of life or death something of great urgency, sometimes involving the possibility that someone will lose their life: *Get the doctor to come quickly — tell him it's a matter of life and death.*

a matter of opinion something about which different people have different opinions or views: *Whether she's clever or not is a matter of opinion.*

not to mince matters *see* **mince.**

meal

make a meal of (something) (*inf*) to take more than the necessary amount of time or trouble over (something) or make (something) seem more complicated than it really is: *He really made a meal of that job — it took him four hours!*

mealy-mouthed (*derog*) not frank or sincere in what one says: *Many politicians are too mealy-mouthed to tell the plain truth.*

a square meal *see* **square.**

means

by all means (*rather formal*) yes, of course: *If you want to use the telephone, by all means do.*

by fair means *see* **fair.**

by no means 1 (*also* **not by any means**) not at all: *I'm by no means certain to win; He's not the best person for the job by any means.* **2** (*formal*) definitely not: *'Can I go home now?' 'By no means!'*

ways and means *see* **way.**

measure

for good measure as something extra or above the minimum necessary: *He ordered half a pound of steak for each guest, and five pounds extra for good measure.* [Literally 'in order not to give short weight to a customer'.]

get/have (someone's) measure/the measure of (someone) (*formal*) to form an idea or judgement of (someone): *He was not a man to be trusted, and she soon had his measure.*

made to measure (of clothing) made to fit the measurements of a particular person: *Was your jacket made to measure?*

measure up (to something) to reach (a certain required standard): *John's performance doesn't measure up (to the others).*

short measure less than the correct or stated amount: *She complained when the shopkeeper gave her short measure.*

meat

be meat and drink to (someone) to be very important in (someone's) life: *She is an old gossip, and scandal is meat and drink to her.*

one man's meat is another man's poison a saying, meaning that something liked by one person may well be disliked intensely by another. [A Latin proverb from Lucretius' *De Rerum Naturae*.]

Mecca

a/the Mecca a place which is very important to a particular group of people, and which they feel they have to visit: *St Andrews is the Mecca of golf.* [From the town in Arabia which is the birthplace of Mohammed, to which all Muslims try to make at least one pilgrimage.]

medicine

a dose/taste of (someone's) own medicine something unpleasant done to a person who is in the habit of doing the same kind of thing to other people: *He's always keeping us waiting, so I think we'll give him a dose of his own medicine and make him wait for us.*

medium

a happy medium *see* **happy.**

meet

meet (someone) halfway *see* **half.**

meet one's match *see* **match.**

meet one's Waterloo *see* **Waterloo.**

there's more to (something) than meets the eye *see* **eye.**

melt

be in the melting-pot to be in the process of changing and forming something new: *This whole area of man's thinking is in the melting-pot.* [The image is of melting down and recasting metal.]

mend

be on the mend (*inf*) to be getting better: *My broken leg is already on the mend; He has been very ill, but he's on the mend now.*

least said, soonest mended *see* **least.**

mend one's ways *see* **way.**

mention

honourable mention an award in a competition *etc* which does not entitle one to one of the prizes: *Mary won first prize at the fête for her jam, and her mother only got an honourable mention.*

not to mention (*often facet*) a phrase used to emphasize something important or to excuse oneself for mentioning something relatively unimportant: *It's far too late for you to go out and play football, not to mention the fact that it's raining.*

mercy

an angel of mercy *see* **angel.**

at the mercy of (something or someone) wholly in the power of or liable to be harmed by (something or someone): *A sailor is at the mercy of the weather; At last he had his enemies at his mercy.*

be thankful for small mercies to appreciate the small benefits, advantages *etc* which are assisting one in a generally difficult situation: *Someone stole my handbag with all my money in it, but my car-keys were in my coat pocket, so I suppose I should be thankful for small mercies.*

leave (someone) to (someone's) tender mercies *see* **tender.**

merry

make merry to enjoy oneself, *usu* in a party of some kind: *A group of young people were making merry in the bar.*

a merry-go-round an activity in which one seems to be busy without making any progress: *Trying to tidy the house while the children are at home is just a merry-go-round.* [From the fairground amusement.]

the more the merrier *see* **more.**

mess

a mess of pottage something one has received in exchange for something more valuable, a reference to the saying **to sell one's birthright for a mess of pottage:** *He has given up his legal studies to work on an oil-rig, and although he's earning a lot, it seems to me that he's sold his birthright for a mess of pottage.* [From the heading to Genesis 25 in the Geneva Bible — 'Esau selleth his birthright for a mess of pottage'.]

message

get the message (*sl*) to understand: *I kept hinting to Simon that it was time he went home, but he didn't seem to get the message.*

method

there is method in his *etc* **madness** although he seems to be doing things in the wrong way, he is in fact following a logical plan: *Despite the odd way he goes about things, he always gets people to do what he wants, so I suppose there's method in his madness.* [A reference to a Shakespearian quotation from *Hamlet*, II. ii — 'Though this be madness, yet there is method in it'.]

mettle

put (someone) on his *etc* **mettle** (*formal*) to rouse or stimulate (someone) to his best efforts: *Everyone else's fine performance put her on her mettle.*

mickey

a Mickey Finn (*sl*) a drugged drink: *They gave him a Mickey Finn and when he was unconscious they tied him up.* [Origin obscure.]

take the mick(ey) (out of someone) (*inf*) to make fun (of) or ridicule (someone or something): *He's always taking the mickey out of his little brother.*

Midas

the Midas touch (*formal*) the ability to make money easily: *He has the Midas touch, and everything he undertakes is immediately successful.* [From a king of Phrygia in Greek legend whose touch turned everything to gold.]

middle

be in the middle of (doing) (something) to be busily occupied (with something) or (doing something): *Please excuse my appearance — I was in the middle of washing my hair when the doorbell rang.*

middle-of-the-road midway between extremes; moderate: *His middle-of-the-road views do not appeal to the extremists of the party.*

midnight

burn the midnight oil to work or study until late at night: *You must have been burning the midnight oil to get that essay finished —*

yesterday you had hardly started it. [Apparently a not uncommon literary image in the 17C.]

midstream

    halt/stop/pause *etc* **in midstream** (*formal*) to pause while doing something busily, *esp* talking: *He stopped speaking in midstream when the door opened.*

midsummer

    midsummer madness (*rather old*) silly behaviour occurring during the hot weather of midsummer: *We suddenly decided to go to Paris for the weekend — I suppose it was midsummer madness, but we went.* [From the old belief that hot weather caused insanity.]

might

    high and mighty *see* **high.**

    with might and main (*liter*) with all the strength and power that one has: *He struggled with might and main to move the stone.* [An Anglo-Saxon phrase — the two words were almost synonymous in Old English, meaning 'power' and 'strength'.]

Mike

    for the love of Mike *see* **love.**

mile

    a milestone a very important event: *The discovery of penicillin was a milestone in medical history.* [Literally, a stone set at the side of the road to show the distance from a given town.]

    a miss is as good as a mile *see* **miss.**

    stand/stick out a mile (*inf*) to be very obvious: *The fact that he was very nervous stuck out a mile.*

milk

    cry over spilt milk *see* **spill.**

    a land of milk and honey *see* **land.**

    milk and water (*derog*) (something) very weak and *usu* lacking in liveliness or interest: *He spoke well, but his speech was milk and water after the fiery rhetoric of the previous speaker.*

    the milk of human kindness (*often facet*) natural kindness and pity towards other people: *She won't get any sympathy from him — he's not exactly full of the milk of human kindness.* [A Shakespearian quotation, from *Macbeth*, I. v.]

mill

    as calm as a millpond very calm: *The sea was as calm as a millpond.* [Probably suggested by the contrast between the still water in a millpond and the often fast-flowing stream which supplies it.]

grist to the mill *see* **grist.**

a millstone round (someone's) neck something that is a heavy burden or responsibility to (someone), and prevents easy progress: *He regarded his mother-in-law as nothing but a millstone round his neck.*

put (someone) through, go through the mill to put (someone) through, or to go through, a series of difficult tests or troublesome experiences: *They really put her through the mill during the inquiry, asking lots of difficult questions.* [The reference is to corn which goes through the grinding process in the mill and emerges in a refined form as flour at the other side.]

run-of-the-mill not special or unusual: *The film on television last night was very run-of-the-mill.* [Originally an American term for ungraded sawn timber as produced by a sawmill.]

million

one in a million (*not formal*) something or *esp* someone that is very special or very good in some way: *His wife has been wonderful throughout his illness — she is one in a million.*

mince

make mincemeat of (someone) (*inf*) to defeat or destroy (someone) completely, or punish them severely: *If I catch you stealing my apples again, I'll make mincemeat of you!* [From the original meaning of *mincemeat* — 'finely chopped meat'.]

not to mince matters/one's words (*formal*) to be entirely frank and open, not trying to make one's words have less effect than they should: *He didn't mince matters — he just told her she was useless.* [The only surviving use of *mince* meaning 'to soften or diminish in strength'.]

mind

bear/keep in mind to remember or take into consideration: *Bear in mind that you'll have to save some money if you want a holiday.*

be, go out of one's mind (*inf*) to be, become mad: *He must be out of his mind to think he can sail round the world in that boat; Stop making that irritating noise before I go out of my mind!*

bring to mind to cause one to remember or think of: *I had forgotten all about him but seeing his brother brought him to mind.*

change one's mind to alter one's intention or opinion (about something): *I used to think he was handsome but I've changed my mind.*

cross (someone's) mind to enter (someone's) mind for a moment only: *It did cross my mind that she might get lost, but I never seriously thought she would.*

give (someone) a piece of one's mind (*inf*) to scold or blame (someone) angrily: *If he does that again, she's going to give him a piece of her mind.*

great minds think alike (*often facet*) a saying, meaning that clever people tend to have the same ideas and opinions, and *usu* said when one discovers that someone else shares yours.

have a good mind to (do something) (*inf*) to feel very much inclined to (do something): *I've a good mind to tell your father what a naughty girl you are!*

have a mind of one's own to be able to think for oneself, not accepting other people's opinions without question: *I don't know if I can persuade my daughter to wear this dress — she may be only seven but she has a mind of her own about clothes.*

have a one-track mind *see* **one.**

have half a mind to (do something) to feel (slightly) inclined to (do something): *I've half a mind to take my holidays in winter this year.*

in one's mind's eye *see* **eye.**

in one's right mind (*usu in neg*) sane: *No-one in his right mind would behave like that.* [An idiom which probably came into widespread use as a quotation from the Bible — Mark 5:15.]

in two minds undecided: *He's in two minds about going/whether to go.*

keep an open mind *see* **open.**

keep in mind *see* **bear in mind** *above.*

keep one's mind on (something) to give all one's attention to (something): *Keep your mind on what you're doing!*

a load off one's mind *see* **load.**

make up one's mind to decide: *They've made up their minds to stay in Africa; Don't try to argue with her — her mind's made up.*

mind one's own business *see* **business.**

mind one's p's and q's *see* **p.**

mind you but (a fact, opinion *etc*) has also to be taken into consideration along with what I have just said: *I didn't believe all he said, mind you, but I suppose there might be some truth in his story; She always avoided him after his divorce — mind you, she had never had much to do with him.*

not to know one's own mind not to know what one really thinks, wants to do *etc*: *The reason she is hesitating about agreeing to marry him is that she doesn't yet know her own mind.*

out of sight, out of mind *see* **sight.**

peace of mind *see* **peace.**

presence of mind *see* **presence.**

put (someone) in mind of (something) to remind (someone) of (something): *This place puts me in mind of a book I once read.*

put/set (someone's) mind at rest to free (someone) from anxiety or worry: *If it will put your mind at rest, I'll phone Mary and make sure she did get home safely.*

put one's mind to (something) to concentrate one's thoughts on (doing something, solving a problem *etc*): *You will get all your homework done before supper if you put your mind to it.*

slip one's mind to be (*usu* temporarily) forgotten: *I meant to ask him if he could come to the party, but it slipped my mind.*

small things please small minds *see* **small.**

speak one's mind to say frankly what one means or thinks: *If you'll allow me to speak my mind, I think your plan is quite unsuitable.*

take (someone's) mind off (something) to turn (someone's) attention from (something); to prevent (someone) from thinking about (something): *A good holiday will take your mind off all the unhappiness of the past few months.*

to my mind (*rather formal*) in my opinion: *To my mind, you're better off working here than in most other places.*

mine

a gold-mine *see* **gold.**

a mine of information a plentiful source of information: *He's a mine of information about insects.*

mint

in mint condition used, but in extremely good condition: *My car is two years old, but it's still in mint condition.* [Literally, in the (unused) condition of a newly-minted coin.]

minute

up to the minute most modern, fashionable, or recent: *Her clothes are always right up to the minute.*

miscarriage

a miscarriage of justice (*formal*) a mistaken decision in a court of law *etc*: *By a miscarriage of justice the wrong man was condemned.*

mischief

do (someone/oneself) a mischief (*inf*) to hurt (someone/oneself): *I almost did myself a mischief when I tried to climb the wall.*

make mischief (*formal*) to cause trouble *etc*: *He tries to make mischief by telling the manager about the other employees' mistakes.*

228

misery

put (someone) out of his *etc* **misery** to end a period of worry, suspense *etc* for (someone) by giving him information which he wants *etc*: *Now that we know the results of the exams, I think we should publish them and put the students out of their misery.* [Originally a euphemism for killing a wounded and suffering man or animal.]

miss

give (something) a miss (*inf*) to leave (something) out, not to go to (something) *etc*: *I think I'll give the party a miss.* [A term from billiards — *to give a miss* is to give away points intentionally, by missing the ball, in order to be able to put the cue-ball in a safe position.]

hit-or-miss *see* **hit.**

a miss is as good as a mile a saying, meaning that if one fails in something it makes no difference how close one came to succeeding. [The proverb originally was *an inch of a miss is as good as a mile*.]

miss the boat/bus (*inf*) to be left behind, miss an opportunity *etc*: *I meant to send her a birthday card but I missed the boat — her birthday was last week.*

a near miss *see* **near.**

never to miss a trick *see* **trick.**

mistake

and no mistake (*inf*) without any doubt: *Henry's mother is a fierce old woman and no mistake — she terrifies me!*

mix

a mixed bag a very varied group or collection (of objects, people *etc*): *The guests at the party were a very mixed bag.* [A shooting term.]

a mixed blessing something which has both advantages and disadvantages: *My mother often looks after my children for me, but it's a mixed blessing, because she gives them too many sweets.*

mocker

put the mockers on (something) (*sl*) to ruin or destroy (a plan, enterprise *etc*), *esp* by bringing bad luck or ill fortune to it: *The terrible weather put the mockers on our church fête.* [An Australian idiom.]

moment

have one's moments (*inf*) to be good, admirable, clever *etc* at times only: *She's not a genius, but she has her moments; The film was rather dull most of the time, but it had its moments.*

the man of the moment *see* **man.**

the moment of truth (*formal or facet*) a moment when one is suddenly forced to face a crisis, make an important decision *etc*: *As the curtain rose she realized that this was the moment of truth — she would have to prove that she was good enough to be a professional singer.* [From the Spanish *el momento de la verdad*, the moment at the climax of a bullfight when the matador kills the bull.]

on the spur of the moment *see* **spur.**

a weak moment *see* **weak.**

money

be in the money (*inf*) to be wealthy: *He's in the money now, since his rich uncle died.* [Literally, to be among the prizewinners in a horse-race *etc*.]

even money *see* **even.**

for my money (*inf*) in my opinion; if I were to choose: *For my money, I'd rather have an amusing friend than an honest one.* [Literally implying that something is what one would choose to spend one's money on.]

get one's money's worth to get full value for one's money: *He didn't get his money's worth at the cinema because the film broke down in the middle.*

have money to burn to have enough money to be able to spend it in ways the speaker thinks are foolish: *If he can afford to pay such a huge sum of money for a new suit he must have money to burn.*

hush money *see* **hush.**

money for jam/old rope (*inf*) money very easily obtained: *They pay me very highly just to give them advice on exporting to Eastern Europe — it's money for jam.* [It has been suggested that *money for jam* — army slang — refers to the enormous quantities of jam supplied to the army in the 1st World War.]

money is no object *see* **object.**

money talks a saying, meaning that rich people are important and have influence simply because they are rich: *Theoretically the fact that a millionaire is involved should not influence the local council, but money talks.*

not for love or money *see* **love.**

put one's money where one's mouth is (*inf*) to supply money for a purpose which one has been saying one supports: *Many important people have been enthusiastic about our proposed day-centre, but not one of them has been prepared to put his money where his mouth is.* [Originally US.]

a (good) run for one's money *see* **run.**

spend money like water (*derog*) to spend money very freely: *She doesn't earn very much, but she spends money like water — I don't know where she gets it from.*

throw good money after bad (*derog*) to spend money in an unsuccessful attempt to get back money one has already lost: *Spending millions on trying to make that factory profitable is just throwing good money after bad.*

monkey

make a monkey out of (someone) (*inf*) to make (someone) appear stupid or ridiculous: *We cannot allow this gang of thieves to make a monkey out of the police force.*

monkey business (*inf*) mischievous or illegal happenings *etc*: *He seems to be involved in some monkey business or other.*

month

a month of Sundays (*inf: usu in neg*) an extremely long time: *You'll never finish that job in a month of Sundays.*

moon

cry for the moon to want or ask for something which is impossible to get: *She's looking for someone to offer her a glamorous, well-paid and undemanding job, but I think she's crying for the moon.*

do a moonlight (flit/flitting) (*Brit sl*) to move away suddenly, *esp* at night (*usu* to avoid people to whom one owes money): *One morning his creditors discovered he had done a moonlight flit and vanished.*

over the moon very happy and excited: *When she found out she was pregnant she was over the moon.*

moral

moral support encouragement, but not actual or physical help: *You don't have to do or say anything, but just come with me for moral support.*

more

more fool you (*inf*) you are/were foolish: *More fool you for believing him.*

more or less approximately or almost: *They've more or less finished the job; The distance is ten kilometres, more or less.*

more's the pity it is a great shame: *They've torn down many of the old buildings, more's the pity.*

the more the merrier a saying, meaning that the more (people or things) there are, the better it will be: *Why don't you come with us? The more the merrier!*

morning

the morning after the night before a morning when one has a hangover from drinking too much the previous night: *From his face, as he staggered into the office, we gathered it was the morning after the night before.*

most

at (the) most taking the greatest estimate: *There were fifty people in the audience at (the) most.*

for the most part *see* **part.**

make the most of (something) to take advantage of (an opportunity *etc*) to the greatest possible extent: *You'll only get one chance, so you'd better make the most of it!*

motion

go through the motions (*inf*) to pretend, or make an unenthusiastic attempt, to do something: *I don't really want to do this, but I suppose I'd better go through the motions (of doing it).*

set the wheels in motion *see* **wheel.**

mould

cast in the same mould (as someone) very similar (to someone): *He's cast in the same mould as his father.* [An idiom from iron-working.]

mountain

make a mountain out of a molehill to exaggerate the importance of a problem *etc*: *You don't have to assume that the child has had an accident just because he's late — you're always making mountains out of molehills.*

mouth

by word of mouth *see* **word.**

down in the mouth miserable or in low spirits: *You haven't been refused the job yet — don't look so down in the mouth!*

foam at the mouth *see* **foam.**

have a big mouth (*sl*) to be in the habit of talking too loudly or too much, or of saying things one shouldn't: *Your sister's got a big mouth — I might have known she would tell everyone our secret!*

put one's money where one's mouth is *see* **money.**

shoot one's mouth off (*sl*) to talk in a careless, loud or boastful manner: *He was in the pub last night, shooting his mouth off about what he would say to the boss if he didn't get a pay-rise.* [Originally US.]

shut/stop (someone's) mouth (*impolite*) to make (someone) be quiet, *esp* about something secret: *If you don't want anyone to know about your plans you'll have to find a way of stopping David's mouth.*

move

get a move on (*inf*) to hurry or move quickly: *Get a move on, or you'll be late!*

move heaven and earth *see* **heaven.**

on the move 1 moving from place to place: *With his kind of job, he's always on the move.* **2** advancing or making progress: *We have heard nothing about our application for weeks, but I think things are on the move at last.*

much

be too much for (someone) to overwhelm (someone); to be difficult *etc* for (someone): *Is the job too much for you?*

make much of (someone or something) to make a fuss of (someone) or about (something): *He made much of his nephew; She makes much of the fact that you lied to her.*

much of a muchness (*inf. usu derog*) (of several things) not very different: *The candidates were all much of a muchness — none of them would be suitable for the job.* [First recorded in a play by Vanbrugh in 1728, from *muchness* = size, greatness.]

not much of a not a very good or great (thing of a particular kind): *I'm not much of a photographer; That wasn't much of a lecture.*

not think much of *see* **think.**

not up to much (*inf*) not very good: *The dinner wasn't up to much.*

so much for (something) (*derog*) that shows the poor quality of (something): *He arrived half an hour late — so much for his punctuality!*

too much (*inf*) more than can be tolerated or accepted: *I can put up with his laziness, but his impudence is too much!*

without so much as (*derog*) without even: *He took my umbrella without so much as asking.*

muck

make a muck of (something) (*slang*) to make a mess of (something): *I made a muck of the interview for that job* (= I didn't do very well at it).

muck in (with someone) (*slang*) to share *eg* accommodation, work *etc* (with someone): *I mucked in with Jim till I found a flat of my own; We all mucked in and finished the job in two days.* [Originally army slang.]

muck-raking (*derog*) the activity of searching for and making public scandalous information about a person or people: *The politician said that the incident referred to in the article had occurred twenty years ago, before he became an MP, and he accused the newspaper* *of muck-raking*. [Originally from 'the Man with the Muck-Rake' in Bunyan's *Pilgrim's Progress*, who was actually an image for greed — the change in meaning came about through the other connotations of *muck*.]

mud

as clear as mud (*inf*) not at all clear: *He has explained to me twice how to do it, but it's still as clear as mud.*

my *etc* **name is mud** (*inf*) I am considered to have misbehaved; I am disapproved of: *I smacked her daughter, so my name is mud.* [*Mud* was an 18C slang term for a fool, and this phrase thus meant 'I am a fool' — but the other associations of *mud* as something worthless have since altered the meaning.]

sling/throw mud at (someone or something) to be insulting about (someone or something); to call (someone or something) names: *Ever since the politician's downfall people have been coming forward to sling mud at his achievements.*

a stick-in-the-mud *see* **stick.**

muddle

muddle through (*inf*) to progress in spite of one's unsatisfactory methods and foolish mistakes: *She is a very disorganized person but she always seems to muddle through.*

mug

a mug's game (*sl*) something which only fools would do or be involved in: *After his second divorce he decided that marriage was a mug's game and resolved not to marry again.*

mule

as stubborn as a mule very stubborn: *You will not persuade her to change her mind — she is as stubborn as a mule.*

multitude

cover a multitude of sins (*often facet*) to be able to be applied to, include or refer to a great number of different things: *He calls himself an advertising executive, which covers a multitude of sins.* [A deliberately misapplied quotation from the Bible — I Peter 3:8 'Charity shall cover the multitude of sins'.]

mum

mum's the word (*rather old*) don't say anything about (a particular subject): *I thought I'd better tell you, but remember — when you see Jane, mum's the word!* [A quotation from a play by the 18C playright George Colman, manager of the Haymarket Theatre and the source of several common phrases.]

mustard

as keen as mustard very eager or enthusiastic: *My young son only took up skiing last year, but he's as keen as mustard and skis every weekend now.* [From *keen* = 'spicy'.]

N

n

to the nth degree to the greatest extent, amount *etc* that can be imagined: *She will get everything organized in time — she is efficient to the nth degree!*

nail

as hard as nails (*derog*) (of a person) very unfeeling and lacking in pity, kindness *etc*, but able to bear a great deal of hardship or trouble: *You won't get any sympathy from Margaret — she's as hard as nails!*

hit the nail on the head to be absolutely accurate (in one's description of something or someone, in an estimate of something *etc*): *You hit the nail (right) on the head when you described her as being naive.*

nail one's colours to the mast *see* **colour.**

a nail in (someone's) coffin something which is very bad for (someone's) health, *eg* a cigarette: *Every cigarette you smoke is another nail in your coffin.*

on the nail (*inf*) immediately: *He paid cash on the nail and took the car away with him.*

tooth and nail *see* **tooth.**

naked

the naked eye *see* **eye.**

name

call (someone) names to insult (someone) by applying rude names to them: *They keep calling her names, shouting things like 'Bighead!' and 'Foureyes!'* (= someone who wears spectacles).

clear (someone's) name to prove that (someone) did not commit a crime *etc* of which they have been accused: *It took him several weeks to clear his name after it had been suggested that he had stolen some of the company's property.*

give (someone or something) a bad name to cause harm to the reputation of (someone or something): *This mix-up is the kind* *of thing that gives our firm a bad name.*

in name alone/only only by title, not really in practice: *They are married in name only, since they have been living apart for years.*

in the name of (someone) (*formal*) by the authority of (someone): *I arrest you in the name of the Queen.*

make a name for oneself to become famous, get a (*usu* good) reputation *etc*: *He made a name for himself as the first man to step on the moon.*

name-dropping mentioning the names of important or well-known persons in a way that suggests that they are one's friends in order to impress people: *Everyone is tired of his name-dropping especially since we are sure that he does not really know any of the people he mentions.*

my *etc* **name is mud** *see* **mud.**

the name of the game (*inf*) the thing that is important, central or essential (about an activity *etc*): *In manufacturing industry the name of the game is efficiency.*

name the day *see* **day.**

no names, no pack-drill if no names are mentioned, no-one will get into trouble (*usu* said to explain that one is not going to mention any names, or to advise someone else not to): *I just want to hear what happened, not who was responsible — no names, no pack-drill.* [An army phrase, from a form of punishment which involved offenders marching up and down carrying full equipment.]

not to have a penny to one's name *see* **penny.**

take (someone's) name in vain *see* **vain.**

their name is legion *see* **legion.**

to one's name owned by one or in one's possession: *He hasn't a penny to his name.*

worthy of the name that deserves to be so called: *Any doctor worthy of the name would have known what was wrong with her; This is a cause which will appeal to any Briton worthy of the name!*

you name it, he *etc* **has, has done** *etc* **it** (*inf*) he has, has done everything you can think of: *Bill has led a very adventurous life — you name it, he's done it.*

nap

catch (someone) napping (*inf*) to meet or find (someone) when they are not prepared: *The first heavy snowfall of the winter caught the roads department napping — they had no grit.* [Literally, to catch someone asleep.]

narrow

narrow-minded (*derog*) unwilling to accept ideas different from one's own: *He is so narrow-minded that he disapproves of all young people.*

a narrow squeak *see* **squeak.**

(on) the straight and narrow (path) *see* **straight.**

nasty

a nasty piece of work (*derog inf*) a person whose character and/or behaviour is extremely unpleasant: *I'm not surprised to hear that her husband is in jail for assault — I always thought he was a nasty piece of work.*

native

go native to live according to the customs, manners *etc* of a country other than one's own: *Since he has moved to Germany he has gone native, and he now eats cheese for breakfast.* [Originally (*derog*) used of white officials *etc* in Africa, India *etc* who chose to live with the native tribesmen and adopt their dress, religion *etc*.]

nature

the call of nature (*facet*) the need to go to the lavatory: *I must answer the call of nature before I leave the house.*

in a state of nature (*euph usu facet*) without any clothes on: *The neighbours were offended when she took to doing exercises on her veranda in a state of nature.*

in the nature of (something) (*formal*) having the qualities of (something): *His words were in the nature of a threat.*

second nature *see* **second.**

near

as near as dammit (*inf*) very nearly: *Our jumble sale raised £500, as near as dammit.*

a near miss something unpleasant that very nearly happened: *That was a near miss — that bus very nearly hit the cyclist.*

near the bone *see* **bone.**

near the knuckle *see* **knuckle.**

a near thing the act or state of just avoiding an accident, punishment *etc*: *I managed to avoid running the child over, but it was a near thing.*

nowhere near *see* **nowhere.**

one's nearest and dearest one's immediate family: *He liked to spend the weekends with his nearest and dearest.*

neck

be in (something) up to one's neck very much and very

seriously involved in (something, *esp* something bad): *She said she knew nothing about the robbery, but I'm sure she's in it up to her neck.*

breathing down (someone's) neck *see* **breathe.**

get it in the neck (*sl*) to be given the blame and be severely scolded or punished (for something one has done *etc*): *Clear up this mess before your father gets home, or you'll really get it in the neck!*

have the brass neck to *see* **brass.**

a millstone round (someone's) neck *see* **mill.**

neck and neck (in a race) exactly equal: *The top two students were obviously neck and neck for the class prize.* [A term from horse-racing.]

this, that *etc* **neck of the woods** (*inf*) a particular place or part of the country: *What do you do in the evenings in this neck of the woods?* [Originally a term for a remote community in the woods of the early 19C American frontier.]

a pain in the neck *see* **pain.**

risk one's neck to do something that puts one's life, job *etc* in danger: *He was aware that in joining the mountaineering expedition he was risking his neck.*

stick one's neck out (*inf*) to take a risk: *I may be sticking my neck out here but I'm willing to volunteer for the job.*

talk through the back of one's neck *see* **back.**

need

in (someone's) hour of need *see* **hour.**

the needful (*sl*) available money: *I would have come home on the train, but I didn't have enough of the needful, so I hitch-hiked.*

needs must (when the devil drives) a saying, meaning that if it is necessary to do something, act in a certain way *etc*, one has to do it even if it is disagreeable.

needle

like looking for a needle in a haystack (of a search) hopeless: *Finding a particular J Smith in the London telephone directory is like looking for a needle in a haystack.*

on pins and needles *see* **pin.**

pins and needles *see* **pin.**

neighbour

in the neighbourhood of (*formal*) approximately: *There must have been in the neighbourhood of five hundred people there.*

nellie

not on your nellie! (*sl*) certainly not: *'Would you ask your boss if we could have a pay-rise?' 'Not on your nellie!'* [Reputedly from *not* *on your puff* (= life) via Cockney rhyming slang *not on your Nellie Duff.*]

nerve

a bag/bundle of nerves a very excitable, anxious, easily frightened person: *Monica cannot work under pressure — she's just a bag of nerves.*

get on (someone's) nerves (*inf*) to irritate (someone): *Her behaviour really gets on my nerves.*

have a nerve (*inf*) to show rudeness and lack of respect in one's words or actions: *He has a nerve coming in here and telling me to make him a cup of tea!*

lose one's nerve to become frightened and lose the ability to continue with a course of action *etc*: *You will never become a good parachutist if you lose your nerve as you are about to jump.*

nest

feather one's (own) nest *see* **feather.**

a mare's nest *see* **mare.**

a nest-egg (*inf*) something saved up for the future, *usu* money: *I have a nest-egg in the bank.* [Literally, a real or artificial egg placed in a nest to encourage hens *etc* to lay more there.]

nettle

grasp the nettle to begin an unpleasant or difficult task in a firm, determined manner: *If the attic has to be cleared out, I think we should grasp the nettle and begin at once.* [From the fact that nettles are less likely to sting one if grasped firmly.]

never

never-never land an imaginary place where conditions are too good ever to exist in real life: *She failed to see disaster approaching as she lived in a never-never land where nothing could ever go wrong.* [From the idealized setting of J M Barrie's *Peter Pan*, itself suggested by the fact that *never-never land* was a 19C name for North Queensland in Australia.]

on the never-never (*inf*) by hire purchase: *They bought a new three-piece suite and a colour television on the never-never.*

new

be a new one on (someone) (*inf*) to be a problem, facet of a situation *etc* that (someone) has not previously heard of (and often does not believe in): *I must admit Mary's delicate health is a new one on me — I always thought she was perfectly fit.*

new blood *see* **blood.**

a new broom a person who has newly been given a job, responsibility *etc* and who is very enthusiastic about working hard, reforming the system *etc*. [From the saying **a new broom sweeps clean,** a new broom being more efficient than an old one.]

the New World North and South America: *Many species of monkey are only found in the New World.*

put new heart into *see* **heart.**

turn over a new leaf *see* **leaf.**

news

be news to (someone) to be a fact *etc* not previously known to (someone): *It may be true that Roger is married, but it is certainly news to me!*

break the news to tell (someone) about something, usually something unpleasant, that has happened: *I had to break the news of her daughter's death.*

no news is good news a saying, meaning that if one has had no information about a person, a project *etc* for some time, it means that all is well, as one would certainly have heard if something bad had happened.

next

next (door) to (*inf*) very nearly; virtually: *His behaviour was next door to absolute rudeness.*

next to nothing (*inf*) almost nothing: *We had a lot of cakes to sell when the sale began, but there's next to nothing left now.*

one's next of kin *see* **kin.**

nick

in good/reasonable nick (*Brit sl*) in good (*esp* physical or working) condition: *He's in very good nick just now — he's been taking a lot of exercise*; *This car's in very good nick.* [Origin obscure.]

in the nick of time at the last possible moment; just in time: *He arrived in the nick of time.* [A reference to measurements marked by notches in a stick *etc*.]

nigger

the nigger in the woodpile a hidden factor, person *etc* that is causing trouble or having a bad effect on something (*esp* deliberately): *The firm investigated its failure to get permission for any extensions to its factory and discovered that one of the local councillors was the nigger in the woodpile.* [A US expression, apparently originally attributing unexplained disappearances of food *etc* to the unseen presence of a runaway slave.]

night

make a night of it *see* **make.**

a nightcap a drink (often alcoholic) taken just before going to bed at night: *Will you have a glass of whisky as a nightcap?* [Literally, a cap worn in bed at night.]

a night-owl a person who is in the habit of staying up late at night: *Alison is a real night-owl — she never goes to bed before 3 am.*

a one-night stand *see* **one.**

nine

dressed up to the nines very carefully and strikingly dressed: *She was dressed up to the nines for her very important interview.* [Origin obscure.]

a nine days' wonder something that amazes and interests everyone for a short time and then is forgotten: *We hope that our brush with the police will prove to be a nine days' wonder and that the press will soon allow us to get back to a normal life.* [From an old saying, referred to by Chaucer, that 'there is no wonder so great that it lasts more than nine days', *ie* even the most amazing events are quickly forgotten.]

a stitch in time saves nine *see* **stitch.**

nineteen

(talk) nineteen to the dozen (*inf*) (to talk) continually or for a long time. [The reference is to someone who manages to get a greater number into a dozen (12) than ought strictly to be possible.]

nip

nip (something) in the bud to stop (something) as soon as it starts: *The managers nipped the strike in the bud.* [From the gardener's method of preventing a plant from flowering.]

nit

get down to the nitty-gritty to begin discussion *etc* of basic practical details: *I'm tired of all these vague plans — isn't it about time we got down to the nitty-gritty and worked out what we can afford?* [Originally US, of unproved etymology, but presumably invented to combine an idea of small size (*nit*) with something basic and intractable (*grit*).]

nit-picking (*inf: derog*) the act of finding unimportant faults in something: *His constant nit-picking irritates me.* [Originally US.]

no

it's no joke *see* **joke.**

no end (of) *see* **end.**

no go (*inf*) unsuccessful; useless; not getting agreement or approval: *I asked if he would agree to our plans, but it's no go, I'm afraid.*

no holds barred *see* **hold.**

a no-man's-land *see* **man.**

no news is good news *see* **news.**

no such thing *see* **thing.**

no thanks to *see* **thank.**

no time (at all) *see* **time.**

no way (*sl*) certainly not; under no circumstances: *She was looking for an invitation, but no way was I inviting her!* [Originally US.]

to no purpose *see* **purpose.**

noble

the noble savage a name for the belief that primitive people are less corrupt and more praiseworthy than civilized people: *He is committed to the idea of the noble savage and his book ignores many unpleasant and even repellent features of the culture of this tribe.* [A quotation from Dryden, developed as a theory by the 18C French philosopher Rousseau.]

nobody

like nobody's business (*inf*) very hard or energetically: *Our secretary works very hard, typing away like nobody's business*; *It was a dreadful day — it rained like nobody's business from dawn to dusk.*

nobody's fool *see* **fool.**

nod

have a nodding acquaintance (with someone or something) to know (someone or something) slightly: *I have only a nodding acquaintance with some of the staff here*; *I have a nodding acquaintance with Greek literature.* [From the greeting once considered correct for a person one knew only slightly.]

the Land of Nod (*old or facet*) sleep: *All the children were in the Land of Nod.* [From a place mentioned in the Bible — Genesis 4:16 — because of the association of nodding with falling asleep.]

nod off (*inf*) to fall asleep: *He nodded off while she was speaking to him.*

on the nod by general agreement, without actually taking a vote: *The resolution was passed by the committee on the nod.*

noise

a big noise (*sl*) a very important person: *He is a big noise in the world of archaeology — I think he discovered a lost civilization.* [Originally US.]

empty vessels make most noise *see* **empty.**

none

none of (something) an expression used to tell a person not to do something or to stop doing something (*usu* something bad): (*I'll have) none of your impertinence* (= Don't be impertinent); *None of that!* (= Stop doing that!)

none other than the very same person as: *The man who had sent the flowers was none other than the man she had spoken to the night before.*

none the wiser *see* **wise.**

none the worse for *see* **worse.**

none too (*slightly facet*) not very: *He lent me a handkerchief which had obviously been in his pocket for weeks and was none too clean.*

nonsense
stuff and nonsense *see* **stuff.**

nook
every nook and cranny (*inf*) everywhere: *They searched in every nook and cranny (of the house).* [*Nook* is 'a corner', *cranny* 'a crack'.]

noose
put one's head in a noose *see* **head.**

nose
cut off one's nose to spite one's face (*derog*) to proceed with an action which harms oneself rather than miss the opportunity which it offers of harming someone else: *Handing in your resignation just because you've had a difference of opinion with the boss would be cutting off your nose to spite your face.*

follow one's nose (*not formal*) to go straight forward: *When you get to the corner just turn right and follow your nose.*

keep one's nose clean (*inf*) to keep out of trouble by not behaving badly or dishonestly: *We don't want the police visiting our premises, so we'd better make sure we keep our noses clean.*

keep (some)one's nose to the grindstone *see* **grind.**

lead (someone) by the nose to make (a person) do whatever one wants: *She leads her husband by the nose.* [The reference is to a bull with a ring in its nose, forced to be docile and obedient.]

look down one's nose at (someone) to think of and/or treat (someone) with contempt: *His mother looks down her nose at his wife.*

a nosey parker (*derog inf*) someone who takes too much interest in other people and what they are doing: *I don't see why I should tell her all my plans — she's just an old nosey parker.* [Origin unknown.]

no skin off one's nose *see* **skin.**

pay through the nose (*sl*) to pay a lot for something: *If you want a really good car you have to pay through the nose for it.*

poke one's nose into (*inf: derog*) to interfere with other people's

243

business: *He is always poking his nose into my affairs.* [The reference is to an animal such as a dog.]

put (someone's) nose out of joint to take (someone's) place as the one loved by someone else: *Their three-year-old is very spoilt — the new baby will certainly put her nose out of joint.*

rub (someone's) nose in it to remind (someone) very often of something they have done wrong: *I know I should have accepted that job when I was offered it, but I do wish you would stop rubbing my nose in it!* [From a frequently recommended method of house-training animals.]

see beyond/further than the end of one's nose (*usu in neg*) to understand more than simply what is happening in the present; to see what future effect one's actions will have *etc*: *If he could see beyond the end of his nose he would know that his strictness will result in his children resenting him.*

thumb one's nose at *see* **thumb.**

turn up one's nose (at something) to treat (something) with contempt: *The child turned up his nose at the school dinner.*

under (someone's) (very) nose 1 right in front of (someone); clearly to be seen by (someone): *The book I was looking for was right under my very nose.* **2** while (someone) is there: *He stole my jewels from under my very nose.*

note

of note (*formal*) famous, distinguished or important; worth mentioning : *No-one of note was at his party.*

strike the right note to say, do *etc* (something suitable or pleasing to someone): *The Prime Minister's speech struck just the right note.* [A musical idiom.]

nothing

be/have nothing to do with (someone) to be something which (someone) should not be interested in: *That letter is/has nothing to do with you.*

come to nothing (*rather formal*) to fail: *His plans came to nothing.*

for nothing 1 free; without payment: *We bought these six chairs, and they gave us the other one for nothing.* **2** (*usu with* **all**) without result; in vain: *I've been working on this book for six years, and all for nothing!*

go for nothing to have no result; to be wasted: *All his notes were destroyed in the fire — three years of research gone for nothing!*

have nothing on (someone) (*inf*) **1** to be not good *etc* enough to compete with (someone): *Mary may be forgetful, but she has* *nothing on my wife!* **2** to have no evidence of (someone's) wrong or immoral behaviour: *The foreman has wanted to dismiss me for years, but he can't because he has nothing on me.*

have nothing to do with (someone or something) to avoid (someone or something) completely: *I will have nothing to do with anything illegal*; *After he came out of prison, many of his former friends would have nothing to do with him.*

like nothing on earth *see* **earth.**

make nothing of (something) (*formal*) not to understand (something): *I can make nothing of this letter.*

next to nothing *see* **next.**

nothing but just; only: *The fellow's nothing but a fool!*; *'Does he drink whisky?' 'Nothing but!'*

nothing doing! (*inf*) an expression used to show a strong or emphatic refusal: *'Would you like to go to the meeting instead of me?' 'Nothing doing!'*

nothing if not certainly; very: *His life has been nothing if not exciting.*

nothing of the kind *see* **kind.**

nothing short of *see* **short.**

nothing to write home about *see* **home.**

nothing ventured, nothing gained a saying, meaning that one cannot achieve anything without taking risks.

stop at nothing *see* **stop.**

sweet nothings *see* **sweet.**

there is *etc* **nothing for it but (to do something)** the only possible thing (to do) is (something): *When the boat hit a rock and sank, there was nothing for it but to swim for the shore.*

there is *etc* **nothing to choose between (two or more people, things etc)** there is hardly any difference of quality *etc* between (two or more people or things): *I don't know whether Jim or Jack will win — there's nothing to choose between them.*

there is nothing to it (*inf*) it is easy: *You'll soon see how to do this job — there's nothing to it!*

think nothing of (something) not to consider it difficult, unusual *etc* (to do something): *My father thought nothing of walking five miles to school every day when he was a boy.*

think nothing of it it doesn't matter; it is not important: *'Thank you so much for your help.' 'Think nothing of it!'*; *'I'm sorry my dog tore your trousers.' 'Oh, think nothing of it.'*

to say nothing of (something) as well as (something); and in addition: *When her mother comes to stay with us, she brings all her jewellery with her, to say nothing of her three fur coats.*

notice

  at short notice *see* **short.**

now

  as of now from this time on: *These new rules apply as of now.*

  every now and then/again sometimes; occasionally: *We go to the theatre every now and then; I see him at the club every now and again.*

nowhere

  get nowhere (*inf*) to (cause someone to) make no progress; to get or produce no results: *Flattering me will get you nowhere.*

  nowhere near (*inf*) not nearly: *We've nowhere near enough money to buy a car.*

nude

  in the nude without clothes: *She always sunbathes in the nude.*

number

  his *etc* days are numbered *see* **day.**

  get (someone's) number (*sl*) to find out what kind of person (someone) is: *He is a very argumentative man — fortunately I had got his number within five minutes of being introduced to him and was careful to agree with everything he said.* [Origin unknown.]

  in penny numbers *see* **penny.**

  his *etc* number is up (*inf*) he is about to die, to suffer something unpleasant *etc*: *When the police arrived, the thieves knew their number was up.* [The reference is to numbers in a lottery, and to the display of winning — or in this case losing — numbers.]

  number one (*inf*) oneself: *No matter how unselfish you are, there comes a time when you have to think first of number one.*

  (someone's) opposite number *see* **opposite.**

  there's safety in numbers *see* **safe.**

nut

  be nuts about (something or someone) (*inf*) to be very enthusiastic or keen (about something or someone), often to a ridiculous extent: *He's nuts about her/cars/football.*

  do one's nut (*sl*) to become extremely angry and show one's anger: *I tore my new dress climbing a tree and my mother did her nut about it.*

  a hard nut to crack a difficult problem: *Finding the money to launch our new firm will be a hard nut to crack.*

  in a nutshell expressed, described *etc* very briefly: *It would take* *hours to describe exactly what happened, but in a nutshell he tried to make us look silly and failed.*

the nuts and bolts (*not formal*) the basic facts or important practical details about something: *After ten years as sales manager he is very familiar with the nuts and bolts of export marketing.*

O

oar

put/stick one's oar in (*derog inf*) to interfere in what another person is saying, doing *etc* by offering opinions *etc* when they are not wanted: *We were quite capable of coming to an agreement without your help — no-one asked you to stick your oar in.* [From an old expression *to have an oar in another man's boat* = to have an interest in someone else's affairs.]

rest on one's oars to rest, *esp* after working very hard: *After the hard work of the last few weeks, I think I am entitled to rest on my oars for a day or two.* [From rowing.]

oats

off one's oats (*slightly facet*) not very well and therefore not eating much: *She hasn't actually been ill in bed, but she has been off her oats for a week or so.* [Literally used of horses.]

sow one's wild oats *see* **wild.**

object

money *etc* **is no object** money is not considered important in the particular circumstances which apply: *He likes to do a job well — time is no object; sometimes he works on a project for months.* [Originally *money is no object* actually meant 'I *etc* am not primarily trying to make money from this' — the present uses arose from misapplications of the phrase, which was much used in advertisements.]

occasion

rise to the occasion to be able to do what is required in an emergency *etc*: *He had never been asked to chair a meeting before, but he rose to the occasion magnificently.*

ocean

a drop in the ocean *see* **drop.**

odd

be at odds (with someone) (*formal*) to be quarrelling, not in agreement *etc* (with someone), *usu* over a particular matter: *He has been at odds with his brother for years over the money their father left them.*

make no odds to be unimportant: *We haven't got quite as much money as we wanted, but that makes no odds.* [In this phrase, and **what's the odds** below, *odds* simply means 'difference'.]

an oddball (*inf*) a person who behaves in a strange way: *A lot of people look on me as a bit of an oddball but I don't care.* [Originally US.]

odd man out/odd one out 1 a person or thing that is different from others: *In this test, you have to decide which of these three objects is the odd man out.* **2** a person or thing that is left over when teams, sets *etc* are made up: *When they chose the two teams, I was the odd man out.* [From a method of selection among an uneven number of people by tossing a coin *etc*.]

odds and ends small objects *etc* of different kinds: *There were various odds and ends lying about on the table; We have moved all our furniture to our new house — we just have to collect the odds and ends.*

over the odds more than expected, normal, necessary *etc*: *I know he has never liked my brother, but some of the things he said to me about him were rather over the odds.* [From horse-racing — literally 'more (money) than one's winning bet actually entitles one to'.]

what's the odds? it's not important; it doesn't matter: *We didn't win the competition but what's the odds?* [See **make no odds** above.]

odour

in bad odour (with someone) having a bad reputation (with someone); disapproved of (by someone): *He is in bad odour with the press because he is always being rude to journalists.*

an odour of sanctity (*derog, usu facet*) an atmosphere of excessive holiness or goodness: *There is such an odour of sanctity about her it is difficult to believe she is really human.* [From a French term for the sweet smell reputed to come from the dead bodies of saints, especially when exhumed some time after burial.]

off

badly, well off *see* **bad, well.**

fall off *see* **fall.**

go off 1 (*inf*) to begin to dislike (someone or something once liked): *I went off that girl when I met her friends.* **2** (of food) to become rotten or less good: *That milk has gone off — we can't drink it.*

have it off *see* **have.**

in the offing (*inf*) about to happen, appear *etc*: *He has a new job in the offing.* [A nautical term — the *offing* is the whole area of sea that can be seen from a particular point on shore.]

off and on/on and off (*inf*) sometimes; occasionally: *I see him off and on at the club.*

the off season the period, at a hotel, holiday resort *etc*, when there are few visitors: *Although the town is busy in the summer, it's very quiet in the off season.*

off the cuff *see* **cuff.**

off the peg *see* **peg.**

off the hook *see* **hook.**

off the rails *see* **rail.**

off the record *see* **record.**

on the off-chance because of a slight chance (that something might be so, happen *etc*): *We waited, on the off-chance (that) he might come.*

put (someone or something) off *see* **put.**

put (someone) off (something) *see* **put.**

put (someone) off his *etc* **stroke** *see* **stroke.**

office

through the (kind) offices of (someone) (*very formal*) with the help of (someone): *I got the job through the kind offices of a friend.*

oil

burn the midnight oil *see* **midnight.**

no oil painting (*inf*) not very attractive to look at: *Mark is a very nice person, but he's no oil painting.*

oil the wheels to make something easier to do or obtain: *It would have taken a long time to get permission to build a new house but fortunately my father knew the chairman of the planning committee and that helped to oil the wheels a bit.* [From the fact that wheels turn more easily when oil is applied to them.]

pour oil on troubled waters to try to calm and soothe a person, a difficult situation *etc*: *He is always getting into arguments with people, and his wife spends a lot of time pouring oil on troubled waters.* [From an old method of calming the sea temporarily.]

strike oil (*not formal*) to be successful, find what one is looking for *etc*: *We've been looking for a suitable house for years and this time I think we've struck oil.*

ointment

a fly in the ointment *see* **fly.**

old

> **any old how** *see* **any.**
>
> **as old as the hills** *see* **hill.**
>
> **money for old rope** *see* **money.**
>
> **an old boy/girl** a former pupil (of a school): *Did you join the old girls' association?*; *The new prime minister is an old boy of our school.*
>
> **the old boy network** a group of people, *usu* upper-class, who are all closely connected and who share information and get jobs *etc* for one another: *It is often maintained that most government departments are staffed by the old boy network.* [An allusion to the fact that the basic connection between such people is often that they were at school together.]
>
> **the old country** the country from which an immigrant or his parents, grandparents *etc* originally came: *Many people emigrating to America settled in the areas that reminded them most of the old country.*
>
> **the old guard** the older and less modern members of a group: *His proposals for reform were vigorously opposed by the old guard.* [From the title — *l'Ancienne Garde* — of the most experienced section of the Imperial Guard, the élite of Napoleon's army.]
>
> **an old hand** (*inf*) a person who is very experienced (at doing something): *He's an old hand at this sort of job.*
>
> **an old maid** (*derog*) a woman who has never married: *She married the first man who proposed to her, for fear of being an old maid.*
>
> **an old master** any great painter or painting of a period before the 19C, especially of the 15C and 16C: *He has a very valuable collection of old masters.*
>
> **the old school** people whose ideas *etc* are the same as those which were important in the past: *Her father is a member of the old school who believe in the importance of obedience to one's parents.*
>
> **an old timer** (*slightly derog*) an old person, *esp* one who has been doing a particular job *etc* for a long time or did it a long time ago: *The new manager's innovations were resented by the old timers on the staff.* [Originally US.]
>
> **a ripe old age** *see* **ripe.**

olive

> **an olive branch** a sign of a wish for peace: *The prime minister's remarks were interpreted as an olive branch held out to all his opponents who had fled the country.* [A symbol for peace in the ancient world.]

on

> **be on to (someone)** (*inf*) to have discovered (someone's) trick, secret *etc*: *The thieves realized that the police were on to them.*

fall on *see* **fall.**

on and off *see* **off.**

once

    give (someone or something) the once-over to look at, study or examine (someone or something) quickly: *I haven't got much time but I'll give your report the once-over.*

    once and for all decisively; finally: *Once and for all, I refuse!* [Originally *once for all*.]

    once in a while occasionally: *I meet him once in a while at the club.*

one

    be at one (with someone) (*formal*) to be in agreement with (someone): *We are at one with the government in this matter.*

    be one up on (someone) (*inf*) to have an advantage over (someone): *We brought out a book on this before our rivals so we're one up on them.*

    have a one-track mind to think of only one thing all the time: *He has a one-track mind — he never talks about anything but politics.*

    not be oneself to look or feel different from usual, because of illness, anxiety *etc*: *I'd better go home — I'm not myself today.*

    number one *see* **number.**

    one and all everyone; all (of a group): *Good evening, one and all; This was agreed by one and all.*

    one by one (of a number of people, things *etc*) each one alone; one after the other: *The boss wants to see each member of staff one by one; He examined all the vases one by one.*

    one for the road *see* **road.**

    a one-horse race a competition *etc* in which one side or person is certain to win: *As the day of the election drew closer it began to look more and more like a one-horse race.* [Racing slang.]

    one in a million *see* **million.**

    one in the eye *see* **eye.**

    a one-man show an activity, planned operation *etc* in which one person appears to be doing everything and getting all the attention: *Anything Paul is involved in tends to become a one-man show, much to everyone else's annoyance.* [A theatrical term.]

    a one-night stand a state of affairs, arrangement, relationship *etc* that lasts only for one evening or night: *He was afraid of getting involved with women and made sure that all his relationships with them were only one-night stands.* [Literally, a single concert *etc* in one place performed by musicians *etc* on tour.]

    one-off (*inf*) (something) made, intended *etc* for one occasion only: *It's just a one-off (arrangement)*.

(just) one of those things *see* **thing.**

one-sided 1 (of a competition *etc*) with one person or side having a great advantage over the other: *That match was rather one-sided — one of the players was much older than the other.* **2** seeing, accepting or representing only one aspect of a subject: *a one-sided view of the problem.*

one way and another *see* **way.**

with one voice *see* **voice.**

onion

know one's onions to know one's job, the subject one studies *etc* well: *It was obvious that the mechanic knew his onions and would have our car working again soon.*

only

only too very: *I'll be only too pleased to come.*

open

bring (something) out into the open to make (something) public: *The affair has been kept secret for too long — it's time it was brought out into the open.* [Literally, 'to bring (something) out from a hiding-place'.]

come (out) into the open to make one's opinions known: *At first, he made no criticism of the government, but eventually he came out into the open and attacked its policies.*

in the open air outside; not in a building: *If it doesn't rain, we'll have the party in the open air.*

keep an open mind to have a willingness to listen to or accept new ideas, other people's suggestions *etc* (*eg* before making a decision): *It doesn't seem to be a very good plan, but I think we should keep an open mind about it for the time being.*

keep open house to be prepared to receive and give food *etc* to anyone who comes or is brought to one's house: *They keep open house for all their children's friends.*

keep one's options open *see* **option.**

lay oneself open to (something) to put oneself in a position where one is likely to receive (blame, criticism, insults *etc*): *If you give him a gift in return for his help, you'll be laying yourself open to charges of corruption.*

open and shut (of a case, problem *etc*) simple, obvious and/or easily decided: *When they found his wife's fingerprints on the murder weapon, the police thought it was an open-and-shut case.*

an open book *see* **book.**

open (someone's) eyes to *see* **eye.**

open fire *see* **fire.**

an open secret something known to many people although supposed to be a secret: *It's an open secret that he is having an affair with the boss's wife.*

with one's eyes open *see* **eye.**

with open arms in a very friendly way: *They received their visitors with open arms.*

operate

the operative word(s) the most important word(s) (in a phrase, document, statement *etc*): *The operative words in that instruction are 'if possible'. If it isn't possible, we don't need to comply with it.* [Literally a legal term for the actual words in a document which express the purpose of the document — *eg* 'devise and bequeath' in a will.]

opinion

a matter of opinion *see* **matter.**

opposite

(someone's) opposite number (*inf*) the person who does the same job *etc* as (someone) in another company, country *etc*: *Our sales manager is having discussions with his opposite number in their firm.*

the Opposition (*Brit*) the main political party which is opposed to the governing party: *The Opposition voted against the bill.*

option

keep one's options open to delay making a definite decision about what one will do *etc* for as long as possible: *Don't refuse the offer immediately — it is always good to keep your options open.*

a soft option *see* **soft.**

order

be in, take (holy) orders (*formal*) to be, or become, a priest, minister *etc*: *Her brother has trained to be a priest and takes orders next month.*

get one's marching orders *see* **march.**

in apple-pie order *see* **apple.**

in (good) running/working order (of a machine *etc*) working well or able to work well: *The car is in good running order; The machines are all in working order.*

in short order quickly and at once: *When the burglars saw the police car they left the factory premises in short order.* [*Short order* is a US term for a portion of food *etc* that can be prepared quickly on request in a cafe *etc*.]

in working order *see* **in (good) running order** *above.*

on order having been ordered but not yet supplied: *We don't have any copies of this book at the moment, but it's on order.*

the order of the day something necessary, normal, common or particularly fashionable at a certain time: *Hats with feathers are the order of the day at fashionable weddings this year.* [Originally the term for the list of items for discussion in Parliament on a particular day.]

out of order 1 not working (properly): *The machine is out of order.* **2** (*formal*) not correct according to what is regularly done, *esp* in meetings *etc*: *The last speaker was out of order in saying that.*

the pecking order *see* **peck.**

a tall order *see* **tall.**

ordinary

out of the ordinary unusual: *I don't consider her behaviour at all out of the ordinary.*

other

every other using, involving *etc* one person or thing in a series, then leaving or not involving the next before going on to the next again: *Leave every other line on the exam paper blank* (= Write on one line, leave the next one blank, then write on the next *etc*); *I work only every other day.*

look the other way *see* **way.**

or other not known or not decided; by some means if not by another: *He must have hidden it somewhere or other; Somehow or other we shall have to get there.*

pass by on the other side *see* **side.**

out

be, go out of one's mind *see* **mind.**

be well out of *see* **well.**

fall out *see* **fall.**

have it out (with someone) *see* **have.**

out and about (of a person who has been ill in bed, in hospital *etc*) well enough to go out, go to work *etc*: *He was very ill for a while, but he's out and about again.*

out-and-out (*rather formal*) complete; very bad: *He's an out-and-out liar.*

out at elbow *see* **elbow.**

out for (something) (*inf*) wanting or intending to get (something): *She is out for a good time* (= enjoyment).

out of commission *see* **commission.**

out of hand *see* **hand.**

out of it (*inf*) not part of, or wanted in, a group, activity *etc*: *I felt a bit out of it at the party since I was the only one who couldn't dance.*

out of mind *see* **out of sight, out of mind** *under* **sight.**

out of order *see* **order.**

out of pocket *see* **pocket.**

out of (all) proportion *see* **proportion.**

out of sight *see* **sight.**

out of sorts *see* **sort.**

out of the ordinary *see* **ordinary.**

out of touch *see* **touch.**

out of turn *see* **turn.**

out of work *see* **work.**

out on a limb *see* **limb.**

out to (do something) (*inf*) determined to (do something): *He is out to win the race.*

out with it! (*inf*) say what you want to say or have to say *etc*: *You obviously know more than you have told us so far — out with it, then!*

take it out of (someone) *see* **take.**

take it out on (someone) *see* **take.**

outside

at the outside (*inf*) at the most: *I shall be there for an hour at the outside.*

outstay

outstay one's welcome *see* **welcome.**

over

be all over (someone) (*usu derog*) to make (too much of) a fuss of (someone); to be (too) friendly towards (someone): *As soon as she realized her guest was a member of the Royal family, she was all over him.*

be over the hump *see* **hump.**

fall over oneself *see* **fall.**

over and above (*formal*) in addition to: *Over and above my normal duties, I have on occasion to assist the office manager.*

over and done with finished; no longer important: *He has behaved very wickedly in the past but that's all over and done with now.*

over and over (again) continually repeated: *He sang the same song over and over (again).*

over my dead body *see* **dead.**

over the hill *see* **hill.**
over the odds *see* **odd.**
over the top *see* **top.**

overboard

go overboard (about/for something) (*inf: often derog*) to be very enthusiastic, often too enthusiastic (about someone or something): *She's gone overboard about that new pop-group; The child has gone overboard for that building toy.*

overdo

overdo it to work too hard: *You've been overdoing it recently — you need a holiday.*

own

be one's own man *see* **man.**

come into one's own to have the chance to show one's good qualities, abilities, intelligence *etc*: *She is very calm and efficient, and really comes into her own when everyone else is panicking during a crisis.* [Literally, to take possession of something to which one has a right.]

do one's (own) thing *see* **thing.**

get one's own back (on someone) (*inf*) to revenge oneself (on someone): *He has beaten me this time, but I'll get my own back (on him).*

get/have one's own way *see* **way.**

hold one's own to be as successful in a fight, argument *etc* as one's opponent: *The others tried to prove that he was wrong, but he managed to hold his own.*

in one's own right *see* **right.**

(just) one of those things *see* **thing.**

(all) on one's own 1 alone: *He lives on his own.* **2** with no-one else's help: *He did it (all) on his own.* [The second meaning is the original.]

own up (to something) to admit (that one has done something): *Who did this? Own up!; He owned up to having broken the window.*

oyster

the world is his *etc* **oyster** he can go anywhere and do anything: *You're talented, young, healthy and wealthy — the world's your oyster!* [A quotation from Shakespeare — *The Merry Wives of Windsor,* II. ii.]

P

p

mind one's p's and q's (*inf*) to be very careful: *Mind your p's and q's if you don't want to annoy him!*

pace

keep pace with (someone or something) to maintain a position of knowledge, understanding, control, equality *etc* with regard to (someone or something): *It is difficult to keep pace with scientific discoveries.* [Literally, in a race, 'to go as fast as someone else'.]

put (someone or something) through his *etc* paces to make (someone or something) show what they are capable of: *The fine weather gave him an opportunity to put his new car through its paces.* [From the standard method of assessing the quality of a horse by watching it move in all four gaits (*paces*).]

set the pace for to go forward at a particular speed which everyone else has to follow: *Her experiments set the pace for future research.* [From racing.]

show one's paces to show what one can do: *The new sales manager was able to show his paces at the sales conference.* [Literally used of horses (*see* **put (someone or something) through his paces** *above*).]

stay the pace to maintain progress in any activity at the same rate as everyone else: *If we are to remain successful as a company we must stay the pace during this period of rapid technological change.*

pack

no names, no pack-drill *see* **name**.

pack it in (*sl*) to stop doing whatever one is doing: *I'm tired of hearing your complaints, so just pack it in!*; *I hate working — I'm going to pack it in and go on holiday.* [From an earlier *pack the game in*, presumably implying 'put away the equipment'.]

packed like herring in a barrel *see* **herring**.

packed like sardines *see* **sardine**.

packed out (*inf*) containing as many people as possible: *The theatre/meeting was packed out.*

pack up (*sl*) to stop working or operating: *We'd only gone five miles when the engine packed up*; *At one point the doctor thought her kidneys were packing up, but she's all right now.* [1st World War army slang, from packing up equipment on ceasing a particular operation *etc*.]

send (someone) packing (*inf*) to send (someone) away firmly

257

and without politeness: *He tried to borrow money from me again, but I soon sent him packing.* [From an old use of *pack* meaning 'to leave in a hurry'.]

paddle

paddle one's own canoe *see* **canoe.**

pain

be at pains/take pains (*formal*) to take great trouble and care (to do something): *She was at pains to explain that she had only been out for five minutes; He took great pains to make sure we enjoyed ourselves; She always takes pains with her work.*

for one's pains (*formal or facet*) as a (poor) reward for one's trouble and effort (in doing something): *She looked after him for years, and all she got for her pains was rudeness.*

on pain of (something) (*formal or facet*) at the risk of being given (some kind of punishment): *The employees were forbidden, on pain of instant dismissal, to tell anyone about their work.*

a pain in the neck (*derog inf*) a person who is constantly annoying: *People who are always complaining are a pain in the neck!* [Originally such a person was said to *give one a pain in the neck*, for reasons which are obscure.]

paint

no oil painting *see* **oil.**

paint the town (red) to go out and enjoy oneself in a noisy and expensive manner: *He inherited a lot of money and proceeded to paint the town (red) with it!* [Originally 19C US.]

pair

pair off to join together with one person to make a pair: *The boys and girls all paired off at the party.*

pale

beyond the pale outside the normal limits of good behaviour, what is acceptable *etc*: *Her behaviour is really beyond the pale!* [*The Pale* was, *esp* in the 16C, the limited area of English government either around Calais or around Dublin, the people who lived outside it in the latter case being regarded as uncivilized barbarians.]

palm

grease (someone's) palm (*sl*) to give (someone) money: *We had to grease the palm of numerous officials before they would allow us to collect our luggage from the airport.*

have an itching palm *see* **itch.**

have (someone) in the palm of one's hand to have (someone) in one's power or ready to act *etc* as one wishes: *He has the local press in the palm of his hand and is never criticized by any of them.*

palm (something or someone) off on (someone) (*inf*) to get rid of (an undesirable thing or person) by giving, selling it *etc* to (someone else): *His car was always breaking down so he palmed it off on his brother.* [From illusion and trickery performed by concealing objects in the palm of one's hand.]

pan
a flash in the pan *see* **flash.**

pants
(be caught) with one's pants/trousers down (*inf*) (to be revealed) at an embarrassing moment, *esp* because one is shown to be completely unprepared to act, respond *etc*: *Judging from his evasive answer to such a pertinent question the politician had obviously been caught with his pants down.*

paper
on paper in theory, but not in practice: *The idea seemed all right on paper, but they soon found that it didn't work.*

paper over the cracks (*inf*) to pretend that no mistake has been made or that there has been no argument: *He was very anxious, after a stormy board meeting, that they should paper over the cracks and present their decision as unanimous.* [From the practice of hiding cracks in the wall of a house with wallpaper.]

par
below par/not up to par 1 not up to the usual standard: *Your work is not up to par this week.* **2** (*inf*) not well: *She had a cold and was feeling below par.*

on a par with (something) as good as (something): *I enjoy cooking, but my results are not on a par with yours.*

par for the course what might have been expected; what usually happens, *esp* if bad: *On our last trip to the beach one of the children got sand in her eye and the other fell in the sea, which was just about par for the course.* [From golf — literally, the number of strokes that would be made in a perfect round on that course.]

paradise
a fool's paradise *see* **fool.**

pardon
beg (someone's) pardon to say one is sorry (*usu* for having offended someone else *etc*): *I've come to beg (your) pardon for being so rude this morning.*

parrot

parrot-fashion (*inf*) without understanding the meaning of what one has learnt, is saying *etc*: *He just repeats what his father says, parrot-fashion.*

sick as a parrot *see* **sick.**

part

for my *etc* **part** (*formal*) as far as I am concerned: *He is very worried, but for my part I can't see anything wrong.*

for the most part (*rather formal*) mainly or chiefly: *For the most part, the passengers on the ship were Swedes.*

part and parcel (*inf*) something which is naturally part (of something): *Doing this is part and parcel of my work.*

part company 1 (*formal*) to go in different directions: *We parted company at the bus-stop.* **2** (*less formal*) to leave each other or end a friendship, partnership *etc*: *My husband and I finally parted company because he was having an affair with another woman.*

the parting of the ways the point at which people must take different decisions, follow different courses of action *etc*: *After ten years of collaboration, I'm afraid we have come to the parting of the ways.* [A Biblical reference — to Ezekiel 21:21.]

take (something) in good part to accept (something) without being hurt or offended: *He took their jokes in good part.*

take (someone's) part to support (someone) in an argument *etc*: *His mother always takes his part.*

take part in (something) to be one of a group of people doing (something); to take an active share in (*eg* playing a game, performing a play, holding a discussion *etc*): *She takes part in many student activities.*

party

the party line the ideas and opinions approved by the leaders of a particular group: *He always follows the party line in his public speeches so it is difficult to know what he really thinks.*

the party's over (*inf*) a particularly happy, favourable, enjoyable *etc* time has come to an end: *The boss is back from his holidays tomorrow, so I'm afraid the party's over as far as the office is concerned.*

pass

in passing (*rather formal*)while doing or talking about something else; without explaining fully what one means: *He told her the story, and said in passing that he did not completely believe it.*

let (something) pass to ignore (something) rather than take the trouble to argue about it: *I didn't quite see the connection he was* making between his health and the weather, but I decided to let it pass.

make a pass at (someone) (*sl*) to try and make (someone) sexually interested in one: *He makes a pass at every girl he meets.* [A fencing term — 'to thrust at (someone) with a fencing foil' — the slang use is originally US.]

pass as/for (something) to be mistaken for or accepted as (something): *Some man-made materials could pass as silk*; *His nasty remarks pass for wit among his admirers.*

pass away (*euph*) to die: *Her grandmother passed away last night.*

pass by on the other side *see* **side.**

pass (something or someone) off as (something or someone) to pretend that (something or someone) is (something or someone else): *He passed the whole embarrassing incident off as a joke*; *He passed himself off as a journalist.*

pass out (*inf*) to faint: *I feel as though I'm going to pass out.* [From a late 19C euphemism for 'to die' — probably as an abbreviation for *pass out of sight* — via 1st World War slang for 'to become unconscious through drink'.]

pass (someone) over (*inf*) to ignore or overlook (someone): *This is the third time he's been passed over for that job.*

pass round the hat *see* **hat.**

pass (something) up (*inf*) not to accept (a chance, opportunity *etc*): *He passed up the offer of a good job in America to come here.*

a pretty pass *see* **pretty.**

ships that pass in the night *see* **ship.**

past

past one's best/(*inf*) **past it** less strong, good, efficient *etc* than one was, because one is getting older: *I used to be quite a good tennis player, but I'm past my best now*; *The silly old fool shouldn't try to dance — everyone knows he's past it!*

a past master (*usu slightly derog*) someone who is extremely skilful (at an activity which requires skill): *She is a past master at the art of getting her own way.* [Literally, 'a person who has held the post of Master in a lodge of freemasons *etc*', but the phrase has been influenced by the expression *passed master* = 'a person who has qualified as a master'.]

I *etc* would not put it past (someone) to (do something) (*derog inf*) I think (someone) is perfectly capable of, *esp* immoral enough to do, (something bad): *I wouldn't put it past Mary to take advantage of my being ill and try to take over my job!*

pat

a pat on the back (*inf*) a demonstration of approval or praise: *We all got a pat on the back from the manager for our hard work.*

patch

hit/strike a bad patch (*inf*) to have a difficult time, meet unfavourable conditions *etc*: *Last year he was the best cricketer in Britain, but he has struck a bad patch in the last few months.*

not to be a patch on (something) (*inf*) to be not nearly as good as (something): *Her cooking is not a patch on my mother's.* [Perhaps deriving from *like a patch on* — 'obviously inferior to' — and originally US.]

patch (something) up (*inf*) to settle (a quarrel): *They soon patched up their disagreement.*

path

beat a path to (someone's) door to visit (someone) very often or in very large numbers: *She became so famous that people from all over the world beat a path to her door.*

cross (someone's) path to be met or noticed casually or accidentally by (someone): *I used to see him quite a lot, but he hasn't crossed my path at all recently.*

patience

enough to try the patience of a saint (*inf*) (something) extremely irritating or annoying: *She is so fussy about her clothes that a day spent shopping with her is enough to try the patience of a saint!*

have the patience of Job to be extremely patient: *To train animals successfully, you have to have the patience of Job.* [From the story of Job in the Bible.]

pause

give (someone) pause (*formal*) to make (someone) hesitate for a moment: *The price marked on the coat gave her pause, but in the end she bought it.* [A Shakespearian quotation — *Hamlet*, III. i.]

pave

pave the way for (something) to make easy or possible for (something to happen): *The scientific discoveries of the eighteenth century paved the way for the Industrial Revolution in Britain.* [From paving roads in order to make traffic faster and easier.]

pay

the devil to pay *see* **devil.**

in (someone's) pay (*inf: usu derog*) employed by, or given money by, (someone), *usu* for a bad purpose: *The judge was in the pay of a group of important criminals.*

pay court to (someone) *see* **court.**

pay (someone) in his own coin *see* **coin.**

pay lip-service *see* **lip.**

pay one's respects *see* **respect.**

pay the earth *see* **earth.**

pay the piper *see* **pipe.**

pay through the nose *see* **nose.**

pay one's way *see* **way.**

put paid to (something) to prevent a person from doing (something he planned or wanted to do): *The rain put paid to our visit to the zoo.* [Apparently from the book-keeping habit of writing 'paid' against accounts *etc* finally settled in a ledger.]

rob Peter to pay Paul *see* **rob.**

pea

as (a)like as two peas (in a pod) exactly alike: *The twins were as alike as two peas.*

peace

hold one's peace (*old or formal*) to remain silent: *He knew what she said was untrue, but he held his peace.*

keep the peace to prevent fighting, quarrelling *etc*: *She tries to keep the peace between her brothers.* [Literally a legal term for not creating a public disturbance.]

make one's peace with (someone) to become friendly again with (someone), or *esp* to get (someone) to be friendly again towards oneself, after a period of quarrelling *etc*: *If you had a difference of opinion with Aunt Anne, I think you should go and make your peace with her before we leave.*

peace of mind freedom from worry, distress *etc*: *After her disturbing meeting with her ex-husband it was a long time before she regained her peace of mind.*

peacock

as proud as a peacock very proud: *The child was as proud as a peacock as she showed me her knitting.*

pearl

cast pearls before swine (*usu facet*) to give or offer something valuable to people who are unable to appreciate it: *Our Latin teacher used to say that teaching us Latin poetry was casting pearls before swine.* [A Biblical reference, to Matthew 7:6.]

peck

keep one's pecker up (*sl*) to remain cheerful and hopeful: *When*

263

things go wrong it is very difficult for me to keep my pecker up. [Probably *pecker* = beak.]

the pecking order the order of importance in a group of people: *I have very little influence on the firm's policy — I'm a long way down the pecking order.* [A translation of a German word — *Hackordnung* — coined in the 1920s for a social system first noticed in domestic hens whereby each bird in a group is allowed to peck the bird next below it in rank and has to submit to being pecked by the bird next above it.]

pedestal

put (someone) on a pedestal (*derog*) to think of and treat (someone) as being much better and more admirable than normal people: *She always puts her boyfriends on a pedestal and won't listen to a word of criticism against them.* [From the method of mounting public statues of heroes *etc*.]

peep

a peeping Tom *see* **Tom.**

peg

bring/take (someone) down a peg (or two) (*inf*) to make (a proud person) more humble: *She thought she was very clever, but she was taken down a peg when she failed the exam.* [The reference is to tuning musical instruments, and dates from the 16C.]

off the peg of clothes, ready to wear: *She has a dressmaker who makes all her clothes, but I buy mine off the peg at the local shop.*

pelt

at full pelt (running) as fast as possible: *They set off down the road at full pelt.*

penny

in for a penny, in for a pound a saying, meaning that once one has decided to take a risk, act in a particular way *etc*, one ought to do so boldly.

in penny numbers a very few, or a very little, at a time: *We couldn't afford the whole dinner-service at once so we decided to buy it in penny numbers.* [From a method of selling encyclopedias *etc* in sections, formerly often at a penny a part.]

not to cost a penny not to cost anything at all: *I'll do the job for you and it won't cost (you) a penny.*

not to have a penny to one's name to have no money at all: *Her parents tried to stop her marrying him, because he hadn't a penny to his name.*

the penny drops (*inf*) I *etc* understand: *He didn't grasp her* *meaning at first, but eventually the penny dropped.* [The reference is to a coin taking a long time to operate the machinery of a slot machine.]

a penny for them what are you thinking about? [In full, **a penny for your thoughts,** a saying recorded in the 16C.]

penny wise and pound foolish saving small amounts of money in everyday matters while wasting large sums in other ways.

a pretty penny *see* **pretty.**

spend a penny (*inf euph*) to urinate: *Do you need to spend a penny before we get on the train?* [From the former long-established price of admission to a cubicle in public lavatories.]

turn an honest penny to earn some money honestly: *I'm glad he's got a job and has decided to turn an honest penny at last after years of living on grants from the state.*

turn up like a bad penny (of someone disliked or unwanted) to reappear, *esp* frequently and/or unexpectedly: *Any time there is the chance of free food, Andrew will turn up like a bad penny to make sure of his share.*

two a penny (*derog*) very common; of little value: *Books like that are two a penny.* [Literally, sold in bulk at a halfpenny each.]

pep

a pep-talk (*inf*) a talk intended to arouse enthusiasm, or to make people work harder, better *etc*: *Morale was rather low in the factory, so the managing director gave all the staff a pep-talk.*

perfect

the pink of perfection *see* **pink.**

to perfection (*formal*) so that (something) is perfect: *The chef cooks veal to perfection.*

peril

at one's peril (*often facet*) at one's own risk: *If the boss tells you not to do that, then you do it at your peril.*

period

a period piece a person or thing (*eg* a play, piece of furniture, painting) that is very typical of the time when he or it was born or made, *esp* if interesting mainly because of this fact: *She had a huge and extremely ornate Victorian sideboard — a real period piece — solidly built and very ugly.*

perish

perish the thought (*usu facet*) I should not think or say such a terrible thing: *I do hope — perish the thought — that she isn't* *bringing her awful children with her!* [A quotation from Colley Cibber's 18C version of Shakespeare's *Richard III*, V. v.]

person

in person personally; one's self, not represented by someone else: *The Queen was there in person.*

the last person *see* **last.**

perspective

in, out of perspective with, without a correct or sensible understanding of something's true importance: *Don't let things get out of perspective*; *Keep things in perspective.* [Literally, of an object in a painting *etc*, having, or not having, the correct size, shape or angle in relation to the rest of the picture.]

petard

be hoist with one's own petard to be the victim of, or ruined by, one's own trick which one intended to ruin or harm someone else: *The councillor who introduced parking restrictions to the town of Southwood was hoist with his own petard when he was himself fined for parking outside the Town Hall.* [A Shakespearian quotation — *Hamlet*, III. iv. A *petard* was a kind of bomb used by military engineers.]

phrase

a turn of phrase *see* **turn.**

phut

go phut (*inf*) (*usu* of something mechanical or electrical) to break or cease to function: *My television has gone phut.* [Probably from the sound accompanying the breakdown.].

pick

pick and choose to select or choose very carefully: *When I'm buying apples, I like to pick and choose (the ones I want).*

pick holes in *see* **hole.**

pick (someone) off to shoot (*esp* people in a group) one by one: *He picked off the enemy soldiers as they tried to leave their hut.*

pick on (someone) (*inf*) **1** to choose (someone) to do a *usu* difficult or unpleasant job: *Why do they always pick on me to do the washing-up?* **2** to speak to or treat (someone) angrily or critically: *Don't pick on me because we didn't get this finished on time — it wasn't my fault.*

pick up the tab *see* **tab.**

picture

get the picture (*sl*) to understand the situation: *You needn't say any more — I get the picture.*

the pictures (*Brit inf*) the cinema: *We went to the pictures last night, but it wasn't a very good film.*

put (someone), be in the picture to give (someone), have all the necessary information (about something): *He put me in the picture about what had happened.*

pie

have a finger in the pie *see* **finger.**

pie in the sky (*derog inf*) something good promised for the future but which one is not certain or likely to get: *He says he will get a well-paid job but I think it's just pie in the sky.* [A quotation — in full, 'You'll get pie in the sky when you die' — from a poem by the American anarchist Joe Hill.]

piece

all of a piece (*inf*) all the same; happening *etc* according to the same rules or principles: *Her rudeness is all of a piece with her lack of respect for authority.*

give (someone) a piece of one's mind *see* **mind.**

go (all) to pieces (*inf*) (of a person) to collapse physically or nervously: *She went to pieces when her husband died.*

a nasty piece of work *see* **nasty.**

a piece of cake *see* **cake.**

pig

buy, get a pig in a poke to buy, get something without knowing whether it is worth anything or not: *The new car we bought was a pig in a poke because we were unable to get a mechanic to check it before we paid for it.* [Allegedly from a fairground trick which involved selling unwary customers a cat in a bag while assuring them it was a piglet. Whether this is true or not, selling a piglet in a bag would make it impossible to check its value.]

go to pigs and whistles to become ruined or worthless: *Ever since my son was offered a job playing in a pop-group, his schoolwork has gone to pigs and whistles.* [*Pigs* here means 'pieces of earthenware' and *pigs and whistles* therefore means 'trifles'.]

make a pig of oneself (*inf*) to eat greedily; to eat too much: *I really made a pig of myself at dinner last night.*

make a pig's ear of (something) (*derog inf*) to do (something) badly or clumsily; to make a mess of (something): *You really made a pig's ear of that piece of work.*

pig-in-the-middle (*inf*) someone who is in a position between two people or groups who are fighting, who disagree *etc*: *Whenever Anne's mother meets Anne's husband, they have an argument and poor*

Anne is always pig-in-the-middle. [From a child's game in which two people throw a ball *etc* from one to another and a third tries to intercept it.]

pigs might fly an expression indicating that one believes that something is very unlikely to happen: *'We might have fine weather for our holiday.' 'Yes, and pigs might fly!'*

pigeon

pigeon-toed (of a person or his manner of walking) with toes turned inwards: *He is pigeon-toed.*

put the cat among the pigeons *see* **cat.**

a stool-pigeon *see* **stool.**

that's (not) my *etc* **pigeon** that is (not) my affair or interest: *I'm not interested in the financial side of our organization — that's my partner's pigeon!* [Strictly, *not my pidgin* — pidgin-English for 'not my business'.]

pikestaff

as plain as a pikestaff very clear or obvious: *It's as plain as a pikestaff that he was embarrassed.* [Apparently originally a play on words, referring to the lack of ornamentation or subtlety of shape in the wooden shaft of a pike.]

pill

sugar the pill *see* **sugar.**

pillar

from pillar to post (*usu* of a person in trouble, difficulty *etc*) from one place to another (*usu* looking fo help *etc*): *He was driven from pillar to post in search of a job.* [An idiom from the game of real tennis.]

pin

for two pins (*inf*) if given the smallest reason, encouragement *etc*; very readily: *For two pins I would cancel the meeting, since no-one wants to go!*

on pins and needles waiting anxiously for something: *The students were all on pins and needles waiting for their exam results.*

pin back one's ears *see* **ear.**

pin (someone) down to make (someone) give a definite answer, statement, opinion, or promise: *I can't pin him down to a definite date for his arrival.*

pin one's hopes/faith on (someone) to rely on (someone); to hope or expect (that someone will do or achieve something): *Britain's athletes have not done very well so far this year, but this afternoon we are pinning our hopes on Lorna Smith.*

pin (something) on (someone) (*inf*) to prove or suggest that (a person) was responsible for (something bad, *esp* a crime): *You can't pin that robbery on me — I've got an alibi!*

pins and needles a tingling feeling (in one's hands, feet or legs): *I've got pins and needles in my arm.*

you could hear a pin drop it is absolutely quiet; no-one is making a sound: *You could have heard a pin drop when the manager announced that he was leaving — no-one wanted to say the wrong thing.*

pinch

at a pinch/if it comes to the pinch (*inf*) in an emergency; if absolutely necessary: *At a pinch, you could get home on foot; If it comes to the pinch, I'll play the piano for you, but I'm not very good.*

feel the pinch (*inf*) to have problems because of lack of money: *Now that my wife has given up her job, we are really feeling the pinch.*

pinch and scrape to live on very little money: *We really have to pinch and scrape to afford a holiday on my husband's salary.*

take (something) with a pinch of salt *see* salt.

pink

be tickled pink *see* tickle.

in the pink (of health) (*old or facet*) very well; in good health: *I've been ill for a few weeks but I feel in the pink now.*

the pink of perfection absolutely perfect: *Everything in her house is always in the pink of perfection — she spends her whole life planning and arranging it.* [A quotation from Goldsmith's *She Stoops to Conquer* — *pink* meaning 'the finest example'.]

pip

give (someone) the pip (*inf*) to annoy, disgust or offend (someone): *That silly laugh of his really gives me the pip!* [*The pip* is a disease of poultry, applied from very early on to vague and generally not very serious human illnesses.]

pipped at the post (*inf*) beaten in the very final stages of a race, competition *etc*: *I thought I was going to win the painting competition, but I was pipped at the post by a friend of mine.* [A term from horse-racing. *Pipped* became a slang term for 'defeated' by extension from the meaning 'blackballed', *ie* denied access to a club *etc* by a vote cast by placing a white (for) or black (against) ball in a box. The black ball was likened to a pip.]

pipe

in the pipeline (*not formal*) in preparation; not yet ready: *Our new orders are still in the pipeline.* [The reference is to crude oil piped from the well to the refinery.]

pay the piper to provide the money for something, and thus have some control over it, a reference to the saying **he who pays the piper calls the tune**: *He feels his fiancée's parents should be allowed to organize the wedding as they want it — after all, they are paying the piper.*

pipe down (*inf*) to stop talking; to be quiet: *Will you pipe down for a moment?*

a pipe dream an idea which can only be imagined, and which would be impossible to carry out: *For most people a journey round the world is only a pipe dream.* [Originally, a vision induced by smoking opium.]

piping hot (*inf*) very hot: *Be careful, the soup is piping hot.*

(you can) put that in your pipe and smoke it! (*inf*) (you can) think about that and see how you like it! (*usu* said of something unpleasant to the hearer): *The boss said this morning my work was better than yours so you can put that in your pipe and smoke it!*

pistol

hold a pistol to (someone's) head to force (someone) to do as one wishes, *usu* by using threats: *I don't want to ask you to repay the money I lent you, but the bank are holding a pistol to my head by refusing to extend my credit.*

pitch

as black as pitch very dark: *It was pouring with rain, and the night was as black as pitch.*

pitch in (*inf*) to (begin to) deal with, do *etc* something: *If everyone pitches in, we'll soon get the job done; There's plenty of food for everyone, so pitch in.*

queer (someone's) pitch *see* **queer**.

place

fall into place (of happenings, facts *etc*) to become easily understood because seen in the proper relationship: *Once we knew he had been in jail his strange remarks and behaviour fell into place.*

give place to (*very formal*) to be followed and replaced by (something): *The horse gave place to the motor car.*

go places (*sl*) to be successful, *esp* in one's career: *That young man is sure to go places.*

in the first place at the very beginning: *I don't mind if I stay behind — I didn't want to go in the first place.*

know one's place to accept one's (low) rank or lack of importance and behave in a suitable manner: *I had no intention of telling my boss his grammar was poor — I know my place!*

pride of place *see* **pride.**

put (someone) in his place to remind (someone), often in a rude or angry way, of his lower social position, or lack of importance, experience *etc*: *He tried to tell her what to do, but she soon put him in his place.*

put oneself in (someone's) place to imagine what it would be like to be (someone else): *If you put yourself in his place, you can understand why he is so careful.*

take place (*formal*) to happen: *The wedding took place as arranged.*

take (someone's) place to do something or go somewhere as a replacement (for someone else): *John is too ill to come, so I'm taking his place.*

take the place of (something) to be used instead of, or to be a substitute for, (something): *I don't think television will ever take the place of books.*

plain

as plain as a pikestaff *see* **pikestaff.**

plain sailing progress without difficulty: *Once we have got the money, it will be plain sailing.* [Probably, by confusion between *plane* and *plain*, from *plane sailing*, a method of making navigational calculations at sea in which the earth's surface is treated as if it were flat.]

plan

go according to plan to happen as arranged or intended: *The journey went according to plan.*

plank

as thick as two short planks (*derog inf*) very stupid: *She's a pretty girl, but as thick as two short planks!*

plate

have (something) handed to one on a plate (*inf*) to get (something) without having to do anything for it: *His father was wealthy, and he had everything handed to him on a plate.*

on one's plate waiting to be dealt with; occupying one's time: *I'd like to help you but I've got too much on my plate at the moment.*

play

all work and no play makes Jack a dull boy *see* **work.**

bring/come into play (*formal*) to (cause to) be used or exercised: *He brought the full range of his intellectual powers into play to solve the many problems he was faced with.*

child's play *see* **child.**

fair play *see* **fair.**

make a play for (something) to try and get (something): *It was obvious that he was making a play for the job as the managing director's assistant.* [An idiom from chess.]

make great play with (something) (*rather formal*) to place great emphasis on (something); to treat or talk of (something) as very important: *She had just got engaged, and was making great play with her fiancé's wealth and aristocratic connections.*

play along with (someone or something) to work together with (someone) or towards (an aim *etc*); to agree with and help (someone), *usu* only for a short while: *They agreed to play along with the kidnappers for the meantime to give the police a chance to find the child.*

play a losing game *see* **lose.**

play one's cards close, right *see* **play.**

play (something) down to try to make (something) appear less important: *He played down the fact that he had failed the exam.*

played out (*inf*) **1** exhausted: *She was very busy spring-cleaning all day, and by the evening she was played out.* **2** no longer of any interest or influence: *Within fifty years the Impressionist style was played out.* [Literally, of theatrical performances, 'played to the end'.]

play fair to act honestly and in an unbiased way; not to cheat: *You're not playing fair! You've taken all the chocolate biscuits and left me the plain ones!*

play fast and loose *see* **fast.**

play for time *see* **time.**

play gooseberry *see* **gooseberry.**

play havoc with *see* **havoc.**

play (merry) hell with *see* **hell.**

play it by ear *see* **ear.**

play it cool *see* **cool.**

play no part in (something) not to be one of the people who are doing (something): *He played no part in the robbery itself.* [From acting in a play.]

play (someone) off against (someone else) to set one person against another in order to gain an advantage: *He played his father off against his mother to get more pocket money.*

play on/upon (someone's feelings, fears *etc***)** to make use of (someone's feelings, fears *etc*): *He played on my sympathy until I lent him £10.*

a play on words a joke, clever saying *etc* based on similarities, associations *etc* between words: *'They went and told the sexton and* *the sexton tolled the bell' is a play on words.*

play possum *see* **possum.**

play safe to take no risks: *He probably won't object, but we had better play safe and ask his permission first.* [From billiards.]

play second fiddle *see* **second.**

play the devil's advocate *see* **devil.**

play the field to spread one's interest, affections *etc* over a wide range of subjects, people *etc* rather than concentrating on any single one: *He decided to play the field a bit before thinking seriously of marriage.*

play the fool *see* **fool.**

play the game *see* **game.**

play one's trump card *see* **trump.**

play up to annoy, cause trouble for or be a nuisance (to): *The children are playing up today; I sprained my ankle last month and it still plays me up occasionally.* [Originally used of horses behaving badly.]

play up to (someone) to flatter or pretend to admire (someone) for one's own advantage: *He is always playing up to the manager.* [Originally theatrical slang for supporting another actor in a play.]

play with fire *see* **fire.**

please

as pleased as Punch *see* **punch.**

if you please (*old or formal*) please: *Come this way, if you please.*

please yourself (*inf*) do what you choose: *I don't think you should go, but please yourself.*

small things please small minds *see* **small.**

pleasure

have had the pleasure (of meeting) (*formal or facet*) to have been introduced to: *'Have you met Mrs Jones?' 'No, I have not had the pleasure.'; I had the pleasure of meeting your daughter yesterday.*

take pleasure in to get enjoyment from doing (something): *He takes great pleasure in annoying me; She takes pleasure in reading aloud to her children.*

plot

the plot thickens (*usu facet*) the affair is becoming more complicated and interesting: *We all thought it was Jim who sent the flowers, but he denies it — the plot thickens!* [A quotation from a Restoration play — *The Rehearsal* by George Villiers, Duke of Buckingham.]

273

plough

plough (something) back to put (money, profits *etc*) back into a business *etc*: *He made a profit last year, but ploughed it back so that he could buy more machinery.* [From ploughing an unimportant crop into the ground to act as fertilizer.]

pluck

pluck up courage *see* **courage.**

plunge

take the plunge to (decide to) start doing something new or difficult: *She was hesitant about trying to learn French, but finally decided to take the plunge.* [Literally 'to dive into water'.]

pocket

burn a hole in (someone's) pocket (*facet*) said of money when one is eager to spend it: *The money the little girl received as a birthday present was burning a hole in her pocket.*

in pocket, out of pocket having gained, lost money over a business deal *etc*: *His last deal has left him out of pocket.*

in (someone's) pocket influenced or controlled by (someone): *Most of the officials in that country are in the pocket of the big oil companies.*

line one's pockets to make money dishonestly from one's job: *The agent was dismissed when the company discovered he had been lining his pockets for the past five years.*

out of pocket *see* **in pocket** *above.*

poetic

poetic justice the suitable but accidental punishing of wrong and, often, rewarding of right: *It was poetic justice that the car broke down after he had taken it without permission.*

point

be beside the point to have no direct connection with, or to be unimportant to, the subject being discussed: *You will have to go. Whether you want to go is beside the point.*

be on the point of (doing something) to be about to (do something): *I was on the point of going out when the telephone rang.*

be to the point (*formal*) to be connected with what is being discussed; to be relevant: *Her speech was very much to the point.*

come to the point to reach the most important matter, consideration in a conversation *etc*: *He talked and talked but never came to the point.*

in point of fact actually; in reality: *He says he can ride, but in point of fact he has never been on a horse before.*

make a point of (doing something) to be especially careful to do something: *I'll make a point of asking her today.*

make one's point to state an opinion *etc* so clearly and persuasively that it has been understood and accepted: *You've made your point — we'll do what you suggest.*

the point of no return the stage in a process *etc* after which there is no possibility of stopping or going back. [Originally the point in an aircraft's flight after which it does not have enough fuel to go back to its place of departure.]

a point of view a way or manner of looking at a subject, matter *etc*: *You must try to look at this matter from your mother's point of view.*

point the finger at (someone) *see* **finger.**

a sore point *see* **sore.**

stretch a point *see* **stretch.**

(someone's) strong point *see* **strong.**

take (someone's) point to understand and accept what (someone) wishes to say, *esp* during an argument, debate *etc*: *I take your point, but I think you have too gloomy a view of our prospects.*

up to a point to a certain extent but not completely: *Your statement is true up to a point.*

when it comes to the point at the moment when something must be done, decided *etc*: *He always promises to help, but when it comes to the point, he's never there.*

poison
a poison-pen letter an anonymous letter saying wicked things about a certain person *etc*: *When she began to get poison-pen letters, she informed the police.*

poke
buy a pig in a poke *see* **pig.**

poke fun at (someone) to laugh unkindly at (someone): *The children often poked fun at him because of his stammer.*

poke one's nose into *see* **nose.**

poker
as stiff as a poker very stiff: *On frosty days the clothes-line is as stiff as a poker.*

pole
be poles apart (*inf*) to be as different or as far apart as possible: *They are poles apart in their attitude to education.*

up the pole (*sl*) **1** in difficulties: *We'll be really up the pole if he doesn't get back in time!* **2** crazy: *If you really intend to go swimming* *in this weather, you must be up the pole!* **3** pregnant: *Don't tell me that she's up the pole again!*

polish

polish (something) off (*inf*) to finish something: *She polished off the last of the food.* [From boxing slang.]

spit and polish *see* **spit.**

pony

on shanks's pony *see* **shanks.**

pop

pop the question *see* **question.**

pop up (*inf*) to appear: *I never know where he'll pop up next.*

top of the pops (*inf*) very much in favour at the moment: *Small hats are top of the pops this summer.* [Originally used of those pop records which are selling best at any given time.]

port

any port in a storm a saying, meaning that one has to accept any possible solution, way out *etc* when one has difficulties.

pose

strike a pose *see* **strike.**

possession

possession is nine points of the law a saying, meaning that if there is a dispute about who should have something, the person who has it at the time is in the strongest position. [The *nine points* are visualized as being out of a hypothetical ten available to be won in a lawsuit.]

what possessed him *etc*? why did he do such a thing?: *What possessed you to buy that hideous coat?* [Literally 'what evil spirit made him . . .']

possum

play possum (*inf*) to pretend to be unavailable, ignorant of a fact *etc* or uninterested in order to protect oneself: *He may be away — he doesn't answer the telephone — but he might just be playing possum.* [From the reputed habit of the possum of pretending to be dead when attacked.]

post

as deaf as a post very deaf: *My uncle won't hear us — he's as deaf as a post.*

from pillar to post *see* **pillar.**

keep (someone) posted (*inf*) to give regular information to (a person): *He always keeps me posted about what he's doing.* [Originally US, from a book-keeping expression meaning 'to keep (ledgers *etc*) fully made up to date'.]

pipped at the post *see* **pip.**

pot

go to pot (*inf*) to become bad; to get worse and worse: *He was under a terrible strain and his work went completely to pot.* [Literally, 'to be made into stew'.]

a pot-boiler (*derog*) a book or other work by a writer, artist *etc*, produced for the sake of money only. [From *keep the pot boiling*, which originally meant 'to earn one's living'.]

the pot calling the kettle black someone who is criticizing someone else for doing something *etc* that he does himself. [From the uniform black colour of all kitchen utensils used over an open fire.]

pot-hunting (*derog*) entering a competition only in order to win a prize: *He won so many small tennis tournaments that his rivals accused him of pot-hunting.*

a pot-shot an easy or casual shot that doesn't need careful aim: *He took a pot-shot at a bird on the fence.* [Originally this term was slightly derogatory and implied that one was shooting birds *etc* solely for food and not in order to exercise one's skill.]

take pot-luck (*inf*) to have a meal as someone's guest without their having prepared special food: *Do come and eat with us, if you don't mind taking pot-luck.* [Literally 'to accept whatever happens to be served to one from the cooking-pot'.]

a watched pot never boils a saying, meaning that when one is waiting for something to happen *etc*, the time seems even longer if one is continually watching and thinking about it.

potato

a hot potato a subject, person *etc* which is extremely difficult and dangerous to handle: *The subject of police brutality is a hot potato.*

pound

get/have one's pound of flesh to obtain everything one is entitled to have, *esp* if this causes difficulties or unhappiness to others: *His ex-wife was determined to have her pound of flesh, even if it meant he would have to sell his house to pay her.* [From the bargain between Shylock and Antonio in Shakespeare's *The Merchant of Venice* whereby Shylock was entitled to a pound of Antonio's flesh if he was unable to repay a loan.]

pour

it never rains but it pours a saying, meaning that when things go wrong, they go disastrously, or frequently, wrong.

pour oil on troubled waters *see* **oil.**

power

do a power of good, harm *etc* to do a lot of good, harm, evil *etc*: *A weekend in the country will do you a power of good*; *A mistake like that can do a power of harm.*

in one's power under one's control and dependent on one's mercy: *I have him in my power at last — I can do what I like with him!*

more power to his *etc* **elbow** I wish him good luck: *If he is really trying to reform the system, more power to his elbow — it badly needs to be reformed.* [Of Anglo-Irish origin — derivation unknown.]

the power behind the throne the person who really runs an organization *etc*, while giving the impression that someone else is in charge: *He is the chairman of the family company, but his wife is the real power behind the throne.*

the powers that be the people in authority: *I have been sacked because the powers that be have decided that I am inefficient.* [A Biblical reference — to Romans 13:1.]

practical

a practical joke a *usu* irritating joke consisting of an action done to someone, rather than a story told: *He nailed my chair to the floor as a practical joke.*

practice

be out of practice not having had a lot of practice recently: *I haven't played the piano for months — I'm very out of practice.*

make a practice of (doing something) to do (something) habitually: *He makes a practice of arriving late at parties.*

practice makes perfect a saying, meaning that if one practises one will eventually be able to do something well, and often said to encourage someone to try again.

put (something) into practice to do (something), as opposed to thinking, planning *etc*: *He never gets the chance to put his ideas into practice.*

sharp practice *see* **sharp.**

practise

practise what one preaches to act or behave oneself as one tells other people they should act or behave: *He says he's a supporter of comprehensive education, but he doesn't practise what he preaches — his son is at boarding-school.*

praise

praise (someone) to the skies *see* **sky.**

sing (someone's) praises to praise (someone) with great enthusiasm: *She was singing the praises of her new secretary, who is apparently absolutely ideal.* [A Biblical phrase.]

preach

practise what one preaches *see* **practise.**

preach to the converted *see* **convert.**

precious

precious few/little (*inf*) very few/little: *Precious few people would agree with you; I've precious little money left.*

prejudice

without prejudice (to something) (*formal*) without any possible harm or danger (to a person's rights, position, prospects *etc*): *You ought to be able to criticize your firm without prejudice to your chances of promotion.* [A legal term.]

premium

be at a premium to be wanted by a lot of people and be therefore difficult to get: *Tickets for the football match were at a premium.* [A financial term — 'sold at more than the nominal value' — the opposite of *at a discount*.]

prepare

be prepared to (do something) to be willing to (do something): *I'm not prepared to lend him any more money!*

presence

presence of mind calmness and the ability to act sensibly (in an emergency *etc*): *He showed great presence of mind in the face of danger.*

present

at present at the present time: *He's away from home at present.*

for the present as far as the present time is concerned: *You've done enough work for the present.*

there's no time like the present *see* **time.**

press

be pressed for (something) (*inf*) to be short of (time, money *etc*): *Do hurry up — I'm a bit pressed for time.*

pressgang (someone) into (doing something) to force (someone) to do (something): *He was pressganged into helping.* [The *press gang* was a group of sailors under an officer formed, *esp* in the 18C, to seize and carry off seamen *etc* and force them to join the navy.]

279

press (someone or something) into service (*formal or facet*) to make use of (a person or thing) in an emergency: *Even the children were pressed into service to prepare for the wedding.* [*Press* here (as in the previous idiom) means 'to force'.]

press (something) on (someone) (*formal*) to urge (someone) to accept (something): *She pressed the money on him.*

pressure

bring pressure to bear on (someone) (*formal*) to try to force (someone) to do something: *They brought pressure to bear on the government to lower taxes.*

a pressure group a group of people who try to get the government *etc* to take notice of certain matters: *The local teachers formed a pressure group.*

pretence

false pretences *see* **false.**

pretty

a pretty kettle of fish *see* **kettle.**

pretty much the same, alike *etc* (*inf*) more or less the same, alike *etc*: *The houses are all pretty much alike.*

a pretty pass a bad state or condition: *Things have come to a pretty pass when you cannot trust your friends.*

a pretty penny (*inf*) a large amount of money: *That car must have cost you a pretty penny.*

pretty well (*inf*) nearly: *I've pretty well finished.*

sitting pretty (*inf*) in a very good position: *These problems don't worry you — you're sitting pretty.*

prey

be prey to (something) to be a sufferer from (something): *He is a prey to anxiety.*

prey on/upon (someone's) mind to cause distress or unhappiness to (someone): *Fears preyed upon her mind.* [Literally, *prey upon* means 'to hunt for food'.]

price

at a price (*inf*) at a high price: *We can get dinner at this hotel — at a price!*

beyond price (*formal*) priceless: *Good health is beyond price.*

a price on (someone's) head a reward offered for (someone's) capture or killing: *He became an outlaw with a price on his head after he had robbed a bank.*

price (something/oneself) out of the market to charge so much for (something or one's services) that no one can afford to pay: *If you ask as much as that for your house, you will price it out of the market.*

what price (something)? (*inf*) what do you think of (something)?; what part does (something) play in all this?: *I hear you've elected yourself our leader — what price democracy, then?*

prick

prick up one's ears (*inf*) to start to pay attention: *He pricked up his ears at the mention of food.* [Literally used of animals.]

pride

be (someone's) pride and joy to be the object of the pride of (someone): *He was his parents' pride and joy.*

pride goes before a fall a saying, meaning that too much confidence and vanity is likely to be followed by misfortune.

pride of place the most important place: *They gave pride of place at the exhibtion to a painting by Canaletto.* [This is apparently a reference to falconry — the *place* was the point from which a hunting falcon begins its dive — coined from Shakespeare, *Macbeth*, II. iv.]

pride (oneself) on (something) to take pride in, or feel satisfaction with, (something one has done, achieved *etc*): *He prides himself on his driving skill.*

swallow one's pride to behave humbly, *eg* by making an apology: *You'll just have to swallow your pride and admit that you made a mistake.*

take pride in (something) to feel pride about (something): *I take pride in my family's achievements; You should take more pride in (= care more for) your appearance.*

prime

the prime mover (*rather formal*) the original force that sets something in motion: *He was the prime mover in the protest against the new motorway.* [In medieval astronomy, the *primum mobile* — 'prime mover' — was the ninth heaven, dividing the motionless, eternal domain of God from the eight spheres containing the stars and the planets, which rotated round the earth. This motion was believed to stem from the rotation of the *primum mobile*.]

principle

in principle in general, as opposed to in detail: *I think it is a good idea in principle, but I must know all the details before I finally agree.*

on principle because of one's principles or moral standards;
He refused to do it on principle.

print

small print *see* **small.**

private

a private eye a private detective: *He employed a private eye to find
out if his wife was having an affair with another man.* [From the
trademark of the Pinkerton Detective Agency.]

pro

the pros and cons the arguments for and against: *Let's hear all
the pros and cons before we make a decision.* [Latin *pro* 'for' and *contra*
'against'.]

probable

in all probability (*rather formal*) most probably; most likely: *In
all probability we shall arrive before them.*

probation

be/put on probation in certain jobs, to spend a period of time
during which one is carefully watched to see that one is capable
of the job: *New members of staff are on probation for a year.* [A legal
term for a system of allowing offenders to go free provided they
commit no more crimes.]

profile

keep a low profile (*inf*) to behave so that one's attitudes,
opinions and actions are not made generally known: *The boss is
angry with me, so I'm trying to keep a low profile and not attract his
attention for a week or so.*

proof

the proof of the pudding is in the eating a saying, meaning
that it is only possible to say whether something is a success or
not when one has found out if it does what it was intended to
do *etc.*

proportion

be, get out of (all) proportion (to something) to (cause to)
have an incorrect relationship (to each other or something else):
His interest in stamp-collecting has grown out of (all) proportion (= it
consumes too great a part of his time, money, interest *etc*); *You've
got this affair out of proportion* (= You think it is more important
than it really is).

a sense of proportion the ability to judge what is important
and what is not: *Don't get so worried about such a trivial matter —
you're losing your sense of proportion.*

proud

do (someone) proud (*inf*) to give (a person) good treatment or entertainment: *We always do them proud when they come to dinner.*

public

public spirit a desire to do things for the good of the community: *He shows a great deal of public spirit.*

puff

puffed out (*inf*) exhausted and out of breath: *She was puffed out by the time she reached the top of the stairs.*

puffed-up (*derog*) conceited: *That puffed-up little man!*

pull

pull a face *see* **face.**

pull a fast one *see* **fast.**

pull (something) off (*inf*) to succeed in doing (something): *He's pulled off a good business deal.*

pull out to abandon a place, situation or course of action which has become too difficult or dangerous: *I think I should pull out of the deal now before I lose any more money by it.*

pull out all the stops *see* **stop.**

pull one's punches *see* **punch.**

pull one's socks up *see* **sock.**

pull (the) strings *see* **string.**

pull (someone) through (*inf*) to (help someone to) survive an illness *etc*: *He is very ill, but he'll pull through; The expert medical treatment pulled him through.*

pull oneself together (*inf*) to control oneself; to regain one's self-control: *At first she was terrified, then she pulled herself together.*

pull up (of a driver or vehicle) to stop: *He pulled up at the traffic lights.*

pull one's weight *see* **weight.**

pulse

keep one's finger on the pulse to keep oneself informed about modern ideas, events *etc*: *He has retired from the firm now, but he still likes to keep his finger on the pulse.* [A medical idiom.]

punch, Punch

as pleased as Punch very happy or pleased: *He was as pleased as Punch when we all said how good his cooking was.* [From the puppet-show character, who is depicted as gleefully triumphant in his antisocial behaviour.]

pull one's punches to use less force in attacking than one is really capable of: *He didn't pull his punches when he criticized her* *work*. [Literally a boxing term for striking blows without using one's full strength.]

punch-drunk dazed and confused: *There had been so many emergencies to deal with that morning that by lunchtime I was quite punch-drunk.* [Literally, suffering from a form of concussion caused by blows to the head and causing one to behave as if drunk — a condition once often found in boxers.]

a punch-up (*inf*) a fight (using fists): *They had a punch-up with the police.*

pup

sell (someone) a pup (*sl*) to cheat (someone): *Someone really sold you a pup when they persuaded you to invest money in that firm — it's about to go bankrupt.*

pure

pure and simple nothing but: *It was an accident pure and simple.*

pure as the driven snow *see* **drive.**

purple

a purple patch an especially brilliant section of something, *orig* (*sometimes derog*) an elaborate piece of writing: *His clear, workmanlike prose is marred by the occasional purple patch.* [From a phrase — *purpurens pannus* — coined by the Latin poet Horace.]

purpose

at cross purposes *see* **cross.**

serve a purpose (*formal*) to be useful in some way: *Keep that bag — it may serve a purpose*; *This is not the tool I wanted but it will serve my purpose* (= do what I need) *very well.*

to good/some purpose with useful results: *His investigations were to some purpose and revealed several ways in which the firm could save money.*

to no purpose (*formal*) with no useful results: *We discussed the problem several times but to no purpose.*

to the purpose (*formal*) relevant; to the point: *His reply was not really to the purpose.*

purse

you can't make a silk purse out of a sow's ear *see* **silk.**

push

be pushed for (something) (*inf*) to be short of (something); not to have enough of (something): *I'm a bit pushed for time/money.*

be pushing forty, fifty *etc* (*inf*) to be nearly forty, fifty in age: *She's very agile and she must be pushing seventy.*

give (someone)/get the push (*sl*) to dismiss (someone)/be dismissed from a job *etc*: *He was the manager of that firm but he got the push*; *His girlfriend had just given him the push*.

push one's luck *see* **luck**.

push off (*impolite inf*) to go away: *I wish you'd push off!*

a push-over (*sl*) a very easy job or task: *The thieves thought the robbery would be a push-over*.

put

put (something) across to convey or communicate (ideas *etc*) to others: *He has a great deal of information but he does not put it across very well*.

put a good face on it *see* **face**.

put a stop to (something) *see* **stop**.

put (something) down to (something) to attribute (*eg* a way of behaviour) to (a particular circumstance): *I put her rudeness down to anxiety*.

put (someone) in his place *see* **place**.

put (someone) in mind *see* **mind**.

put oneself in (someone's) place *see* **place**.

put (someone) in the picture *see* **picture**.

put (something) into practice *see* **practice**.

put one's finger on (something) *see* **finger**.

put one's mind to *see* **mind**.

put (someone's) nose out of joint *see* **nose**.

put (someone or something) off to postpone: *She wanted to come today but I put her off till tomorrow*.

put (someone) off (something) to cause (someone) to feel disgust *etc* for (something): *The conversation about illness put me off my dinner*.

put (something) on to make a false show of (something); to feign (something): *She said she felt ill, but she was just putting it on*.

put on an act *see* **act**.

put one across (someone) *see* **across**.

put (someone) out (*inf*) to cause bother or trouble to (someone): *Are we putting you out?*; *Don't put yourself out for my sake!*

put (someone) right *see* **right**.

put (something) right *see* **right**.

put the cat among the pigeons *see* **cat**.

a put-up job (*inf*) something done to give a false appearance, in order to cheat or trick someone: *The trial was just a put-up job*.

put upon (someone) to make use of (someone) for one's own benefit to an unreasonable extent: *She is very helpful and tends to* *be put upon by the lazier members of her family.*

put (someone) up to (doing something) to persuade (a person) to (do something): *Who put you up to writing that letter?*; *Did he put you up to it?*

put up with (something) to bear (something) patiently; to tolerate (something): *I cannot put up with all this noise.*

stay put *see* **stay.**

pyjamas

the cat's pyjamas *see* **cat.**

Pyrrhic

a Pyrrhic victory (*formal*) a situation where one is successful but where the cost of winning is so great that it was not worth it: *Winning the court case turned out to be a Pyrrhic victory, as his health was shattered by the experience and he died shortly afterwards.* [From the costly victory of Pyrrhus, king of Epirus, over the Romans at Heraclea in 280 BC.]

Q

quantity

an unknown quantity a person or thing whose characteristics, abilities *etc* cannot be predicted: *We do not know how he will react — he's an unknown quantity.* [A mathematical term — the definition of *x, etc*, in algebra.]

quarter

at close quarters from or at a position nearby: *He was staying in our hotel, so I had an opportunity of observing him at close quarters.* [A military term.]

queer

in Queer Street in difficulties, *esp* in debt or very short of money: *If I don't get my money back from Henry, I shall be in Queer Street before the end of the month.* [In the early 19C *queer* was an element in many slang terms for shady or criminal persons, activities *etc*.]

a queer fish *see* **fish.**

queer (someone's) pitch (*inf*) to spoil (someone's) plans; to make it impossible for (someone) to do something: *He had persuaded her to go and live with him but her sister queered his pitch by telling her that he was married.* [A showman's term — a *pitch* is the place where a stall, circus *etc* is set up (from pitching tents) and anything that went wrong, *esp* interference from the police, was said to *queer* it.]

question

beg the question *see* **beg.**

call (something) into question (*formal*) to raise doubts about (something): *The company's ability to survive has been called into question.*

in question (*formal*) being talked about: *The matter in question can be left till next week.*

a loaded question *see* **load.**

out of the question not to be thought of as possible; not to be done: *It is quite out of the question for you to go out tonight.*

pop the question (*inf*) to ask (a woman) to marry one: *She said that her boyfriend had popped the question as they drove home from his sister's wedding.*

a rhetorical question *see* **rhetorical.**

the sixty-four (thousand) dollar question *see* **sixty.**

a vexed question *see* **vex.**

queue

jump the queue to move ahead of others in a queue without waiting for one's proper turn: *Many wealthy or important people try to jump the queue for hospital beds.*

qui

on the qui vive very alert: *Mary, who was the only one on the qui vive, heard his car draw up and ran out to greet him.* [From the standard challenge of a French sentry: *Qui vive?* — 'Long live who?', *ie* 'Which side are you on?'.]

quick

as quick as lightning *see* **lightning.**

cut (someone) to the quick to hurt (someone's) feelings very much: *His lack of consideration cut her to the quick.* [The *quick* is the living, sensitive part of *eg* a fingernail.]

a quick one (*inf*) a quick drink: *We've just time for a quick one before the pubs close.*

quick on the uptake *see* **uptake.**

quid

quids in (*sl*) in a very good or favourable position: *If your fiancé's mother likes you, you'll be quids in!*

quit

be quits with (someone) to be even with (someone), neither owing them anything nor being owed anything by them: *You hit him and he hit you back, so you are quits.*

call it/cry quits (*inf*) to agree with someone that neither person owes the other person anything: *This fight has been going on for years — why don't you two call it quits and be friends?*

quite

quite something (*inf*) something special, remarkable or very good: *Her apple pie is quite something!*

R

r

the three Rs reading, writing and arithmetic, thought of as the most necessary parts of a basic education: *It is often said that modern education spends too much time on unimportant activities and not enough on the three Rs.* [From reading, writing and a-rithmetic.]

race

a one-horse race *see* **one.**

the rat race *see* **rat.**

rack

go to rack and ruin to get into a state of neglect and decay: *The castle has gone to rack and ruin now.* [*Rack* here means 'destruction'.]

rack one's brains *see* **brain.**

rag

glad rags *see* **glad.**

like a red rag to a bull *see* **red.**

lose one's rag (*Brit inf*) to lose one's temper: *The teacher really lost his rag when the children started to laugh.* [Origin uncertain.]

rage

(all) the rage (*inf*) very much in fashion: *Fur hats are (all) the rage this winter.*

rail

off the rails (*Brit inf*) not sensible; slightly mad: *I think he has gone a bit off the rails with some of these suggestions.* [The reference is to a railway train.]

rain

as right as rain (*inf*) perfectly all right; completely well: *Your daughter has a slight cold. Keep her in bed and she'll be (as) right as* *rain in a couple of days*. [A pun on the original meaning of *right* = straight.]

keep/save *etc* **(something) for a rainy day** to keep (something, *esp* money) until one needs it or in case one may need it: *I don't spend my whole salary — I put some in the bank for a rainy day.* [The reference is to money-making activities only possible on days when the sun shines.]

rain or shine whatever the weather is like: *He goes for a long walk every morning, rain or shine.*

rain cats and dogs *see* **cat**.

raise

raise a stink *see* **stink**.

raise Cain/hell *etc* (*inf*) to make a great deal of noise: *She raised hell when she discovered what the children had done.*

raise (someone's) hopes *see* **hope**.

raise the wind *see* **wind**[1].

raise one's voice *see* **voice**.

rake

as thin as a rake very thin: *Since his illness he has been as thin as a rake.*

rake (something) up to find out and tell or remind people about (something, *usu* something unpleasant that would be better forgotten): *The newspaper reporters raked up a story about the politician stealing £20 from a shop when he was a boy.* [From *muckraking* — *see at* **muck**.]

rally

rally round to come together for a joint action or effort, *esp* of support: *When John's business was in difficulty, his friends all rallied round (to help) him.*

ram

ram (something) down (someone's) throat *see* **throat**.

rampage

be/go on the rampage to rush about angrily, violently or in excitement: *The boss is on the rampage because people keep coming in late.*

random

at random without any particular plan or system: *The police were stopping cars at random and checking their brakes.*

rank

break ranks to cease to take united defensive action: *Eventually* *the strikers will break ranks and go back to work because they have no money.*

close ranks to act together as a defensive measure: *The staff have closed ranks and refuse to discuss the matter.* [Literally used of soldiers *etc*, meaning 'to move closer together'.]

the rank and file ordinary people: *The rank and file in a trade union do not always agree with their officials.* [Literally, *ranks* and *files* are the horizontal and vertical lines in which battalions of soldiers were once drawn up in the field and on parade.]

ransom

hold (someone) to ransom to use threats *etc* to try to persuade (someone) to do as one wishes: *He tried to hold the shop to ransom by threatening to buy all his office furniture elsewhere if they did not allow him a discount.* [Literally, to keep someone as a prisoner until a sum of money is paid for his release.]

a king's ransom a vast amount of money: *She would not marry him for a king's ransom.* [Literally, the amount of money that would be demanded as ransom for a king, if captured.]

rant

rant and rave to talk angrily about something: *He's still ranting and raving about the damage to his car.*

rap

take the rap (for something) (*sl*) to take the blame, punishment *etc* (for a crime, mistake *etc*): *She is always taking the rap for things other people have done because she refuses to tell tales.*

raring

raring to go (*inf*) very keen to begin, go *etc*: *He always arrives early, full of energy and raring to go.* [A dialectal form of *rearing* — *ie* in eagerness.]

rat

rat on (someone) to betray (one's friends, colleagues *etc*): *The police know we're here. Someone must have ratted on us.*

the rat race (*inf*) a fierce, unending competition for success, wealth *etc* in business, society *etc*: *He grew tired of the rat race and retired to live in the country.* [A nautical phrase for a fierce tidal current — both *rat* and *race* are forms of the French *ras* = a tide-race.]

smell a rat (*inf*) to have a feeling that something is not as it should be, but is wrong or bad: *The police set up a trap, but the thieves smelt a rat and drove away.* [The reference is to a terrier hunting.]

rate

at any rate 1 whatever may happen or have happened: *It's a pity it has started to rain, but at any rate we can still enjoy ourselves at the cinema.* **2** that is to say; at least: *He is a very good artist, at any rate for someone who is colour-blind; The Queen is coming to see us — at any rate, that's what John says.*

at a rate of knots *see* **knot.**

at this, at that rate if this or if that is the case; if this or if that continues: *He says that he isn't sure whether we'll be allowed to finish, but at that rate we might as well not start.*

raw

in the raw in the natural state; exactly as it is, without anything to make it look nicer: *You see nature in the raw in the jungle.*

a raw deal (*inf*) unfair treatment: *His secretary thinks she got a raw deal, since everyone got an increase in salary except her.*

raw material something out of which something else can be made: *Her experiences in India provided the raw material for the novels she was to write in later life.* [Literally, the naturally-occurring products out of which manufactured goods are made.]

razor

as sharp/keen as a razor 1 very sharp: *The edge of the leaf was as keen as a razor and cut my hand.* **2** very quick-witted and intelligent: *She is ninety-nine years old, but her mind is still as sharp as a razor.*

read

read between the lines *see* **line.**

read (something) into (something) to understand (a statement *etc*) to have a meaning which is not actually stated, and may not be intended: *You're reading more into his speech than he intended.*

read the riot act *see* **riot.**

read up on (something) (*inf*) to learn (something) by study: *I must read up on this before my exam.*

take (something) as read to assume (something) without checking it, doing it *etc*: *Can we take it as read that this has all been verified, or do we need to make further enquiries?* [Literally used of the minutes of a previous meeting which are accepted without being formally read over.]

real

for real (*esp US: sl*) genuine; true: *He says he's got a new bike, but I don't know if that's for real.*

in reality really; actually: *He pretends to be busy, but in reality he has very little to do.*

the real McCoy/Mackay (*inf*) something genuine, *esp* of very good quality, as contrasted with all other (inferior) things called by the same name: *I have been in many so-called 'Chinese restaurants', but this one is the real McCoy.* [Origin unknown.]

rear

bring up the rear (*formal*) to come last: *One of the most experienced climbers brought up the rear.* [A military term.]

rear its ugly head *see* **head.**

reason

have (good) reason to (believe, think *etc*) (*formal*) to feel justified in (believing *etc* something): *I have (good) reason to think that he is lying.*

it stands to reason (that) anyone who thinks about (a subject) will come to the conclusion (that something is true, probable *etc*): *If you go on smoking sixty cigarettes a day, it stands to reason that you'll get lung cancer.*

listen to reason to allow oneself to be persuaded to do something more sensible than what one was going to do; to pay attention to common sense: *He was so angry that he was going to resign, but I got him to listen to reason.*

lose one's reason (*formal*) to become mad or insane.

see reason to (be persuaded to) be more sensible than one is or has been: *He's so impulsive that it's sometimes difficult to make him see reason.*

within reason within the limits of good sense: *I'll do anything/ go anywhere within reason.*

rebound

on the rebound (*inf*) soon after, and as the result of suffering, a great disappointment, *esp* the end of a love affair: *His fiancée left him, and he married the girl next door on the rebound.* [An idiom from ball-games.]

recall

beyond recall unable to be changed, stopped *etc*: *The matter is beyond recall.*

reckon

reckon on (something) to depend on or expect (something): *I was reckoning on meeting him tonight.*

reckon with to expect trouble, difficulties *etc* from (a person *etc*): *He's a man to be reckoned with.*

record

break the record to do something better, faster, more often *etc* than anyone else has done: *He has just broken the record for the number of pork pies eaten in half an hour.*

for the record (*formal*) in order to be sure that the facts are recorded correctly: *Just for the record, I would like to make it clear that I do not agree with the committee's decision.*

off the record (of information, statements *etc*) not intended to be repeated or made public: *The Prime Minister admitted off the record that the country was going through a serious crisis.*

on record written down or recorded for future reference: *I wish to go/be put on record as disagreeing with all these decisions*; *This is the coldest winter on record* (= since records were started).

set the record straight (*formal*) to put right a mistake or misunderstanding: *You have got a false impression of my opinion on this matter, and I am glad of this opportunity to set the record straight.*

(someone's) track record *see* **track.**

red

catch (someone) red-handed to find (someone) in the act of doing wrong: *The police caught the thief red-handed.* [The reference is to finding a murderer with blood still on his hands.]

in the red (*inf*) in debt: *I am/My bank account is in the red.* [From the use of red ink to make entries on the debit side of a ledger.]

like a red rag to a bull (*inf*) certain to make (a person) angry: *Criticizing the Liberal Party in front of him is like a red rag to a bull.* [From the widespread belief that the sight of the colour red makes bulls angry. In fact, bulls are colour-blind.]

on red alert in a state of being warned and ready for an immediately approaching danger: *When smoke was seen rising from the volcano, the whole area was put on red alert.* [Originally a military term for use *esp* in mobilizing civilians during an air-raid *etc*. *Yellow, blue* and *red alerts* represented increasing degrees of readiness for an attack.]

paint the town red *see* **paint.**

red-blooded active; manly; full of strong, *usu* sexual desires: *He was a red-blooded male who could not be expected to live like a monk.*

a redbrick university (*sometimes derog*) any of the universities founded in England in the late nineteenth century, *usu* contrasted with Oxford and Cambridge: *He didn't get into Cambridge — he's going to one of the redbrick universities.*

(the) red-carpet treatment great respect and honour given to important guests or visitors: *The Prime Minister was given the red-carpet treatment when he visited the town.* [From the practice of rolling out a red carpet for important guests to walk on.]

a red herring a false clue intended or tending to mislead someone: *The evidence about the missing gun, over which the police spent so much time, turned out later to be a red herring — it was not the murder weapon.* [Red herring, a type of smoked herring, were occasionally used to lay trails for hunting dogs to follow. The scent of a red herring which had been dragged across the trail of genuine animal-scent, however, could also be used to mislead the dogs.]

red-hot (*inf*) very enthusiastic: *a red-hot socialist.*

a red-letter day a day which will always be remembered because something particularly pleasant or important happened on it: *The day I won a prize on the football pools was a real red-letter day.* [From the medieval custom of using red ink for saints' days when writing out a calendar.]

reds under the bed (*derog*) (the belief that everything bad that happens to one's country is caused by) the secret activities of Communists: *Politicians who are always looking for reds under the bed are unlikely to discover much about the real causes of industrial unrest.*

red tape (*derog*) (the strict attention to and following of) annoying and unnecessary rules and regulations: *I need a new passport, but because of all the red tape, I won't get it in time for my holiday.* [From the 'red' — actually pink — tape used by government offices *etc* to tie up bundles of papers.]

see red (*inf*) to become angry: *When he started criticizing my work, I really saw red.* [Probably the same origin as **like a red rag to a bull,** *above.*]

redeem
a redeeming feature something which compensates (for something which is bad or wrong): *It's an ugly house — its one redeeming feature is its position on the hill.*

redress
redress the balance (*very formal*) to make things (more nearly) equal again: *The general claimed that the enemy had many more missiles than our allies and that the government must somehow redress the balance.*

reed
a broken reed *see* **broken.**

reel
reel off (something) to say or repeat (something) quickly and

easily without pausing: *He reeled off the list of names/the parts of the verb 'to be'.*

refresh

refresh one's (someone's) memory to, or to cause (someone) to, think about, read *etc* the facts or details of something again so that they are clear in the mind: *Let me refresh your memory about the details of our plans in case anyone asks any awkward questions.*

refusal

first refusal the opportunity to buy, accept *etc* or refuse (something) before it is offered, given, sold *etc* to someone else: *If you ever decide to sell your caravan, will you give me (the) first refusal?*

regard

as regards (something) (*formal*) as far as (something) is concerned; turning our attention to (something): *That answers your first question. As regards your second question, I feel that it is ridiculous.*
with regard to (something) (*formal*) about; concerning: *I have no complaints with regard to his work.*

region

in the region of (*formal*) about; near: *The cost of the new building will be somewhere in the region of £50000.*

regular

regular as clockwork *see* **clock.**

rein

give (free) rein to (something) (*formal*) to allow oneself, one's mind *etc* great freedom (to act, think *etc* as one pleases): *In writing that novel she gave free rein to her imagination.* [From riding or driving horses.]
keep a tight rein on (someone or something) (*formal*) to keep strict control of (a person, thing *etc*): *I have to keep a tight rein on my wife's spending.* [As previous idiom.]

relieve

relieve (someone) of (something) (*facet*) to take (something) from (someone) unwillingly, *esp* to steal it: *The thief relieved her of £10000 worth of jewellery; A man at the door relieved us of £2 entrance fee, which we thought very expensive.*

repeat

repeat oneself to say the same thing more than once: *Listen carefully because I don't want to have to repeat myself.*

reputation

live up to one's reputation to behave in the way that people

295

say one behaves; to do what people expect one to do: *He has the reputation of being a fool, and he is really living up to it.*

repute

of repute (*formal*) well thought of and respected by many people: *He is a man of some repute in this town.*

reserve

have, keep *etc* **(something) in reserve** (*formal*) to have or keep (something) in case or until it is needed: *If you go to America please keep some money in reserve for your fare home.*

resort

as a/in the last resort when all other methods *etc* have failed: *If we can't get the money in any other way, I suppose we could, as a last resort, sell the car.* [Originally a legal term referring to a hearing in a court from which there was no appeal.]

resource

leave (someone) to his own resources to leave (someone) to amuse himself, or to find his own way of solving a problem *etc*: *After they had finished interviewing him they left him to his own resources.*

respect

be no respecter of persons not to be influenced by the importance, wealth *etc* of the people involved: *Old age is no respecter of persons — even millionaires cannot stay young for ever.* [A Biblical reference — to Acts 10:34.]

in respect of (something) (*formal*) as far as (something) is concerned: *This report is fine in respect of information but the spelling is dreadful.*

pay one's respects (to someone) to visit (someone) as a sign of respect to him: *I've come to pay my respects (to your father).*

with respect to (something) (*formal*) about or concerning (something): *With respect to your request, we regret that we are unable to assist you in this matter.*

rest

come to rest to stop moving: *The ball came to rest under a tree.*

for the rest as far as everything else is concerned; when thinking of everything else: *I make sure he never speaks to any of my family, and for the rest I don't really care what he does!*

God rest his soul a wish that a dead person's soul may be at peace: *My father, God rest his soul, was out fishing on the very day he died.*

(someone's) last resting-place (*formal*) (someone's) grave: *He died in London, and his last resting-place is in Westminster Abbey.*

lay (someone) to rest (*formal euph*) to bury (someone) in a grave: *She was laid to rest in the village where she was born.*

rest assured (*formal*) to be certain: *You may rest assured that we will take your views into consideration.*

rest on one's laurels *see* **laurel.**

rest on one's oars *see* **oar.**

retreat

beat a (hasty) retreat to leave or go away in a hurry: *The children beat a hasty retreat when they saw the headmaster coming.* [A military phrase, from the former practice in infantry regiments of transmitting orders by means of different drum signals.]

return

by return (of post) (*formal*) (of an answering letter *etc*) immediately; (sent) by the very next post: *Please reply by return of post.*

in return (for something) as an exchange (for something): *We'll send them whisky and they'll send us vodka in return; They'll send us vodka in return for whisky.*

many happy returns (of the day) an expression of good wishes (said to a person on his birthday): *He visited his mother on her birthday to wish her many happy returns.*

the point of no return *see* **point.**

rhetorical

a rhetorical question a question which the speaker answers himself, or which does not need an answer: *When you said 'What next will she do?', was it a rhetorical question or do you expect me to answer it?* [From the use of such stylized questions as one of the commonest and most effective elements of formal speech-making.]

rhyme

without rhyme or reason without sense, reason or a logical system: *His method of classifying books seems to be without rhyme or reason.*

rich

strike it rich (*inf*) to make a lot of money: *He did not make much money in his new business at first but he finally struck it rich.* [An idiom from gold-mining.]

rid

be, get rid of (someone or something) to have removed, to remove (someone or something); to free oneself from (a problem, worry *etc*); to make (someone or something) go away: *I thought I'd never get rid of these stains/weeds/people/debts.*

good riddance (to someone or something) (*inf*) I am happy to have got rid of (someone or something): *I've thrown out all those old books, and good riddance (to the lot of them).*

ride

be/come/go along for the ride (*inf*) to join a group of people *etc* simply out of interest, not to take part oneself in what they are doing: *Unlike the others I was not performing at the concert, but as it promised to be an interesting evening I decided to go along for the ride.* [Originally used of joining other people on a journey which they were obliged to make.]

let (something) ride (*inf*) to do nothing about (something); to let (something) continue as it is: *I can foresee a lot of problems with his plans, but we'll let that ride for the time being.*

ride out (something) to survive until (a period of difficulty) is past: *I think we'll ride out the crisis.* [Literally, of a ship, 'to keep afloat throughout (a storm *etc*)'.]

ride up (of a skirt *etc*) to move gradually up out of its correct position: *I can't wear this skirt when I go into town as it rides up when I walk.*

riding for a fall behaving in a manner likely to cause a disaster to oneself: *She has begun to be very impertinent to the manager recently — I think she's riding for a fall.* [A hunting metaphor.]

riding high very successful; in a high position *etc*: *She has just been promoted, so she is riding high at the moment.* [A phrase often used literally of the moon *etc*.]

take (someone) for a ride (*inf*) to trick, cheat or deceive (someone): *He doesn't actually work for a charity at all, so the people who have sent him money have been taken for a ride.* [Originally American gangsters' slang for killing someone, from a common practice of doing so in a moving car to avoid attracting attention.]

rift

a rift in the lute (*liter*) a small disagreement, problem *etc* that shows signs of developing into something which will destroy a project or relationship: *They did not realize then that the argument they had just had was the rift in the lute that would eventually lead to divorce.* [A quotation from Tennyson's *Idylls of the King*.]

right

as right as rain *see* **rain.**

by right(s) rightfully: *By rights, I ought to be in charge of this department.*

get, keep on the right side of (someone) to make (someone) feel, or continue to feel, friendly or kind towards oneself: *If you want a pay rise, you'd better get on the right side of the boss.*

get (something) right to understand, do, say *etc* (something) correctly: *Did I get the answer right?*; *The movements in this dance are quite difficult, so you won't get them right at your first attempt.*

go right to happen as expected, wanted or intended; to be successful or without problems: *Nothing ever goes right for him.*

in one's own right 1 not because of someone else; independently: *She is a baroness in her own right* (= because she has inherited the title or has received it as an honour, not because she is married to a baron). **2** because of one's own ability, work *etc*: *She's married to a writer, but she is a novelist in her own right.* [A medieval legal term.]

in one's right mind *see* **mind.**

in the right correct in what one says or does: *I will support you because I believe you are in the right.*

keep (someone) right to prevent (someone) from making mistakes: *This book of instructions will keep you right.*

Mr Right (*often facet*) the perfect man for someone to marry: *She believes that one day Mr Right will come and sweep her off her feet.*

not (quite) right in the head (*inf*) (slightly) mad: *He cannot be right in the head — making incredible suggestions like that!*

on the right track *see* **track.**

put (someone) right 1 to tell (someone) the truth, the correct way of doing something *etc*: *I used to think he was a fool but John put me right about him.* **2** to make (someone) healthy again: *I had an upset stomach, but that medicine soon put me right.*

put (something) right 1 to repair (something); to remove faults *etc* in (something): *There is something wrong with this kettle — can you put it right?* **2** to put an end to or change (something that is wrong): *He hasn't been paid for the last job he did, but we can soon put that right.*

(someone's) right arm *see* **arm.**

a right-hand man a person's most trusted and useful assistant: *I couldn't do without William — he is my right-hand man.*

right off immediately; without delay: *I just asked David and he gave me the information right off.*

right you are (*inf*) certainly; very well: *'I'll put this box over here.' 'Right you are.'*

serve (someone) right to be what a person deserves (*usu* something bad): *If you fall and hurt yourself, it'll serve you right for climbing* *up there when I told you not to!*

set (something) to rights to put (something) into the correct order, place *etc*, or into a good or desirable state: *The room was in a dreadful mess, and it took us the whole day to set it to rights.*

strike the right note *see* **note.**

take (something) in the right spirit *see* **spirit.**

ring

a dead ringer for (someone or something) (*sl*) almost identical to (some other person or thing): *I saw a woman yesterday who was a dead ringer for my music teacher.* [An American phrase probably connected with the use of the word *ringer* to mean a person sent to vote illegally in a district where he is not entitled to vote, and later to mean a horse substituted for another horse of less ability in a race.]

have a ringside seat (*inf*) to be in a position where one can see clearly something which is happening: *Since the incident involving the two cars happened right outside my window, I had a ringside seat.* [Probably from boxing.]

ring a bell *see* **bell.**

ring down the curtain *see* **curtain.**

ring off to end a telephone call: *'I will never forgive you!' she said, and rang off before I could reply.* [From the method of ending a call in the early days of the telephone, by alerting the operator by means of a bell.]

ring the changes *see* **change.**

ring true to sound or seem to be true or false: *His story does not ring true.* [From the practice of testing the quality of metal or glass by striking it and listening to the resultant sound.]

ring (someone or something) up 1 to telephone (someone): *I'll ring you up tonight.* **2** to record (the price of something sold) on a cash register: *You've rung up £5 and this sweater costs only £3.*

riot

read the riot act to tell (someone) angrily that they have done wrong and warn them that their bad behaviour must stop: *The teacher read the riot act when he found one of the boys cheating in their exams.* [The Riot Act of 1715 decreed that when a group of twelve or more people assembled in one place were considered to be a threat to the peace, the magistrates should read part of the Act to them, commanding them to disperse in the King's name, after which action could be taken against them if they did not.]

riotous living (*usu facet*) living in a very extravagant and energetic manner: *She is exhausted after all the riotous living of the Christmas holidays.* [A Biblical reference, to the parable of the Prodigal Son, Luke 15:13.]

run riot to act, speak *etc* in an uncontrolled way: *When the teacher left the room the children ran riot.* [A hunting term for hounds which are following the scent of the wrong animal, from the Old French word for a dispute.]

ripe

a ripe old age a very old age: *He lived to the ripe old age of ninety-five.*

rise

give rise to (something) (*formal*) to cause (something): *This plan has given rise to serious problems.*

rise and shine! (*inf: usu facet*) an instruction to someone to get out of bed quickly, *esp* in the morning: *Come on, girls, rise and shine!* [The image is of the sun.]

rise to the occasion *see* **occasion.**

take/get a rise out of (someone) (*inf*) to make (a person) angry *etc* by teasing or annoying him: *Just ignore him when he makes fun of your nose — he's just trying to take a rise out of you.*

risk

at (someone's) own risk with (the person concerned) agreeing to accept any loss, damage *etc* involved: *Cars are parked here at your own risk* (= The owners of the car park will not pay for any damage *etc* to parked cars).

risk one's neck *see* **neck.**

run/take the risk (of doing something) to do (something which involves a risk): *I took the risk of buying that jumper for you in the sales — I hope it fits.*

river

sell (someone) down the river to betray (someone): *The gang found that they had been sold down the river by one of their associates.* [An American phrase, from the former custom of slave-owners in the upper Mississippi states of selling unsatisfactory household slaves to the much harsher life on the cotton and sugar plantations of Louisiana.]

road

get the show on the road *see* **show.**

in, out of the/(someone's) road (*inf*) in or out of the/(someone's) way: *Get out of my road!*

one for the road (*inf*) a last alcoholic drink before leaving (to go somewhere): *It's about time we were heading home — let's just have one for the road and then we'll go.*

on the road to recovery getting better after an illness: *He had a very bad attack of flu, but he's on the road to recovery now.*

a road-hog a person who drives carelessly or selfishly, causing trouble and annoyance to other drivers. [From the proverbial greediness and bad manners of pigs.]

roaring

do a roaring trade (*inf*) to have a very successful business; to sell a lot of (something): *She and her friends have started selling home-made cakes and they're doing a roaring trade.*

roaring drunk (*inf*) very drunk.

roast

a dripping roast *see* **drip.**

rob

daylight robbery (*inf*) the charging of prices which are too high: *Asking £5 for a book like that is daylight robbery.*

rob Peter to pay Paul to get enough money *etc* to pay one debt or get one thing done by using the money *etc* which one actually needs to pay another debt or do something else: *If you use your rent money to pay the interest on your bank loan, isn't that robbing Peter to pay Paul?* [Probably from the fact that St Peter and St Paul share the same feast-day — 29 July — and have alliterating names.]

rock

as steady as a rock very steady and unmoving: *Although he had had quite a lot to drink, his hand was as steady as a rock.*

off one's rocker (*sl*) mad; crazy: *If you think he'll lend you £100, you must be off your rocker.* [The reference is to a broken rocking-chair.]

on the rocks (*inf*) **1** (of a marriage) in(to) a state where the husband and wife wish to separate or be divorced: *Their marriage is (going) on the rocks.* **2** (of a *usu* alcoholic drink) served with ice cubes: *I'll have a Scotch on the rocks, please.* **3** (of a business firm) in(to) a state of great financial difficulty, having no, or not enough, money: *The firm is on the rocks.* [A reference to a shipwreck.]

rod

make a rod for one's (own) back to do something which is going to cause trouble for oneself: *That child's mother is making a* *rod for her back by spoiling him like that.* [Literally, 'to provide a stick for oneself to be beaten with' — a medieval image.]

rule with a rod of iron *see* **iron.**

spare the rod and spoil the child a saying (once generally believed) meaning that it is a mistake to treat children too mildly.

rogue

a rogues' gallery (*sl*) a police collection of photographs of known criminals: *The police hoped she would be able to identify her attacker from their rogues' gallery.*

roll

roll in (*inf*) to come in or be got in large numbers or amounts: *They've started selling home-made cakes, and the money is just rolling in.*

a rolling stone gathers no moss a saying, meaning that people who have never stayed long in one place generally have no responsibilities and few possessions.

roll on (a time, day *etc*) may (a given time) come soon: *Roll on the day when I can afford to buy a new car!*

roll up 1 (*inf*) to arrive: *John rolled up ten minutes late.* **2** (*usu* to a crowd *eg* in a market, at a fair) come near: *Roll up! Roll up! Come and see the bearded lady!*

to be rolling in (something) (*inf*) to have large amounts of (something, *usu* money): *He doesn't have to worry about money — he's rolling in it.*

Rome

Rome was not built in a day a saying, meaning that a difficult or important aim cannot be achieved quickly or all at once.

when in Rome, do as the Romans do a saying, meaning that one is wise to copy the behaviour of people who are used to the circumstances, places *etc* in which one finds oneself. [A saying of St Ambrose.]

romp

romp home (*inf*) to win easily: *After scoring the first goal, the team romped home to an easy victory.*

roof

go through the roof/hit the roof (*inf*) to become very angry: *When he saw all the mistakes his secretary had made, he really hit the roof; Your father will go through the roof when you tell him you have crashed his car.*

have a roof over one's head to have somewhere to live: *My* *new house is not a palace, but at least it means I have a roof over my head.*

room

    room to swing a cat *see* **cat.**

roost

    (chickens) come home to roost (of a *usu* bad action) to have an unpleasant effect on the person who did the action: *All his lies have come home to roost.* [From the motto of Robert Southey's poem *The Curse of Kehama* — 'Curses are like young chickens, they always come home to roost'.]

    rule the roost to be the person in a group, family *etc* whose orders, wishes *etc* are obeyed: *In that family there is no doubt that the grandmother rules the roost.* [An alteration of the obscure **rule the roast**, of which the origin is unknown.]

root

    be rooted in (something) (*formal*) to have (something) as a cause; to originate in (something): *His difficulties are rooted in his lack of education.* [From plants.]

    the grass roots *see* **grass.**

    root and branch (*formal*) completely and absolutely: *This evil system must be destroyed root and branch!* [A phrase derived from the Bible — Malachi 4:1 — and much used in the early 1640s in connection with the attempt at that time to abolish episcopacy in the Church of England.]

    rooted to the spot *see* **spot.**

    root (something) out to destroy (something) completely: *We must do our best to root out disease and poverty.*

    take root to grow firmly; to become established: *The new business took root.* [From plants.]

rope

    know the ropes to understand the detail and procedure (of a job *etc*): *He'll be very good once he knows the ropes a bit better.* [A nautical idiom, from the practical implications of getting used to working on board ship.]

    money for old rope *see* **money.**

    rope (someone) in (*inf*) to include (someone); to persuade (someone) to join in doing something: *We roped him in to help.* [Originally US, from the use of lassoes to catch and collect cattle in the American West.]

rose

    a bed of roses *see* **bed.**

everything's coming up roses (*not formal*) everything is proving to be successful, happy, lucky *etc* (for a particular person): *He has been very unfortunate in the past, but since he got married everything's coming up roses for him.*

look at/see (something) through rose-coloured spectacles to have a very ideal, optimistic view of (something): *She looks at marriage through rose-coloured spectacles.*

rough

be rough on (someone) (*inf*) to be bad luck or unfortunate for (someone): *It's rough on her, to have to stay behind when her husband goes to Paris.*

cut up rough (*slang*) to behave in an unpleasant, angry manner: *He'll cut up rough when he hears about the damage to his car.*

ride roughshod over (someone) (*inf*) to treat (someone) without any regard for his feelings: *He is so ambitious that he rides roughshod over everyone.* [Literally, *roughshod* is used of a horse, and means 'provided with roughened horse-shoes' — to give better grip on roads.]

rough-and-ready 1 not carefully made or finished, but good enough: *His speech at the dinner was a bit rough-and-ready.* **2** (of people) friendly enough but without politeness *etc*: *He's rather rough-and-ready but you'll like him.*

rough-and-tumble a (*usu* friendly) fight; a scuffle: *The children were having a rough-and-tumble in the garden.* [Originally boxing slang for a kind of fight in which the normal rules did not apply.]

a rough diamond *see* **diamond.**

rough it (*inf*) to live primitively, without the usual comforts of life: *We had no money for a hotel so we had to rough it and camp out.*

rough (something) out to draw or explain (a rough sketch *etc* or idea): *He roughed out the plan to the others.*

sleep rough to sleep out-of-doors: *He spent his holiday hitch-hiking through Greece, sleeping rough and eating in small cafés.*

take the rough with the smooth to accept the disadvantages of a person, situation *etc* with the advantages: *I don't like living in the town, but with a new job you have to take the rough with the smooth.*

round

an all-rounder in games *etc*, a person who can play any position, *eg* who can bat as well as bowl in cricket.

get round to (something) (*inf*) to manage to do (something);

to find enough time to do (something): *I don't know when I'll get round to painting the door.*

go the rounds (*inf*) to be handed from one person to another or from place to place: *His first novel went the rounds for a year before he finally found a publisher for it.*

in the round (*formal*) visible from all sides: *Sculpture should be seen in the round.*

round figures/numbers the nearest convenient or easily remembered numbers: *Tell me the cost in round figures* (*ie* £20 rather than £19.87 or £5000 rather than £5123).

round (something) off to complete (something) successfully; to make a successful ending to (something): *He rounded off his career by becoming president; He rounded the meal off with a glass of port.*

round on (someone) (*formal*) to attack (someone) (*usu* in words): *He rounded on her, demanding to know where she had been.*

round the twist *see* **twist.**

a round trip a journey to a place and back again: *She drove to Aberdeen and back again, a round trip of 90 miles.*

round (something) up 1 to collect (something) together: *The farmer rounded up the sheep.* **2** to raise (a number) to the nearest convenient figure, *usu* ten, one hundred *etc*: *The total came to £2.89, which we rounded up to £3.00 and divided among the six of us.*

talk (someone) round *see* **talk.**

row

have a hard row to hoe to have to lead a life full of difficulties and hardship: *Mary had a hard row to hoe, with an invalid husband, five children and very little money to live on.*

in a row one after the other: *She won the championship three years in a row.* [Originally US.]

rub

rub along (with someone) (*inf*) to get on fairly well (with someone); to be fairly friendly (with someone): *I rub along all right with my relations.*

rub (something) in (*inf*) to keep reminding someone of (something unpleasant): *I know I've lost my job — you don't have to keep rubbing it in!*

rub (someone's) nose in it *see* **nose.**

rub off on (to) (someone) to pass to (someone) through close contact *etc*: *Jane is such a polite child — I hope some of her manners will rub off on to my daughter if they play together often.*

rub salt into the wound *see* **salt.**

rub shoulders with *see* **shoulder.**

rub (someone) (up) the wrong way (*inf*) to annoy or irritate someone: *He's always rubbing me (up) the wrong way.* [The reference is to an animal's coat.]

there's the rub (*rather formal*) that is where the difficulty lies: *Once we have manufactured the product we have to sell it, and there's the rub — we have no sales force.* [A Shakespearian quotation — *Hamlet*, III. i.]

rubber

rubber-stamp (*derog*) to give official approval to a decision actually made by somebody else: *The President was accused of merely rubber-stamping policies devised by his political advisors.* [From the practice of using a rubber stamp instead of an individually written signature.]

Rubicon

cross the Rubicon to do something which commits one to a particular course of action: *He had always wanted to work free-lance, and decided to cross the Rubicon by giving up his present job.* [See **the die is cast** at **die**. As the Rubicon was the boundary between Cisalpine Gaul and Italy, into which generals were not permitted to bring their armies, Caesar's crossing of the river in 49 BC committed him to a war with the Senate.]

ruffle

ruffle (someone's) feathers *see* **feather.**

rug

pull the rug (out) from under (someone) to do something suddenly which leaves (someone) in a very weak position: *She was just about to appeal to the bishop for support when he pulled the rug out from under her by saying that he found her attitude unchristian.*

ruin

go to rack and ruin *see* **rack.**

rule

as a rule usually: *I don't go out in the evening as a rule.*

the exception proves the rule *see* **except.**

golden rule *see* **gold.**

rule of thumb a method of doing something based on experience rather than theory or careful calculation: *I usually work by rule of thumb.* [From the use of one's thumb to make rough measurements.]

rule out (something) to leave out or not to consider (something): *We mustn't rule out the possibility of bad weather*. [Literally, to judge officially that (something) is not allowable, possible *etc*.]

rule the roost *see* **roost.**

rule with a rod of iron *see* **iron.**

run

an also-ran (*derog inf*) an unsuccessful or unimportant person (*esp* compared with someone else): *He was an also-ran in the race for promotion*; *He is a bit of an also-ran*. [A racing term for a horse which was not placed in a race.]

a dry run *see* **dry.**

in, out of the running having a, no chance of success: *She's in the running for promotion*.

in the long run *see* **long.**

on the run escaping; running away: *He's on the run from the police*.

run across (someone) (*inf*) to meet (someone) by chance: *I ran across an old friend*.

run along (*inf*) to go away: *Run along now, children!*

run a tight ship *see* **tight.**

run away with (something) to win (a prize *etc*) easily: *He was so brilliant that he simply ran away with the championship*.

run down tired or exhausted because one has worked too hard: *He felt run down so he had a holiday*.

run for it (*inf*) to try and escape: *Quick — run for it!*

a (good) run for one's money a good show or performance; something worth having in return for the effort, money *etc* one has spent: *We've had a good run for our money, so we can't complain if we have to stop now*; *Our team did not win, but they gave the opposition a run for their money*. [A racing term — indicating that the horse one has bet on has actually raced, although it has not won, as opposed to being withdrawn and not running at all.]

run high *see* **high.**

run (someone or something) in 1 to get (a new engine *etc*) working properly: *I only bought the car last month, so I am still running it in*. **2** (*inf*) to arrest (someone): *The policeman ran him in for dangerous driving*.

run in the family *see* **family.**

the runner-up a person, thing *etc* that is second in a race or competition: *My friend won the prize and I was the runner-up*.

run-of-the-mill *see* **mill.**

run out 1 (of a supply) to come to an end; to finish: *The food has run out*. **2** (*with* **of**) to have no more: *We've run out of money*.

run out of steam *see* **steam.**

run out on (someone) (*sl*) to leave or abandon (someone): *His wife ran out on him.*

run (something) over (of a vehicle or driver) to knock down or drive over (something): *Don't let the dog out of the garden or he'll get run over.*

run riot *see* **riot.**

run the show *see* **show.**

run through (something) to look at (something), deal with (something) *etc* from beginning to end: *He ran through their instructions.*

run to (something) to be or have enough of something (*esp* money) to do or have (something): *We can't run to a new car this year; It is a comfortable hotel, but it doesn't run to private bathrooms.*

run to earth *see* **earth.**

run (something) up 1 (*inf*) to make (something) quickly or roughly: *I can run up a dress in a couple of hours.* **2** to make (money) increase; to accumulate (money): *He ran up an enormous bill.*

run wild *see* **wild.**

take a running jump! (*sl*) to go away!: *I wish she would tell that dreadful woman to take a running jump!*

a trial run *see* **trial.**

rush

  be rushed off one's feet *see* **feet.**

  rush one's fences *see* **fence.**

  the rush hour a period when there is a lot of traffic on the roads, *usu* when people are going to or leaving work: *I got caught in the rush hour this morning.*

rustle

  rustle (something) up (*sl*) to get or make (something) quickly: *He rustled up some food and clean clothes.* [Originally US.]

rut

  in(to) a rut having a fixed, monotonous, firmly established way of life: *I felt that I was (getting) in a rut, so I changed my job.* [The reference is to a cartwheel which is unable to change direction easily if it is running in a rut in the track.]

S

sack

   get the sack (*inf*) to be dismissed from one's job *etc*: *I'll get the sack if I arrive at the office late!* [A French idiom, probably from the bag in which a workman carried his tools from one job to another.]

   give (someone) the sack (*inf*) to dismiss (someone) from their job *etc*: *They gave Jones the sack for being drunk on duty.* [As previous idiom.]

sacred

   a sacred cow (*derog*) a custom, tradition, body of people *etc* that is regarded (by a group of people *etc*) with so much respect that one is not allowed even to criticize it freely: *The politician said that he was aware that the policy he was attacking was one of the government's sacred cows and that he was therefore unlikely to succeed in changing it.* [From the fact that cattle are regarded as sacred by Hindus.]

saddle

   in the saddle in a position of power or control: *The new manager had not been in the saddle long when the trouble occurred.* [From horse-riding.]

   saddle (someone) with (something) (*inf*) to give (a person) something annoying, difficult *etc* to deal with: *I can't do very much shopping when I'm saddled with the children.*

safe

   as safe as houses *see* **house.**

   be on the safe side to avoid risk or danger: *I don't think we'll need much money but I'll take my cheque-book just to be on the safe side.*

   play safe *see* **play.**

   safe and sound unharmed: *He returned safe and sound from his exciting adventure.*

   there's safety in numbers a saying, meaning that it is fairly safe to do something, even if it may seem risky, if a (large) number of other people are also doing it.

sail

   plain sailing *see* **plain.**

   sail close to the wind *see* **wind**[1].

   take the wind out of (someone's) sails *see* **wind**[1].

saint

   enough to try the patience of a saint *see* **patience.**

salad

> **(someone's) salad days** the time when (someone) was young and inexperienced: *I often walked five miles home from a dance in my salad days*. [A Shakespearian quotation — *Antony and Cleopatra*, I. v. — from the association of greenness with youth.]

salt

> **go through (something) like a dose of salts** *see* **dose**.

> **rub salt into the wound/(someone's) wounds** to make (someone's) sorrow, shame, regret *etc* worse, often deliberately: *I was very disappointed at having to miss the concert, and my friends kept rubbing salt into the wound by telling me how good it was*. [Aboard ship *etc*, salt was often used as an antiseptic.]

> **salt (something) away** (*inf*) to store up (*esp* money) for future use: *He has a pile of money salted away*. [From preserving meat or fish in salt.]

> **the salt of the earth** (a) very good or worthy person or persons: *She would do anything to help someone in trouble — people like that are the salt of the earth*. [A Biblical reference — to Matthew 5:13.]

> **take (something) with a grain/pinch of salt** to receive (a statement, news *etc*) with a slight feeling of disbelief: *I took his story with a pinch of salt, because he has a tendency to exaggerate*.

> **worth one's salt** deserving the pay that one gets: *If he can't even do that, he's not worth his salt*. [The reference is to the salt eaten by a servant *etc*.]

Samaritan

> **a good Samaritan** someone who helps others who are in need: *When my car broke down I would have been stranded if a good Samaritan had not stopped and offered me a lift*. [A Biblical reference to the parable in Luke 10.]

same

> **all/just the same** nevertheless; in spite of this: *I'm sure I locked the door, but, all the same, I think I'll go and check*.

> **at the same time** nevertheless; still: *Mountain-climbing is fun, but at the same time we must not forget the danger*.

> **be all the same to (someone)** (*inf*) to make no difference to, or be a matter of no importance to (someone): *I'll leave now, if it's all the same to you*.

> **much the same** not very much changed or different: *'How is your mother?' 'Much the same (as she was).'*

> **not to be in the same street as** *see* **street**.

> **the same as always/ever** not at all changed: *I was in London last*

week — it was the same as ever.

same here (*inf*) I think, feel *etc* the same: *'This job bores me.'* *'Same here.'*

the same old story *see* **story.**

sand

as happy as a sand-boy (*inf*) very happy and cheerful: *My husband is as happy as a sand-boy when he's working on his car.* [Apparently a *sand-boy* was a young seller of sand — why such people should be particularly jolly is obscure.]

build on sand to try to establish something without enough security or support: *Their marriage was built on sand because they had absolutely nothing in common.* [A Biblical reference to Matthew 7:26.]

sardine

packed like sardines crowded very close together: *The train was so full we were packed like sardines.* [From the practice of selling sardines very tightly packed in tins.]

sausage

not a sausage (*inf*) nothing at all: *'Did you get anything from them?'* *'Not a sausage!'*

savage

the noble savage *see* **noble.**

save

saved by the bell *see* **bell.**

save (one's/someone's) face *see* **face.**

save (something) for a rainy day *see* **rain.**

save one's skin *see* **skin.**

save the day *see* **day.**

scrimp and save *see* **scrimp.**

sauce

what's sauce for the goose is sauce for the gander a saying, meaning that a rule, method of treatment *etc* which applies to one person must also apply to others, *esp* to the person's wife or husband.

say

have (something, nothing *etc***) to say for oneself** to be able/ unable to explain one's actions *etc*: *Your work is very careless — what have you to say for yourself?*

I say! words expressing surprise or protest or used to attract someone's attention: *I say! What a surprise!*; *I say! Look at those birds!*

I wouldn't say no to (something) (*inf*) I would like (something): *I wouldn't say no to an ice-cream.*

it goes without saying (that) *see* **go.**

it is said/they say expressions used in reporting rumours, news that is not yet definite *etc*: *They say he hasn't much money.*

say the word *see* **word.**

that is to say in other words; I mean: *He was here last Thursday, that's to say the 4th of June.*

there's no saying it is impossible to guess: *There's no saying what will happen next.*

to say nothing of *see* **nothing.**

what would you say to (something) (*inf*) would you like (something): *'What would you say to a cup of tea?' 'I'd love one!'*

you can say that again! (*inf*) you're absolutely right!: *'He's crazy.' 'You can say that again!'*

scales

tip the scale(s) to be the (*usu* small) fact, happening *etc* which causes events to happen in a certain way, a certain decision to be made *etc*: *The match was a very close one, but Martin's experience finally tipped the scales in his favour.*

tip/turn the scales at (a certain weight) (*inf*) to weigh (a certain amount): *The boxer tipped the scales at 140 pounds on the day of the fight.*

scarce

make oneself scarce (*inf*) to run away or stay away, *esp* in order to avoid trouble or difficulty: *As soon as his mother-in-law arrived, he made himself scarce.*

scare

scare (someone) out of his wits *see* **wit.**

scare (someone) stiff *see* **stiff.**

scarlet

a scarlet woman (*facet*) an immoral and dangerous woman, *esp* a prostitute: *My next-door neighbour disapproves of me — he thinks I'm a scarlet woman because I have so many male visitors.* [A Biblical reference, to the woman in Revelation 17.]

scene

behind the scenes out of sight of the audience or public: *It would be interesting to know what goes on behind the scenes at the White House.* [A theatrical idiom — the *scenes* are the flat pieces of scenery *etc* forming the set on stage.]

come on the scene to arrive: *We were enjoying ourselves till you came on the scene.* [A theatrical idiom.]

not to be (someone's) scene (*inf*) not to be the kind of thing (someone) likes, is good at *etc*: *I'm afraid politics is not my scene — I hate arguments.*

set the scene to discuss the background to an event *etc*: *Before the ceremony began, the television commentator spent half an hour setting the scene for the viewers.* [A theatrical phrase — 'to prepare the stage for the beginning of the action'.]

scent
put/throw (someone) off the scent to give (someone) wrong information so that he will not find the person, thing *etc* he is looking for: *She told the police a lie in order to throw them off the scent.* [Literally used of dogs distracted while tracking a prey.]

schedule
according to schedule as planned: *The work is going according to schedule.*

ahead of, behind, on schedule before, later than, or by, the arranged time: *The plane is two hours behind schedule; They finished the work on schedule.*

school
the old school *see* **old.**

score
know the score (*inf*) to know the facts of the situation; to know exactly how difficult the situation is and what the risks are *etc*: *We knew the score, but we had to try to rescue the trapped men whatever the danger.* [Literally, 'to know how unlikely one is to win the game from one's present position'.]

on that score for that reason: *He's perfectly healthy, so you don't need to worry on that score.* [A figurative use of *score* meaning 'a record or list'.]

score off (someone) (*inf*) to make (someone) appear foolish, *esp* in conversation: *He's always scoring off his wife in public.*

settle old scores to get revenge from someone for past wrongs: *I have some old scores to settle with you.*

scot
scot-free (*derog*) unhurt or unpunished: *The older of the two boys was fined but the younger got off scot-free.* [An old legal term — literally 'free from tax'.]

scrape
scraping the (bottom of the) barrel *see* **barrel.**

scratch

backscratching *see* **back.**

scratch the surface *see* **surface.**

start from scratch to start (an activity *etc*) from nothing, from the very beginning, or without preparation or the advantage of previous experience: *He now has a very successful business but he started from scratch*; *He decided to start writing the novel again from scratch.* [Literally, to begin a race from the starting-line (originally scratched on the track) rather than from a position further down the course determined by any handicap the competitor might have.]

up to scratch (*not formal*) at or to the required or satisfactory standard: *Your work does not come up to scratch.* [From the mark up to which prize-fighters were once obliged to make their way at the beginning of each round.]

screw

have a screw loose (*inf*) (of a person) to be slightly mad: *She must have a screw loose to go skiing at her age!* [The reference is to unreliable machinery.]

put the screws on (someone) (*inf*) to use force or pressure in dealing with (someone): *If he won't give us the money, we'll have to put the screws on (him).* [*The screws* are thumbscrews, an old instrument of torture.]

screw up one's courage *see* **courage.**

scrimp

scrimp and save to be thrifty or very careful with money: *She scrimps and saves for her sons' education.* [*Scrimp* literally means 'to be mean with money'.]

Scrooge

a Scrooge (*derog*) a person who is mean with money: *The boss could afford to pay us all more, but he's just an old Scrooge.* [From the main character in Dicken's *A Christmas Carol* (1843).]

sea

at sea puzzled or bewildered: *Can I help you? You seem all/completely/rather at sea.*

get one's sea legs (*inf*) to become accustomed to the motion of a ship: *I felt seasick at first, but I soon got my sea legs.* [Originally, this phrase meant only 'to be able to walk steadily on a heaving deck'.]

seal

set one's seal on/to (something) to give one's authority or agreement to (something): *The Prime Minister has finally set his seal to the proposals for Parliamentary reforms*. [Literally, to sign by attaching a wax seal to (something).]

seam

come/fall apart at the seams to become completely ruined, useless or unworkable: *When one of the gang was stopped by the police, their whole plan began to come apart at the seams and they eventually had to abandon it.* [Literally, used of a garment *etc* which is badly sewn together.]

the seamy side (of life) the roughest, most unpleasant side or aspect (of human life): *As a social worker, you certainly see the seamy side of life.* [A Shakespearian metaphor — *Othello*, IV. ii. — referring to the wrong side of a garment, on which the seams show.]

search

search me! (*inf*) I really don't know!: *'Why does the manager want to see us?' 'Search me!'*

season

the compliments of the season *see* **compliment.**

the off season *see* **off.**

the silly season *see* **silly.**

seat

have a ringside seat *see* **ring.**

in the hot seat *see* **hot.**

take a seat (*rather formal*) to sit down: *Please take a seat!*

second

at second hand through or from another person: *I heard the news at second hand.*

come off second best to be the loser in a struggle: *That cat always comes off second best in a fight.*

get one's second wind (*often fig*) to recover one's natural breathing after breathlessness: *Once she got her second wind, she found it easier to run the next few laps; I've been awake for twenty hours, but I'm beginning to get my second wind, so I don't feel tired.*

play second fiddle (to someone) (*derog*) to be a supporter or follower (of someone) in an activity, rather than a leader: *He disliked playing second fiddle to anyone and soon left the firm to start his own business.* [From the rôles of *first* and *second fiddle* in a chamber orchestra *etc*.]

(someone's) second childhood (*derog*) the return to childish habits and behaviour that occurs in some elderly people: *He's in his second childhood.*

a second-class citizen a member of a group, community *etc* who does not have full (political) rights, privileges *etc*: *In some countries, women are treated as second-class citizens.*

second nature a firmly fixed habit: *It was second nature to/with him to think carefully before spending even 10p.* [From a Latin proverb, *consuetudo est secunda natura* = habit is a second nature.]

second-rate (*derog*) inferior; not of the best quality: *The play was pretty second-rate.* [Originally applied literally to warships, which were graded in seven *rates* according to size, number of guns *etc*.]

second sight the power of seeing into the future or into other mysteries: *They asked a women with second sight where the dead body was.*

second thoughts a change of opinion, decision *etc*; an opinion reached after thinking again about something: *I'm having second thoughts about selling the piano*; *On second thoughts, I'd rather stay here.*

second to none better than every other (person, thing *etc*) of the same type; very good: *His roast pheasant is second to none*; *As a portrait painter, he is second to none.*

a split second *see* **split.**

secret

an open secret *see* **open.**

see

(I'll) be seeing you (*inf*) goodbye.

let me see used to indicate that one is trying to find an answer, trying to remember something, make a decision or do a calculation *etc*: *I think I could let you have the money in — let me see — ten days.*

see about (something) to attend to, or deal with (a matter): *Will you see about putting the children to bed?*

see daylight *see* **day.**

see double to see two images of everything instead of only one: *When I first met the twins, I thought I was seeing double, they were so alike.*

see eye to eye *see* **eye.**

see further than the end of one's nose *see* **nose.**

see here! a phrase used, *usu* in anger, when telling a person what he ought (not) to do or have done: *See here! When I ask for tea, I don't expect to be given coffee!*

see how the land lies *see* **land.**

see how/which way the wind blows *see* **wind**[1].

seeing is believing a saying, meaning that it is only possible to believe fully in something which can be demonstrated and seen.

seeing that since; considering that: *Seeing that he's ill, he's unlikely to come.*

see life *see* **life.**

see (someone) off 1 to accompany (someone starting on a journey) to the airport, railway station *etc* from which he is to leave: *He saw me off at the station.* **2** (*inf*) to chase (someone) away: *There were some children stealing my apples but my dog soon saw them off.*

see (someone) out 1 to lead or accompany (someone) to the door or exit of a building *etc*: *The maid will see you out.* **2** (*inf*) to last longer than (someone): *These old trees will see us all out.*

see over (something) to visit and inspect (*eg* a house that is for sale): *We'll see over the house on Friday.*

see red *see* **red.**

see stars *see* **star.**

see the last of *see* **last.**

see things *see* **thing.**

see (something) through to give support to (a person, plan *etc*) until the end is reached: *She had a lot of difficulties, but his family saw her through.*

see through (someone or something) not to be deceived by (a person, trick *etc*): *We saw through him and his little plan.*

see to (someone or something) to attend to or deal with (someone or something): *I must see to the baby; I can't come now — I've got this job to see to.*

see to it that (*formal*) to ensure or make certain that: *See to it that this never happens again!*

see one's way to (doing) *see* **way.**

see with half an eye *see* **eye.**

see you later (*inf*) goodbye.

I *etc* **will see** I shall wait and consider the matter later: *'May I have a new bicycle?' 'We'll see.'; 'Did he agree?' 'He said he'll see.'*

I *etc* **will see what I can do** I will do what I can to help: *I can't promise to get you a seat for the concert, but I'll see what I can do.*

you see 1 a phrase used when giving an explanation: *I can't meet you tomorrow — I'm going away, you see.* **2** a phrase used to draw attention to the correctness of what one has said: *You see! I told you he wouldn't help us.*

seed

go to seed 1 (of a person) to become careless about one's clothes and appearance: *Don't let yourself go to seed when you reach middle age!* **2** (of a place) to become rather shabby and uncared for: *This part of town has gone to seed in the past twenty years.* [Literally, of a plant, to produce seeds after flowering and therefore, if a leaf vegetable, to become unfit for use as food.]

seize

seize on (something) to accept (an idea, suggestion *etc*) with enthusiasm: *I suggested a cycling holiday, and he seized on the idea.*

seize up (of machinery *etc*) to get stuck and stop working: *The car engine seized up because it overheated.*

self

self-possessed calm in manner or mind, and able to act confidently in an emergency: *She was so calm and self-possessed we never suspected that she was nervous.*

self-righteous (*derog*) having too high an opinion of one's own goodness, and intolerant of other people's faults: *'I'm never late for work,' he said in a self-righteous voice.* [A theological term.]

self-willed (*derog*) determined to do, or have, what one wants: *I can't control that child — he's so self-willed.*

sell

sell (someone) a pup *see* **pup.**

sell (someone) down the river *see* **river.**

a sell-out (*inf*) **1** an event, *esp* a concert, for which all the tickets are sold: *His concert was a sell-out.* **2** a betrayal: *The gang realized it was a sell-out and tried to escape.*

See also **sold.**

send

send away/off for (something) to order (goods) by post: *I've sent away for some things that I saw in the catalogue.*

send (someone) down to expel (a student) from university: *He was sent down for setting fire to the university buildings.*

send (someone) packing *see* **pack.**

send (someone) to Coventry *see* **Coventry.**

send (something) up (*inf*) to ridicule (something), *esp* through satire or parody: *In his latest play, he sends up university teachers.*

sense

bring (someone) to his *etc* senses to make (someone) understand that they must behave, think *etc* more sensibly: *He is behaving stupidly, but his wife may be able to bring him to his senses.*

come to one's senses to realize that one must behave more sensibly, or that facts *etc* are not as one thought they were: *He had gambled away most of his money before he came to his senses and decided to stop gambling.*

horse sense *see* **horse.**

in a sense in a certain way, or to a certain extent, but not complete: *What you said was right in a sense, but the problem is rather more complex than you seem to think.*

out of one's senses not in a normal or sane state of mind: *How could he do such a crazy thing? He must be out of his senses!*

a sense of proportion *see* **proportion.**

a sixth sense *see* **six.**

take leave of one's senses to become slightly mad: *What did she say that for? She must have taken leave of her senses!*

sepulchre

    a whited sepulchre *see* **white.**

serve

    serve a purpose *see* **purpose.**

    serve its turn *see* **turn.**

    serve (someone) right *see* **right.**

service

    at your *etc* **service** (*often facet*) ready to help or be of use: *I'm at your service if you want my help*; *My bicycle is at your service.*

    be of service to (someone) (*formal*) to help (someone): *Can I be of service to you?*

    have seen good service to have been well used: *This bicycle has seen good service.*

    press into service *see* **press.**

set

    all set (to) ready or prepared (to do something); just on the point (of doing something): *We were all set to leave when the phone rang*; *Are we all set? Let's go, then!*

    be set on (something) to want (to do something) very much; to be determined (to do something): *He was set on going to university.*

    get set (of runners in a race) to get ready to start running: *Get ready! Get set! Go!*

    set about (someone or something) 1 to begin (something): *How will you set about this task?* **2** (*formal*) to attack (someone): *When I refused to give him money, he set about me with a stick.*

set (someone) against (someone) (*formal*) to cause (a person) to dislike (another person): *She set the children against their father.*

set (someone) by the ears *see* **ear.**

set (someone) by the heels *see* **heel.**

set one's cap at *see* **cap.**

set one's face against *see* **face.**

set one's heart on *see* **heart.**

set in (of weather, seasons, feelings *etc*) to begin or become established: *Winter has set in early; Boredom soon set in among the children.*

set (something or someone) on (someone) to cause (*eg* dogs) to attack (someone): *He set his dogs/men on me.*

set one's seal on *see* **seal.**

set one's sights on *see* **sight.**

set (someone's) teeth on edge *see* **teeth.**

set the record straight *see* **record.**

set the pace *see* **pace.**

set the wheels in motion *see* **wheel.**

set to to start to do (something) (vigorously): *They set to, and finished the work the same day.*

a set-to (*inf*) an argument or fight: *There was a set-to between two of the office staff.*

set (something) to rights *see* **right.**

set to work *see* **work.**

settle

settle down to (begin to) work, live *etc* in a quiet, calm *etc* way: *He is settling down well in his new school/job; Isn't it time you got married and settled down?*

settle for (something) to accept (something that is not completely satisfactory): *We wanted two single rooms at the hotel, but had to settle for a room with two beds instead.*

settle old scores *see* **score.**

settle (something) on (someone) (*formal or legal*) to give (money, property *etc*) to (a person) for his use: *He settled £2000 a year on his daughter.*

settle up (with someone) to pay money (owed to someone): *He asked the waiter for the bill, and settled up; We shall have to settle up with the travel agent tomorrow.*

seven

at sixes and sevens *see* **six.**

in (the) seventh heaven *see* **heaven.**

sew

sewn up (*inf*) completely settled or arranged: *We've definitely got the contract — it's all sewn up.*

shack

shack up with (someone) (*sl*) to live with (someone one is not married to): *He has been shacked up with his secretary for years.*

shade

put (someone or something) in the shade to cause (a person, a piece of work *etc*) to seem unimportant: *His piano-playing puts me and my playing in the shade.* [Literally, to make (someone *etc*) appear dark by being much brighter oneself.]

shades of (someone or something)! that reminds me of (a particular person or thing)!: *Shades of school! We were all treated at the conference as if we were children.* [Originally a humorous calling up of the spirit of someone who is dead but who would have an interest in what is happening.]

shadow

worn to a shadow made thin and weary through *eg* hard work: *She was worn to a shadow after months of nursing her sick husband.*

shaggy

a shaggy-dog story (*inf*) a kind of joke which relies for its effect on being very long and having a sudden ridiculous ending. [From the subject of many of the best-known jokes.]

shake

no great shakes (*inf*) not very good or important: *He has written a book, but it's no great shakes.* [Perhaps from the shaking of dice.]

shake off (someone or something) to rid oneself of (something unwanted): *By running very hard he managed to shake off his pursuers.*

two shakes (of a lamb's tail) a very short time: *I'll find Mr Brown for you in two shakes, if you would like to wait.* [19C US.]

shame

a crying shame *see* **cry.**

put (someone or something) to shame to make (a person) feel ashamed of his work or to make (the work) seem to be of poor quality by showing greater excellence: *She works so hard that she puts me to shame.*

shame on you *etc*! (*often facet*) you should be ashamed!: *You mean you don't make your own jam? Shame on you!*

shanks

on shanks's pony/mare on foot: *If my car won't start I have to get to work on shanks's pony.* [From *shank* = leg.]

shape

get/knock (something) into shape (*inf*) to put (something) into the desired condition: *I must try to knock the team into shape*; *A couple of day's work will get the garden into shape.*

in any shape or form at all: *I don't accept bribes in any shape or form.*

in, out of shape in good, bad physical condition: *I have to be in shape for this race.*

in the shape of in the form of: *Help arrived in the shape of a passing motorist.*

lick into shape *see* **lick**.

shape up to develop or become formed: *The team is shaping up well.*

take shape to develop or grow into a definite form: *My book/ garden is gradually taking shape.*

share

go shares with (someone) (*inf*) to share expenses, profits *etc* with (someone): *I went shares with him in the cost of the meal.*

share and share alike (to own, use, pay for *etc* something) with everyone having an equal share: *We divided the money between us, share and share alike.*

sharp

as sharp as a razor *see* **razor**.

look sharp (*inf*) to be quick or to hurry: *Bring me the books and look sharp (about it)!*

sharp practice (*derog*) dishonesty or cheating: *There has been some sharp practice over this contract.*

a sharp tongue (*derog*) the tendency to be bad-tempered or sarcastic in speech: *He could bear his wife's sharp tongue no longer.*

sheep

as well be hanged for a sheep as a lamb a saying, meaning that if one is going to do something wrong, likely to be disapproved of *etc*, one might as well do something much worse which will benefit oneself more. [From the fact that at one time stealing a lamb was punishable by death.]

separate the sheep from the goats to make it possible to distinguish good, useful *etc* people in a group from the bad, useless *etc* ones: *We have plenty of support for our plan now, but there are difficulties ahead which will separate the sheep from the goats.* [A Biblical reference, to Matthew 25:32.]

a wolf in sheep's clothing *see* **wolf**.

sheet

as white as a sheet very pale: *He was as white as a sheet after the accident.*

shelf

on the shelf (*derog inf*) (of an unmarried woman) no longer likely to attract a man enough for him to want to marry her: *Some girls seem to think they're on the shelf if they're not married by the age of eighteen.*

shell

come out of one's shell to become more confident and less shy: *She was very quiet and reserved when she first went to school, but she's coming out of her shell a bit now.* [The reference is to a tortoise, or a crab *etc*.]

shell out (*inf derog*) to pay out (money): *I refuse to shell out any more money on a project that's bound to fail.*

shift

shift for oneself (*formal*) to do as well as one can; to manage without help: *I may be old and my legs may be a bit shaky, but I can still shift for myself.*

shift one's ground *see* **ground.**

shilling

take the king's shilling *see* **king.**

shine

take a shine to (**someone**) (*inf*) to become fond of (someone): *The boss took a shine to the new girl.* [Originally US.]

ship

run a tight ship *see* **tight.**

shipshape (and Bristol fashion) in good order; neat: *She left everything shipshape in her room when she went away.* [A nautical term.]

ships that pass in the night people who only meet once, by chance: *I meet a lot of people, working in a hotel, but in most cases we're ships that pass in the night.* [An image from a poem by Longfellow.]

spoil the ship for a ha'porth of tar to spoil something valuable by trying to save money *etc* and not buying or doing something very small but necessary: *That door needs another coat of paint, and since we've spent so much time and money redecorating the room it would be a pity to spoil the ship for a ha'porth of tar.* [Presumably from the use of tar to make boats watertight.]

when my *etc* **ship comes in** when I become rich: *We'll buy a big house in the country when our ship comes in.*

shirt

in one's shirt-sleeves without a jacket or coat: *I don't like wearing a jacket when I'm working — I prefer to wear a jersey or work in my shirt-sleeves.*

keep one's shirt on (*inf*) not to become angry: *Keep your shirt on — I'm not accusing you of anything.*

put one's shirt on (a horse) (*sl*) to bet everything one has on (a racehorse).

a stuffed shirt *see* **stuff.**

shiver

the shivers (*inf*) a feeling of horror: *The thought of working for him gives me the shivers.*

shoe

in (someone's) shoes in (someone's) place: *I wouldn't like to be in your shoes when they find out what you've done!*

on a shoestring with or using very little money: *We organized this party on a shoestring and had very little food to spare.*

step into dead men's shoes *see* **dead.**

shoot

shoot a line *see* **line.**

shoot one's mouth off *see* **mouth.**

the whole shoot (*inf*) the whole lot: *Don't try to sort out those papers — just throw the whole shoot in the fire.*

shop

all over the shop spread out everywhere: *Her office is very untidy — books and papers all over the shop.*

set up shop to begin doing something: *She set up shop as a singing teacher.* [Literally, to open a shop.]

shop around to compare prices, quality of goods *etc* at several shops before buying anything: *This isn't exactly what I want, so I think I'll shop around a bit before I make any decision.*

shut up shop to stop doing something, working *etc*: *This is the last lot of envelopes we've to address — after this we can shut up shop.*

a talking-shop *see* **talk.**

talk shop to talk about one's work: *We agreed not to talk shop at the party.*

short

at short notice without much warning time for preparation *etc*: *He had to make the speech at short notice when his boss suddenly fell ill.*

be in short supply *see* **supply.**

bring (someone) up short to cause (someone) suddenly to stop what he is doing: *I was casually reading the newspaper when I was brought up short by the headline about the murder.*

by a short head by a very small amount: *In the jam-making competition, my mother won by a short head from her next-door neighbour.* [A racing term for the shortest distance by which a horse can be judged to have won a race — once under *a length*, the distances are *half a length*, *a neck*, *a head* and *a short head*.]

caught/taken short (*inf*) having a sudden need to urinate: *It would be very embarrassing to be taken short in the middle of the meeting.*

fall short *see* **fall.**

for short as an abbreviation: *His name is Victor, but we call him Vic for short.*

give (someone or something) short shrift to waste little time or consideration on (someone or something), *usu* in an unpleasant or unfriendly way: *He came to me with some crazy plan, but I gave him/it very short shrift!* [*Short shrift* was the short time given to a criminal for confession and absolution before his execution.]

go short to cause or allow oneself not to have enough of something, *eg* in order to allow someone else to have some: *If you can lend me some bread, I'd be grateful, but I don't want you to go short.*

have (someone) by the short hairs *see* **hair.**

in short (often used after listing complaints, reasons *etc*) in a few words: *In short, I didn't like the film at all.*

in short order *see* **order.**

little/nothing short of (something) (almost) the same as, or as bad as (something else): *Charging prices like that is little short of robbery; To do that would be nothing short of suicide!*

make short work of (something) to settle, or dispose of (something) very quickly: *The children made short work of the cream cakes.*

run short 1 (of a supply) to become insufficient: *Our money is running short.* **2** (*with* **of**) not to have enough: *We're running short of money.*

sell (someone or something) short to belittle (a person or thing): *Tell them about your achievements — don't sell yourself short.* [Literally, not to sell the correct amount (*ie* enough) of (something).]

short and sweet (*ironic*) very short and emphatic: *His reply was short and sweet: 'Get out!' he shouted.* [A 16C proverb, meaning in effect 'the shorter the better'.]

326

short for (something) an abbreviation of (something): *'Vic' is short for 'Victor'*; *'Phone' is short for 'telephone'*.

short measure *see* **measure.**

short of 1 not as far as or as much as: *Our total came to just short of £1000*; *We stopped five miles short of London.* **2** without doing something as bad, unpleasant *etc* as (something else): *Short of murdering her, I'd do anything to get rid of her.*

short on (something) (*inf*) lacking in (a particular thing, quality *etc*): *The book is rather short on illustrations, but has some useful information.*

short-tempered easily made angry: *My husband is very short-tempered in the mornings.*

stop short of *see* **stop.**

to cut a long story short *see* **story.**

shot

a big shot (*inf*) an important person: *He's one of the big shots in the organization.*

call the shots (*inf*) to be in control of what is happening: *I'll do my best to get an agreement, but I'm afraid our opponents are calling the shots at present.* [Literally used of target shooting — to say, as a shot is fired, where on the target it will strike.]

like a shot very quickly; eagerly: *He accepted my invitation like a shot.*

a long shot (*inf*) a guess, attempt *etc* unlikely to be right or succeed, but worth trying: *Guessing he would stay at home was a long shot, but it paid off!*

a shot across the bows something intended to be a warning: *I think the solicitor's letter he sent us was merely a shot across the bows.* [From naval warfare.]

a shotgun marriage/wedding a forced marriage: *I think theirs was a shotgun wedding — the bride was certainly pregnant at the time.* [From the idea that such a wedding might well be arranged solely because the bride's father threatened the bridegroom with a shotgun.]

a shot in the arm the addition of new ideas, money *etc* to a failing business *etc* in the hope of reviving it: *This loan is a shot in the arm for the economy.* [Literally, an injection in the arm.]

a shot in the dark (*inf*) a guess based on little or no information: *The detective admitted that his decision to check the factory had just been a shot in the dark.*

shoulder

give (someone) the cold shoulder *see* **cold.**

have a chip on one's shoulder *see* **chip.**

have a head on one's shoulders *see* **head.**

have broad shoulders to be able to accept a great deal of responsibility: *Blame me if you like — I've got broad shoulders.*

put one's shoulder to the wheel (*inf*) to begin to work very hard: *We'll have to put our shoulders to the wheel if we are going to finish by Christmas.*

rub shoulders with (someone) to mix or associate with (someone): *He rubs shoulders with some very strange people in his job.*

a shoulder to cry on (*slightly derog*) a sympathetic listener: *She doesn't want advice, she only wants a shoulder to cry on.*

shoulder to shoulder close together; side by side: *We'll fight this battle shoulder to shoulder, and we'll show the management that they can't treat their staff like slaves.'*

shout

be all over bar the shouting (*inf*) (of a happening, contest *etc*) to be almost completely finished, over or decided: *If you have decided to give up supporting us, then it's all over bar the shouting, I'm afraid.*

shout (someone) down to make it impossible for (a speaker) to be heard (*eg* at a meeting) by shouting, jeering *etc* very loudly: *The meeting had to be abandoned because certain people in the audience were determined to shout down all the speakers.*

shove

shove off (*inf: sometimes impolite*) to go away: *Shove off and leave me alone!*; *I think I'll shove off now.* [Literally a nautical term meaning 'to push a boat away from the shore'.]

show

for show in order to give the appearance of something special: *They did it just for show, to make themselves seem more important than they are*; *His sword is just for show — it's very blunt.*

get the show on the road (*inf*) to get a plan, organization *etc* into operation; to begin a planned activity *etc*: *If everyone is here, let's get the show on the road — we haven't a lot of time.* [Originally used of a theatre company *etc* going on tour.]

give the show away *see* **give.**

good show! (*inf*) that's good; I'm pleased: *So you've finished that already! Good show!*

on show obvious and able to be watched by a lot of people: *Do remember you're on show as the wife of the principal speaker.*

run the show to be in control or charge of a plan, organization *etc*: *Your campaign is very successful — you must have some clever people running the show.* [A theatrical idiom.]

show one's face *see* **face.**

show one's hand *see* **hand.**

show oneself in one's true colours *see* **colour.**

show off (*inf derog*) to try to impress others with one's possessions, ability to do something *etc*: *She is just showing off — she wants everyone to know how well she speaks French.*

a show of hands at a meeting, debate *etc*, a vote expressed by people raising their hands: *The union leaders called for a show of hands to decide whether or not to come out on strike.*

show one's paces *see* **pace.**

show one's teeth *see* **teeth.**

show the flag *see* **flag.**

show the white feather *see* **feather.**

show up 1 to make obvious (faults *etc*): *This kind of light really shows up the places where I've mended this coat.* **2** (*inf*) to reveal the faults, mistakes *etc* of (a person): *Mary was so neat that she really showed me up.* **3** (*inf*) to appear or arrive: *I waited for hours, but she never showed up.*

steal the show to attract the most admiration, attention *etc* during an event of some kind: *The bride was very pretty, but the bridegroom's sister stole the show by appearing in an enormous scarlet hat covered in ostrich feathers.* [A theatrical term for attracting the most applause during a performance.]

to show for (something) having been got as a profit, advantage *etc*: *I've worked for this firm for twenty years and what have I got to show for it? Nothing!*

shrift

give (someone or something) short shrift *see* **short.**

shrug

shrug (something) off to get rid of or dismiss (something) or treat it as unimportant: *She shrugged off all criticism and calmly went on with the project.*

shut

shut (someone's) mouth *see* **mouth.**

shut up (*inf*) to (cause to) stop speaking: *Tell them to shut up!*; *That'll shut him up!*

shy

> **fight shy (of)** *see* **fight.**

sick

> **make (someone) sick** (*inf*) to make (someone) feel very annoyed, upset *etc*: *It makes me sick to see him waste money like that.*
>
> **sick and tired/sick of the sight/sick to death (of something)** (*inf derog*) very tired (of something); wishing to have, hear, see *etc* no more (of something): *I'm sick of the sight of the shawl I'm trying to knit; I'm sick and tired of hearing about your problems!; I'm sick to death of her moaning!* [*Sick to death* once literally meant 'suffering from a mortal illness'.]
>
> **sick as a parrot** (*inf*) suffering from a disappointment: *I'm sick as a parrot about having to cancel our holiday.*
>
> **sick at heart** *see* **heart.**
>
> **worried sick** (*inf*) very worried: *I'm worried sick about my exams.*

side

> **get, keep on the right side of** *see* **right.**
>
> **get on the wrong side of** *see* **wrong.**
>
> **let the side down** (*inf*) to disappoint and hinder one's associates by acting, performing *etc* less well than they have done: *His colleagues felt he had let the side down by appearing drunk at the office party.*
>
> **on, from all sides** in, from all directions: *They were trapped, with enemies on all sides; People were running towards him from all sides.*
>
> **on the long, short, tight** *etc* **side** (*inf*) rather too short, long, tight *etc*: *This shirt is a bit on the small side for me.*
>
> **on the side** (*sl*) in another way than through one's ordinary occupation: *He is earning quite a lot on the side as a singer.*
>
> **on the side of the angels** *see* **angel.**
>
> **pass by on the other side** not to help someone in trouble *etc*, *esp* to pretend one has not noticed them: *Most people's response to the plight of drug addicts seems to be to pass by on the other side.* [A Biblical reference, to the action of the priest and the Levite in the parable of the Good Samaritan — Luke 10.]
>
> **pick/choose sides** to select the people for each team *etc* before a game: *Let's pick sides and start the game.*
>
> **put (something) on one side** to leave (a plan, problem *etc*) to be considered later: *I have been so busy I have had to put my holiday plans on one side for a month or two.*
>
> **side by side** beside one another; close together: *They walked along the street side by side.*

a sidekick (*derog sl*) a partner, assistant or special friend: *He has some sort of sidekick he calls his 'financial adviser'*.

side with (someone) to give support to (a person, group *etc*) in an argument *etc*: *Don't side with him against us!*

take sides to choose to support a particular opinion, group *etc* against another: *Everybody in the office took sides in the dispute*.

sieve

have a head/memory like a sieve to be very forgetful: *I'd better write the date of the meeting in my diary — I've got a head like a sieve*.

sight

catch sight of (someone or something) to get a brief view of (someone or something); to begin to see (someone or something): *He caught sight of her as she came round the corner*.

have (something) in one's sights to be preparing to try to get (something): *I've had that job in my sights ever since I heard it would be available*. [The reference is to the sights of a gun.]

have/set one's sights on (something) to try to get (something): *I have set my sights on the manager's job*. [As previous idiom.]

keep sight of (someone or something) to remain close enough to see (someone or something): *He kept sight of her as she walked along the street*; *We must keep sight of our original intention*.

know (someone) by sight to be able to recognize (someone) without ever having spoken to them: *I know her by sight, but we've never been introduced*.

lose sight of (someone or something) 1 to stop being able to see (someone or something): *She lost sight of him in the crowd*. **2** to forget about (a purpose *etc*): *He became so involved in discussing the details of his plan that he lost sight of his original intentions*.

not to be able to stand the sight of (someone) (*inf*) to dislike (someone) very much: *She's quite nice, but I can't stand the sight of her husband*.

out of sight, out of mind a saying, meaning that one ceases to think about someone who is absent or something that is no longer obvious.

second sight *see* **second.**

set one's sights on *see* **have one's sights on** *above*.

a sight for sore eyes (*inf*) a most welcome sight: *You're a sight for sore eyes!*

silence

silence is golden a saying, *usu* meaning that it is better to say nothing in a particular situation — from the proverb **speech**

is silver, silence is golden = it is good to speak and even better not to.

silent

the silent majority the people, making up most of the population, whose opinions are moderate and reasonable, but who do not make them known: *It is time the views of the silent majority in this country were considered by our politicians!*

silk

you can't make a silk purse out of a sow's ear a saying, meaning that one cannot make something good out of materials which are by nature bad and *usu* implying that a certain result is the best that can be expected.

silly

the silly season (*rather old: derog*) a time of year, *usu* late summer, when the newspapers, television *etc* spend a lot of time on unimportant things because there is a lack of important news: *I see from today's paper that the silly season is here again — nothing in it but rubbish!*

silver

be born with a silver spoon in one's mouth to be born into a wealthy family: *What does he know about hardship — he was born with a silver spoon in his mouth!* [Probably from the custom of godparents giving a silver spoon to a child as a christening present.]

every cloud has a silver lining *see* **cloud**.

sin

as ugly as sin very ugly: *She's very beautiful, but I would still love her if she was as ugly as sin!*

cover a multitude of sins *see* **multitude**.

live in sin (*usu facet*) to live together without being married: *Are they married or are they by any chance living in sin?*

sing

sing (someone's) praises *see* **praise**.

single

not a single not (even) one: *There's not a single person that I can trust.*

single-handed working *etc* by oneself, without help: *He runs the restaurant single-handed.*

single-minded (of a person) having one aim or purpose only: *He is single-minded about his work.*

single (someone or something) out to choose or pick (someone or something) out for special treatment: *He was singled out to receive special thanks for his help.*

sink

be sunk (*sl*) to be defeated, in a hopeless position *etc*: *If he finds out that we've been disobeying him, we're sunk.*

sink our, your *etc* **differences** to forget mutual disagreements *etc*: *For the next six months, we're going to sink our differences and work together.*

sit

sit at (someone's) feet *see* **feet.**

sit back to rest and take no part in an activity: *He just sat back and let it all happen.*

sit in on (something) to be present at (a meeting *etc*) without being an actual member: *The inspector sat in on the trainee teacher's lesson.*

sit on the fence *see* **fence.**

sit tight *see* **tight.**

sit (something) out to remain inactive and wait until the end of (an unpleasant episode): *They'll try to sit out the crisis.*

a sitting duck someone or something likely to be attacked and unable to put up a strong defence: *He wants to criticize someone, and I'm afraid his secretary is a sitting duck.* [From shooting. A duck on the water/ground is easier to shoot than one in the air.]

sitting pretty *see* **pretty.**

a sitting target someone or something that is in an obvious position to be attacked: *If they're reducing staff, he's a sitting target.* [As **a sitting duck** above.]

sit up 1 to remain awake, not going to bed: *I sat up until 3 a.m. waiting for you!* **2** (*inf*) to pay attention: *That'll make them all sit up!*

six

at sixes and sevens (*inf*) in confusion; completely disorganized: *On the day before the wedding, the whole house was at sixes and sevens.* [From playing dice, originally meaning 'having gambled on the high numbers only' and thus 'in disarray'.]

knock (someone) for six (*inf*) to overcome or defeat (someone) completely; to take (someone) totally by surprise: *The news just knocked me for six!* [A cricketing idiom — literally to score six runs off a ball bowled by (someone).]

six of one and half a dozen of the other (of two things, possibilities *etc*) equally to blame, responsible, important, relevant *etc*: *There's no point in wondering whether to go by train or by car — it really is six of one and half a dozen of the other.* [From the fact that half a dozen = six.]

six of the best (*old*) six strokes with a cane (as a punishment at school *etc*): *The old man said that in his youth schoolboys got six of the best for such behaviour.*

a sixth sense an ability to feel or realize something apparently not by means of any of the five senses: *He couldn't hear or see anyone, but a sixth sense told him that he was being followed.* [From the fact that there are five normal senses — sight, hearing, touch, taste and smell.]

sixty

the sixty-four (thousand) dollar question (*inf facet*) a most important and/or difficult question: *We know we didn't leave the office window open, so the sixty-four thousand dollar question is — who did?* [From a US quiz game in which the contestant won $1 for answering the first question, $2 for the second, $4 for the third *etc*, up to the last question when he won $64 or lost it all.]

size

cut (someone) down to size (*inf*) to reduce someone's sense of their own importance: *I'll cut this cheeky young rascal down to size!*

of a size of the same size: *Your coat should fit me — we're very much of a size.*

the size of it (*inf*) a description of the situation or state of affairs which exists at the moment: *'You mean we're trapped?' 'That's about the size of it.'*

size up (someone or something) (*slightly inf*) to form an opinion about the worth, nature, *etc* of (a person, situation *etc*): *I'm not very good at sizing people up quickly; He sized up the situation and acted immediately.*

try that on for size! (*inf*) what do you think of that!: *Mary wants us to have lunch with a wealthy American friend, so try that on for size!*

skate

get one's skates on (*inf*) to hurry up: *I'd better get my skates on if I want to get to the cinema by nine o'clock.*

skate over (something) (*inf*) to pass over (a subject, difficulty *etc*) quickly, trying to avoid taking it into consideration: *He always skates over the problems attached to his plans.*

skeleton

a skeleton in the cupboard/closet a closely-kept secret concerning a hidden cause of shame: *Aunt Mary's affair with the milkman is the skeleton in the family cupboard.*

skid

put the skids under (someone) (*inf*) to cause (someone) to hurry: *Tell him he's fired unless he finishes the work by Friday — that'll put the skids under him!*

skin

by the skin of one's teeth very narrowly; only just: *We escaped by the skin of our teeth.*

get under (someone's) skin (*inf*) to annoy and upset (someone) greatly: *Don't let his comments get under your skin.*

jump out of one's skin (*inf*) to get a great fright or shock: *I was daydreaming so I nearly jumped out of my skin when he spoke to me.*

no skin off one's nose (*inf*) something about which one is not concerned, or does not care, because it is not inconvenient to one or benefits one: *You can sit in the hall and wait for my boss as long as you like — it's no skin off my nose.*

save one's skin to save one's life: *When they were attacked by armed men, he managed to save his skin by pretending to be dead.*

skin and bone (*inf*) very thin: *She was just skin and bone after her illness.*

skin-deep (*formal or liter*) on the surface only: *His sorrow was skin-deep; Beauty is skin-deep.*

a skinflint (*derog*) a very mean person.

thick-skinned *see* **thick.**

thin-skinned *see* **thin.**

skull

the skull and crossbones (*hist*) (a design displayed on) a pirate's flag.

sky

pie in the sky *see* **pie.**

praise (someone) to the skies (*slightly facet*) to praise (someone) very highly: *He should be good — his last boss praises him to the skies.*

sky-high very high: *The car was blown sky-high by the explosion; The prices in that shop are sky-high.*

the sky's the limit (*inf*) there is no upper limit eg to the amount of money that may be spent: *Choose any present you like — the sky's the limit!*

slang

a slanging-match (*inf*) an angry quarrel or argument in which rude expressions are used by both sides: *I could hear our next-door neighbours having a slanging-match, because the dividing wall is very thin.*

slap

slap and tickle playful and not very serious lovemaking: *He said that just because he liked a bit of slap and tickle now and then, there was no reason to accuse him of immorality.*

a slap in the face (*inf*) an insult or rebuff: *The miners' decision to strike was a slap in the face for the government.*

a slap on the wrist (*derog usu facet*) a mild scolding: *He said he would probably get a slap on the wrist for taking the day off, but that no-one would be really angry.*

slapstick a kind of humour which depends for its effect on very simple practical jokes *etc*: *Throwing custard pies turns a play into slapstick.* [From the double stick once carried by a harlequin and used to make a slapping noise on stage.]

slap-up (*inf*) (of a meal *etc*) splendid; excellent: *The firm gave its employees a slap-up dinner in the local hotel.*

slate

on the slate on credit: *He ordered two double whiskies and told the barman to put them on the slate.*

slave

a slave-driver a person who expects too much work from his employees, pupils *etc*: *My son's teacher is a real slave-driver — she gives him so much homework.* [Literally, a man in charge of getting slaves to work.]

sleep

lose sleep over (something) (*inf*) to worry about (something): *Don't lose any sleep over the problem!*

put (someone or something) to sleep 1 (*inf*) to cause (a person or animal) to become unconscious by means of an anaesthetic; to anaesthetize: *The doctor will give you an injection to put you to sleep.* **2** (*euph*) to kill (an animal) painlessly, *usu* by the injection of a drug: *As she was so old and ill my cat had to be put to sleep.*

sleep around (*inf often derog*) to be in the habit of having sexual intercourse with a number of different people; to be promiscuous: *She finally got married and stopped sleeping around.*

sleep in (*Brit*) to sleep late in the morning; to oversleep: *I slept in by mistake and was very late for work.*

sleep like a log *see* **log.**

sleep like a top *see* **top.**

sleep (something) off to recover from (something) by sleeping: *She's in bed sleeping off the effects of the party.*

sleep on (something) (*inf*) to put off making a decision about (something): *I'll sleep on it and let you know tomorrow.*

sleep with (someone) (*euph*) to have, or be in the habit of having, sexual intercourse with (someone): *His wife has a lot of male friends but I don't think she ever sleeps with any of them.*

sleeve

have/keep (something) up one's sleeve to keep (a plan *etc*) secret for possible use at a later time: *I'm keeping this idea up my sleeve for the time being.* [From cheating at cards by having extra cards hidden in one's sleeve.]

laugh up one's sleeve to laugh secretly: *I had the feeling she was laughing up her sleeve at something I didn't understand.*

slice

a slice of the cake (*not formal*) a share of something valuable which has been gained: *The company is now very profitable, and the workers are demanding a larger share of the cake.*

slide

let (something) slide (*inf*) to neglect and not to bother about (something): *I tend to let things slide during the holidays.*

slight

not in the slightest not at all: *You haven't upset me in the slightest; That doesn't worry me in the slightest; 'Am I disturbing you?' 'No, not in the slightest.'*

sling

sling mud at *see* **mud.**

slip

a Freudian slip *see* **Freud.**

give (someone) the slip (*inf*) to escape from or avoid (someone) in a secretive manner: *The crooks gave the policemen the slip.*

let (something) slip 1 to miss (an opportunity *etc*): *I let the chance slip, unfortunately.* **2** to say (something) unintentionally: *He let slip that his mother had been criticizing me; She let slip some remark about my daughter.*

slip (someone) (something) (*inf*) to pass (money *etc*, *usu* intended as a bribe) to (a person): *I slipped the barman a pound-note to serve us first.*

slip one's mind *see* **mind.**

a slip of the tongue a word *etc* said by mistake when the speaker meant something else: *I didn't mean to call you a fool — it was just a slip of the tongue.*

slip up to make a mistake; to fail to do something: *They certainly slipped up badly over the new appointment.*

there's many a slip 'twixt cup and lip a saying, meaning that a plan can easily go wrong before it is carried out and that it is therefore unwise to praise, depend on, *etc* anything before it is completed.

slope

slope off (*sl*) to go away, *esp* secretively and without warning: *When I next looked round for him, he had taken his chance and sloped off.*

slow

go slow (*Brit*) (of workers in a factory *etc*) to work less quickly than usual, *eg* as a form of protest: *All our mail is being delayed as the postal workers are going slow.*

in slow motion (*inf*) very much slower than normal: *He does everything in slow motion, so he always takes ages!* [Literally used of movement in films made very slow by running the film very slowly.]

slow on the uptake *see* **uptake**.

sly

on the sly secretly, without informing others: *I think he's helping himself to the firm's stationery on the sly.*

smack

a smack in the eye (*very inf*) an insult or rebuff: *The miners' decision to strike was a real smack in the eye for the government!*

small

feel/look small to feel or look foolish or insignificant: *He criticized her in front of her colleagues and made her feel very small.*

in a small way 1 with little money or stock: *He is an antique-dealer in a small way.* **2** quietly, without extravagance: *We celebrated in a small way at home.*

it's a small world a phrase used to indicate surprise, interest *etc* at some unexpected coincidence, contact between unconnected people one knows *etc*: *It's a small world — the people we met on holiday in Majorca turned out to be the son and daughter-in-law of one of my wife's schoolfriends.*

small fry *see* **fry**.

the small hours the hours immediately after midnight: *She works into the small hours every night.* [From the fact that the numbers involved are small — one o'clock, two o'clock *etc.*]

small-minded having, or showing, narrow interests or intolerant and unimaginative opinions: *Am I just being small-minded in objecting to nudity on television?*

the small print the place in a document *etc* where important information is given without being easily noticed: *You must always read the small print on your insurance policy to make sure you are covered for all risks.*

small talk (polite) conversation about very unimportant matters: *I refuse to go to the party and indulge in small talk all evening.*

small things please small minds (*derog*) a saying, meaning that mean and petty people are pleased by mean and petty subjects, victories *etc.*

small-time (of a thief *etc*) not working on a large scale: *He is only a small-time crook/thief.*

small wonder (it is) not really surprising: *Considering how rude you were, it is small wonder he dislikes you; Small wonder he dislikes you, when you dislike him.*

smart

look smart to be quick: *Get those files into my office, and look smart about it!*

a smart Alec(k)/Alick (*derog sl*) a person who thinks he is cleverer than others: *Many road-accidents are caused by smart Alecks doing dangerous things other people wouldn't dream of.* [Originally US, *c* 1870, of unknown derivation.]

smash

a smash-and-grab (raid/robbery) a robbery in which the window of a shop is smashed and goods grabbed from behind it: *There was a smash-and-grab robbery at the jeweller's last night.*

a smash hit (*inf*) a song, show *etc* that is a great success: *This play was a smash hit in New York.*

smear

a smear campaign an attempt to damage someone's reputation by making a number of accusations in speech or writing: *The politician accused the press of conducting a smear campaign against him.*

smell

smell a rat *see* rat.

smell of the lamp *see* lamp.

smile

be all smiles to be, or look, very happy: *He was all smiles when he heard the good news.*

smile on (someone or something) (*rather liter*) to be favourable to (someone or something): *Fate smiled on us.*

smoke

go up in smoke (*inf*) **1** to vanish very quickly, leaving nothing behind: *All his plans have gone up in smoke.* **2** to lose one's temper: *He'll go up in smoke when he hears about this.* [Literally, to burn.]

smoke out (something or someone) to discover (something or someone): *The police were determined to smoke out the criminals.* [Literally, to drive (an animal) from a hiding-place with smoke or fire.]

there's no smoke without fire a saying, meaning that there is always a basis for any rumours, talk *etc* however untrue they may appear.

snail

at a snail's pace very slowly: *She knits beautiful jumpers — but she does them at a snail's pace.*

snake

a snake in the grass (*derog inf*) a person who cannot be trusted: *Beware of him — he's a real snake in the grass.* [An image from one of Virgil's *Eclogues*.]

snap

make it/look snappy (*inf*) hurry up: *I want an answer, and make it snappy!*

snap out of it (*inf*) to make oneself quickly stop being miserable, depressed *etc*: *I was getting very depressed so I decided to snap out of it and go on holiday.*

snap (something) up to grab (something) eagerly: *I saw this bargain in the shop and snapped it up straight away.*

sneeze

not to be sneezed at (*inf*) (of a chance, opportunity *etc*) not to be ignored: *This is an offer that's not to be sneezed at.*

sniff

sniff (something) out (*inf*) to discover or detect (something): *I'll see if I can sniff out the cause of the trouble.* [The reference is to a tracker dog.]

snook

cock a snook at (someone) *see* **cock.**

snow

as pure as the driven snow *see* **drive.**

not to have a snowball's chance in hell *see* **hell.**

snowed under overwhelmed *eg* with a great deal of work: *Last week I was absolutely snowed under with work.*

so

so-and-so 1 an unnamed, unidentified person: *If I said I would meet so-and-so, I would do it.* **2** (*derog*) used as a substitute for an offensive term for a person or thing: *I've had another letter from those so-and-sos at the bank!*

so-so (*inf*) neither very good nor very bad: *His health is so-so.*

so what? (*impolite inf*) what of it?; does it really matter?: *'He doesn't like you.' 'So what?'*

soap

a soap opera (*usu derog*) a radio or television serial broadcast weekly, daily *etc, esp* one that continues from year to year, that concerns the daily life, troubles *etc* of the characters in it. [From the fact that such series originated in the US where they were often sponsored by soap manufacturers.]

sob

a sob-story (*derog inf*) a story of misfortune *etc* told in order to gain sympathy: *She asked me to lend her five pounds, telling me a sob-story about her purse being stolen and her children needing food.*

sober

stone-cold sober *see* **stone.**

sock

pull one's socks up to make an effort to do better: *You'd better pull your socks up if you want to succeed in this business!*

put a sock in it! (*sl*) be quiet!: *I wish you two would put a sock in it — you've been quarrelling all day!*

sock it to (someone) (*sl*) to speak to or behave towards (someone) in a very strong or impressive manner: *Now it's your turn to make a speech — go on, sock it to them!*

soft

have a soft spot for (someone or something) (*inf*) to have a weakness for (someone or something) because of great affection: *He's always had a soft spot for his youngest son.*

soften (someone) up (*inf*) to weaken (someone) to make them less able to resist something which follows: *He sent his aunt a bunch of flowers to soften her up before asking for a loan.*

soft in the head *see* **head.**

341

softly-softly (*sl*) careful, cautious and gentle: *The police adopted a softly-softly approach to juvenile crime.*

a soft option (*inf*) a choice, alternative *etc* which is easier or more pleasant than the others: *He decided to go to college because he thought it was a soft option, but he soon found he had to work very hard.*

soft-pedal (*inf*) not to make evident or acknowledge the importance *etc* of (something): *The government is soft-pedalling (on) the wages issue until after the election.* [From the action of the *soft pedal* on a piano, which makes it play more quietly.]

a soft touch/mark (*sl*) a person who is easily deceived, used *etc*: *She always asks her father for things rather than her mother, because he's a soft touch.*

sold

be sold on (something) (*sl*) to be enthusiastic about: *I'm sold on the idea of a holiday in Canada.*

be sold out 1 to be no longer available, because all have been sold: *The second-hand records are all sold out.* **2** (*sometimes with* **of**) to have no more (of something) available to be bought: *The concert is sold out; We are sold out of children's socks.*

soldier

soldier on to keep going despite difficulties *etc*: *There have been several power-cuts in the office, but we are trying to soldier on (despite them).*

some

be/have something to do with (something) to be connected with (something): *Calculus has/is something to do with mathematics, hasn't/isn't it?*

make something of (something) (*inf*) to understand (something): *I apologize for the untidiness of my letter, but I hope you can make something of it.*

make something of oneself (*inf*) to become important or successful in some way: *He's a clever boy — I hope he'll make something of himself.*

or something used when the speaker is uncertain or being vague: *Her name is Mary or Margaret or something; I like to knit or something while I watch television.*

something tells me I have reason to believe; I suspect: *Something tells me she's lying.*

song

for a song (*inf*) for a very small amount of money: *He bought* *the lamp for a song.* [Probably derived from an image of Shakespeare's — *All's Well that Ends Well*, III. iii.]

make a song and dance about (something) to make an unnecessary fuss about (something): *I don't know why you're making such a song and dance about the accident — no-one was hurt, after all.* [From the expanding of an incident into a musical number in a stage or film musical.]

(someone's) swan song *see* **swan.**

soon

no sooner said than done (of a request, promise *etc*) immediately fulfilled: *She asked him to get her a drink of water. This was no sooner said than done.*

sooner or later eventually: *He'll come home sooner or later, I suppose.*

the sooner the better as quickly as possible: *'When shall I tell him?' 'The sooner the better!'*

speak too soon to say something that takes a result *etc* for granted before it is certain: *I don't want to speak too soon, but I know she'll win that scholarship.*

sore

a sight for sore eyes *see* **sight.**

a sore point a subject which it annoys or offends one to speak about: *Gambling has been a sore point with him since he lost a fortune betting on horses.*

stick out like a sore thumb to be too noticeable, painful, awkward *etc* to be ignored: *You can't be the only person at the parade not wearing a uniform — you'll stick out like a sore thumb!*

sorrow

drown one's sorrows *see* **drown.**

more in sorrow than in anger (*often facet*) more disappointed and unhappy than angry (at someone's bad behaviour *etc*): *The headmaster told her, more in sorrow than in anger, that she was a disgrace to the entire school and he felt he had failed to teach her right from wrong.*

sorry

be/feel sorry for (someone) to pity (someone): *I'm really sorry for that poor woman.*

sort

it takes all sorts (to make a world) a saying, meaning that one should be tolerant towards everyone, whatever their views, behaviour *etc*.

not a bad sort (*inf*) quite a nice person: *The headmaster's not a bad sort when you get to know him.*

of a sort/of sorts of a (*usu* poor) kind: *She threw together a meal of sorts but we were still hungry afterwards.*

out of sorts (*inf*) **1** slightly unwell: *I felt a bit out of sorts after last night's heavy meal.* **2** not in good spirits or temper: *He's been a little out of sorts since they told him to stay at home.* [Possibly from the use of the phrase as a printing term — literally, 'with some of the letters of the alphabet used up and unavailable'.]

sort of (*inf*) rather; in a way; to a certain extent: *He was sort of peculiar!*; *I feel sort of worried about him.*

sort (something or someone) out 1 to separate (one lot or type of) things from a general mixture: *I'll try to sort out some books that he might like.* **2** to correct, improve, solve *etc* (something): *You must sort out your business affairs before you are forced to close down.* **3** (*sl*) to attend to (someone), *usu* by punishing or reprimanding: *I'll soon sort you out, you evil little man!*

soul

God rest his soul *see* **rest.**

not to be able to call one's soul one's own to be organized and controlled by someone else: *His wife is so bossy he can't call his soul his own.*

the soul of (something) a perfect example of (a quality *etc*): *She's the soul of honour/discretion.*

soul-searching the examination of one's own conscience to find out *eg* whether one's motives are genuine: *He went through a lot of soul-searching before he finally decided to leave the priesthood.*

sound

sound off (*derog sl*) to speak loudly and freely, *esp* while complaining: *She was sounding off about the price of tea.*

sound (someone) out to try to find out (someone's) thoughts and plans *etc*: *Will you sound out your father on this?*

soup

in the soup (*sl*) in serious trouble: *If she's found out about it, we're all in the soup!* [Originally US.]

souped-up (*sl*) (of a car *etc*) made more powerful: *He roars about in a souped-up black Mini.* [Originally US, *c* 1945.]

sour

sour grapes *see* **grape.**

sow[1]

sow one's wild oats *see* **wild.**

sow[2]

you can't make a silk purse out of a sow's ear *see* **silk.**

space

in the space of (a minute, hour *etc*) in as little as (a minute, hour *etc*): *She contradicted herself twice in the space of five minutes.*

spade

call a spade a spade to say plainly and clearly what one means, not softening anything by trying to use polite words: *The trouble with doctors is that they never call a spade a spade — I sometimes find it difficult to know what they mean.* [From a 16C mistranslation of a passage in one of Plutarch's works.]

spadework hard work done at the beginning of a project *etc*, serving as a basis for the future: *Most of the spadework has already been done, so we should progress quite well with our task.* [From the fact that digging is a main constituent of the first stage of any building project.]

spanner

throw a spanner in the works to frustrate or ruin (a plan, system *etc*): *You'd better not let your sister know what you intend, because she never misses an opportunity to throw a spanner in the works — she's jealous of you.* [A reference to engines.]

spar

a sparring-partner (*inf*) a person with whom one enjoys a lively argument: *His sparring-partner in the debate was an old friend of his.* [Literally, a person with whom a boxer practises.]

spare

go spare (*sl*) to become angry or upset: *If your father sees the mess you've made of his workshop he'll go spare!*

a spare tyre (*inf*) a roll of fat around the middle of one's body: *I must go on a diet and try to get rid of my spare tyre.*

(and) to spare in larger numbers or quantities than is needed; extra: *Go to the exhibition if you have time to spare; I haven't much money to spare; She has enough and to spare.*

speak

be on speaking terms (with someone) to be friendly enough (with someone) to speak (to him): *She's not been on speaking terms with me since I broke her favourite ornament.*

generally speaking in general: *Generally speaking, men are stronger than women.*

so to speak if one may use such an expression; in a way; it could be said: *Our dog is a member of the family, so to speak.*

speak for (someone) to give an opinion *etc* on behalf of (someone else): *I myself don't have any objections to your suggestions, but I can't speak for Liz and Frank.*

speak for itself/themselves to have an obvious meaning; not to need explaining: *The situation speaks for itself; The facts speak for themselves.*

speak one's mind *see* **mind.**

speak out to say boldly what one thinks: *I don't like to make a fuss, but I feel the time has come to speak out.*

speak the same language *see* **language.**

speak too soon *see* **soon.**

speak up to speak (more) loudly: *Speak up! We can't hear you!*

speak volumes *see* **volume.**

speak with a forked tongue *see* **fork.**

to speak of worth mentioning: *He has no talent to speak of.*

to speak to (*inf*) well enough to have a conversation with: *I don't know him to speak to.*

spec

on spec (*inf*) taking a chance in the hope of achieving something *etc*: *I didn't have an appointment, but I went along on spec and they were able to give me one.* [An abbreviation of *on speculation* = as a gamble.]

spectacles

look at (something) through rose-coloured spectacles *see* **rose.**

spell

spell (something) out to give a highly detailed explanation of (something): *He's a bit stupid — you'll have to spell it out for him.*

spend

spend a penny *see* **penny.**

spend money like water *see* **money.**

spice

variety is the spice of life *see* **variety.**

spick

spick and span neat, clean and tidy: *In half an hour she had the whole house spick and span.* [The original phrase was *spick and span new*, literally, 'with even the nails and chips of wood brand-new'.]

spike

spike (someone's) guns *see* **gun.**

spill

cry over spilt milk to waste time regretting an accident, loss *etc* that cannot be put right: *You wouldn't have torn your skirt if you* *had opened the gate instead of trying to climb the fence, but there's no point in crying over spilt milk.*

spill the beans *see* **beans.**

spin

in a flat spin *see* **flat.**

spin a yarn *see* **yarn.**

spin (something) out to cause (something) to last a (*usu* unnecessarily) long or longer time: *He spun out his speech for an extra five minutes.* [The image is of spinning a long thread from a short bundle of fibres.]

spirit

out of spirits (*formal or liter*) feeling depressed: *He is rather out of spirits today.*

public spirit *see* **public.**

spirit (someone or something) away to carry away or remove (someone or something) secretly and suddenly, as if by magic: *The actress left the hotel by a back door and was spirited away before the reporters discovered the plan.*

the spirit is willing (but the flesh is weak) a saying, meaning that it is not always physically possible to do everything one would like to, often used to explain one's failure to do something. [A quotation from the Bible — Matthew 26:4.]

take (something) in the right spirit not to be offended by (something): *He took the joke/criticism in the right spirit.*

spit

the dead spit/the spitting image (of someone) (*inf*) an exact likeness (of someone): *He's the dead spit of his father; The twins are the spitting image of each other.*

spit and polish very careful cleaning of equipment, furniture *etc*: *This office could do with a bit of spit and polish — the woodwork is filthy!* [From the practice of using spit along with polish to clean boots *etc*, *esp* in the army.]

splash

make a splash (*inf*) to attract a lot of notice, *esp* deliberately: *He has made quite a splash in his new career as an actor.*

splash down (of spacecraft *etc*) to land in the sea at the end of a trip: *Apollo 17 is expected to splash down in the South Atlantic tomorrow.*

splash out on (something) (*inf*) to spend a lot of money on (something): *I haven't bought any clothes for months so I decided to splash out on a new dress.*

spleen
 vent one's spleen to express the anger and frustration one feels (often by attacking someone innocent): *A quarrel with your wife is no reason to vent your spleen on me!* [In medieval medicine, the spleen was thought to be the source of spite, melancholy and resentment.]

splice
 splice the mainbrace (*sl*) to serve out alcoholic drinks: *It's six o'clock — I think it's about time we spliced the mainbrace, don't you?* [Naval slang, originally a euphemism.]

splinter
 a splinter group a group (*esp* a political group) formed by breaking away from a larger one: *He's a member of a left-wing splinter group formed by ex-supporters of the Radical Party.*

split
 do the splits to sit down on the ground with one leg straight forward and the other straight back: *The pavements are very icy today — I nearly did the splits twice on the way to work.* [From the gymnastic exercise.]
 split hairs *see* **hair.**
 a split second a fraction of a second: *For a split second she thought she saw a face at the window, and then it vanished.*
 split the vote *see* **vote.**

spoil
 be spoiling for (something) (*inf*) to be eager for (*esp* a fight): *Be careful what you say to Jim — he seems to be spoiling for a fight!* [Originally US.]
 spoil the ship for a ha'porth of tar *see* **ship.**
 too many cooks spoil the broth *see* **cook.**

spoke
 put a spoke in (someone's) wheel to put difficulties in the way of what (someone) is doing: *It's time someone put a spoke in his wheel — he always seems to get what he wants.* [From a Dutch idiom deriving from the practice of jamming a cartwheel with a bar — in Dutch, *spaak* — to act as a brake when going downhill.]

sponge
 throw up the sponge to give up a struggle, argument *etc*: *I can see we are going to be defeated — I think we should throw up the sponge.* [From a method of conceding defeat in a boxing match.]

spoon

be born with a silver spoon in one's mouth *see* **silver.**

spoon-feed (*derog*) to teach or treat (a person) in a way that does not allow him to think or act for himself: *Some of these students expect to be spoon-fed with information rather than being made to find it themselves.* [Literally, 'to feed with a spoon'.]

sport

make sport of (someone or something) (*formal*) to make fun of or ridicule (a person, efforts *etc*): *They made sport of his attempts to start a conversation with one of the girls.*

a sporting chance a reasonably good chance: *If our train is on time, we have a sporting chance of getting home before midnight.*

spot

have a soft spot for *see* **soft.**

in a spot (*inf*) in trouble: *His failure to return the papers on time put her in a spot.*

knock spots off (someone) (*inf*) to do something much better, faster *etc* than (someone): *That little girl can knock spots off her elder brother at tennis.* [Originally US.]

on the spot (*inf*) **1** at once: *She liked it so much that she bought it on the spot.* **2** in the exact place referred to; in the place where one is needed: *He felt he was the best person to deal with the crisis as he was on the spot.*

put (someone) on the spot (*not formal*) to place (someone) in a dangerous, difficult or embarrassing position: *The interviewer's questions really put the Prime Minister on the spot.* [1920s' US gangsters' slang for 'to decide to assassinate (someone)'.]

rooted to the spot (*inf*) unable to move, because of fear, surprise *etc*: *I shouted to her to run, but she seemed to be rooted to the spot.*

spot on (*inf*) very accurate or exactly on the target: *His description of Mary was spot on!* [2nd World War RAF slang.]

a tight spot *see* **tight.**

spout

up the spout (*sl*) **1** completely ruined, useless or damaged beyond repair: *My wife has to go into hospital for an operation, so our summer holiday is up the spout.* **2** (*vulg*) pregnant: *His girlfriend has gone to the doctor — she thinks she's up the spout.* [Originally this phrase meant 'at the pawnbroker's' — allegedly from a pawnbroker's method of checking articles in by passing them up a spout to the back shop.]

sprat

> **a sprat to catch a mackerel** something small granted, conceded *etc* in order to make a large gain: *The investment we have made in our new oil field is just a sprat to catch a mackerel.*

spread

> **spread like wildfire** *see* **wild.**
>
> **spread one's wings** *see* **wing.**

spring

> **spring (something) on (someone)** (*inf*) to tell or propose (something) suddenly to (a person), so that he is surprised: *He sprang the news of his divorce on me.*

spur

> **on the spur of the moment** suddenly; without previous planning: *We decided to go to Paris on the spur of the moment.*
>
> **spur (someone) on** to cause (someone) to make greater efforts: *The thought of the prize spurred her on.* [Literally, to urge a horse to go faster, using spurs.]
>
> **win one's spurs** to achieve something important; to become recognized: *As a politician, he won his spurs by his masterly handling of the firemen's strike.* [When a man was knighted in the Middle Ages, he was presented with a pair of spurs by his sponsor.]

spurt

> **put a spurt on/put on a spurt** (*inf*) to run or go faster *eg* towards the end of a race: *He put on a sudden spurt and passed the other competitors.*

spy

> **spy on (someone)** to watch (a person *etc*) secretly: *Our next-door neighbours are always spying on us.*
>
> **spy out the land** to investigate or examine (*eg* an area of land, a matter *etc*) before proceeding further: *Before the firm entered into negotiations with the French, they sent two of their executives to spy out the land.*

square

> **go back to square one** (*inf*) to start again at the beginning: *If this experiment fails, we'll have to go back to square one.* [From a common instruction on board games.]
>
> **a square deal** (*inf*) an honest bargain, transaction *etc*: *You always get a square deal in that shop.*
>
> **a square meal** a good nourishing meal: *Her children never seem to get a square meal.*
>
> **square up (with someone)** (*inf*) to settle an account (with

someone): *I'll pay for the meal and we can square up/you can square up with me afterwards.*

square up to (something) to face (something) honestly and try to deal with it: *We've got to square up to the problem of our overspending.*

squeak

a narrow squeak a narrow escape: *Phew! That was a narrow squeak.*

squib

a damp squib *see* **damp.**

stab

have a stab at (doing) (something) (*inf*) to try (to do) (something: *I must have a stab at mending this machine.*

stab (someone) in the back to behave treacherously towards someone: *He always pretends to be her friend but he stabbed her in the back by applying for her job when she was in hospital.*

a stab in the back a treacherous act: *The government's refusal to allow a pay-rise is a stab in the back.*

stable

lock the stable door after the horse has bolted to take action to stop something from happening after it has already happened once: *After we had that terrible fire in the kitchen, I bought a fire extinguisher, although it did seem rather like locking the stable door after the horse had bolted.*

stack

stack the cards against *see* **card.**

staff

the staff of life (*old or facet*) bread.

stage

stage fright the nervousness felt by an actor *etc* when in front of an audience, *esp* for the first time: *She always suffered from stage fright when she stood up to make a speech, and found it difficult to begin.*

stage-manage to be in charge of the organization of (*eg* a military operation, a large-scale robbery *etc*): *The police failed to arrest the man who had stage-managed the escape of the prisoners.* [Literally, to be in charge of the scenery and equipment for a play *etc.*]

a stage whisper a loud whisper that is intended to be heard by people other than the one to whom it is addressed: *'I wish someone would offer me a drink,' said David to me in a stage whisper.* [From the fact that whispers on stage must be audible to the audience.]

stair

below stairs (*old*) in the part of a house *etc* where the servants live and work: *Her book is a vivid account of life below stairs in an Edwardian mansion.*

stake

at stake 1 to be won or lost: *A great deal of money is at stake.* **2** in great danger: *The peace of the country/Our children's future is at stake.*

have a stake in (something) to have an investment in (a business *etc*) or an interest or concern in (something): *He has a stake in several companies*; *We all have a stake in the future of the world.*

stake a claim to assert or establish one's ownership or right to something: *You ought to stake your claims to the property.* [From gold and silver mining.]

stake (someone or something) out (*sl*) to watch (a person, place *etc*) carefully: *The police staked out the gang's headquarters and waited for them to appear.*

stamp

a stamping-ground (*often facet*) a place where a person or people can usually be found: *The auction rooms are his stamping-ground*; *He's changed his stamping-ground — he's looking for a new girlfriend.* [Literally used of animals.]

stamp (something) out to crush or subdue (a rebellion *etc*): *The new king stamped out all opposition to his rule.* [Literally, to extinguish (a fire) by stamping on it.]

stand

it stands to reason *see* **reason.**

know where one stands to know what one's position or situation is (in some particular sense): *Once we've looked through all these financial reports, we'll know how we stand as far as money is concerned.*

make a stand to resist something one believes to be wrong *etc*: *We must make a firm stand against the lowering of educational standards.* [A military phrase, literally 'to stop and offer resistance'.]

not to be able to stand the sight of *see* **sight.**

on stand-by (*inf*) ready for action if necessary: *Two fire-engines went directly to the fire, and a third was on stand-by.*

stand by 1 to watch something happening without doing anything: *I couldn't just stand by while he was hitting the child.* **2** to be ready to act: *The police are standing by in case of trouble.* **3** to support or maintain: *She stood by him throughout his trial.*

stand corrected to agree that one has been wrong and accept the correction given to one: *Mr Brown now tells me that his complaint* *was made in December, not in January — I stand corrected, but it makes no difference to my case.*

stand down to withdraw from a contest: *Two of the candidates have stood down.*

stand fast/firm to refuse to yield: *I'm standing firm on/over this issue.*

stand for (something) (*inf*) to tolerate (something): *I won't stand for her rudeness.*

stand one's ground *see* **ground.**

stand in for (someone) to take (another person's) place, job *etc* for a time: *Could you stand in for me as chairman of the meeting?*

a standing joke a subject that causes a laugh whenever it is mentioned: *Aunt Eileen's cooking is a standing joke in the family — she's hopeless.*

stand (someone) in good stead *see* **stead.**

stand-offish (*derog*) (of a person or his manner *etc*) unfriendly: *The neighbours were rather stand-offish when we first moved into this house.* [From the naval term *stand off* = 'to keep away from the shore' (of a ship) and thus (of a person) 'to keep away from other people'.]

stand on ceremony *see* **ceremony.**

stand or fall by (something) to be completely committed to (an idea *etc*); to depend completely on (something): *I stand or fall by my belief in the brotherhood of man!*

stand out 1 to be noticeable because exceptional: *They were all pretty, but she stood out among them.* **2** (*formal*) to go on resisting or to refuse to yield: *The garrison stood out (against the besieging army) as long as possible.*

stand out a mile *see* **mile.**

stand (someone) up (*sl*) not to keep a promise to meet (*eg* a girlfriend): *You've stood me up three times this week!*

stand up and be counted to make one's opinions public, *esp* if they are only held by a minority of people or are unpopular: *It is time for those of us who are dissatisfied with the government to stand up and be counted!*

stand up for (someone or something) to support or defend (someone or something) in a dispute *etc*: *I thanked him for standing up for me/my proposals.*

stand up to (someone or something) to show resistance to (someone or something): *He stood up to the bigger boys who tried to bully him; These chairs have stood up to very hard wear.*

star

    see stars (*inf*) to see flashes of light as a result of a hard blow on the head: *I banged my head on the car door and saw stars.*

stare

    be staring (someone) in the face *see* **face.**

start

    a false start *see* **false.**

    for a start (used in argument *etc*) in the first place, or as the first point in an argument: *You can't have a new bicycle because for a start we can't afford one.*

    for starters (*inf*) in the first place; to begin with: *Everything's wrong with this dress — it doesn't fit me, for starters.* [Literally 'as the first course of a meal'.]

    get off to a good, bad start to start well or badly in a race, business *etc*: *The new scheme got off to a good start.*

    get started on (something) (*inf*) to start doing *etc* or talking about (something): *I'd better get started on (making) the supper.*

    start from scratch *see* **scratch.**

state

    get into a state (*inf*) to become very upset or anxious: *Don't come home late, or Mother will get into a state!*

statistics

    (someone's) vital statistics *see* **vital.**

status

    the status quo (*formal or legal*) the situation as it now is, or as it was before a particular change: *The committee voted not to change the status quo with regard to hospital visiting.*

    a status symbol a possession which people are supposed to get in order to show their high social position: *A house with a swimming-pool is a status symbol among business executives.*

stay

    stay put (*inf*) to remain where placed: *Once a child can crawl, he won't stay put for long.*

    stay the course to continue going to the end (of a race, period of training *etc*): *The race/training was strenuous, and few people managed to stay the course.*

    stay the pace *see* **pace.**

stead

    stand (someone) in good stead (*formal*) to be useful to (a person) in a time of need: *His knowledge of French stood him in good stead when he lost his money in France.*

steady

    as steady as a rock *see* **rock.**

    go steady (of a girl and boy not yet engaged to be married) to got out together regularly; to have a steady relationship: *He's going steady with his friend's sister.*

    steady (on)! (*inf*) don't be so angry, upset *etc*!: *Steady on! You mustn't shout at her — she's only a child!* [Apparently a nautical term.]

steal

    steal a march on *see* **march.**

    steal the show *see* **show.**

    steal (someone's) thunder *see* **thunder.**

steam

    full steam ahead at the greatest speed possible: *The building programme was going full steam ahead.* [Literally, an instruction for maximum forward speed conveyed to the engine-room of a steamship.]

    get, be (all) steamed up (*inf*) to get or be very upset or angry: *It is useless to get all steamed up about it.*

    get up steam to collect energy to do something: *I was just getting up steam to reach the summit of the mountain.* [Literally, to increase the pressure of steam in an engine before putting it into operation.]

    let off steam (*inf*) to release or get rid of excess energy, emotion *etc*: *A noisy quarrel can be a way of letting off steam.* [Literally, to release steam from an engine into the air and thus reduce the pressure.]

    run out of steam (*inf*) to lose energy, or become exhausted: *He ran out of steam shortly before the end of the race.* [Literally used of a steam engine.]

    under one's own steam (*inf*) by one's own efforts, without help from others: *John gave me a lift in his car, but Mary arrived under her own steam.*

steer

    steer clear of (something) to avoid (something): *You should steer clear of her — she is not trustworthy.*

step

    a false step *see* **false.**

    in, out of step with (someone) able, unable to share (someone's) interests and attitudes: *He feels he is out of step with today's young people.*

step by step gradually: *He improved step by step.*

step down (*not formal*) to give up a position, advantage *etc* in order to let someone else have it: *Mr Grant, our chairman, has decided that it is time he stepped down in favour of a younger man.*

step in to intervene: *The children began to quarrel, and I thought it was time I stepped in.*

step on it (*inf*) to hurry: *We'll have to step on it!*. [Originally, to drive a car faster by pressing harder on the accelerator pedal.]

step out of line *see* **line.**

step (something) up to increase (something), *esp* to raise it to a higher level: *The firm must step up production this year.*

take steps to take action: *I shall take steps to prevent this happening again.*

watch one's step to behave with care and caution (so as not to make mistakes): *She had better watch her step or she will be sacked for incompetence.*

stew

be, get in a stew to be or become very anxious and worried: *My mother will get in a stew if we're late home.*

stew in one's own juice *see* **juice.**

stick

get (hold of) the wrong end of the stick to misunderstand a situation, something said *etc*: *I got the wrong end of the stick and thought you wouldn't be coming till tomorrow.*

give (someone) stick (*inf*) to punish, criticize or scold (someone): *The Prime Minister got a lot of stick from Opposition MPs over the government's failure to reduce unemployment.*

in a cleft stick *see* **cleft.**

stick around (*sl*) to remain (in a place), *usu* in the hope of some future advantage *etc*: *If you stick around, we might have a job for you in a week or two.*

stick at (something) to hesitate, or refuse, *eg* to do (*esp* something wrong): *He probably wouldn't stick at murder to get what he wants.*

stick by (someone) (*inf*) to support or be loyal to (a person): *His friends stuck by him when he was in trouble.*

a stick-in-the-mud (*inf derog*) a person who can never be persuaded to do anything new: *She has become a terrible stick-in-the-mud since she got married.*

stick in (someone's) throat *see* **throat.**

stick it out (*inf*) to endure a situation for as long as necessary: *Will you manage to stick it out until I can find someone to help you?*

stick one's neck out *see* **neck.**

stick one's oar in *see* **oar.**

stick out a mile *see* **mile.**

stick out for (something) (*inf*) to refuse to accept less than (something): *The men are sticking out for a fifteen per cent pay rise.*

stick out like a sore thumb *see* **sore.**

stick to one's guns *see* **gun.**

stick up for (someone) to speak in defence of (a person *etc*): *When my father is angry with me, my mother always sticks up for me.*

sticky

come to a sticky end (*inf*) to have an unpleasant death or to end a period of one's life in an unpleasant way: *He'll come to a sticky end if he isn't more careful!*

on a sticky wicket in difficult circumstances, *esp* in a position where one's actions may be illegal, immoral *etc*: *Considering that you assaulted the manager, I think you would be on a sticky wicket trying to prove that they were wrong to dismiss you.* [A cricketing idiom — *sticky* here meaning 'muddy'.]

sticky-fingered (*derog inf*) in the habit of stealing things: *This firm has lost a great deal of money recently through the activities of sticky-fingered employees.*

stiff

as stiff as a poker *see* **poker.**

bore, scare (someone) stiff (*inf*) to bore or frighten (a person) very much: *His driving scares me stiff; I was bored stiff at the lecture.*

keep a stiff upper lip *see* **lip.**

sting

take the sting out of (something) to make (a disappointment *etc*) less painful: *The kindness of his manner took the sting out of the disappointing news he was relating.*

stink

like stink (*sl*) very much; very strongly: *You'll have to work like stink if you're going to win the prize!*

raise a stink (*sl*) to cause trouble: *He will raise a stink if he finds out what you have done!*

stir

stir one's stumps *see* **stump.**

stitch

he *etc* **hasn't got a stitch on/isn't wearing a stitch** (*inf*) he is completely naked: *It is difficult to appear dignified when you haven't got a stitch on.*

in stitches (*inf*) laughing a great deal: *His stories kept us in stitches* (= caused us to laugh a lot) *all night*.

a stitch in time saves nine a saying, meaning that one can save oneself a great deal of work by repairing something, putting something right *etc* as soon as the fault is noticed, and before it gets worse.

stock

on the stocks still being made, prepared, arranged *etc*: *A new expansion plan for the car industry is now on the stocks*. [Literally used of a ship, which is supported on *stocks* — a wooden framework — while being built.]

(someone's) stock-in-trade the standard ideas, methods *etc* used by (someone): *Sarcasm is too often part of a teacher's stock-in-trade*.

stock up (on something) to accumulate a supply (of something): *The boys were stocking up on chocolate and lemonade for their walk*.

take stock to form an opinion (about a situation *etc*): *He had no time to take stock of the situation*. [Literally, 'to make a list of goods in stock'.]

stomach

have a strong stomach *see* **strong**.

have no stomach for (something) (*formal*) not to have any desire, enough courage *etc* for (something): *I had no stomach for the fight*. [From the medieval belief that the stomach was the source of physical courage.]

turn (someone's) stomach (*inf*) to make (someone) feel disgusted, sick or angry: *The way he treats his staff turns my stomach!*

stone

leave no stone unturned to try every possible means: *The police left no stone unturned to (try to) find the child*.

stone-cold sober (*inf*) completely sober and not under the influence of alcohol.

a stone's throw a very short distance: *They live only a stone's throw away from here*.

stonewall to obstruct or impede progress intentionally: *I tried to get her to tell me what was wrong but she stonewalled me*. [A cricketing term for 'to play defensively'.]

stool

fall between two stools to lose both of two possibilities by hesitating between them or trying to achieve both: *That book falls between two stools — it is neither fiction nor biography.*

a stool-pigeon (*inf derog*) an informer or spy *esp* for the police: *The police received information about the planned robbery from a stool-pigeon.* [Originally US — a shooting term for a pigeon tied to a stool and used as a decoy.]

stop

come to a full stop to stop completely: *I'm afraid our plans for redecorating the kitchen have come to a full stop.* [Literally, to arrive at the full stop at the end of a sentence.]

pull out all the stops to act *etc* with as much energy, determination or emotion as possible: *I'll pull out all the stops to contact your wife before she arrives at her destination; He pulled out all the stops to make his story as pathetic as he could.* [From the stops of an organ — pulling them all out makes the organ play at full volume.]

put a stop to (something) to make sure that (something) does not continue: *We must put a stop to his disobedience.*

stop at nothing to be willing to do anything unworthy, in order to get something: *He'll stop at nothing to get what he wants.*

stop dead to stop completely: *I stopped dead when I saw him.*

stop (someone's) mouth *see* **mouth.**

stop off (*inf*) to make a halt on a journey *etc*: *We stopped off at Edinburgh to see the castle.*

stop over (*inf*) to make a stay of a night or more during a journey: *We're planning to stop over in Amsterdam.*

stop short of (something) to be unwilling to go beyond (a certain limit in one's conduct): *He wouldn't stop short of murder if his children were starving.*

store

in/into cold storage kept aside ready for use, but not used immediately: *The sudden crisis meant that our plans for a holiday in Germany had to be put into cold storage.*

in store coming in the future: *There's trouble in store for her!; If you've never been to York, that's a treat in store* (= a future pleasure) (*for you*).

set great store by (something) to value highly (*eg* a person's approval, opinion *etc*): *She sets great store by her husband's approval.*

storm

any port in a storm *see* **port.**

a storm in a teacup a fuss made over an unimportant matter: *We thought that they had decided not to get married but their quarrel was* *just a storm in a teacup*. [The title of a farce written by William Bernard in 1854.]

take (someone or something) by storm to impress (someone or something) greatly and immediately: *The singer took the audience by storm*. [Literally a military term — to capture (a fort *etc*) by making a sudden violent attack.]

weather the storm to survive a difficult time: *The next year or two will be very difficult for our firm, but I think we will weather the storm*.

story

    cut a long story short to describe something *etc* briefly: *We started off by getting up late because the alarm clock had stopped — to cut a long story short, we were late for everything all day*.

    the same old story something that happens or has happened in the same way often: *It's the same old story — Mary's in hospital with bronchitis again*.

    the story goes (that) people say (that): *The story goes that he beats his wife*; *He's been married before, or so the story goes*.

    a success story *see* **success.**

    a tall story *see* **tall.**

straight

    get (something) straight to get the facts right, so that (a situation) is fully understood: *Let's get this straight — you gave her the message, but she forgot to give it to me*.

    go straight (*inf*) (of a former criminal) to lead an honest life: *He got out of prison last year, and now he is going straight*.

    set the record straight *see* **record.**

    (on) the straight and narrow (path) (leading) a good and admirable way of life: *He was a very wild young man, but now he's married his wife keeps him on the straight and narrow*. [A variation on a Biblical reference — Matthew 7:4 — 'Strait is the gate, and narrow is the way, which leadeth unto life'.]

    straight away immediately: *Do it straight away*.

    straight from the horse's mouth *see* **horse.**

    straight off (*inf*) without deliberation: *I knew straight off that she was telling a lie*.

    straight out (*inf*) frankly: *I told her straight out that she was talking nonsense*.

    straight talking frank and honest conversation: *The time has come for some straight talking*. [From the idea that *straight*, like *level* and *square*, implies rightness and fairness.]

strait

strait-laced (*derog*) strict and severe in attitude and behaviour: *Her parents are rather strait-laced.* [Literally, having one's corset laced up very tightly.]

strange

be a stranger to (something) (*liter or formal*) to have no experience of (a condition, quality *etc*): *He is no stranger to misfortune* (= has had a lot of misfortune); *He is a stranger to fear* (= is very brave); (*euph*) *He is a stranger to the truth* (= tells lies).

strangely enough it is strange (that): *He lives next door, but strangely enough I rarely see him*; *'Did you recognize him?' 'Strangely enough, yes.'*

strange to say/tell/relate surprisingly: *Strange to say, he did pass his exam after all.*

straw

clutch at straws to hope that something may happen to help one in a difficult, dangerous situation *etc* when this is extremely unlikely: *They hoped the operation might save the child's life although they knew they were clutching at straws.*

the last straw *see* **last.**

a straw in the wind a small incident *etc* that shows what kind of thing may happen in the future: *The events of that year were straws in the wind which might have warned the government of the revolution which was soon to follow.*

a straw poll a vote taken unofficially, *eg* within a trade union, to get some idea of the general opinion: *The results of the BBC's straw poll show that there should be a substantial majority for the government in the by-election.*

the straw that breaks the camel's back *see* **the last straw** *at* **last.**

streak

be on a winning streak to have a series of successes in gambling *etc*: *I think I'll go on playing cards for a while — I'm on a winning streak.*

street

be on the street (*inf*) to be homeless: *We'll find ourselves on the street if we don't pay the rent.*

be streets ahead of (someone or something) (*inf*) to be much better than (someone or something): *Your work is streets ahead of hers.*

be (right) up (someone's) street (*inf*) to be exactly suitable for (a person): *That job is just up her street.*

go on the streets (*sl*) to become a prostitute: *Many girls have gone on the streets in the hope of becoming rich.*

in Queer Street *see* **queer.**

the man in the street *see* **man.**

not to be in the same street as (someone or something) to be completely different, *usu* worse, in quality than (someone or something): *She's not in the same street as you when it comes to organizing meetings.*

strength

go from strength to strength to move forward successfully from one achievement, triumph *etc* to another: *The society was founded in 1894 and after a slow start it has gone from strength to strength.*

in strength in large numbers: *The police were at the meeting in strength.*

on the strength (*not formal*) included as a member of a staff, group *etc*: *Our firm employs many highly-qualified people and has more than one university lecturer on the strength.*

on the strength of (something) relying on (something): *On the strength of this offer of money, we plan to start building soon.*

a tower of strength *see* **tower.**

stretch

at a stretch continuously: *He can't work for more than three hours at a stretch.*

at full stretch using all one's powers, energy *etc* to the limit in doing something: *They're working at full stretch trying to complete the job in time.*

stretch a point to go further, in giving permission, than the rules allow: *The children are only allowed two sweets a day but we might stretch a point today.*

stretch one's legs (*inf*) to go for a walk for the sake of exercise: *I need to stretch my legs.*

stride

get into/hit one's stride to reach one's normal or expected level of skill or success at something: *Once she gets into her stride she can get through a tremendous amount of work.* [An idiom from running.]

make great strides to progress well: *He's making great strides in his piano-playing.*

take (something) in one's stride to accept or cope with (a matter) successfully without worrying about it: *She takes difficulties in her stride*. [Literally used of a horse, runner *etc* jumping an obstacle without altering stride to do so.]

strike

come, be within striking distance of (something) to get or have got reasonably close to (something or doing something): *He didn't come within striking distance of passing the exam* (= He didn't even nearly pass the exam).

strike a bad patch *see* **patch.**

strike a balance to find an acceptable and satisfactory compromise between two extremes: *The manager tried to strike a balance between being too strict and too lenient with his staff.*

strike a bargain/an agreement to make a bargain; to reach an agreement: *We struck a bargain with each other.*

strike a chord *see* **chord.**

strike an attitude/pose to place oneself in a particular *usu* rather showy pose, as an actor does, or to express an opinion *etc* strongly and *usu* insincerely: *He's always striking attitudes, but he doesn't really mean what he says.*

strike fear/terror *etc* **into (someone)** to fill (a person) with fear *etc*: *The sound struck terror into them/their hearts.*

strike it rich *see* **rich.**

strike (it) lucky *see* **luck.**

strike (someone) off to remove or erase (*eg* a doctor's name) from a professional register *etc* for misconduct: *He/His name was struck off after his crimes were revealed.*

strike terror into (someone) *see* **strike fear into (someone)** above.

strike the right note *see* **note.**

strike up 1 to begin to play a tune *etc*: *The band struck up (with) 'The Red Flag'*. **2** to begin (a friendship, conversation *etc*): *He struck up an acquaintance with a girl on the train*. [The first meaning is the original one.]

strike while the iron is hot *see* **iron.**

string

have more than one string to one's bow *see* **bow**[2].

have (someone) on a string (*inf*) to have (a person) under one's control: *He seems to have his poor mother on a string — she agrees with everything he says.*

pull strings (*inf*) to use one's influence or that of others to gain an advantage: *His father had to pull strings to get him that job.*

pull the strings (*inf*) to be the person who is really, though *usu* not apparently, controlling the actions of others: *The government pulls the strings when the Bank of England decides to change the bank rate.* [The image is of manipulating a puppet.]

string (someone) along (*sl*) to keep (a person) attached to oneself without being seriously committed to him/her: *You're just stringing me along till you find a girl you like better.*

string (someone) up (*sl*) to hang (someone): *The gang threatened to seize the prisoners from the jail and string them up.*

strung up (*inf*) very nervous: *She's a bit strung up about her exam.*

with no strings attached (*inf*) without any conditions being made: *The money was lent to them with no strings attached* (= without instructions or conditions about how it was to be spent).

strip

strip off (*inf*) to remove one's clothes: *He stripped off and had a shower.*

tear a strip off (someone)/tear (someone) off a strip (*inf*) to rebuke (a person) very angrily: *He tore a strip off his secretary for arriving at the office half an hour late.*

stroke

at a stroke with a single effort: *He solved the problem at a stroke.*

on the stroke of (a time) punctually at (a time): *They arrived on the stroke of seven.* [From the striking of a clock.]

put (someone) off his *etc* stroke to make it impossible for (someone) to proceed smoothly with what they are doing: *The interruption put the teacher off her stroke and she found it difficult to continue with the lesson.* [A rowing idiom — to upset the rhythm with which a rower is completing each stroke.]

strong

be still going strong (*inf*) to continue to be successful, healthy *etc*: *Our business/grandfather is still going strong.*

be (someone's) strong suit (*formal*) to be the thing in which (someone) is expert or excels: *Being agreeable to ladies is his strong suit.* [An idiom from card games.]

have a strong stomach to be not easily made sick or disgusted: *A police surgeon needs to have a strong stomach to deal with some of his cases.*

strong-arm methods/tactics the use of violent methods to solve a problem *etc*: *He was suspected of resorting to strong-arm tactics to get what he wanted.* [Originally US.]

strong language (*formal or facet*) swearing or abuse: *The workman* *used strong language and embarrassed the old lady.*

(someone's) strong point a quality *etc* in which (someone) excels: *His ability to talk to strangers is one of his strong points.*

stubborn
as stubborn as a mule *see* **mule**.

stuck
get stuck in (*sl*) **1** to start working hard (at a job *etc*): *It's time we got stuck in.* **2** to start eating: *Dinner's ready — get stuck in!*

stuck for (something) (*inf*) unable to go on doing (something) because of the lack of (something): *We would like to expand our business, but unfortunately we are stuck for money at the moment.*

stuck on (something or someone) (*inf*) very fond of (someone or something): *He is stuck on Renaissance art.*

stuck with (something) (*inf*) unable to escape from or avoid (a burden, task *etc*): *She doesn't want to get stuck with (looking after) her husband's mother permanently.*

stuff
a bit of stuff (*derog sl*) a girl or woman: *He went to the party with a very flashy looking bit of stuff he had picked up in a pub.*

do one's stuff (*inf*) to perform in the expected way, or show what one can do: *They watched him while he did his stuff on the trapeze.*

get stuffed! (*impolite sl*) an angry expression rejecting or dismissing someone or their opinions, requests *etc*: *Get stuffed! I'm not going to do you any favours!*

hot stuff *see* **hot**.

kid's stuff *see* **kid**.

knock the stuffing out of (someone) (*inf*) to make (someone) weak, less strong *etc*: *His last illness knocked the stuffing out of him; The death of his wife knocked the stuffing out of him.* [From stuffed toys.]

know one's stuff (*inf*) to have skill and knowledge in one's chosen subject, job *etc*: *He's a good lecturer, as he really knows his stuff.*

stuff and nonsense! (*slightly old*) that's nonsense!: *You're too tired to work? Stuff and nonsense!*

a stuffed shirt (*derog inf*) a pompous person: *He never looks as though he is enjoying himself — he is such a stuffed shirt!* [Literally, a dummy.]

that's the stuff (*inf*) that's just what is wanted!: *Come on — sing a bit louder! That's the stuff!* [Originally US, probably popularized in Britain as used in the song 'Boiled Beef an' Carrots' (*c* 1910).]

stumble

a stumbling-block a difficulty that prevents progress: *The scheme would be excellent, but its cost is the main stumbling-block.* [A Biblical reference — to Romans 14:13.]

stump

on the stump (*sl*) taking part in a (political) speech-making tour or campaign: *The President is at the moment on the stump in New England.* [Originally US, from the use of tree-stumps as impromptu platforms.]

stir one's stumps (*inf*) to start moving: *We've only twenty minutes to catch the train, so you'd better stir your stumps!* [*Stumps* here = legs.]

stump up (*inf*) to pay (a sum of money), often unwillingly: *We all stumped up £1 for his present; We're always being asked to stump up.*

style

cramp (someone's) style (*usu facet*) to prevent (someone) from showing their ability to the full: *Having a wife and child has certainly cramped his style* (= prevented him from having such a carefree life as before).

do (something), live *etc* **in style** to do (something), or live, in a luxurious, elegant way without worrying about the expense: *The bride arrived at the church in style, in a horse-drawn carriage.*

subject

be subject to (something) (*formal*) **1** to be liable to or likely to suffer from, or have a tendency towards (something): *He is subject to colds/infection; The programme is subject to alteration.* **2** to depend on (something): *These plans are subject to your approval.*

change the subject to start talking about something different: *I mentioned the money to her, but she changed the subject.*

success

a success story the story of someone's rise to fame, wealth *etc*: *The life-history of my grandfather is one of the great success stories of Scottish literature.*

such

such-and-such used in discussing unreal or hypothetical situations, to refer to an unnamed person or thing: *Let's suppose that you go into such-and-such a shop and ask for such-and-such.*

such as it is, they are (*ironic*) though it hardly deserves the name: *You can borrow our lawnmower, such as it is.*

366

suck

suck up to (someone) (*derog inf: esp* used by schoolchildren) to try to gain a person's favour by flattery *etc*: *He's just trying to suck up (to you).*

sudden

all of a sudden suddenly or unexpectedly: *All of a sudden the lights went out.*

suffer

on sufferance (*formal*) with permission but without welcome: *He's here on sufferance, and if he does anything wrong he'll have to leave.*

suffer fools gladly (*usu in neg*) to be sympathetic and patient with foolish people: *He's an irritable man and doesn't suffer fools gladly.* [A Biblical reference — to II Corinthians 11:19.]

suffice

suffice it to say (*very formal*) I need only say: *Suffice it to say that the manager is on the whole pleased with the work.*

sugar

a sugar daddy (*derog sl*) an elderly man who has a young girlfriend to whom he gives generous presents: *She doesn't have to work — she has a wealthy sugar daddy.*

sugar the pill to make an unpleasant experience as pleasant as possible: *Whenever we went to the dentist as children my parents used to sugar the pill by taking us to the zoo afterwards.*

suit

be (someone's) strong suit *see* **strong.**

follow suit *see* **follow.**

suit one's actions to one's words (*liter or formal*) to do immediately what one is promising or threatening to do: *The father said he would smack the child if she disobeyed and he suited his actions to his words.*

suit (someone) down to the ground *see* **ground.**

suit oneself (*inf*) to do what one wants to do, without considering other people *etc*: *You can suit yourself whether you come or not.*

sum

the sum total the complete or final total: *The sum total of the cost/damage cannot be calculated.*

summer

an Indian summer *see* **Indian.**

one swallow doesn't make a summer *see* **swallow**[1].

sun

catch the sun (*inf*) to become sunburnt: *You've certainly caught the sun today! Your nose is red!*

under the sun (*inf*) in the whole world: *I'm sure that he must have visited every country under the sun.*

Sunday

a month of Sundays *see* **month.**

(someone's) Sunday best the smart, formal garments that a person wears for going to church or for other special occasions: *She was all in her Sunday best.*

sundry

all and sundry everybody: *This announcement concerns all and sundry.*

sunk

sunk *see* **sink.**

supply

be in short supply (of goods *etc*) to be scarce: *Cabbages/Good joiners are in short supply.*

sure

be/feel sure of oneself to be confident: *He's never very sure of himself amongst people he doesn't know.*

be sure to/(*inf*) **and** don't fail to (do something *etc*): *Be sure to/and switch off the television.*

for sure definitely or certainly: *We don't know for sure that he's dead.*

make sure to act so that, or check that, something is certain or sure: *Arrive early at the cinema to make sure of (getting) a seat!*

sure enough in fact, as was expected: *I thought it would rain, and sure enough it did.*

to be sure (*old or dial*) certainly; of course: *He's a nice person, to be sure, but not very clever.*

surface

scratch the surface only to deal with a very small part of a subject, problem *etc*: *What our organization can do to help the homeless only scratches the surface of a vast problem.*

surprise

take (someone) by surprise to catch (someone) unawares: *The news took me by surprise.* [Literally a military term — to capture a fort *etc* by a sudden, unexpected attack.]

(much, greatly *etc*) **to (someone's) surprise** causing (someone) great surprise: *Much to my surprise it had stopped raining by the time I wanted to go out.*

suspicion
 be above suspicion (*formal*) to be too highly respected ever to arouse suspicion: *A country's police force should be above suspicion.*

swallow[1]
 one swallow doesn't make a summer a saying, meaning that one should not be too quick to assume that a single success, opinion *etc* indicates that the success, opinion *etc* will be general. [From the fact that swallows arrive in Britain at the beginning of summer.]

swallow[2]
 swallow one's pride *see* **pride.**

swan
 swan around/off (*inf derog*) to wander about or go travelling in a leisurely and rather irresponsible way: *He swans around doing nothing while his wife works.*
 (someone's) swan song (*formal or facet*) the last work or performance of *eg* a poet, musician *etc* before his death or retirement: *The actor's performance as Othello proved to be his swan song.* [From the ancient legend that the swan, which is usually silent, sings only once in its life, as it is dying.]

sway
 hold sway (*formal*) to have control or influence; to rule: *Rome held sway over a huge empire for several hundred years.*

swear
 swear by (something) (*inf*) to put complete trust in (a certain remedy *etc*): *She swears by aspirin for all the children's illnesses.* [Literally, to use the name of something as an oath.]
 swear (someone) in to introduce (a person) into a post or office formally, by making him swear an oath: *The new Governor is being sworn in next week.*
 swear like a trooper *see* **trooper.**

sweat
 a cold sweat (coldness and dampness of the skin when a person is in) a state of shock, fear *etc*: *I was in a cold sweat; The horrible sound brought me out in a cold sweat.*
 no sweat (*sl*) no trouble: *I'll do that for you, no sweat!* [Originally US.]
 sweat blood (*inf*) to work hard; to use a great deal of effort: *I sweated blood to finish that essay last night.*

sweat it out (*inf*) to endure or bear a difficult or unpleasant situation: *He'll just have to sweat it out by himself.*

the sweat of one's brow (*often facet*) one's effort and hard work: *I can proudly say that I earned all my money by the sweat of my brow.*

sweep

make a clean sweep *see* **clean.**

sweep (someone) off his *etc* **feet** *see* **feet.**

sweep (something) under the carpet *see* **carpet.**

sweet

be (all) sweetness and light to appear to be gentle and reasonable: *His wife is all sweetness and light in public, but she has a terrible temper.*

have a sweet tooth (*inf*) to like sweet things to eat: *My friend has a sweet tooth, so I always give her chocolates.*

sweet nothings (*rather old*) loving but unimportant things whispered to someone attractive of the opposite sex: *He was whispering sweet nothings into the ear of the prettiest girl there.*

the sweets of (something) (*liter*) the delights of (*eg* life, success *etc*): *He was enjoying the sweets of victory.*

swim

be in the swim (*inf*) to be involved in, or aware of, the latest fashion or trend of affairs, business *etc*: *He and his wife always like to be in the swim.*

swing

get into the swing (of things) (*inf*) to begin to understand, and fit into, a routine or rhythm of work *etc*: *He took a few days to get back into the swing of things after his illness.*

in full swing going ahead, or continuing, busily or vigorously: *The work/party was in full swing.*

room to swing a cat *see* **cat.**

swing the lead *see* **lead**[2].

what you win on the swings you lose on the roundabouts a saying, meaning that a gain in one place is usually cancelled out by a loss in another. [The reference is to a fairground.]

switch

be switched on (*sl*) **1** to be aware of and in sympathy with all the activities and developments that are up to date and fashionable: *My grandmother's really switched on — she enjoys pop music.* **2** to take drugs for stimulation; to be under the influence of such drugs.

switch over to (cause to) change: *We're switching over from coal-gas to North Sea gas.*

swollen

    swollen-headed (*derog*) too pleased with oneself; conceited: *He's very swollen-headed about his success.*

swoop

    at one fell swoop all at the same time; in a single movement or action: *The new manager got rid of several unwanted employees at one fell swoop.* [A Shakespearian quotation — from *Macbeth*, IV. iii. The reference is to a hawk swooping on poultry.]

sword

    cross swords to quarrel or disagree: *I try not to cross swords with my boss but he is a most unreasonable man.* [From fencing.]

    the sword of Damocles a disaster which may happen at any moment: *The sword of Damocles has been hanging over us ever since we discovered my husband has cancer.* [From the story of Damocles, who was forced by Dionysius of Syracuse to sit through a banquet with a sword suspended over him held up only by a single hair.]

symbol

    a status symbol *see* **status.**

system

    get (something) out of one's system to stop oneself permanently from thinking *etc* about (something), *esp* by expressing one's feelings: *Tell me all about your problem — it'll help you to get it out of your system.* [A medical reference.]

T

t

    to a T (*inf*) exactly; very well: *This job suits me to a T.* [Origin obscure — possibly from *to a tittle* = to the last dot (in writing *etc*).]

tab

    keep tabs on (someone or something) to keep a check on (someone or something); to watch (someone or something): *I like to keep tabs on what is happening at home when I'm on holiday.* [Originally US, from an American use of *tab* to mean 'account'.]

    pick up the tab (*US inf*) to pay the bill (for something): *He insisted on picking up the tab for the meal.* [As previous idiom.]

table

drink (someone) under the table (*inf*) to remain conscious after having drunk an amount of alcohol that makes (someone else) unconscious: *He's a very heavy drinker — he could drink us all under the table.*

turn the tables on (someone) to reverse a situation *etc* and put (someone) in a totally different position, *esp* one where he has lost his previous advantage: *I'll turn the tables on you one day, and I will be the boss.* [From the medieval game of *tables* — of which backgammon is a form — in which turning the board round would exactly reverse the position of the players.]

tag

tag along (*inf: sometimes derog*) to follow or go (with someone), often when one is not wanted: *We never get away from him — everywhere we go, he insists on tagging along (with us)!*

tail

tail-end Charlie (*inf*) someone who is last in a competition, series or group of people *etc*: *My daughter won't be out of school yet — she's always a tail-end Charlie.* [RAF slang for the rear-gunner in an aircraft and hence for the last aircraft in a group.]

with one's tail between one's legs in a very miserable and ashamed manner: *I gave the child a severe scolding and he went away with his tail between his legs.* [From the behaviour of an unhappy dog.]

take

be taken with (something) (*inf*) to find (something) pleasing or attractive: *He was very taken with the village and its inhabitants.*

take after (someone) (*inf*) to be like (someone, *esp* a parent or relation) in appearance or character: *She takes after her father.*

take (something) as read *see* **read.**

take one's cue from (someone) *see* **cue.**

take (someone) for (someone or something) to believe (mistakenly) that (someone) is (someone or something else): *I took you for your brother; I took him for an intelligent person.*

take (someone) for a ride *see* **ride.**

take heart *see* **heart.**

take (someone) in (*inf*) to deceive or cheat someone: *I was told the picture was very valuable, but I soon found out I'd been taken in; He took me in with his story.*

take it (*with* **can/could**) to be able to bear suffering, trouble, difficulty *etc*: *Tell me the bad news. Don't worry, I can take it.*

take it easy *see* **easy.**

take it from me (that) you can believe me when I say (that): *Take it from me — this company is heading for bankruptcy.*

take it from there (*inf*) to deal with events as they happen, not following any plan of action: *I think we should offer him the job and take it from there.*

take it or leave it to accept something or refuse to accept it, without trying to alter what one is being offered, the price *etc*: *I want £50 for that coat — take it or leave it.*

take it out of (someone) (*inf*) to tire or exhaust (someone): *The long walk really took it out of me.*

take it out on (someone) (*inf*) to be angry with or unpleasant to (someone) because one is angry, disappointed *etc* oneself: *I know you're upset, but there's no need to take it out on me!*

take (someone's) mind off *see* **mind.**

take off (*inf*) to begin suddenly to improve or get bigger: *I think the computer business is about to take off.* [From the launching of rockets.]

take (someone) off (*inf*) to imitate someone (often unkindly): *He used to take off his teacher to make his friends laugh.*

take place *see* **place.**

take (someone's) place *see* **place.**

take sides *see* **side.**

take steps *see* **step.**

take the floor *see* **floor.**

take the place of *see* **place.**

take the risk *see* **risk.**

take one's time *see* **time.**

take up arms *see* **arm.**

take (someone) up on (something) (*inf*) to accept (someone's offer *etc*): *'Why don't you come and stay with us one day?' 'I might take you up on that.'*

take (something) upon oneself to take responsibility for (something): *I took it upon myself to make sure she arrived safely.*

take up the cudgels *see* **cudgel.**

take up with (someone) (*inf*) to become friendly with or associate with (someone): *She has taken up with some very strange people.*

take (something) up with (someone) (*formal*) to discuss (*esp* a complaint): *I shall take the matter up with my MP.*

tale

tell its own tale to show clearly what has happened: *There was* no sign of James, but the suicide note and the pile of clothes on the beach told their own tale.

tell tales (*derog*) to give away secret or private information about the (*usu* wrong) actions of others: *You must never tell tales about your friends to the teacher.*

thereby hangs a tale there is a story connected with that which could be told: *I was very late getting back from Bristol, and thereby hangs a tale.* [A pun on *tail*, a favourite of Shakepeare's which appears in several of his plays.]

talk

money talks *see* **money.**

now you're talking (*inf*) at last you are saying something important or to the point: '*How about if I paid you to do this for me?*' '*Now you're talking!*'

straight talking *see* **straight.**

talk about (something) this is an excellent example of (something): *Talk about bad manners! She left the party without saying a word to the hostess!*

talk back to (someone) (*derog*) to answer (someone) rudely: *Don't talk back to me!*

talk big (*inf*) to talk as if one is very important; to boast: *He's always talking big about his job.*

talk down to (someone) to speak to (someone) as if they are much less important, clever *etc*: *Children dislike being talked down to.*

talk one's head off to talk a great deal: *The two friends talked their heads off when they eventually met again.*

talking of (something) (*inf*) while we are on the subject of (something): *Talking of food, what time are we having dinner?*

a talking-shop (*derog inf*) a place or meeting where things are discussed but no action is ever decided on or taken: *They claimed that the Emergency Committee was just a talking-shop and achieved nothing.*

talk (someone) into, out of (doing) (something) to persuade (someone) to do, not to do (something): *He talked me into changing my job; She tried to talk her husband out of going.*

talk nineteen to the dozen *see* **dozen.**

the talk of the town someone or something that everyone (in society) is talking about: *Their divorce is the talk of the town.*

talk (something) over to discuss (something): *We talked the whole idea over at great length.*

374

talk (someone) round to persuade (someone): *She didn't want to do it but I managed to talk her round.*

talk shop *see* **shop.**

talk through one's hat *see* **hat.**

talk through the back of one's head/neck *see* **back.**

talk turkey *see* **turkey.**

tall

a tall order something very difficult to do: *Finding somewhere for fifty children to stay tonight is rather a tall order.* [Originally US, from a slang use of *tall* = large.]

a tall story a story which is hard to believe: *He says the Queen has invited him to Buckingham Palace, but that's just one of his tall stories.* [Originally US.]

tan

tan (someone's) hide *see* **hide.**

tangent

go off at a tangent to go off suddenly in another direction or on a different line of thought, action *etc*: *It is difficult to have a sensible conversation with her, as she keeps going off at a tangent.* [A *tangent* is a line which touches a curve at one end — the reference is to something which is rotating in a circle round a point and which suddenly breaks loose and flies out of the circle into space.]

tap

on tap ready for immediate use: *You're lucky to live near a library and have all that information on tap.* [Literally used of beer *etc* which is in a cask fitted with a tap and thus ready to be drawn off as required.]

tape

have (someone or something) taped 1 to understand (something, *esp* a person's character and abilities) very clearly: *He was trying very hard to impress me, but I soon had him taped.* **2** to have got (a matter) arranged as one wants: *I'm to start a new job next month — I've got it all taped.* [The implication is probably 'measured with a tape'.]

red tape *see* **red.**

tar

be tarred with the same brush to have the same faults (as someone else): *My brothers are both tarred with the same brush — they're both extremely lazy.* [From the use of tar to cover sores on sheep, *esp* considered as members of a flock.]

spoil the ship for a ha'porth of tar *see* **ship.**

target

a sitting target *see* **sit.**

tart

tart (someone or something) up (*derog sl*)) to make (a person, thing *etc*) more attractive, *esp* in a showy or tasteless way: *She was tarting herself up in front of the mirror*; *Their house was nicer before it was tarted up.*

task

take (someone) to task (*formal*) to blame or criticize (a person): *She took him to task for his rudeness to her mother.* [Literally, 'to accept (the correction of someone *etc*) as one's allotted task'.]

taste

to taste (used in recipes *etc*) in whatever quantity is desired: *Add salt and pepper to taste.*

to one's taste (in a way that is) pleasing to one: *The furniture was at last arranged to her taste*; *A walking holiday would not be to his taste.*

tea

(someone's) cup of tea *see* **cup.**

not for all the tea in China certainly not; not at all: *I wouldn't be married to that nasty man for all the tea in China!* [From the fact that for a long time China was the source of all the world's tea.]

a storm in a teacup *see* **storm.**

teach

teach one's grandmother to suck eggs *see* **egg.**

I, that *etc* will teach (someone) to be, do *etc* (something bad) I, that *etc* will punish a person, or be a person's punishment, for doing something bad: *I'll teach you to be rude to me!*; *That'll teach you to disobey me.*

tear[1]

tear a strip off (someone) *see* **strip.**

tear[2]

crocodile tears *see* **crocodile.**

teeth

armed to the teeth (*old or facet*) carrying all the weapons, armour, equipment *etc* possible (for a fight or struggle): *He arrived for the interview armed to the teeth with statistics and documents supporting his point of view.* [A medieval idiom.]

by the skin of one's teeth *see* **skin.**

cut one's teeth on (something) to get valuable experience from (something): *The famous mountaineer said he had cut his teeth on rock-climbing in the Lake District.* [Literally, of a child, to use (something) to chew on in order to help new teeth to break through the gum.]

draw the teeth of (someone or something) to make (someone or something) no longer dangerous (*esp* to oneself): *He knew that his unexpected offer had drawn the teeth of his opponent's plan of action.* [Literally, to remove (an animal's) teeth.]

fed to the back teeth *see* **fed.**

get one's teeth into (something) to tackle (something serious) in a determined manner: *He likes to work on a really difficult problem that he can get his teeth into.*

gnash one's teeth (*rather facet*) to be angry and disappointed: *The criminals escaped in a speedboat and the police were left on the jetty to gnash their teeth.* [A Biblical reference — to Matthew 8:12.]

grit one's teeth (to try) not to show one's feelings: *He gritted his teeth and tried to speak calmly and pleasantly although he was very angry.*

in the teeth of (something) (*formal*) against or in opposition to (something): *They were walking in the teeth of a gale.*

lie in one's teeth *see* **lie**[1].

set (someone's) teeth on edge to cause an unpleasant feeling of discomfort *etc* to someone: *These sour grapes set my teeth on edge; That shrill bell set everyone's teeth on edge.*

show one's teeth to show one's anger and power to resist; to act decisively *etc*: *The government soon showed its teeth to the rebels.*

teething troubles problems experienced at the beginning of a new plan, operation *etc*: *We have had our teething troubles but the new system is working very well now.* [From the fact that a baby is often unwell and uncomfortable for a short time very early in its life while its teeth are coming in.]

tell

all told (*rather formal*) altogether; including everything or everyone: *This has been a very successful day all told; There was an audience of nine all told.* [*Told* here means 'counted'.]

I told you so I told or warned you that this would happen, had happened *etc*, and I was right: *'He's made a complete mess of this.' 'I told you so, but you wouldn't believe me.'*

take a telling (not) to do what one is told, warned *etc* (not) to do: *I warned you not to climb trees, but you just won't take a telling, will you?*

tell its own tale *see* **tale.**

tell (someone) off (*inf*) to scold (someone): *The teacher used to tell me off for not doing my homework.* [Probably from the older meaning, 'to separate or detach from others (for a purpose)', and its use in the army.]

tell on (someone) 1 to have a bad effect on: *The strain of looking after her invalid mother is obviously telling on her.* **2** (*inf*) to give information about (a person, *usu* if they are doing something wrong): *I'm late for work — don't tell on me!*

tell tales *see* **tale.**

tell (someone) where to get off *see* **get.**

there's no telling it is impossible to know: *There's no telling what he'll do if you make him angry!*

to tell the truth *see* **truth.**

you never can tell it is possible: *It might rain — you never can tell*; *You might be a millionaire one day — you never can tell.*

you're telling me! (*inf*) certainly; that is definitely true: *'It's cold today.' 'You're telling me (it is)!'* [Originally US, probably from Yiddish idiom.]

temper

  keep, lose one's temper not to show, to show, anger: *He lost his temper and shouted at me.*

tender

  leave (someone) to (someone's) tender mercies to leave (someone) to be dealt with by (someone hostile, unattractive, inefficient *etc*): *I didn't want to leave your visitor to Miss Harris's tender mercies, so I brought him into my office to wait for you.* [A Biblical reference, to Psalm 25:6.]

tenterhooks

  be on tenterhooks (*inf*) to be uncertain and anxious about what is going to happen: *We were all on tenterhooks waiting to hear the result of the general election.* [*Tenterhooks* were hooks for stretching newly-woven cloth on a frame or *tenter* — the idiom thus means 'very tense or tightly-stretched'.]

term

  be on speaking terms *see* **speak.**

  come to terms with (something) to find a way of living with or tolerating (some personal trouble or difficulty): *He managed to come to terms with his illness.* [A phrase from diplomacy — 'to reach an agreement with'.]

  in terms of something using (something) as a terminology, a

378

means of expression, a means of assessing value *etc*: *He thought of everything in terms of money; Give the answer in terms of a percentage.*

terror

strike terror into (someone) *see* **strike.**

test

put (someone or something) to the test to test (someone or something): *He decided to put her loyalty to the test by sending someone to question her.*

tether

at the end of one's tether *see* **end.**

thank

be thankful for small mercies *see* **mercy.**

have only oneself to thank for (something) to be the cause of (something unfortunate which has happened to one): *If his wife is angry with him he only has himself to thank — he should have let her know he would be late.*

I'll thank you *etc* **to (do something)** (*impolite*) please (do something) (used to indicate that the speaker is angry): *From now on I'll thank you to keep your nose out of my business!*

no thanks to (*inf*) in spite of (a person's help, lack of help *etc*): *We eventually managed to finish the job, no thanks to him and his stupid ideas.*

thanks to because of: *Thanks to the bad weather, our journey was very uncomfortable; Thanks to your generous donation, we can rebuild our laboratory.*

thank you for nothing (*inf: ironic*) an expression indicating that the speaker is not pleased by the information he has been given, the job he has been asked to do *etc*: *'I've made an appointment with the dentist for you.' 'Thank you for nothing!'*

a vote of thanks *see* **vote.**

that

and all that (*inf*) and all the rest of that kind of thing: *He said he was sorry and didn't want to hurt anyone, and all that, but I didn't think he really meant it.*

at that in addition; when everything has been considered: *He's a novelist, and a good one at that; It wasn't such a bad idea at that, but it didn't work.*

(just) like that (*inf*) immediately, without further thought, discussion *etc*: *You don't expect me to give up my job and go to America just like that, surely?*

that's/there's a (good) boy, girl, dog *etc* (*inf*) an expression used to praise or encourage a child, animal *etc*: *You finish your soup now — there's a good boy.*

that's that an expression used to show that a decision has been made, that something has been completed, made impossible *etc*: *He has said that we can't do it, so that's that; 'The car has broken down.' 'That's that then. We won't reach Glasgow tonight.'*

then

then and there/there and then (*inf*) at that very time or moment: *He asked me then and there; She began to take all her clothes off right there and then.*

there

so there (*inf*) an expression used, *esp* by children, to indicate that the speaker thinks he has an advantage of some kind over the person he is speaking to and wishes to make it obvious: *The teacher says my spelling is better than yours, so there!; I don't care what the teacher says, so there!*

there and then *see* **then**.

there's a (good) boy, girl, dog *etc see* **that**.

there you are 1 used to express satisfaction when something one said would happen does happen: *There you are! I told you you would fall in!* **2** used to indicate that something is a feature of life that cannot be changed: *We can't really afford to run a car, but there you are — when you live in the country, you need one.*

thick

as thick as thieves (*inf*) very friendly: *They didn't like each other at first, but they're as thick as thieves now.*

as thick as two short planks *see* **plank**.

a bit thick (*inf*) more than a person can tolerate; not just or fair: *He expected me to do his work for him — that's a bit thick, isn't it?*

give (someone) a thick ear to strike (a child *etc*) on the ear, *usu* as a punishment: *If I find my son has been involved in this, I'll give him a thick ear!*

lay it on thick to go beyond the truth in what one is saying, *esp* in praising something: *I thought she was laying it on a bit thick when she said his house was the loveliest house she'd ever seen, but he was really pleased.*

the plot thickens *see* **plot**.

thick and fast frequently and in large numbers: *The bullets/ insults were flying thick and fast.*

thick-skinned not easily hurt by criticism or insults: *You won't upset her — she's very thick-skinned.*

through thick and thin (*inf*) whatever happens; in spite of all difficulties: *They were friends through thick and thin.* [An idiom from hunting — the reference is to thick and thin vegetation.]

thief

set a thief to catch a thief a saying, meaning that the best way to outwit a deceitful person is to employ another deceitful person to do it.

as thick as thieves *see* **thick.**

thin

as thin as a rake *see* **rake.**

be thin on top (*inf*) to be becoming bald: *He is still a handsome man, although he is a little thin on top.*

on thin ice *see* **ice.**

thin air nowhere: *He disappeared into thin air; The magician seemed to produce coins out of thin air.* [A Shakespearian quotation — from *The Tempest*, IV. i.]

the thin end of the wedge *see* **wedge.**

thin on the ground rare: *Real experts are thin on the ground.*

thin-skinned sensitive; easily hurt or upset: *Be careful what you say — she's very thin-skinned.*

a thin time (*inf*) a difficult or not very pleasant time, *eg* because of a lack of money: *She's had rather a thin time of it since her husband died; Her husband is very suspicious and gives her a thin time if she is ever out late.*

thing

all things being equal if none of the other facts of the matter make/made any difference: *I'm younger than him and, all things being equal, I should outlive him.*

be all things to all men (*slightly derog*) to be able to fit in with the attitudes *etc* of whoever one is with, *esp* by constantly changing one's opinions to agree with one's companions: *I never really trusted her — I felt she was all things to all men and didn't mean what she said.* [A Biblical reference to I Corinthians 9:22.]

do one's (own) thing (*sl*) to behave in a way which is natural to one or to do something which one is good at: *We believe that our youth club provides facilities for youngsters to do their own thing, whatever that may be.*

first thing *see* **first.**

for one thing used to introduce the first reason (for (not) doing something): *I can't go — for one thing, I have no money, and for another, I have too much work.*

have a thing about (something or someone) (*inf*) to be especially fond of, keen on, annoyed by, frightened by (something or someone) *etc*: *I've got a thing about men in uniforms; She's got a thing about spiders.*

hear things *see* **see things** *below*.

know a thing or two (*inf*) to be wise and show good practical judgement: *George wouldn't sign a document he hadn't read — he knows a thing or two.*

make a thing of (something) (*inf*) to make a fuss about (something): *Don't make a thing of leaving early, it's not important.*

a near thing *see* **near**.

no such thing 1 something quite different: *He said he was a lawyer, but he turned out to be no such thing.* **2** no, not at all: *I expected him to be waiting for us, but no such thing — he'd gone.*

not to know the first thing about *see* **first**.

(just) one of those things something that must be accepted: *Being ill on holiday was just one of those things.*

see, hear things to see or hear something that is not there: *'That man has two heads!' 'Don't be silly — you're seeing things!'; I keep hearing things — it's very frightening.*

a stupid, wise *etc* **thing to do** a stupid, wise *etc* action: *That was a silly thing to do, wasn't it?*

the thing is ... (*inf*) the important fact or question is; the problem is: *The thing is, is he going to help us?; The thing is, I haven't any money.*

the very thing *see* **very**.

think

have (got) another think coming (*derog inf*) to be mistaken (in what one thinks): *If you think I'm going to work for you without being paid, you've got another think coming!*

I should think so, not that is, is not what one should do *etc*; certainly (not): *'I've come to apologize for being rude to you.' 'I should think so, too!'; 'I never drink when I'm going to be driving.' 'I should think not!'*

not think much of *see* **think little of** *below*.

put on one's thinking cap (*inf*) to think about, and try to solve, a problem *etc*: *We've got to find some way of improving our sales figures, so we'd better put on our thinking-caps.*

I *etc* **shouldn't think of (something)** I *etc* should not do (something) under any circumstances: *I shouldn't think of taking your money!*

think better of (someone or something) 1 to think again and decide not to (do something); to reconsider (something): *He was going to ask for more money, but he thought better of it.* **2** to think that (someone) would not be so bad *etc* as to act in a certain way: *I thought better of you than to suppose you would lie to me.*

think little of/not think much of (something) to have a very low opinion of (something): *He didn't think much of what I had done; He thought little of my work.*

think nothing of it *see* **nothing.**

think (something) out to plan (something); to work (something) out in the mind: *I haven't thought out the details of the operation yet.*

think (something) over to think about (something) carefully; to consider all aspects (of an action, decision *etc*): *He thought it over, and decided not to go.*

think the world of *see* **world.**

think twice *see* **twice.**

think (something) up to invent or devise (something): *He thought up a new way of making polythene.*

third

give someone the third degree *see* **degree.**

third time lucky a saying, expressing the belief that one usually succeeds in something the third time one tries, and usually said to encourage a third attempt, as one begins a third attempt, or to draw attention to a success at the third attempt.

this

this and that/this, that and the other various unimportant objects, actions *etc*: *I spent the morning in the office doing this, that and the other while I waited for his phone call.*

Thomas

a doubting Thomas *see* **doubt.**

thorn

a thorn in (someone's) flesh/side something or someone that continually irritates (someone): *His sister is a thorn in his flesh.* [A Biblical reference, to II Corinthians 12:7.]

thought

food for thought *see* **food.**

perish the thought *see* **perish.**

second thoughts. *see* **second.**

thrash

thrash (something) out to discuss (a problem *etc*) thoroughly and solve it: *They thrashed it out between them, and finally came to an agreement.* [Literally, to separate the grains of corn from the stalk by threshing.]

thread

hang by a thread to be in a very precarious, dangerous state: *His life is hanging by a thread.* [Probably a reference to the story of Damocles — *see* **sword of Damocles** *at* **sword.**]

lose the thread to cease to understand the connection between the details of a story *etc*: *I'm sorry — I'm afraid I've lost the thread of what he was saying.*

three

the three Rs *see* **r.**

thrill

thrilled to bits very greatly delighted and excited: *The children were thrilled to bits at the thought of going to America.*

throat

at each other's throat quarrelling violently: *He can't get on with his brother-in-law — they're always at each other's throats.* [The reference is to fighting dogs.]

cut one's own throat to act in a way which damages oneself: *I think you'll be cutting your own throat if you refuse to take that job.*

have a frog in one's throat *see* **frog.**

jump down (someone's) throat (*inf*) to attack (someone) verbally in a violent way before they can explain themselves: *She jumped down my throat before I had a chance to apologize.*

ram (something) down (someone's) throat (*derog inf*) to (try to) force (someone) to believe or accept (a statement, idea *etc*, *esp* one they are unwilling to believe or accept).

stick in (someone's) throat (*inf*) to be impossible to believe, accept *etc*: *Opening other people's letters really sticks in my throat; I don't usually criticize other people's behaviour but the way she carries on really sticks in my throat.* [Literally, to be impossible to swallow.]

throe

in the throes of (something) (*formal or facet*) in the (difficult) process of: *The country is in the throes of a minor revolution.* [Literally, 'in labour' — the reference is to producing something new with difficulty and effort, but the emphasis has shifted from the creativity to the suffering involved.]

throne

  the power behind the throne *see* **power.**

through

  fall through *see* **fall.**

  pull through *see* **pull.**

  see through *see* **see.**

  through and through completely: *He was a gentleman through and through.*

  through with (someone or something) (*inf*) finished with (someone or something): *Are you through with the newspaper yet?*; *I'm through with working*; *I'm through with him.* [From US usage, although existent also in older and dialectal British English.]

throw

  throw cold water on/over *see* **cold.**

  throw (something) in (*inf*) to include or add (something) as a gift or as part of a bargain: *When I bought his car he threw in the radio and a box of tools.*

  throw in one's hand *see* **hand.**

  throw in the towel *see* **towel.**

  throw (something) off to get rid of (something): *She finally managed to throw off her cold*; *They were following us, but we managed to throw them off.*

  throw (someone) over (*inf*) to leave, abandon (a girlfriend, boyfriend *etc*): *She threw him over for someone with more money.*

  throw (someone) to the lions *see* **lion.**

  throw up 1 (*sl*) to vomit: *She had too much to eat, and threw up on the way home.* **2** (*inf*) to give up or abandon: *He threw up his job.*

  throw up the sponge *see* **sponge.**

  throw one's weight about *see* **weight.**

thumb

  rule of thumb *see* **rule.**

  stick out like a sore thumb *see* **sore.**

  thumb a lift to ask for or get a lift in someone's car *etc* by signalling to the driver with one's thumb: *He thumbed a lift outside the hospital.*

  thumb one's nose at (someone) to express defiance or contempt towards (someone), originally by means of a rude gesture: *The police must do something to prevent these criminals thumbing their noses at the authorities and getting away with it.*

  thumbs down (a sign indicating) disapproval or failure: *I asked the boss, but I'm afraid it's thumbs down for our proposed scheme.* [From the Latin *pollice verso* — which probably means 'thumbs up' rather than 'thumbs down' as has been assumed — the signal made by a Roman crowd voting for the death of a gladiator.]

thumbs up (a sign indicating) hope of, or wishes for, success: *He could see that the team manager was signalling thumbs up from the edge of the football pitch.* [The opposite of the previous idiom.]

twiddle one's thumbs (*inf*) to do nothing: *He spent six months twiddling his thumbs while he waited for a job.* [Literally, to rotate one's thumbs round each other, a pointless activity indicating boredom.]

under (someone's) thumb controlled or greatly influenced by someone: *She is completely under her husband's thumb.*

thunder

steal (someone's) thunder to prevent (someone) from receiving congratulations, getting publicity *etc* for something, by using it, making it public *etc* before they do: *He was looking forward to telling his family the news and was annoyed to find that his cousin had phoned them and stolen his thunder.* [From an incident in the 17C theatre when a machine invented by the playwright John Dennis for simulating thunder on stage was pirated and used in a rival play.]

tick

on tick (*Brit inf*) on credit, promising to pay later: *He bought the books on tick.* [From *on ticket*, *ticket* once being the usual name for a formal acknowledgement of money owed.]

tick (someone) off/give (someone) a ticking-off (*inf*) to scold (someone) (*usu* mildly): *The teacher gave me a ticking-off for being late.* [Army slang.]

tick over to run quietly and smoothly at a gentle pace: *Our sales are ticking over nicely at the moment.* [Literally used of a car engine.]

ticket

just the ticket (*slightly old inf*) exactly right, ideal *etc*: *A cup of hot tea is just the ticket on a cold day.* [Possibly from the US use of this word to mean 'a party's list of candidates for an election'.]

tickle

be tickled pink (*inf*) to be very pleased (by something): *He was tickled pink when she asked him for his autograph.*

tickle (someone's) fancy (*inf*) to attract (someone) mildly in some way: *The amusing toy tickled his fancy, so he bought it for his daughter.*

tide

    tide (someone) over (*inf*) to help (someone) for a time: *He gave me £10 to tide me over until I could get to the bank.* [Literally, to carry (someone) over an obstacle, as the tide does.]

tie

    be tied up 1 (*inf*) to be busy; to be involved (with): *I can't come to the party this evening — I'm a bit tied up tonight; I can't discuss this matter just now — I'm tied up with other things.* **2** connected (with): *His state of depression isn't just because of his job — it's tied up with his home life.*

    tie (someone) down 1 to limit (someone's) freedom *etc*: *The baby ties her down a bit; Her work tied her down.* **2** to make (someone) come to a decision: *He managed to tie them down to a definite date for the meeting.*

    tie (up) in knots *see* **knot.**

    tie in with (something) (*inf*) to be linked or joined logically to (something): *This doesn't tie in with what he said earlier.*

tight

    keep a tight rein on *see* **rein.**

    run a tight ship (*not inf*) to be in control of an efficient, well-run organization or group: *He prided himself on being concerned with his employees' welfare and on running a tight ship.* [A nautical idiom.]

    sit tight (*inf*) to keep the same position or be unwilling to move or act: *The best thing to do is to sit tight and see if things improve.*

    a tight corner/spot a difficult position or situation: *His refusal to help put her in a tight corner/spot.*

    tighten one's belt *see* **belt.**

tile

    have a tile loose (*inf*) to be a little mad: *His wife is very odd — in fact I sometimes think she has a tile loose.* [The reference is to a roof.]

    on the tiles (*sl*) away from home drinking, dancing *etc*: *They decided to go out for a night on the tiles.* [The reference appears to be to cats spending the night out on the roof.]

tilt

    (at) full tilt (at) full speed: *He rushed down the street at full tilt; He rushed round the corner and ran full tilt into the headmaster.* [From the flat-out gallop at which knights competed in a joust or *tilt*.]

    tilt at windmills *see* **windmill.**

time

    about time not too soon; the correct time or rather late (to do something): *Here comes John — and about time too. I was beginning to think he was lost.*

ahead of one's time having ideas *etc* which are too advanced to be acceptable at the time: *He was a brilliant man but he was ahead of his time and his theories were rejected by his contemporaries.*

all in good time soon enough: *The work will be finished all in good time.*

one, two *etc* **at a time** singly, or in groups of two *etc*: *They came into the room three at a time.*

at one time at a time in the past: *At one time there was a village here, but there is no sign of it now.*

at the same time *see* **same.**

behind the times not modern; old-fashioned: *We have made changes here — we don't want to be accused of being behind the times.*

bide one's time to wait for a good opportunity: *I'm just biding my time until he makes a mistake.* [*Bide* means literally 'to await'.]

the big time (*sl*) the top level in any kind of activity: *She was a struggling actress for many years before she finally made the big time.* [Originally US.]

do time (*sl*) to be in prison: *He's doing time in Pentonville.*

for the time being meanwhile: *I am staying at home for the time being.*

from time immemorial *see* **immemorial.**

from time to time occasionally; sometimes: *From time to time he brings me a present.*

gain time to cause something to be delayed in order to give oneself more time to do something else: *He knew that his work would not be ready for the meeting so he pretended to be ill in order to gain time.*

half the time (*inf*) frequently; very often: *I hate going to parties — half the time I don't even know the host very well.*

have a time of it (*inf*) to have to deal with problems, difficulties *etc*: *We had quite a time of it trying to find your house — no-one knew where you lived.*

have no time for (someone or something) to despise (someone or something): *I have no time for people of that sort.*

have the time of one's life (*inf*) to enjoy oneself very much; to have a wonderful time: *They are having the time of their lives in London.*

in good time (*inf*) early enough; before a set time (for an appointment *etc*): *We arrived in good time for the concert.*

in (someone's) own good time (*slightly derog*) at whatever time or however quickly is convenient to (someone): *I suppose Marion will return the book she borrowed in her own good time.*

in (someone's) own time 1 (someone's) spare time, when not at work: *I have so much work to do, I have to finish a lot of it in my own time.* **2** at the speed which is natural to one: *Don't hurry over this job — just finish it in your own time.*

in the fullness of time *see* **full.**

in the nick of time *see* **nick.**

in one's time at some past time in one's life, *esp* when one was at one's best: *He has been a good footballer in his time, but he's getting old now.*

in time early enough: *He arrived in time for dinner; Are we in time to catch the train?*

keep time 1 (of a clock *etc*) to show the time accurately: *Does this watch keep (good) time?* **2** (*with* **with**) to perform an action in the same rhythm (as someone else): *She doesn't keep time with her partner when she dances.*

kill time (*inf*) to find something to do to use up spare time, such as a period of waiting: *I'm just killing time until I hear whether I've got a job or not.*

make good time to travel as quickly or more quickly than one had expected or hoped: *We got caught in a traffic jam in Glasgow, but we made good time on the rest of the journey.*

mark time to allow time to pass without making any progress oneself: *He's only marking time in this job until he gets one more suited to his qualifications.* [Literally, of soldiers, to move the feet up and down as if marching but without going forwards, in order to retain marching rhythm.]

not before time (*inf*) not too soon; rather late: *They've decided to mend our roof, and not before time — it has been leaking all winter.*

no time (at all) (*inf*) a very short time indeed: *He arrived in no time; The journey took no time (at all).*

an old timer *see* **old.**

on time at the right time: *The train left on time; He was on time for his appointment.*

play for time to delay an action, decision *etc* in the hope or belief that conditions will be better at a later time: *Play for time — tell them we need more information from them before we can make a decision.* [Literally, to play a game, such as cricket, in such a way as to avoid defeat by playing defensively until the game ends.]

a stitch in time saves nine *see* **stitch.**

take one's time to do (something) as slowly as one wishes, often more slowly than someone else wishes: *Take your time — there's no hurry; I wish he would hurry up — he's rather taking his time about making a decision.*

there's no time like the present a saying, meaning that if an action has been decided on, it is best to do it immediately. [A quotation from a play of *c* 1700.]

a thin time *see* **thin.**

time and (time) again/time after time again and again; repeatedly: *I asked her time and (time) again not to do that.*

time and tide wait for no man a saying, meaning that life moves on without any delay for people to make decisions, plans *etc* and that therefore opportunities must be taken when they arise because they may not be available for long.

time flies a saying, meaning that time passes very quickly — *usu* expressing surprise at the amount of time that has passed without one noticing it. [From the Latin *tempus fugit*, a quotation from one of Virgil's *Georgics*.]

time is getting on (*not formal*) time is passing; it is getting late: *Time is getting on — we ought to be leaving soon.*

time out of mind (*formal*) during the whole time within human memory. [A translation of **time immemorial,** *see* at **immemorial.**]

time was (*rather formal*) there was once a time (when): *Time was when I would have come sailing with you, but I'm too old now.*

tin

put the tin lid on (something) *see* **lid.**

a tin god (*derog inf*) a person who thinks he is very important and orders other people about: *Our manager is a tin god who makes everyone else's life a misery.*

tinker

not to give a tinker's cuss/damn for (something) (*inf*) not to care anything at all about (something): *I don't give a tinker's damn how wealthy his parents are — I don't like him.* [It has been suggested that this phrase originated in a pun, from the fact that tinkers used a *dam* made from a pellet of bread to keep the solder from escaping while they mended a hole in a pan, and that the dam — which was worthless and expendable — was discarded when the repair was complete.]

tinkle

give (someone) a tinkle (*Brit inf*) to call (someone) on the telephone: *I'm not absolutely certain if Jennifer is coming tomorrow — I'd better give her a tinkle.* [A humorous variant of *give (someone) a ring* from the sound made by early telephone bells.]

tip

be on the tip of one's tongue to be almost, but *usu* not, spoken or said: *Her name is on the tip of my tongue* (= I can't quite remember it); *It was on the tip of my tongue to tell him* (= I almost told him).

just/only the tip of the iceberg *see* **ice.**

tip (someone) off (*sl*) to give information or a hint to (someone); to warn (someone): *He tipped me off about her arrival.*

tip the scales *see* **scales.**

tip (someone) the wink *see* **wink.**

tit

tit for tat (*inf*) blow for blow; repayment of injury with injury: *He tore my dress, so I spilt ink on his suit. That's tit for tat.* [This phrase may represent *tip for tap* — 'blow for blow', the Dutch *dit voor dat* — 'this for that', or French *tant pour tant* — 'equal for equal'.]

to

to and fro backwards and forwards: *They ran to and fro in the street.*

toing and froing going backwards and forwards in an anxious way, or without apparently achieving anything: *There was much toing and froing between our house and the one next door on the morning of the fête.*

toast

as warm as toast very warm: *My new coat keeps me as warm as toast.*

tod

on one's tod (*inf*) alone: *If you won't come with me, I'll have to go on my tod.* [From Cockney rhyming slang *on one's Tod Sloan* — on one's own. Tod Sloan was an American jockey.]

toe

be on one's toes (*inf*) to be ready; to be prepared for action: *We are all on our toes and just waiting for the order to start.*

toe the line (*inf*) to act according to the rules: *He isn't allowed to do as he likes in that firm — they make him toe the line.*

tread on (someone's) toes (*inf*) to offend or upset (someone): *I would like to help to organize the fête but I am afraid to suggest it in case I tread on someone's toes.*

toffee

not for toffee (*inf*) not at all: *I can't sing for toffee.*

token

by the same token (*formal*) also; in addition: *By the same token, we should like to thank your wife.*

told

told *see* **tell.**

Tom

any/every Tom, Dick or/and Harry anybody at all: *But you can't go on holiday with any Tom, Dick or Harry you happen to meet!* [From the fact that all three have always been common English names.]

a peeping Tom (*derog*) a man who spends his time watching women who are naked, undressing *etc, usu* through the windows of their houses: *The police have arrested the peeping Tom who was causing such distress in our neighbourhood.* [From the story of Lady Godiva, who is said to have ridden naked through the streets of Coventry in 1040 as part of a bargain made with her husband Leofric, Earl of Mercia, to persuade him to lift a tax he had imposed on his tenants. A late addition to the legend says that only one citizen of Coventry — 'Peeping Tom' — looked out to see her pass, and he was immediately struck blind.]

tone

tone (something) down to make (something) softer, less harsh *etc*: *The painters added white to tone down the colour of the green paint.*

tongue

be on the tip of one's tongue *see* **tip.**

hold one's tongue (*inf*) to remain silent or stop talking: *There were a lot of things I wanted to say, but I thought I'd better just hold my tongue.* [An idiom which existed in Old English.]

a sharp tongue *see* **sharp.**

a slip of the tongue *see* **slip.**

speak *etc* **with/have one's tongue in one's cheek** to say something that one does not intend literally or seriously: *He said it with his tongue in his cheek.*

tooth

be, get *etc* **long in the tooth** (*inf*) (of a person or animal) to be, become *etc*, old: *I'm getting a bit long in the tooth to climb mountains.* [From the receding gums of elderly horses and the practice of assessing the age of horses by examining their teeth.]

have a sweet tooth *see* **sweet**.

tooth and nail fiercely and with all one's strength: *They fought tooth and nail.*

top

at the top of one's voice *see* **voice**.

be thin on top *see* **thin**.

be top dog (*inf*) to be the most important or powerful person: *He always likes to be top dog in any group.* [From the hierarchical structure of dog packs.]

blow one's top (*inf*) to become very angry: *She blew her top when he arrived home late.* [Originally US. The reference is probably to an oil-well.]

off the top of one's head *see* **head**.

on top of the world *see* **world**.

out of the top drawer *see* **drawer**.

over the top (*inf*) too much, too strong or too great: *I know we said our statement should be forceful, but I think what you are suggesting is over the top.*

sleep like a top to sleep very soundly: *I was afraid I wouldn't sleep well, but in fact I slept like a top.* [A pun on the specialized meaning of *sleep* when applied to a top = 'to spin steadily without wobbling'.]

the top brass *see* **brass**.

the top of the ladder/tree (*inf*) the highest point in one's profession: *He has reached the top of the ladder/tree.*

top of the pops *see* **pop**.

top (something) up to fill (a cup *etc* that has been partly emptied) to the top: *Let me top up your glass/drink.*

torch

carry a/the torch for (someone) to be in love with (someone) who does not appear to be in love with oneself: *Is she still carrying a torch for Brian? I though she had got over him.* [The reference is to love as a flame.]

torn

be torn between (one thing and another) to have a very difficult choice to make between (two things): *He was torn between* *obedience to his parents and loyalty to his friends*.

that's torn it! (*inf*) that has spoilt everything!; that's most unfortunate!: *That's torn it! We've missed the last train home.*

toss

argue the toss (*inf*) to dispute a decision: *I won't argue the toss with you.* [The image is of someone arguing about the result of having tossed a coin.]

it's a toss-up (whether) (*inf*) it is a matter of uncertainty (whether): *It's a toss-up whether we shall get there in time.* [Literally, as uncertain as tossing a coin.]

toss (something) off (*inf*) **1** to drink (something) quickly: *He tossed off a pint of beer.* **2** to produce (something) quickly and easily: *He tossed off a few verses of poetry.*

toss up (*inf*) to toss a coin to decide a matter: *We tossed up (to decide) whether to go to the play or the ballet.*

win, lose the toss to guess rightly, or wrongly, which side of the coin will fall uppermost: *He won the toss so he started the game of cards first.*

touch

finishing touches *see* **finish.**

in touch in communication (with); able to talk (to): *I have kept in touch with my schoolfriends; I'll get in touch with you again about this matter; Good-bye! We'll be in touch!*

it's touch-and-go (whether) it's very uncertain (whether): *It was touch-and-go whether he would survive the operation.*

lose touch to stop communicating (with): *If you don't write regularly, you will soon lose touch with him; I used to see him quite often but we have lost touch.*

the Midas touch *see* **Midas.**

out of touch 1 not in communication (with): *We have been out of touch for years.* **2** not sympathetic or understanding (towards): *Older people sometimes seem out of touch with the modern world.*

touch a chord *see* **chord.**

touch down (of aircraft) to land: *The plane should touch down at 2 o'clock.*

touch (someone) for (something) (*inf*) to persuade (someone) to lend (money): *I touched him for £5.*

touch (something) off to cause (something) to begin to happen vigorously: *His remark touched off an argument.* [Literally, to ignite gunpowder *etc* by touching with a flame.]

touch (something) up to improve (*eg* paintwork, a photograph *etc*) by small touches: *He took a brush and touched up the paintwork*; *The photograph had been touched up.*

touch wood *see* **wood.**

tough

a tough customer (*inf*) a person who is difficult to deal with: *I couldn't persuade him — he's a real tough customer.*

tough luck bad luck: *That was tough luck.*

tow

have (someone) in tow (*inf*) to have (someone) in one's charge: *He came to the meeting with a party of students in tow.*

towel

throw in the towel (*inf*) to give up and admit defeat: *If we cannot raise any money to carry on our campaign, we shall have to throw in the towel.* [From a method of conceding defeat in a boxing match.]

tower

an ivory tower *see* **ivory.**

a tower of strength someone who is a great help or encouragement: *He was a tower of strength to me when my father died.* [A Shakespearian metaphor — from *Richard III*, V. iii.]

town

go out on the town (*inf*) to have a good time eating, drinking, dancing *etc*: *Let's go out on the town tonight!*

go to town (*inf*) to do something very thoroughly or with great enthusiasm or expense: *He really went to town on* (*preparing*) *the meal.* [Originally US, probably implying that to go to town on some business was to take a great deal of trouble over it.]

paint the town *see* **paint.**

the talk of the town *see* **talk.**

track

be on (someone's) track/be on the track of (someone or something) to be following, pursuing, or looking for (someone or something): *I'm on the track of a valuable painting*; *The police are already on the track of the murderer.*

have a one-track mind *see* **one.**

in one's tracks (*inf*) where one stands or is: *He stopped dead in his tracks.*

keep, lose track of (someone or something) (*inf*) to keep, not to keep, oneself informed about (the progress or whereabouts of) (someone or something): *I find it difficult to keep track of my old friends*; *I've lost track of what is happening.*

make tracks (for) (*inf*) to depart, or set off (towards): *We ought to be making tracks (for home).*

on the right, wrong track progressing in a way which is, is not, going to achieve what one wants; working, not working, correctly: *The new evidence which has emerged shows that the police have been on the wrong track from the beginning.*

track (someone or something) down to pursue or search for (someone or something) until it is caught or found: *I managed to track down an old copy of the book.*

(someone's) track record the history of (someone's) success or lack of success in an activity, *esp* their job: *He seems a likely candidate for the post — his track record in his last job was very impressive.* [From athletics.]

trade

trade (something) in to give (something) as part-payment for something else: *We decided to trade in our old car and get a new one.*

trade on (something) (*derog*) to take *usu* unfair advantage of (something): *He traded on her kindness.*

trail

blaze a trail (*formal*) to lead or show the way towards something new: *His discoveries blazed a trail in the field of nuclear power.* [Literally, to mark a trail by *blazing*, *ie* stripping sections of bark from trees.]

tread

tread on (someone's) corns *see* **corn.**

tread on (someone's) toes *see* **toe.**

tread water *see* **water.**

tree

a family tree *see* **family.**

not to be able to see the wood for the trees *see* **wood.**

tremble

be/go in fear and trembling (of) (*esp facet*) to be very afraid: *I was in fear and trembling in case you made a mistake; They go in fear and trembling of their father.* [A Biblical reference — to Philippians 2:12.]

trial

trial and error the trying of various methods, alternatives *etc* until the right one happens to appear or be found: *He found the best way of driving through London by trial and error.* [The name of a method of solving mathematical problems.]

a trial run a rehearsal, first test *etc* of anything, *eg* a play, car, piece of machinery *etc*: *He decided to give the car a trial run before buying it.*

triangle

    the eternal triangle *see* **eternal.**

tribute

    be a tribute to (something) to be the (praiseworthy) result of: *The success of the scheme is a tribute to his hard work.*

trice

    in a trice (*rather old*) in a very short time; almost immediately: *He returned in a trice.* [From an old word meaning 'to tie up' — literally 'in the time taken to make a single tug'.]

trick

    a bag of tricks *see* **bag.**

    a confidence trick *see* **confidence.**

    do the trick (*inf*) to do or be what is necessary: *I need a piece of paper — this old envelope will do the trick*; *I had a very bad headache but I feel better now — that aspirin did the trick.*

    how's tricks (*sl*) how are you: *Hello Jim, how's tricks!*

    never to miss a trick to be very alert and not to miss any opportunities to profit: *I might have known Bill would make money out of this deal — he never misses a trick.* [From card games.]

    a trick of the trade (*sometimes derog*) one of the ways of being successful in a job *etc*: *Remembering the customers' names is one of the tricks of the trade.*

    up to one's tricks (*inf: often derog*) behaving in one's usual (deceitful, amusing *etc*) way: *He's up to his old tricks again — he's been getting money from people by pretending to be blind.*

trigger

    trigger-happy (*inf*) too ready or likely to use guns (or general violence): *I hope that they don't elect him president — he is so trigger-happy that he will certainly start a war.*

trooper

    swear like a trooper (*derog*) to swear very often or very strongly: *She pretends to be very refined, but I've heard her swearing like a trooper when she spilt tea over herself.* [A trooper was an ordinary cavalry soldier.]

trot

    on the trot (*inf*) **1** one after the other: *He ate four ice-creams on the trot.* **2** continually moving about; busy: *My job keeps me on the trot.*

    trot (something) out (*inf derog*) to bring (something) out (*usu* to show to someone): *He is always trotting out the same excuses for being late*. [Literally to make a horse trot that one is attempting to sell, in order to show how it moves.]

trouble

be asking for trouble *see* **ask**.

fish in troubled waters *see* **fish**.

trousers

wear the trousers (*derog inf*) (of a wife) to be the person who makes the decisions *etc* in her household: *He looks like a tough, strong-minded man, but actually it's his wife who wears the trousers.*

(be caught) with one's pants/trousers down *see* **pants**.

trowel

lay it on with a trowel (*inf*) to say very obviously flattering things: *I tried my best to put him in a good mood — I really laid it on with a trowel.* [From a remark made by Charles Dickens.]

truck

have no truck with (something) (*formal*) to have nothing to do with (something); not to take part in (something): *My father would have no truck with politics.* [From *truck* = bartering, *ie* business dealings.]

true

come true (of a dream, hope *etc*) to really happen: *Her dreams finally came true.*

out of true not straight or not properly positioned *etc*: *The drawer did not fit because one of its sides was out of true.*

ring true *see* **ring**.

trump

play one's trump card to use something powerful and influential which one has saved in order to use it when really necessary: *When they refused to allow him into the football match he finally played his trump card, saying he was the manager's brother.* [From certain card games, in which a *trump* is a card of whichever suit has been declared to be higher-ranking than any of the others for the purposes of the hand being played.]

turn up trumps (*inf*) to behave or do one's work well when things are difficult, *esp* unexpectedly: *When I lost my job my friends really turned up trumps, helping me with my rent and so on.* [As above — the reference is to drawing a trump from the pack in the course of one's turn.]

trumpet

blow one's own trumpet (*inf*) to boast, praise oneself greatly

etc: *He really isn't very clever but he is always blowing his own trumpet.*
[From the herald who formerly would announce the arrival of an important person with a fanfare on a trumpet.]

trust

take (someone or something) on trust to accept or believe (someone or something) without checking: *He always takes his friends on trust*; *He took it on trust that he would be made president.*

truth

a home truth *see* **home.**

to tell the truth (*inf*) really; actually: *To tell the truth I forgot it was your birthday last week.*

truth will out a saying, meaning that it is impossible to conceal the truth about something for ever.

try

try one's hand at *see* **hand.**

try it on (*inf*) to attempt to do (something); to indulge in (a certain kind of behaviour) *etc* in order to see whether it will be allowed: *Take no notice of the child's behaviour — he's just trying it on.*

try (something) on to put on (clothes *etc*) to see if they fit: *I've bought a dress but I haven't tried it on yet.*

try (something) out to test (something) by using it: *He tried out the bicycle*; *We are trying out new teaching methods.*

try that on for size! *see* **size.**

tuck

tuck in (*inf*) to eat greedily or with enjoyment: *They sat down to breakfast and started to tuck in straight away.*

tuck into (something) (*inf*) to eat (something) eagerly: *He tucked into his tea.*

tug

tug at the heartstrings *see* **heart.**

tumble

tumble to (something) (*inf*) to understand or realize (something) (suddenly): *All at once he tumbled to my plan*; *He has been deceiving her for many years but she has still not tumbled to it* (= realized that he has been deceiving her).

tune

call the tune (*inf*) to be the person who gives the orders: *He calls the tune in this office.* [From the saying *he who pays the piper calls the tune* = the person who is paying has a right to choose what is done with his money — *see also* **pay the piper** *at* **pipe.**]

change one's tune (*inf*) to change one's attitude, opinion *etc*: *He said he liked travelling by train, but after six hours standing in the corridor he changed his tune.*

in tune (with something or someone) agreeing or fitting in (with something or someone): *The sunny weather was in tune with his happy mood.* [A musical idiom — literally 'adjusted so as to be at the same pitch (as)'.]

to the tune of (*inf*) amounting to the sum or total of: *He received bills to the tune of £20.*

tune in to tune a radio (to a particular station or programme): *We usually tune (the radio) in to the news.*

turkey

talk turkey (*esp US*) to talk honestly and openly, *esp* about business: *The oil executive seemed to have stopped making vague statements and was prepared to talk turkey.* [Originally US, of unknown derivation.]

turn

at every turn (*formal or liter*) everywhere, at every stage *etc*: *She encountered difficulties at every turn.*

do (someone) a good turn to do something helpful for (someone): *He did me several good turns.*

done to a turn (*inf*) cooked to exactly the right degree: *The meat was done to a turn.* [This phrase originally applied to meat roasted on a spit, and implied that if the spit had been turned once more the meat would have been overcooked.]

in turn/by turns one after the other; in regular order: *They answered the teacher's questions in turn.*

on the turn 1 (of the tide *etc*) in the process of turning: *The tide is on the turn.* **2** (*inf*) (of milk *etc*) on the point of going sour: *This cream is on the turn.*

out of turn out of the correct order or not at the correct time: *He answered a question out of turn* (= when it was not his turn to do so); *I'm sorry if I spoke out of turn.*

serve its turn (to be useful or good enough) to achieve a particular result, help to do a particular job *etc*: *The stick did not make a very good crutch but it served its turn until the injured climber reached help.*

take a turn for the better, worse (of things or people) to become better, or worse: *His fortunes have taken a turn for the better; Her health has taken a turn for the worse.*

take turns (of two or more people) to do something one after

400

the other, not at the same time: *We took turns at pushing the pram.*

turn a blind eye to *see* **eye.**

turn (and turn) about one after the other, each taking his turn: *They drove the car turn (and turn) about.*

turn against (someone or something) to become dissatisfied with or hostile to (people or things that one previously liked *etc*): *He turned against his friends.*

turn an honest penny *see* **penny.**

turn one's coat *see* **coat.**

turn (something) down to say 'no' to (something); to refuse (something): *He turned down her offer/request.* [Originally US slang.]

turn one's hand to *see* **hand.**

turn (someone's) head *see* **head.**

turn in (*inf*) **1** (*Brit*) to go to bed: *I usually turn in at about 11 o'clock.* **2** to hand over (a person or thing) to people in authority: *They turned the escaped prisoner in to the police.*

turn (someone) off (*sl*) to create feelings of dislike, repulsion, disgust *etc* in (someone): *People with loud voices turn me off.*

turn of phrase a way of expressing things: *He has a very blunt turn of phrase.*

a turn of speed an ability to move fast for a short period: *For a fat man, he had an amazing turn of speed.*

the turn of the month, year, century the end of one month or year or century and the beginning of the next: *He hasn't been to Leeds since the turn of the year.*

turn (someone) on (*sl*) to create feelings of excitement, interest, lust, pleasure *etc* in (someone): *Music really turns me on.*

turn on one's heel *see* **heel.**

turn on the heat *see* **heat.**

turn out 1 (of a crowd) to come out; to get together for a (public) meeting, celebration *etc*: *A large crowd turned out to see the procession.* **2** to happen or prove to be: *He turned out to be right; It turned out that he was right; The weather turned out (to be) fine; You said we shouldn't trust him, and you were right, as it turns out.*

turn over a new leaf *see* **leaf.**

turn (someone's) stomach *see* **stomach.**

turn the corner *see* **corner.**

turn the scales at *see* **scales.**

turn the tables *see* **table.**

turn to (good) account *see* **account.**

turn up (*inf*) **1** to appear or arrive: *He turned up at our house.* **2** to be found: *Don't worry — it'll turn up again.* **3** to discover (facts) *etc*: *The police have apparently turned up some new evidence.*

a turn-up for the book(s) (*inf*) something which happens unexpectedly: *He's won a lot of money — what a turn-up (for the book)!* [19C racing slang.]

turn up one's nose (at) *see* **nose.**

turn up trumps *see* **trump.**

a U-turn *see* **u.**

turtle

turn turtle (of a boat *etc*) to turn upside down; to capsize: *The boat turned turtle in the rough sea.* [Literally, to make a turtle easy to kill by turning it on its back.]

twice

think twice to be very careful about considering (doing) something): *We thought twice about travelling in bad weather; I wouldn't think twice about sacking him.*

twiddle

twiddle one's thumbs *see* **thumb.**

twinkle

in the twinkling of an eye/in a twinkling in a moment; immediately: *He arrived in the twinkling of an eye.* [A Biblical image, from I Corinthians 15:51.]

twist

get one's knickers in a twist *see* **knickers.**

round the twist (*sl*) slightly mad: *If you expect me to believe you, you must be round the twist!*

twist (someone's) arm *see* **arm.**

twist (someone) round one's little finger *see* **finger.**

two

as (a)like as two peas in a pod *see* **pea.**

for two pins *see* **pin.**

in two minds *see* **mind.**

put two and two together (*inf*) to realize or work out something from what one sees, hears *etc*: *You won't be able to keep your marriage a secret — people will soon put two and two together.* [Literally, to be able to solve the sum 2 + 2 = ?]

there are no two ways about it *see* **way.**

two a penny *see* **penny.**

two heads are better than one *see* **head.**

two of a kind (*often derog*) of the same type, similar in character, outlook *etc*: *He behaves just like his father — they are two of a kind*.

two's company (three's a crowd) a saying, meaning that a third person who joins a couple to do something is often unwanted.

two shakes (of a lamb's tail) *see* **shake**.

two ticks (*inf*) a very short time: *I'll be ready in two ticks*. [The reference is to a clock.]

two-time (*sl*) to deceive (a boyfriend or girlfriend) by having a relationship with another person.

tyre

a spare tyre *see* **spare**.

U

u

a U-turn a turn, in the shape of the letter U, made by a motorist *etc* in order to reverse his direction: *He made a swift U-turn and went back the way he had come*.

ugly

ugly as sin *see* **sin**.

an ugly duckling a member of a family who at first lacks beauty, cleverness *etc* but later becomes the most beautiful or successful. [From the story by Hans Andersen of the duckling who is rejected by ducks for being ugly by their standards, but turns out eventually to be not a duck but a swan.]

umbrage

take umbrage to feel, and show that one is, offended by another person's action *etc*: *He took umbrage because I forgot to introduce him to my mother*. [Originally 'to feel overshadowed (and thus threatened)'; from Latin *umbra* = shade.]

uncle

like a Dutch uncle *see* **Dutch**.

Uncle Sam (*usu derog*) the United States of America: *The money for most of these weapons has come from Uncle Sam*. [Coined in Troy, NY in 1812, probably from the initials U.S. which were stamped on government supplies *etc* and possibly also because someone actually called Uncle Sam was employed in handling such supplies.]

under

take (someone) under one's wing *see* **wing**.

under (someone's) (very) nose *see* **nose.**

under one's own steam *see* **steam.**

under the weather *see* **weather.**

under (someone's) thumb *see* **thumb.**

under way *see* **way.**

understand

  give (someone) to understand that (*formal*) to cause (someone) to think that: *I was given to understand that you were coming at two o'clock.*

unknown

  an unknown quantity *see* **quantity.**

unsound

  of unsound mind (*esp legal*) insane: *The coroner's verdict was that he had committed suicide while of unsound mind.*

unstuck

  come unstuck (*inf*)to fail: *Our plans have come unstuck.*

up

  be in (something) up to one's neck *see* **neck.**

  be one up on *see* **one.**

  be on the up-and-up (*inf*) to be progressing very successfully, *esp* financially: *The firm is on the up-and-up now.*

  be up (with someone) (*inf*) to be wrong (with someone): *Something's up!*; *What's up with her?*

  be/come up against (something) to be faced with (difficulties *etc*): *I'm up against a problem*; *You may come up against several difficulties.*

  be (well) up in/on (something) (*inf*) to know a lot about (a subject): *Are you well up on mythology?*; *He is well up in astrology.*

  be up in arms *see* **arm.**

  be up to (someone) to be the duty or privilege of: *It's up to you to decide*; *The final choice is up to him.*

  be up to (something) 1 (*inf*) to be busy or occupied with (an activity *etc*): *What is he up to now?*; *I'm sure that man is up to no good* (= he is planning to do something bad or evil). **2** (*inf*) to be capable of: *She wasn't up to cooking a meal*; *He isn't quite up to the job.* **3** to reach the standard of: *This work isn't up to your best.*

  be up to no good *see* **good.**

  be up to the mark *see* **mark.**

  it is all up with (someone) there is no hope for the survival of (someone): *If the soldiers had seen them, it would have been all up with them.*

not up to much *see* **much.**

his *etc* **number is up** *see* **number.**

up-and-coming (of *eg* a person starting a career) progressing well: *He was well-known as an up-and-coming young scientist.* [Originally US.]

up and doing (*not formal*) to be active and occupied: *I like to be up and doing early when I have guests for lunch.*

ups and downs (*inf*) times of good and bad luck: *We all have our ups and downs.*

the upshot (*inf*) the result or end (of a matter): *What was the upshot of that affair?* [Literally, the last shot in an archery competition.]

upstage (*inf*) to take people's interest or attention away from (someone or something): *She upstaged all the other girls at the party in her fashionable new dress.* [A theatrical term, from the fact that an actor who is *upstage of* — further towards the back of the stage than — another has the advantage, as his companion, in order to face him, has to act with his back to the audience.]

up the pole *see* **pole.**

up the wall *see* **wall.**

up to a point *see* **point.**

up to the minute *see* **minute.**

upper

have, get the upper hand (of/over someone) (*inf*) to have or win an advantage (over someone): *I've got the upper hand over you; Our team managed to get the upper hand in the end.*

keep a stiff upper lip *see* **lip.**

on one's uppers (*inf*) very short of money: *He hasn't had a job for months — he must really be on his uppers.* [Literally, with the soles completely worn off one's shoes so that one is walking on the uppers.]

upper-crust (*inf derog*) of the upper classes: *His accent sounds rather upper-crust.* [The population is pictured as a closed pie with a lower and upper crust and a filling in the middle.]

upside

be, get upsides with (someone) (*inf*) to be or become level or equal with (someone): *He was always trying to get upsides with his clever elder brother.* [Originally a Scots dialect phrase.]

turn something upside down to put something into confusion: *The burglars turned the house upside down.*

uptake

quick, slow on the uptake quick, or slow, to understand: *She's inexperienced, but very quick on the uptake*. [Originally a Scots phrase.]

use

come in useful to become useful: *My French came in useful on holiday*. [*See* **come in handy** *at* **handy**.]

have no use for (someone or something) (*inf*) to despise (someone or something): *I have no use for such silliness/silly people*.

in, out of use able, or not able, to be used: *How long has the gymnasium been out of use?*

it's no use it's impossible or useless: *He tried in vain to start the car, then said 'It's no use'*.

make (good) use of (something)/put (something) to (good) use to use (something) to one's advantage: *He makes use of his training*; *He puts his training to good use in that job*.

V

vain

take (someone's) name in vain (*formal or facet*) to use someone's (*esp* God's) name in an insulting or blasphemous way: *Who has been taking His name in vain?*; *Someone has been taking my name in vain*. [From the phraseology of the Ten Commandments in the Bible — Exodus 20.]

value

at face value *see* **face**.

variety

variety is the spice of life a saying, meaning that the many different things, situations, opportunities *etc* that occur, and the constant changes, are what make life interesting. [A quotation from a poem by William Cowper.]

veil

draw a veil over (something) (*often facet*) not to discuss, mention *etc* (something), or to hide (a fact *etc*), because one feels it is better forgotten: *I will draw a veil over our conversation, as it was neither interesting nor intelligent*.

velvet

the velvet glove *see* **the iron hand** *at* **iron**.

vengeance

with a vengeance in a very great or unexpected degree; violently; thoroughly: *If the plans for the redevelopment scheme are approved, they'll start knocking houses down with a vengeance.* [Literally, 'with a curse'.]

vent

  give vent to (something) to express (an emotion *etc*) freely: *He gave vent to his anger in a furious letter to the newspaper.*

  vent one's spleen *see* **spleen.**

venture

  nothing ventured, nothing gained *see* **nothing.**

very

  the very thing exactly what is wanted or needed: *That dress is the very thing to wear to Anne's wedding!*

vessel

  empty vessels make most noise *see* **empty.**

vested

  a vested interest a biased and *usu* personal interest (in continuing or suggesting a particular scheme *etc*): *She has a vested interest in suggesting that we sell our shares in the company, since she would make a huge profit if we did.* [A legal term.]

vex

  a vexed question a problem that is discussed a great deal, without being solved: *We still have not solved the vexed question of who is to pay for the improvements to our school.*

vicious

  a vicious circle (*inf*) a bad situation whose results make it worse: *He works hard, gets tired, gets behind with his work, and has to work harder still — it's a vicious circle.* [In logic, the term for the fallacy of proving one statement by the evidence of another which itself is only valid if the first statement is valid.]

victory

  a landslide victory *see* **land.**

  a Pyrrhic victory *see* **Pyrrhic.**

view

  in view of (something) (*formal*) taking (something) into consideration; because of (something): *In view of the committee's criticisms of him, he felt he had to resign.*

  a point of view *see* **point.**

  take a serious, kindly *etc* **view of (something)** to adopt a serious, kindly *etc* attitude to (something): *Fortunately the headmaster took a benevolent view of his behaviour.*

  with a view to (something) (*formal*) with the aim of (doing something): *He's started walking to work with a view to cutting down expenses.*

villain

the villain of the piece (*formal or facet*) the person or thing responsible for some evil: *Who is the real villain of the piece in this scandal?* [A theatrical idiom.]

virtue

by virtue of (something) (*formal*) because of (something): *By virtue of the position he held, he was able to move about freely; She is allowed to do as she wishes by virtue of the fact that she is the manager's daughter.*

vital

(someone's) vital statistics (*facet inf*) a woman's chest, waist and hip measurements: *If you enter the beauty contest you will have to give your vital statistics.* [Originally statistics dealing with population — *eg* births, marriages and deaths.]

voice

at the top of one's voice very loudly: *They were shouting at the top(s) of their voices.*

in good voice (*not inf*) having one's voice in good condition for singing or speaking: *The choir was in good voice tonight.*

lose one's voice to be unable to speak *eg* because of having a cold, sore throat *etc*: *When I had 'flu I lost my voice for three days.*

raise one's voice to speak more loudly than normal *esp* in anger: *I don't want to have to raise my voice to you again.*

with one voice (*formal*) simultaneously or unanimously: *They asked for his resignation with one voice.*

volume

speak volumes (*rather liter*) to have a great deal of meaning: *She said nothing but her face spoke volumes.*

vote

put (something) to the vote to decide (a matter) by voting: *There is disagreement about whether we should close the school — let us put it to the vote.*

split the vote to cause an opponent *etc* to be elected by giving supporters a choice of two things, people *etc* to vote for instead of only one: *It is thought that his candidacy will split the Left-wing vote and allow the Right-winger to be elected.*

a vote of confidence a vote taken to establish whether the government or other body or person in authority still has the majority's support for its/his policies.

a vote of thanks an invitation, *usu* in the form of a short speech, to an audience *etc* to show gratitude to a speaker *etc* by applauding *etc*: *Mrs Smith proposed a vote of thanks to the organizers of the fête.*

vulture
culture vulture *see* **culture.**

W

wade
wade in/into (someone or something) (*inf*) to attack (someone, a task *etc*) with enthusiasm and without hesitation: *He waded into the discussion without thinking.*

wagon
on the wagon not allowed or prepared to take alcoholic drink: *She only drinks soft drinks — she's on the wagon until her baby is born.* [Originally US, in full *on the water wagon.*]

wait
waiting in the wings *see* **wing.**

wake
in the wake of (something) immediately after (and *usu* caused by) (something): *He made several valuable business deals in the wake of his appearance on television.* [From the strip of disturbed water left by the passage of a ship.]
in (someone's) wake close behind (someone more noticeable or important): *He came into the dining-room in Mrs Barlow's wake.* [As previous idiom.]

walk
cock of the walk *see* **cock.**
walk all over (someone) (*derog inf*) to pay no respect to (a person's) rights, feelings *etc*: *He'll walk all over you if you let him.*
walk away/off with (something) (*inf*) to win (prizes *etc*) easily: *Of course you'll win — you'll walk away with all the prizes.*
walk it (*inf*) to win or succeed easily: *I'm not anxious about his exam — I know he'll walk it.*
a walk of life (*formal*) a way of earning one's living; an occupation or profession: *People from all walks of life went to the minister's funeral.*
walk on air (*inf*) to feel extremely happy *etc*: *She's walking on air since he asked her to marry him.*

walk out on (someone) (*derog*) to abandon (someone): *He's walked out on his wife/responsibilities.*

wall

go to the wall to be defeated in (*esp* business) competition: *Several small firms went to the wall in the past financial year.* [An old phrase of obscure origin.]

have one's back to the wall see **back**.

send/drive *etc* **(someone) up the wall** (*inf*) to make (someone) angry, confused *etc*: *This business is sending/driving me up the wall!*; *He's going up the wall about the mess they've made of his garden!*

walls have ears a saying, meaning that a secret conversation may still be overheard even if it seems impossible.

I *etc* **would like to be a fly on the wall** *see* **fly**.

the writing on the wall *see* **write**.

Walter

a Walter Mitty (*derog*) a person who makes up stories to make his life seem more exciting than it really is: *I had come to the conclusion that he was a Walter Mitty whose accounts of his past history were almost entirely imaginary.* [From the main character in a short story by James Thurber.]

wane

on the wane (*formal*) becoming less: *His power is on the wane.* [Literally used of the moon.]

want

be found wanting (in something) (*formal*) to be seen to be lacking (certain things): *When it came to the time when courage was necessary, he was found wanting*; *You won't find her wanting in charm.* [A Biblical idiom.]

want for (something) to lack (something): *She wants for nothing* (= She has everything she could wish for).

war

carry the war into the enemy's camp to proceed with an argument *etc* by attacking one's opponent strongly: *'Never mind what I was doing—what were you doing in my house at midnight?' she demanded, carrying the war into the enemy's camp.* [A military reference.]

have been in the wars (*inf facet*) to have been injured (*usu* slightly) in some rough activity: *He came back from the rugby match looking as if he'd really been in the wars.*

on the warpath (*inf*) in a very angry mood: *The boss is on the* *warpath this morning, so be careful!* [A Red Indian expression = going to war.]

war to the knife a fierce, pitiless struggle: *After such an exchange of insults, it was war to the knife between them.* [From the Spanish phrase *guerra al cuchillo*.]

warm

as warm as toast *see* **toast.**

warm the cockles of the heart *see* **cockle.**

wart

warts and all including all the faults, disadvantages or unattractive parts: *They've adopted our system of government, warts and all.* [From the story that Oliver Cromwell instructed Sir Peter Lely — who was commissioned to paint his picture — that he wanted the portrait to show him as he really was, and to include the warts which disfigured his face.]

wash

come out in the wash to work out satisfactorily in the end: *Never mind, these problems will all come out in the wash.* [Literally, of a stain *etc*, to be removed by washing.]

wash one's dirty linen *see* **linen.**

washed-out (*inf*) completely lacking in energy *etc*: *I feel washed-out today.* [Literally, of garments, having lost colour as a result of washing.]

wash one's hands of *see* **hand.**

wash (something) out (*esp* of rain) to ruin, prevent *etc* (something): *Heavy rain washed out twenty football matches today in southern England.*

washed-up (*sl*) defeated, finished, failed *etc*: *You're all washed-up in advertising, so find yourself another job!* [The reference is apparently to a shipwreck.]

waste

go/run to waste (to be allowed) to be wasted: *All this good land is going to waste simply because there's nobody to farm it.*

lay waste (*formal or liter*) to destroy or ruin (a town, country *etc*) by force: *The invaders laid waste a huge area of excellent farmland.*

waste not, want not a saying, meaning that if one is careful not to waste anything, one is unlikely ever to find oneself short of anything.

watch

be on the watch for (something or someone) to stay alert in order to notice (something or someone); to look out for (some-

411

thing or someone): *The staff are always on the watch for shoplifters.*

a watched pot never boils *see* **pot.**

watch it! (*inf*) be careful!: *Watch it! Next time you do that you'll be sacked!*

watch (someone) like a hawk *see* **hawk.**

watch out to be careful (of): *Watch out (for the cars)!*; *Watch out! The police are coming!*

watch over (someone or something) (*formal*) to guard or take care of (someone or something): *The mother bird is watching over her young.*

watch one's step *see* **step.**

water

be like water off a duck's back to have no effect: *There's no point being sarcastic to Mark — it's like water off a duck's back.* [From the fact that water runs straight off a duck's oily feathers without wetting them.]

hold water (*formal*) to be correct or accurate and bear examination: *His explanation doesn't hold water.*

in deep water *see* **deep.**

like a fish out of water *see* **fish.**

milk and water *see* **milk.**

of the first water *see* **first.**

pour oil on troubled waters *see* **oil.**

spend money like water *see* **money.**

throw cold water on/over *see* **cold.**

tread water to keep oneself afloat in an upright position by moving the legs (and arms): *The swimmer trod water before beginning the long swim to the shore.*

water (something) down to make (something) less strong: *He watered down his comments so that they became less offensive.* [Literally, to dilute with water.]

water under the bridge something that is past and cannot now be altered, is not worth worrying about or regretting *etc*: *We were very friendly until we had that terrible quarrel — but that's all water under the bridge now.* [From the saying *a lot of water has passed under the bridge* (= a lot has happened) *since* . . .]

Waterloo

meet one's Waterloo (*rather facet*) to be finally defeated: *The thief met his Waterloo when he tried to rob our local judo champion.* [From the Battle of Waterloo (1815) in which Napoleon was defeated for the last time. The phrase was coined by Wendell Phillips.]

wave

> **on the (same) wavelength (as someone)** having the same
> attitude of mind, opinions, sympathies *etc* as someone: *She and
> her mother are not on the same wavelength; I can't understand her — I'm
> just not on her wavelength.*

way

> **by the way** incidentally, in passing, while I remember *etc*: *By
> the way, I'm leaving on Thursday.*
>
> **by way of (something)** for, or as if for, the purpose of (doing)
> (something): *He did it by way of helping me.*
>
> **come (someone's) way** to become available to, possible for *etc*
> (someone): *He takes every opportunity that comes his way.*
>
> **get into, out of the way of (doing) (something)** to become
> accustomed to doing, not doing (something); to get into, out of
> the habit of doing (something): *They got into the way of waking up
> early when they were on holiday; I have got out of the way of working
> in an office.*
>
> **get/have one's own way** to do, get *etc* what one wants: *That
> child always cries if he doesn't get his (own) way.*
>
> **go a long way to(wards) (something)** to help greatly in (achiev-
> ing something): *These measures go a long way towards solving the
> problem.*
>
> **go out of one's way** to do more than is really necessary: *He
> went out of his way to help us.*
>
> **go one's own way** to act as one likes, *esp* in a manner different
> from others: *You must allow your children to go their own way — you
> can't always tell them what they must do.*
>
> **go the way of all flesh** (*usu facet*) to die or disappear finally:
> *They eventually decided that the man they were searching for must have
> gone the way of all flesh.* [A Biblical reference, to the dying words
> of David — II Kings 2:2 — in a medieval mistranslation.]
>
> **have a way with (someone or something)** to be good at
> dealing with or managing (someone or something): *She has a way
> with children.*
>
> **have a way with one** (*formal or facet*) to have an attractive
> manner: *'He's very charming.' 'Yes, he certainly has a way with him!'*
>
> **have everything/it (all) one's own way** to get one's own way
> in everything/something: *He likes to have everything his own way;
> Oh, have it your own way — I'm tired of arguing.*
>
> **have it both ways** to get the benefit from two actions, situations
> *etc*, each of which excludes the possibility of the other: *'She wants*

to divorce him, but she doesn't want to lose the importance she gets from being married to him.' 'Well, she can't have it both ways.'

in a bad way (*inf*) unhealthy or in a poor state: *The nation's economy is in a bad way.*

in a big way (*inf*) strongly and with enthusiasm: *She went in for entertaining in a big way and often had twelve people for dinner.*

in a way from a certain point of view: *In a way I think this book is her biggest success, although it has serious faults.*

in, out of (the/someone's) way blocking, not blocking (someone's) progress, or occupying, not occupying, space that is needed (by someone): *We had to stop the car because there was a fallen tree in the/our way; Don't leave your bicycle where it will get in the way of pedestrians; He moved out of the way to let her pass.*

lead the way *see* **lead**[1].

look the other way to ignore or pretend not to notice something wrong, illegal *etc*: *As long as she is discreet in the conduct of her love affairs, her husband is prepared to look the other way.*

lose one's way to stop knowing where one is, or in which direction one ought to be going: *The child lost his way in the woods.*

make one's way 1 (*formal*) to go: *They made their way towards the centre of the town; You should make your way to the coast.* **2** to get on in the world: *He has made his own way — his father has not helped him at all.*

make way (for something) to stand aside and leave room (for something): *The crowd parted to make way for the ambulance.*

mend one's ways (*old or formal*) to improve one's behaviour: *A good beating will soon make him mend his ways.*

no way *see* **no.**

one way and another (*not formal*) when one considers various qualities, features *etc* of something: *This has been a very trying week, one way and another.*

on the way coming; about to happen; being prepared: *There is a new baby on the way in our family; He phoned to say he was on the way here; It looks as if there's a storm on the way.*

the parting of the ways *see* **part.**

pave the way *see* **pave.**

pay one's way to pay one's own expenses; never to owe money: *No matter how poor he was, he has always managed to pay his way.*

see one's way to (doing) (something) to be able and willing to (do) (something): *Can you see your way to lending me £5?; He said he couldn't see his way to it.*

there are no two ways about it it is not a matter about which it is possible to have different attitudes, opinions *etc*: *There are no two ways about it — the man is a thief.*

under way moving, in progress *etc*: *Her plans are under way.* [A nautical phrase = moving.]

ways and means methods, *esp* of providing money: *You must use any ways and means you can think of.*

wayside

fall by the wayside to fail to continue with something until the end: *During the election campaign, many of our party supporters fell by the wayside, but a small number went on campaigning up to the very last moment.* [A Biblical reference — to the parable of the Sower, Luke 8:5.]

weak

as weak as a kitten *see* **kitten.**

have a weakness for (something) (*inf*) to have a liking for (something): *She has a weakness for plain chocolate biscuits*; *He has a weakness for blondes.*

a weak moment a moment of weakness: *In a weak moment I agreed to help him.*

wear

wear one's heart on one's sleeve *see* **heart.**

wear off (of effects *etc*) to become less: *The effect of the anaesthetic began to wear off*; *The pain is wearing off.*

See also **worn.**

weather

keep a weather eye (open) to remain alert or watchful: *You should keep a weather eye open for signs of difficulties ahead.* [A nautical term — one's weather eye is the eye one keeps on the weather.]

make heavy weather *see* **heavy.**

under the weather (*inf*) in poor health; unwell: *I'm feeling a little under the weather this week.* [Literally, affected by (thundery) weather — originally US.]

weave

get weaving (*sl*) to start working or moving quickly: *We'll have to get weaving if we want to catch that train.*

wedding

a shotgun wedding *see* **shot.**

wedge

the thin end of the wedge a small beginning (*usu* of something bad) that will certainly lead to greater (and worse) things: *This* *demand is only the thin end of the wedge — soon they'll want more and more.*

weed

    weed (something) out (*inf*) to remove (things which are unwanted) from a group or collection: *We'll weed out all the unsuitable candidates and then interview the rest.*

weep

    weep buckets *see* **bucket**.

weight

    carry weight *see* **carry**.

    pull one's weight (*inf*) to take one's fair share of work, duty *etc*: *Some of the workers are not pulling their weight.*

    throw one's weight about (*derog inf*) to use one's power in an unsubtle way; to be bossy or domineering: *He's always throwing his weight about.*

    weigh in to join in a discussion, project *etc* with enthusiasm: *She weighed in with a long list of complaints*; *Mr Smith has weighed in with an offer of help.*

    weigh (something) up to calculate or assess (a probability *etc*): *He weighed up his chances of success*; *She weighed the situation up and decided she could win easily*; *She's good at weighing up people.*

    worth its/one's weight in gold extremely valuable: *My secretary is worth her weight in gold.*

welcome

    be welcome to (do, have) (something) to be gladly given permission to (do, have) (something): *You're welcome to stay as long as you wish*; (*ironic*) *You're welcome to marry him — I don't want him!*

    make (someone) welcome to welcome (someone): *I like visiting them — they always make us welcome.*

    outstay one's welcome to stay too long: *I must go — I don't want to outstay my welcome.* [Literally 'to remain after one's welcome has gone'.]

well

    all very well apparently satisfactory (but really not satisfactory for some reason): *What you are saying is all very well, but it doesn't answer my question.*

    as well (*inf*) in addition; too: *If you will go, I'll go as well.*

    as well as in addition to: *She works in a restaurant in the evenings as well as doing a full-time job during the day.*

    be as well (to) to be advisable or sensible (to do something):

It would be as well to go by train — the roads are very icy.

be just as well (that) it is fortunate or advantageous (that); it is no cause for regret (that): *It's just as well that you didn't go — the meeting was cancelled.*

be well out of (something) to be lucky because one has got out of (an unfortunate situation *etc*): *You're well out of that firm — the police have arrested the owner for fraud.*

do well out of (something) (*inf*) to make a profit or get some other advantage from (something): *You did well out of that deal.*

well and good (that is) quite acceptable (*usu* as opposed to something else which is not): *If you want to come, well and good, but you mustn't interfere.*

well off 1 rich: *He is very well off.* **2** (*inf*) in a fortunate position: *You do not know when you are well off.*

well up (in/on something) (*inf*) knowing a great deal (about something): *He's very well up in antiques, you know.*

west

go west (*sl*) to become useless; to be destroyed: *I'm afraid this jacket has finally gone west; That's all hopes of winning gone west!* [1st World War airmen's slang.]

wet

be wet behind the ears (*derog*) to be young, inexperienced and easily fooled: *In those days I was still wet behind the ears and I didn't realize he was dishonest.* [The reference is to a young animal washed by its mother.]

a wet blanket *see* **blanket.**

wet one's whistle *see* **whistle.**

whale

have a whale of a time (*inf: slightly old*) to enjoy oneself very much: *We had a whale of a time at the party.*

what

give (someone) what for (*inf*) to scold or punish (someone) severely: *If I find you playing in the coal cellar again, I'll give you what for!*

know what (something) is to have experienced (something, an emotion, *etc*): *If you had lived in our town in the 1930s, you would know what poverty is.*

know what's what to be able to tell what is important: *He'll make a sensible decision — he knows what's what.*

or whatever (*inf*) or something of that sort: *You can practise singing while you wash the dishes, clean the house or whatever.*

what about? (*inf*) used in asking whether the listener would like (to do) something: *What about a glass of milk?*; *What about going to the cinema?*

what all/what have you/whatnot (*inf*) and similar things; and so on: *He told me all about publishing and whatnot*; *The cupboard was full of books, boxes and what all.*

what in the world? *see* **world.**

what of it? (*inf*) used in replying, to suggest that what has been done, said *etc* is not important: *'You've offended him.' 'What of it?'*

what price (something)? *see* **price.**

what's the odds? *see* **odd.**

what with (*inf*) because of: *What with having no exercise and being overweight, he had a heart attack.*

wheel

oil the wheels *see* **oil.**

put a spoke in (someone's) wheel *see* **spoke.**

put one's shoulder to the wheel *see* **shoulder.**

set the wheels in motion to arrange for the beginning of a process *etc*: *If I'm to get a permit, I'd better set the wheels in motion at once.* [The reference is to a large piece of machinery.]

wheeling and dealing making intelligent but possibly immoral business deals *etc*: *There was a lot of wheeling and dealing involved in the election of the last chairman to our local council.*

wheels within wheels circumstances which create a very complicated situation affected by several different influences: *It would seem reasonable to deal with the problem as you suggest but there are unfortunately wheels within wheels.* [A Biblical reference, to Ezekiel 1:16.]

whet

whet (someone's) appetite (for something) to make (someone) eager to have more (of something): *Reading Shakespeare's Sonnets whetted his appetite for poetry at an early age.* [Literally, to increase someone's desire for food.]

while

once in a while *see* **once.**

worth (someone's) while worth (someone's) time and trouble: *It's not worth your while reading this book, because it isn't accurate*; *If you do this job for me I'll make it worth your while* (= I'll see that you are paid or get some other advantage).

whip

have the whip hand (over someone) to have control, or hold an advantage (over someone): *He has the whip hand in all these situations.* [The reference is to driving coach-horses.]

a whipping-boy someone punished because of someone else's mistakes: *Our manager always has to have a whipping-boy for his mistakes.* [Literally, a boy once educated with a royal prince and punished for the prince's mistakes because it was not permitted for the tutor to strike a member of the royal family.]

whisker

the cat's whiskers *see* **cat.**

do (something) by a whisker to barely manage to do (something): *The government won by a whisker.*

whisper

a stage whisper *see* **stage.**

whistle

as clean as a whistle very clean or cleanly: *Everything in her kitchen was as clean as a whistle.*

blow the whistle on (someone) (*sl*) to expose or make public (someone's) illegal or deceitful schemes: *He made quite a lot of money out of selling faulty electric goods before someone finally blew the whistle on him.*

wet one's whistle (*old inf*) to have a drink: *We stopped at a pub to wet our whistles.*

whistle for (something) (*sl*) to ask for (something) with no hope of getting it: *If you want me to give you fifty pounds, you can whistle for it.* [Probably a reference to the sailors' superstition that a wind can be summoned by whistling.]

white

as white as a sheet *see* **sheet.**

show the white feather *see* **feather.**

a whited sepulchre (*rather formal*) someone who is bad, but who pretends to be very good and moral: *I always felt that my pious uncle was a whited sepulchre with an unsavoury past.* [A Biblical reference, to Matthew 23:27.]

a white elephant *see* **elephant.**

a white lie a not very serious lie: *I'd rather tell my mother a white lie than tell her the truth and upset her.*

whizz

a whizz-kid (*inf: sometimes derog*) a very bright person who gains quick promotion: *The new headmaster is a real whizz-kid.* [Originally US.]

whole

go the whole hog *see* **hog.**

on the whole taking everything into consideration: *I think our trip was very successful on the whole; On the whole I am quite satisfied with the experiment.*

the whole shoot *see* **shoot.**

whoop

whoop it up (*sl: slightly derog*) to celebrate or enjoy oneself in a noisy, extravagant manner: *After working very hard for his exams, he spent his summer whooping it up in Paris.*

why

the whys and the wherefores (*inf*) all the reasons (for an action *etc*) or details of (a situation *etc*): *I don't want to know the whys and the wherefores, I just want to know what you have decided.*

wick

get on (someone's) wick (*sl*) to annoy someone greatly: *His constant complaining gets on my wick!*

wicket

on a sticky wicket *see* **sticky.**

widow

a grass widow *see* **grass.**

wild

run wild to behave without control or discipline: *They let their children run wild.*

sow one's wild oats (*usu* of young men) to live a life of wild enjoyment before settling down to a quieter, more serious and respectable life: *The students sowed their wild oats before leaving university to become teachers, doctors etc.*

spread like wildfire (of *eg* news) to spread extremely fast: *The news of the invasion spread like wildfire.* [*Wildfire* was apparently originally a furious fire caused by lightning.]

a wild-goose chase an attempt to catch or find something one cannot possibly obtain (*esp* because it does not exist or is not there): *The false clue sent us north on a wild-goose chase, while the criminals escaped southwards.* [From a kind of 16C horse race in which each horse had to follow exactly the erratic course of the leader, forming a string like that of geese in flight.]

wild horses would not (do something *etc***)** certainly nothing at all would be able to (do something etc): *Wild horses would not drag his secret from him; Wild horses would not get me to go there again!*

wilderness

crying in the wilderness giving opinions or making suggestions that are not (likely to be) followed: *We keep stressing the need to save money, but I'm afraid we're crying in the wilderness*. [A Biblical reference, to Isaiah 40:3.]

will

at will as, or when, one chooses: *The soldiers fired at will; You are free to leave the house at will*.

a willing horse *see* **horse**.

with a will (*formal*) eagerly and energetically: *They set about (doing) their tasks with a will*.

with the best will in the world however hard one tries or wishes to do something: *With the best will in the world, I couldn't do that job, because I don't know anything about electronics*.

willies

give (someone) the willies, get the willies (*sl*) to give (someone) or get an uncomfortable, eerie or fearful feeling: *This dark, mysterious house gives me the willies!*

win

be on a winning streak *see* **streak**.

win (someone) over to succeed in gaining the support and sympathy of (someone): *At first he refused to help us but we finally won him over*.

win one's spurs *see* **spur**.

win the day *see* **day**.

win the toss *see* **toss**.

win through to succeed in getting (to a place, the next stage *etc*): *It will be a struggle, but we'll win through in the end*.

wind[1]

cast/throw (caution *etc*) to the wind(s) to abandon (caution *etc*), often recklessly: *She cast caution to the winds and bought a new dress although she could not afford it*.

get one's second wind *see* **second**.

get/have the wind up (*inf*) to become nervous or anxious: *She got the wind up when she realized how close we were to the edge of the cliff*.

get/have wind of (something) (*inf*) to get a hint of or hear indirectly about (something): *The police got wind of an attempt to rob the bank, so they surrounded the building*. [Literally 'to smell (something) in the wind'.]

in the wind about to happen: *Government officials seem to think that a change in policy is in the wind.*

it's an ill wind (that blows nobody any good) *see* **ill.**

like the wind very quickly: *The horse galloped away like the wind.*

put the wind up (someone) to cause (someone) to become nervous or anxious: *We'll pretend to be the police — that will put the wind up them!*

raise the wind (*old inf*) to get enough money (to do something): *I will buy some shares in his company if I can raise the wind.*

sail close to the wind nearly to break a rule of acceptable behaviour *etc*: *Some of the students in the hostel sail very close to the wind with their all-night parties.* [Literally, in a sailing boat, to sail as nearly straight into the wind as possible.]

see which way/how the wind blows to wait before making a decision *etc* to find out what the situation is going to be: *Before we decide on our expansion plans for the firm, I think we should see which way the wind blows.* [A nautical idiom.]

a straw in the wind *see* **straw.**

take the wind out of (someone's) sails to take an advantage away from (someone); to make (someone) feel silly, embarrassed *etc*: *She was about to tell him her secret when he took the wind out of her sails by saying that he already knew it.* [A nautical idiom — a ship takes the wind out of another's sails by passing close to it on the windward side.]

wind[2]

wind up *see* **wound**[2].

windmill

tilt at windmills to struggle against imaginary opponents or imaginary opposition: *You are tilting at windmills — none of us disagrees with you.* [From an episode in Cervantes's *Don Quixote*, in which the hero mistakes a row of windmills for giants and attacks them.]

window

window-dressing (*derog*) the giving to something of an appearance which makes it seem more favourable, good *etc* than it really is: *The encyclopaedia is almost the same as it was, but they've modernized a few obvious things as window-dressing.* [Literally, the arranging of goods in a shop window.]

window-shopping looking at things in shop windows, but not actually buying anything: *I really intended just to go window-shopping but I bought a new dress.*

wine

wine and dine (someone) to give (someone) expensive meals: *He always wines and dines his clients before discussing business with them.*

wing

clip (someone's) wings to take away from (someone) the power of doing something: *She used to go to a lot of parties but having to look after a baby has clipped her wings.* [From a method of preventing domestic birds from flying away.]

spread one's wings to try to carry out one's plans and ideas for oneself *etc*: *You can't keep your children at home for ever — you must let them spread their wings.*

take (someone) under one's wing to take (someone) under one's protection and/or guidance: *The older girl took the younger one under her wing and looked after her at school.* [From the way in which birds protect their offspring.]

waiting in the wings ready to do something, *esp* to take over someone else's job: *He has to succeed as chairman because there are at least three people waiting in the wings if he should fail.* [Literally, in a theatre, waiting at the side of the stage ready to go on.]

wink

forty winks *see* **forty.**

tip (someone) the wink (*inf*) to give (someone) information privately or secretly: *He tipped me the wink that the house was for sale.* [Originally criminals' slang.]

wipe

wipe (someone or something) out 1 to remove or get rid of (someone or something): *You must try to wipe out the memory of these terrible events.* **2** to destroy (someone or something) completely: *They wiped out the whole regiment in one battle.*

wipe the floor with (someone) *see* **floor.**

wire

have one's wires crossed to misunderstand one another: *I'm sorry, I think we got our wires crossed — I thought you were coming tomorrow.* [From telecommunications.]

live wire *see* **live**[2].

wise

be wise after the event to know what one should have done *etc* after a situation has passed: *It's all very well being wise after the event, but what we really need is to be able to act decisively when an emergency arises.*

be wise to (something) (*inf*) to be aware of or know the purpose of (something): *He thinks I'm going to give him some money, but I'm wise to his plan; I used to trust him but I'm wise to him now.* [Originally US.]

none the wiser not knowing any more than before: *She didn't know what the meeting was to be about before she went, and she's still none the wiser.*

put (someone) wise (*inf*) to let (someone) know or give (someone) information (about): *Before he makes a mistake, you'd better put him wise to the current situation; He thought that he was going to be in charge but I soon put him wise.* [Originally US.]

a wise guy (*derog inf*) a person who (shows that he) thinks that he is smart, knows everything *etc*: *All right, wise guy, if you know so much about it, you mend the car!* [Originally US.]

wish

wishful thinking the belief or hope that something unlikely will happen merely because one wishes that it should: *His belief that she will marry a poor man like him is only wishful thinking.*

wish (someone) joy of (something) (*usu ironic*) to wish that (something) will be a pleasure or advantage to someone: *You can take this horrible plant away — I wish you joy of it.*

wit

at one's wits' end utterly confused and desperate: *I'm at my wits' end with this terribly complicated situation.*

frighten/scare (someone) out of (someone's) wits to frighten someone greatly, (almost) to the point of madness: *The sight of the gun in his hand scared me out of my wits.*

have/keep one's wits about one to be cautious, alert and watchful: *You have to keep your wits about you in a dangerous situation.*

live by one's wits (*formal*) to live by cunning rather than by hard work: *He does not work — he lives by his wits.*

witch

a witch-hunt a search for, and persecution of, people whose views are regarded as being evil: *The McCarthy witch-hunt in the United States from 1950-54 sought out members of the Communist Party.* [Originally US, from the organized hunts for witches which took place in America and in Britain, *esp* in the 17C.]

with

be with (someone) (*inf*) **1** to understand (someone): *Are you with me so far?* **2** to support (someone): *I'm with you all the way in your effort to be elected.*

with it (*sl: sometimes facet*) fashionable: *He's very with it*; *Although he's middle-aged he tries to be with it.*

without

    without rhyme or reason *see* **rhyme.**

    without so much as *see* **much.**

woe

    woe betide him *etc* (*liter or facet*) he will regret it: *Woe betide you if you forget!* [*Betide* = happen to.]

    woe is me (*usu facet*) I am unhappy, unlucky *etc*: *You're all going to Paris and leaving me behind — woe is me!*

wolf

    cry wolf to give warning of an imaginary danger: *She's cried wolf so often about her children's health that no-one believes her any longer.* [A reference to the fable of the shepherd boy who amused himself by rousing his village to beat off attacks on his sheep from non-existent wolves. He did this so often that at last, when the sheep were indeed attacked by wolves, no-one would come to help him and all his sheep were killed.]

    keep the wolf from the door to keep away poverty or hunger: *The job I have is not very exciting, but the money will help to keep the wolf from the door.*

    a lone wolf *see* **lone.**

    a wolf in sheep's clothing a dangerous, ruthless person who appears to be gentle and harmless: *I always suspected that his meek little wife was a wolf in sheep's clothing.* [A Biblical reference, to Matthew 7:15.]

wonder

    a nine days' wonder *see* **nine.**

    no wonder (*inf*) it isn't surprising (that): *No wonder you couldn't open the door — it was locked!*; *'He says he feels sick.' 'No wonder, after eating all that ice-cream!'*

    small wonder *see* **small.**

wood

    this, that *etc* **neck of the woods** *see* **neck.**

    the nigger in the woodpile *see* **nigger.**

    not to be able to see the wood for the trees not to understand exactly the nature and purpose of a situation *etc* because of too much concern with the details of it: *If you are too much involved with the day-to-day organization of a new project, there is a danger of not being able to see the wood for the trees and forgetting the point of the whole scheme.*

out of the wood(s) out of danger: *We're not out of the wood(s) yet by a long way.* [From a proverb — *do not shout until you are out of the wood* = do not celebrate prematurely.]

touch wood (*used as an interjection*) to touch something made of wood superstitiously, in order to avoid bad luck: *None of the children has ever had a serious illness, touch wood!*

wool

pull the wool over (someone's) eyes to deceive (someone): *She tried to pull the wool over his eyes with some ridiculous excuse.* [Originally US.]

wool-gathering absentmindedness or daydreaming: *I'm tired of his constant wool-gathering — I wish he would concentrate on his work.* [From collecting tufts of wool from hedges, which obliges one to wander to and fro in a haphazard manner.]

word

be as good as one's word *see* **good.**

break, keep one's word to fail to keep, keep one's promise: *If you break your word he will never trust you again; You must keep your word if you promised to take the children to the cinema.*

by word of mouth by one person telling another in speech, not in writing: *She gets a lot of information from the newspapers, and some by word of mouth.*

eat one's words to admit humbly that one was mistaken in saying something: *I'll make him eat his words!*

from the word go *see* **go.**

get a word in edgeways (*inf*) to break into a conversation *etc* and say something: *She couldn't get a word in edgeways — those two kept shouting at each other.*

have a word in (someone's) ear to tell (someone) something confidentially: *Have a word in his teacher's ear and tell her that he is worrying about his school-work.*

have a word with (someone) to have a short conversation with (someone): *I shall have to have a quick word with my secretary before I leave.*

have words (*inf*) to argue or quarrel: *He's in a foul mood — I think they've been having words.*

in a word to sum up briefly: *In a word, I don't like him.*

in so many words stating very clearly or bluntly: *He said in so many words that he was sick to death of me; 'Did he tell you to leave?' 'Not in so many words, but that was what he meant.'*

keep one's word *see* **break one's word** *above.*

the last word *see* **last.**

a man of his word *see* **man.**

mum's the word *see* **mum.**

not the word for (something) (*inf*) not a strong enough word to describe (something): *You should see my son's bedroom — untidy isn't the word for it!*

(a man, woman *etc*) **of few, many words** (someone) who talks little, a lot: *The farmer was a man of few words, but what he did say was sensible.*

the operative word *see* **operative.**

a play on words *see* **play.**

put in/say a good word (for someone) to say something pleasant to someone (about someone else): *John's going to put in a good word for me in the hope that his boss will give me a job.*

put words into (someone's) mouth to say or suggest that (someone) has said something which they did not: *Don't put words into my mouth — you know that wasn't what I said.*

say the word (*inf*) I'm ready to obey your wishes: *If you'd like to go with me, say the word.*

take (someone) at his *etc* **word** to believe (someone) without question and act accordingly: *When she said that she would like them to visit her they took her at her word and arrived the following week.*

take the words out of (someone's) mouth to say something which is exactly what (someone) was about to say or would have said if asked: *'Donald doesn't trust her — do you, Donald?' 'You took the words out of my mouth.'*

take (someone's) word for it to assume that what someone says is correct (without checking): *I'll have to take his word for it that the train leaves at 10 o'clock — I haven't got a timetable; You'll have to take the child's word for it that he did the work by himself.*

word for word in the exact, original words; verbatim: *That's precisely what he told me, word for word.*

words fail me I cannot describe my feelings: *Words fail me when I think of what you have done!*

work

all in a/the day's work not causing extra or unusual effort or trouble: *She thanked him for attending to her problems so kindly, but he assured her that it was all in the day's work.*

all work and no play makes Jack a dull boy a saying, meaning that it is not good for people to work, or do something disagreeable, all the time and that they should not do so.

give (someone) the works (*inf*) to give someone the full treat-ment: *They've certainly given her the works at the hairdresser's — she's had her hair cut, tinted and permed.* [Originally US gangsters' slang for 'to kill (someone)'.]

go to work on (something) to begin work on (something): *We're thinking of going to work on an extension to the house.*

gum up the works *see* **gum.**

have one's work cut out to be faced with a difficult task: *You'll have your work cut out to beat the champion.* [Literally, to have (a lot of) work already prepared for one to start.]

in working order *see* **order.**

a nasty piece of work *see* **nasty.**

out of work having no employment: *He's been out of work for months.*

set to work to start work: *I'll have to set to work on this mending this evening.*

throw a spanner in the works *see* **spanner.**

worked-up excited, nervous, annoyed *etc*: *He became/got very worked-up about the whole problem.*

a work of art a painting, sculpture *etc*: *The Royal Gallery houses many works of art.*

work (something) off to get rid of (something unwanted or unpleasant) by taking physical exercise *etc*: *He tried to work off some of his excess weight by doing exercises every day.*

work out to happen successfully: *Don't worry — it will all work out in the end.*

work (something) out to solve or calculate (something) cor-rectly: *I can't work out how many should be left.*

world

all the world and his wife (*old inf*) a very large number of people: *It looked as if all the world and his wife had been invited to Judy's wedding.*

dead to the world *see* **dead.**

for all the world exactly, quite *etc*: *He looked for all the world as though he had slept in his clothes.*

have the best of both worlds *see* **best.**

it's a small world *see* **small.**

it takes all sorts to make a world *see* **sort.**

a man of the world *see* **man.**

the New World *see* **new.**

not long for this world *see* **long.**

on top of the world feeling very well and happy: *She's on top of the world — she's just got engaged to be married.*

out of this world (*inf*) unbelievably marvellous: *His cooking is just out of this world.*

think the world of (someone) to be very fond of (someone): *He thinks the world of his wife.*

what in the world? (*often derog*) used for emphasis when asking a question: *What in the world have you done to your hair?*; *What in the world did you do that for?*

with the best will in the world *see* **will.**

the world is his *etc* **oyster** *see* **oyster.**

worm

the worm turns a patient, long-suffering person decides not to be patient and long-suffering any longer: *She made her husband's life a misery for twenty years until the worm finally turned and he ordered her out of the house.* [From a saying — *tread on a worm's tail and it will turn.*]

worn

worn(-)out 1 so damaged by use as to be unfit for further use: *I don't want to hear any of your worn-out excuses.* **2** very tired: *His wife is worn out after looking after the children.*

worn to a shadow *see* **shadow.**

worse

none the worse for (something) not in any way harmed by (something): *The baby's none the worse for being left out in the cold.*

the worse for wear (*inf*) tired (and untidy *etc*): *You look a bit the worse for wear after last night's party.*

worse luck! *see* **luck.**

worst

do one's worst to do the most evil *etc* thing that one can do: *Do your worst — you'll never manage to defeat me.*

get the worst of (something) to be affected more unpleasantly *etc* than someone else by (something); to lose (something): *If you argue with him, you'll get the worst of it.*

if the worst comes to the worst if the worst possible thing happens: *If the worst comes to the worst and your business fails, you can always sell your house.*

the worst of it is (that) the most unfortunate *etc* aspect of the situation is (that): *It's a terrible situation but the worst of it is, I didn't even know she was married!*

worth

for all one is worth using all one's efforts, strength *etc*: *When the boat sank, he swam towards the shore for all he was worth.*

for what it is worth used to suggest that what is being said is doubtful or does not deserve consideration: *For what it's worth, John told me that quite the opposite was true; For what it's worth, I like it even if nobody else does.*

worth one's salt *see* **salt**.

worth its/one's weight in gold *see* **weight**.

worth (someone's) while *see* **while**.

worthy of the name *see* **name**.

wound¹

rub salt into the wound *see* **salt**.

wound²

be, get wound up (*inf*) to be, or get, in a very excited or anxious state: *He gets very wound up about going to the dentist.* [The reference is to winding up a spring.]

wrap

keep (something) under wraps (*inf*) to keep (something) secret: *They're keeping the new design under wraps until August.*

wrapped up in (something) (*inf*) giving all one's affection or attention to (something): *She's very wrapped up in her work/thoughts these days.*

wrap (something) up (*inf*) to finish (something) completely: *I went to Aberdeen to wrap up my firm's deal with the oil companies.* [Originally US.]

wrist

a slap on the wrist *see* **slap**.

write

write (something) off 1 to regard (something) as lost for ever: *They wrote off the whole amount that had been spent on the new project.* **2** (*inf*) to destroy (something) completely or damage it beyond repair: *He wrote his car off in a bad accident.* [A term from finance — to deduct the value (of something) from an account *etc* as being a complete loss.]

the writing on the wall something which shows that a disaster or failure is about to happen: *The criminal saw the writing on the wall and left the country just before the police arrived to arrest him; I'd like to think our company can survive, but I'm afraid this year's sales figures are the writing on the wall.* [From the Biblical story of Belshazzar's Feast — Daniel 5:5–31 — at which a mysterious hand appeared and wrote words on the wall which Daniel interpreted as foretelling Belshazzar's death and the downfall of his kingdom. The words the hand actually wrote were *Mene, Mene, Tekel, Upharsin*.]

wrong

get off on the wrong foot *see* **foot.**

get on the wrong side of (someone) to make (someone) dislike one or be hostile to one: *James isn't usually bad-tempered — you must have got on the wrong side of him.*

get (hold of) the wrong end of the stick *see* **stick.**

get (something) wrong (*inf*) to misunderstand (something): *I must have got it wrong — I thought you were coming tomorrow.*

go wrong 1 to go astray, badly, away from the intended plan *etc*: *Everything has gone wrong for her in the past few years.* **2** to stop functioning properly: *The machine has gone wrong — I can't get it to stop!* **3** to make a mistake: *Where did I go wrong in that sum?*

in the wrong guilty of an error or injustice: *She is completely blameless. You're the one who's in the wrong!*

not to put a foot wrong *see* **foot.**

on the wrong track *see* **track.**

put (someone) in the wrong (*formal*) to cause (someone) to seem to be in the wrong: *Whenever he explains to anyone why we didn't arrive, he always puts me in the wrong.*

wrongfoot (someone) (*inf*) to cause (someone) to be unprepared to deal with an unexpected problem; to attack (someone) in an unexpected manner: *By calling a meeting during a holiday weekend, the chairman of the council wrongfooted most of his opponents, who were not prepared to argue their case.* [Literally a sporting term — to attack in such a way that one's opponent has his weight on the wrong foot to defend effectively.]

Y

yarn

spin a yarn to tell a long story, *esp* one that is not true: *He managed to spin a yarn of some sort to account for his lateness.*

year

year in, year out all the time, every year without exception.

yesterday

    not born yesterday (*inf*) experienced and wise, not stupid or easily fooled: *Surely you don't expect me to believe that rubbish — I wasn't born yesterday, you know!*

yet

    as yet up to the time referred to, *usu* the present: *I haven't had a book published as yet.*

Z

zero

    zero hour (*inf*) the time at which something is fixed to begin: *Zero hour is at midnight.* [From military use.]

    zero in on (something) (*inf*) to aim accurately for (something one wants *etc*): *The journalists zeroed in on the filmstar as she stepped off the plane.* [From target-shooting.]